An Introduction to
Hospitals and Inpatient Care

Eugenia Siegler, MD, is a graduate of Johns Hopkins University School of Medicine. She completed an internal medicine residency at Bellevue and Tisch Hospitals and a Fellowship in Geriatrics and General Internal Medicine at the University of Pennsylvania.

She has served as a member of the faculty at the University of Pennsylvania and as Chief of Geriatrics at Brooklyn Hospital Center, where she directed its United Hospital Fund-supported Hospital-Based Palliative Care Initiative. Dr. Siegler is presently Associate Professor of Clinical Medicine at the Weill Medical College of Cornell University and is the Medical Director of the Geriatrics Inpatient Service at the Cornell Campus of the New York Presbyterian Hospital.

Saeid Mirafzali, MD, MHSA, is a graduate of Michigan State University College of Human Medicine. He completed an internal medicine residency at Henry Ford Hospital and a Master's in Health Services Administration at the University of Michigan School of Public Health in Ann Arbor.

He has served as a member of the faculty at the Henry Ford Hospital and as Director of the Inpatient Medical Division, where he directed the hospitalist program. Dr. Mirafzali is presently Assistant Professor of Clinical Medicine at the Weill Medical College of Cornell University. He also serves as the Director of General Internal Medicine Hospitalist Services and as Assistant Chair for Inpatient Operations for the Department of Internal Medicine at the Cornell Campus of the New York Presbyterian Hospital.

Janice B. Foust, PhD, RN, is Assistant Professor of Nursing at the University of New Hampshire. She received her Bachelor of Science degree from the University of New Hampshire, a Master of Science degree from Boston College, and a Doctor of Philosophy degree from the University of Pennsylvania. Prior clinical positions include Clinical Director of Nursing Practice at the University of Pennsylvania Health System and Clinical Nurse Specialist and Primary Nurse at Beth Israel Hospital. Dr. Foust has also been an Assistant Professor at Temple University, teaching in the graduate and undergraduate nursing programs. Her research interests are focused on discharge planning and transitional care of older adults.

An Introduction to
Hospitals and
Inpatient Care

Eugenia L. Siegler, MD
Saeid Mirafzali, MD
Janice B. Foust, PhD, RN

Editors

 Springer Publishing Company

Springer Publishing Company, Inc.
536 Broadway
New York, NY 10012-3955

Acquisitions Editor: Ruth Chasek
Production Editor: Jeanne Libby
Cover design by Joanne Honigman

03 04 05 06 07 / 5 4 3 2 1

Library of Congress Cataloging-in-Publication Data

An introduction to hospitals and inpatient care / Eugenia L. Siegler, Saeid Mirafzali, Janice B. Foust, editors.
    p. cm.
    Includes bibliographical references and index.
    ISBN 0-8261-2194-2
    1. Hospitals—Administration. 2. Hospital care. 3. Hospital patients—Services for. I. Siegler, Eugenia L. II. Mirafzali, Saeid. III. Foust, Janice B.

RA981.A2 I5526 2003
362.1'1'068—dc21

2002036656

Printed in the United States of America by Maple-Vail Book Manufacturing Group.

Contents

Part III   Facilitating Continuity of Care

Part IV   Common Social and Ethical Issues

Part V Improving Quality of Care

Contributors

Shantanu K. Agrawal, BS, BA
Medical Student
Weill Medical College of Cornell
 University
New York, NY

Elizabeth A. Ayello, PhD, RN, CS, CWOCN
Assistant Clinical Professor
John A. Hartford Foundation
 Institute for Geriatric Nursing
Division of Nursing, School of
 Education
New York University
New York, NY

David S. Battleman, MD, MSc
Assistant Professor
Departments of Public Health and
 Medicine
Weill Medical College of Cornell
 University
New York, NY

Rebecca Berlin, MSN, CRNP
Nurse Consultant
Philadelphia, PA

Joseph R. Betancourt, MD, MPH
Senior Scientist, Institute for Health
 Policy
Director for Multicultural Education,
 Multicultural Affairs Office
Massachusetts General Hospital—
 Harvard Medical School
Boston, MA

Kenneth S. Boockvar, MD, MS
Assistant Professor
Brookdale Department of Geriatrics
 and Adult Development
Mount Sinai School of Medicine
Attending Physician, the Jewish
 Home and Hospital
New York, NY

Melissa M. Bottrell, MPH, PhD(c)
Project Director
Division of Nursing, School of
 Education
New York University
New York, NY

Abraham A. Brody
Senior Research Assistant
Hartford Institute for Geriatric Nursing
Division of Nursing, School of
 Education
New York University
New York, NY

Mark A. Callahan, MD
Division Chief
Outcomes and Effectiveness Research
Departments of Public Health and
 Medicine
Assistant Professor
Departments of Public Health and
 Medicine
Weill Medical College of Cornell
 University
New York, NY

Maria Camargo, MD, PhD
Clinical Assistant Professor
Mount Sinai School of Medicine
Attending Physician, the Jewish
Home and Hospital
New York, NY

David A. Campbell, MPhil
Doctoral Student
Department of Medical Informatics
Columbia University
New York, NY

Elizabeth Capezuti, PhD, RN, CS, FAAN
Associate Professor
Independence Foundation-Wesley
Woods Chair in Gerontologic
Nursing
Nell Hodgson Woodruff School of
Nursing, Emory University
Wesley Woods Health Center
Atlanta, GA

J. Emilio Carrillo, MD, MPH
Medical Director, New York-
Presbyterian Healthcare System
Executive Director, New York—
Presbyterian Community
Health Plan
New York, NY

Robert Cato, MD
Chief, General Internal Medicine
Presbyterian Medical Center
Assistant Professor of Medicine
University of Pennsylvania School
of Medicine
Philadelphia, PA

Charlene Compher, PhD, RD, FADA, CNSD
Assistant Professor
University of Pennsylvania School
of Nursing
Nutrition Support Service
University of Pennsylvania Health
System
Philadelphia, PA

Margaret Dimond, ACSW
Regional Administrator
Henry Ford Medical Group
Detroit, MI

Molla Sloane Donaldson, DrPH
Outcomes Research Branch, ARP,
DCCPS
National Cancer Institute
Bethesda, MD

Barbara Doyle, MSN, CRNP
Product Manager, CareScience, Inc.
Philadelphia, PA

Sona Euster, MSSA, ACSW
Assistant Adjunct Professor
of Social Work
Columbia University School of
Social Work
Director, Department of Social Work
New York Presbyterian Hospital
New York, NY

Joseph J. Fins, MD
Director of Medical Ethics
New York Presbyterian Hospital,
Cornell Campus
Associate Professor of Medicine
Associate Professor of Medicine
in Psychiatry
Weill Medical College
New York, NY

Barry Gallison, GNP
Nurse Practitioner, Geriatric
  Inpatient Service
New York Presbyterian Hospital,
  Cornell Campus
New York, NY

Sandy B. Ganz, PT, MS, GCS
Associate in Research, Hospital for
  Special Surgery
Director of Rehabilitation
Amsterdam Nursing Home
New York, NY

Kyle L. Grazier, PhD
Associate Professor
Department of Health Management
  and Policy
School of Public Health
University of Michigan
Ann Arbor, MI

Alexander R. Green, MD
Assistant Attending Physician
Instructor in Medicine
Weill Medical College of Cornell
  University
New York, NY

Alice Herb, JD
Assistant Clinical Professor of Family
  Practice
SUNY Health Science Center
  at Brooklyn
Brooklyn, NY

Lisa Honkanen, MD
Fellow, Division of Geriatrics and
  Gerontology
Weill Medical College of Cornell
  University
New York, NY

Margaret Horgan, MSN, RN
Director, CareScience, Inc.
Philadelphia, PA

Nathaniel Hupert, MD, MPH
Assistant Professor
Departments of Public Health
  and Medicine
Weill Medical College of Cornell
  University
New York, NY

Havva Idriss, MPH
Vice Dean for Administration
Weill Cornell Medical College
  in Qatar
New York, NY

Bruce Kinosian, MD
Associate Professor of Medicine
University of Pennsylvania School
  of Medicine
MIRECC
Philadelphia Veterans Affairs
  Medical Center
Philadelphia, PA

**Christine T. Kovner, RN, PhD,
  FAAN**
Professor
Division of Nursing
New York University
New York, NY

Veronica LoFaso, MD
Assistant Professor of Medicine
Weill Medical College of Cornell
  University
New York, NY

Mark S. Pecker, MD
Professor of Clinical Medicine
Vice Chairman, Educational Affairs
Director, Internal Medicine
  Residency Program
Department of Medicine
Weill Medical College of Cornell
  University
New York, NY

Barrie G. Raik, MD
Geriatric Fellowship Program Director
Assistant Professor of Medicine
Department of Medicine
Weill Medical College
New York, NY

Bharathi Raman, MD
Assistant Professor of Medicine
Department of Medicine
Weill Medical College
New York, NY

Brian K. Regan, PhD
Vice President, Professional Services
The Brooklyn Hospital Center
Brooklyn, NY

Robert J. Rosati, PhD
Director of Outcomes Analysis
  and Research
Center for Home Care Policy
  and Research
Visiting Nurse Service of New York
New York, NY

Jessica B. Scholder, MPH
Project Coordinator
Hartford Institute for Geriatric
  Nursing
Division of Nursing, School of
  Education
New York University
New York, NY

Freddi I. Segal-Gidan, PA, PhD
Director, Stroke Rehabilitation
Rancho Los Amigos National
  Rehabilitation Center
Associate Clinical Professor
Department of Neurology
Keck School of Medicine
University of Southern California
Los Angeles, CA

Peter D. Stetson, MD
Assistant Attending in Clinical
  Medicine
Division of General Medicine
Columbia University
Postdoctoral Research Fellow
Department of Medical Informatics
Columbia University
New York, NY

Beryl C. Vallejo, RN, MPH, DrPH
Clinical Consultant
The Institute for Management
  Development (IMD)
Houston, TX

Sharon Stahl Wexler, MA, RNC, CS
Adjunct Clinical Instructor
Division of Nursing, School
  of Education
New York University
New York, NY

Foreword

Health care today has reached a level of complexity that challenges all providers, leadership, and frontline health-care workers. Over the last few years, finance, quality, patient satisfaction, and operational efficiency have been the top priorities of most health-care organizations. It is a daily challenge to stay abreast of the latest areas of change and to integrate vast ranges of knowledge into the health-care delivery model with the goal of providing the highest level of care to each patient served. In this environment, many individuals who possess very specific, unique knowledge and expertise are interacting in multiple ways. This book presents key elements of the health care process and serves as a common platform for various constituencies to understand processes that extend beyond one's particular area of expertise. The chapters touch on topics that should be understood by a wide audience who work together in the patient care process. A common understanding will ensure greater cooperation and facilitate the provision of care for patients and their families. This book will be most beneficial for young health-care providers and will serve as a reference tool for experienced health-care leaders and workers.

The compilation of information that is presented emphasizes many topics not commonly covered in technical or didactic studies. The selection of topics is also unique and the areas are carefully chosen. The relationship of these topics with a common understanding by the health care team can result in higher levels of patient satisfaction as well as provider satisfaction. Functioning with a better understanding of areas such as hospital-based teams, cultural competence, restraint management, and preventing errors provides tools and insights to raise the bar for all aspects of care and will facilitate overall outcomes for the patients we serve.

I recommend this book as required reading for our young health-care team and consideration of this for inclusion in management orientation for all leadership.

STEPHEN H. VELICK, PHD
CEO, Community Hospital Division
Henry Ford Health System
Detroit, Michigan

Preface

Because such a large proportion of medical and nursing education takes place in the hospital, it is hard to imagine why a student would be unfamiliar with any aspect of inpatient care. Nonetheless, although training offers abundant opportunities to learn how to manage acute illness, it leaves much unsaid about all of the other things that occur when a person is admitted to the hospital. We often field questions about topics like insurance or discharge planning, but we have also noted that new clinicians may be so focused on mastering specific clinical skills that they have little time to observe or question the whole process of care.

Originally, we had wanted to assemble answers to nonclinical questions that residents and students often asked, but as we realized that many equally important topics went undiscussed, the book evolved into something different that is perhaps best thought of as IAQ—infrequently asked questions about inpatient care. In essence, it is a plea to look beyond the acute disease not just to the patient but also to the environment of care, how it works, how it doesn't work, and how it might improve.

We have deliberately avoided trying to serve as a textbook of inpatient medicine or nursing and left management of illnesses to other texts. The exceptions are delirium and skin care; we have observed that these clinical problems are often ignored and merit extra attention. We also recognize that we could have included a variety of other general clinical topics in the book—palliative care and integrative medicine are two examples. We did not feel that we could do justice to topics such as these, which merit texts of their own.

This book is aimed at hospital neophytes—medical students, house officers, physician assistants, and nurses. Keeping our very busy and often overwhelmed readership in mind, we asked our contributors to favor brevity and practicality over comprehensiveness. Our goal is to provide an overview and broaden a perspective here and there. We thank our students and house staff for inspiring the book and our contributors for sharing their expertise.

EUGENIA L. SIEGLER
SAEID MIRAFZALI
JANICE B. FOUST

Part I
The Hospital Setting

■ 1
Hospitals: From Stand-Alone to Networks and Systems

Havva Idriss

Today's physicians and nurses in training are much more adaptable to change than their immediate forerunners, who have had to face dramatic shifts in conditions of practice and reimbursement after years of relative stability and income growth. Practitioners and hospitals are no longer separate entities; all components of the health care system, particularly doctors and hospitals, are forced to integrate their respective functions even though their economic incentives are not always aligned. This phenomenon is driven by economic pressures and by the advocacy of public-interest research groups such as the Institute of Medicine to deliver good health care that will cease to "harm too frequently and fail to deliver potential benefits routinely" (Institute of Medicine, 2001). Clinicians must work with administrators, insurance plans, and policy makers to design and develop an effective health care delivery system. To do this, they must understand the evolution of the structures of contemporary hospitals and the forces shaping these changes.

FORCES DRIVING CHANGES IN HOSPITAL STRUCTURE

For a significant part of the nineteenth century, the American hospital was an asylum for the indigent. The last quarter of the twentieth century marked the beginning of the transformation of hospitals into modern scientific institutions (Stevens, 1989), with growth in their complexity and numbers throughout the century. The tradition of patients who had the means paying for hospital services dates as far back as 1751 when Pennsylvania Hospital, the first hospital in the United States, was established. Although surgeons and small town doctors were seen to set up small hospitals for their private patients even in those early days, they much preferred to admit their patients to hospitals run by others. This practice had economic and professional benefits, as it relieved physicians of "the burden of capital costs, fund-raising, and any hospital operating losses, as well as from the headaches of hospital administration" (Stevens, 1989).

As the technological advances of the twentieth century turned hospitals into complex institutions of care, payment sources for health care also expanded in scope and complexity. Over the past 40 years, most health care expenditures have been covered by either the public sector through the Medicare and Medicaid programs or by the private sector through employee health plans. In the 1980s, the U.S. government and the business community recognized that neither could continue to pay for health care under the traditional indemnity plan model that lacked incentives to control costs. American corporations were facing global competition and could no longer afford to have a significant portion of their expenses consumed by employee health care. Twenty years after the initiation of Medicare, longer life expectancy and an unchecked increase in health expenditures fueled projections that at least one of the two Medicare funds—the one covering hospital-related expenses (Part A)—would be depleted in the initial years of the twenty-first century.

These developments spurred market forces and legislative initiatives. In the public sector, Medicare reimbursement policy for hospital services changed in the mid-1980s from a hotel-type per-diem payment scheme, which placed no limitation on the number of days spent in the hospital per episode of acute illness, to a DRG (diagnosis related group) or per-diagnosis-type payment, which fixed the total reimbursable amount by diagnosis, regardless of the patient's length of stay.

In the private sector, because employers demanded reduced health care premium costs, the insurance industry developed products that managed care, that is, influenced or controlled utilization and cost of services. Insurance companies extracted discounted rates from a limited group of hospitals and physicians in each market with the promise of increased volume that would result from directing cases to these preferred providers. This limited the choices available to consumers. Despite initial resistance, hospitals and doctors, particularly in markets with an excess supply of beds and physicians, often offered discounts to insurance plans in order to beat their competitors to the promised volume of referrals.

Government, employers, the insurance industry, and providers focused on strategies with immediate economic returns and for the most part failed to pursue a coordinated, enduring system of health care delivery that would ensure acceptable levels of access and quality. The wide array of organizational structures that developed reflects this confused response to market pressures.

THE ASSAULT ON HOSPITAL FINANCING

As a result of changes in reimbursement policies by the public and private sectors, hospitals faced an assault on their financing system in reimbursement and utilization, and many found themselves yielding to deals they later regretted. Many hospitals suffered severe financial losses, while others closed down altogether.

Commercial insurance plans that had traditionally offered the most favorable hospital reimbursement were not willing to pay the DRG rates but were seeking discounted per diem rates, while concurrently providing physicians with economic incentives to reduce the average length of stay in the hospital. They were also aggressively monitoring utilization by requiring preadmission clearance of hospital admissions. In addition, hospitals were required to justify the necessity of each day of a patient's hospital stay in order to be reimbursed. Because these plans covered a working population that was for the most part young and relatively healthy, it was not clinically challenging to reduce the overall rate of hospitalization or the number of days of hospitalization per acute episode. As a result, hospital admissions and days per admission declined dramatically. Hospitals found themselves providing only the most highly labor- and capital-intensive days of care; they had lost the ability to spread their costs across the less acute days of recovery. Moreover, in the early days of managed care, some hospitals had unwittingly given discounts on per diem rates to insurance plans that were *less* than their average daily costs. This occurred partly because hospitals lacked good cost-accounting systems and could not discretely measure the specific costs associated with each unique day of care. The best they could do was deal with averages. Another destabilizing factor was the effort to execute as many managed care contracts as possible, in order to undercut other hospitals and gain volume to counter the rapid declines in occupancy.

Medicare, which had historically been viewed as a poor source of reimbursement, suddenly became the preferred payer. Because Medicare was paying the full DRG rate, those hospitals able to monitor and manage reduction of the average length of stay for this population could experience a positive margin, or at least break even (i.e., cover costs) on these admissions. The effort to reduce the average length of stay in the hospital spurred an escalating demand for lower-intensity care settings that could monitor the convalescent phase of recovery from the acute episode that had precipitated the hospitalization. As a consequence, the federal agency that oversees

Medicare, the Health Care Financing Administration (HCFA; now known as Centers for Medicare and Medicaid Services, or CMS), experienced skyrocketing utilization in home health care and post-acute, or short-stay use, of nursing home beds. Faced with these forces that diminished overall utilization and coupled with declines in reimbursement rates, many hospitals sought refuge in numbers and started forming various types of alliances with other hospitals and other types of health care institutions and caregivers.

LEGAL AND REGULATORY FACTORS

Legal and regulatory impediments hampered the formation of new alliances. Health care in general and hospitals in particular have traditionally been very highly regulated at the federal, state, and local levels. Hospitals interested in collaborating with sister institutions for the purpose of managed care contracting faced various antitrust impediments unless they were organized under a common corporate entity. Similarly, because physicians are the basic source of hospital admissions, certain antitrust and fraud provisions precluded hospitals from entering into particular types of economic arrangements with them. Yet, particularly in the early stages of managed care, physicians played a critical role because many were resistant to signing managed care contracts. Hospitals that were willing to give discounts and sign managed care contracts could not expect to see patients covered by these contracts admitted to their institutions unless they had physicians on their staff who had also signed contracts with the same companies. Hospitals, especially community hospitals, were at an advantage if they could secure exclusive arrangements with those physicians who were prepared to contract with managed care companies. Further, all hospitals, and particularly academic medical centers, found it essential to have more primary care physicians with exclusive commitments to their institution in order to ensure the referrals to faculty specialists, who in turn admitted the more complex and therefore more highly reimbursable cases. These factors drove many hospitals to purchase physician practices outright in order to circumvent the risk of fraud or antitrust violations. Many hospitals would neglect to structure the compensation of these physicians with the necessary incentives for productivity and would find themselves burdened with failing practices.

These legal and regulatory barriers put the lawyers to work developing creative models for their client hospitals and physicians to achieve the particular objective in each case. This led to the proliferation of a variety of alliance models, running the entire spectrum from legally binding to very loose contractual relationships. Regardless of the model or the composition of participants, the initiators of these alliances were, for the most part, hospitals.

HOSPITAL-LED ALLIANCES

Hospitals had started forming strategic combinations as long ago as the early 1980s. In 1982, 19% of urban hospitals were in local systems compared to 28% in 1989 (Luke & Begun, 1996). By 1995, however, the Annual Survey Data of the American Hospital Association revealed that 72% of United States hospitals belonged to a *health network* or a *health system* (Shortell, Bazzoli, Dubbs, & Kralovec, 2000). The authors define *networks* as aggregations where members retain their individual ownership, and *systems* as groups led by a parent organization that has unified ownership of assets. In practice, however, hospitals engaging in such alliance formation gave no particular definition to the meaning of these terms, as they often incorporated "network" or "system" into the name of their alliance, nor did they clearly articulate the strategic purpose of each such initiative. Rather, groups of providers across the nation started forming relationships in a variety of models, inconsistently calling them networks or systems.

It was expected that these alliances would allow hospitals to consolidate and reduce costs of administrative and clinical services. Hospital executives also assumed that these lowered costs, coupled with collaboration among network/system member institutions on managed care contracting, would permit hospitals to develop market power in negotiating with managed care companies. These expectations, along with other factors such as local market dynamics, caused the differentiation of two types of alliances: *horizontal* and *vertical*. Similar institutions providing the same level of service, such as hospitals, would come together in horizontal alliances to realize economies of scale through consolidation of like services. In other cases, combinations of entities providing different levels of service, such as hospitals, nursing homes, and physicians, would organize into a vertical alliance. Some of the vertical alliances went so far as to form their own insurance product in order to engage in direct contracting with employers, and many marketed themselves as *integrated delivery systems (IDS)*, purporting to offer services integrated across different levels of care and to avoid unnecessary duplications and inefficiencies. HCFA sought to have these integrated delivery systems insure Medicare beneficiaries as well. The effectiveness of these initiatives in eliminating inefficiencies, thereby reducing cost and delivering coordinated care, remains unproven. Reports on the performance of these organizational structures and measures of their achievements will be discussed further later in the chapter.

Quality was clearly a secondary consideration during these changes. Nonetheless, the value statement developed by the Henry Ford Health System gained popularity and was frequently quoted among hospital systems. The statement claimed that improved quality and value are implicit in cost reduction, as expressed by the formula Value = Quality/Cost. This would allow hospital executives to justify network/system development from a quality perspective, even as these alliances were intended to reduce inefficiencies and excess cost.

THE CURRENT DEFINITION OF HOSPITALS

As Shortell et al. (2000) point out, for a significant portion of the twentieth century, hospitals were described by their ownership (for profit, voluntary, sponsored by a religious order, etc.), size (number of beds), teaching status, and location (urban, community). With the proliferation of alliances and new hospital structures, these traditional definitions and measures proved less relevant. The 1995 American Hospital Association survey results revealed that 2,467 hospitals belong to one of 306 networks, and 3,017 belong to one of 297 systems. Approximately 72% of hospitals belong to a network or system, and 22% hold membership in both (Shortell et al., 2000). This is often attributable to a hospital's participation in a local or regional network that may have one or more nonsystem hospitals. A similar analysis undertaken with 1994 survey data had comparable findings (Bazzoli, Shortell, Dubbs, Chan & Kralovec, 1999). In comparing the 1994 survey data with that of 1995, Bazzoli et al. (1999) found that over the 1-year period, networks tended to become more centralized in their arrangements, but little change was observed among systems.

As a result of these data that describe the complexity of relationships among members of networks and systems and the significant amount of restructuring that has occurred within the health care delivery system in the U.S., Shortell et al. (2000) have identified the need for new measures and descriptors for hospitals. They argue appropriately that in the absence of a new classification system, it will not be possible to assure equitable payment policies for providers, to develop comprehensive regulations that cover the full range of activities of the respective entities, to identify where accountability rests, or to longitudinally track changes in the United States health care system.

Under current conditions, providers tend to commit errors of underidentification, as they are inclined to view their situation as being unique and different from others. Policy makers and regulators on the other hand tend to overidentify, or prefer to see most, if not all, fall within the same organizational category, due to the difficulty of tailoring legislation to individuals or numerous groups (Shortell et al., 2000). The authors argue that health care executives would also find a classification system useful as they assess various strategic options for their organizations, such as risk assumption, potential alliance partners, and merger and acquisition opportunities.

Shortell et al. (2000) propose that the new taxonomy be based on structure and process measures that reflect the complex relationships among hospitals, physician groups, and insurance plans. The methodology would specifically measure the degrees of differentiation, centralization, and integration. *Differentiation* measures the type and scope of services offered, for example, acute care, long-term care, tertiary care. *Centralization* identifies the extent to which activities are organized centrally versus at dispersed locations. Finally, *integration* determines the extent to which services are being provided by member institutions themselves as opposed to contracted entities external to the system.

Shortell et al. (2000) reported that by applying these measures, important and meaningful similarities were found to exist among many of the hospital-led systems and networks. The measures were applied to hospital-physician relationships and the insurance products owned by the networks and systems under study. The use of cluster analysis techniques yielded five categories of networks and systems: (a) centralized health networks/systems; (b) centralized physician/insurance health systems; (c) moderately centralized health networks/systems; (d) decentralized health networks/systems; and (e) independent health networks/systems (see Table 1.1). Shortell et al. (2000) propose that these clusters, or categories, provide a sound foundation on which to base certain assessments such as a network or system's readiness to assume risk, that is, to accept a fixed payment in order to manage the health of a population of subscribers.

WHAT HAVE HOSPITAL NETWORKS/SYSTEMS DELIVERED?

In spite of the similarities found among health networks and systems (Shortell et al., 2000), there is no conclusive evidence that these structures in fact delivered what they promised. Although Coile (2001) forecasts that over the next two decades 75% to 80% of United States hospitals will be in networks or integrated health systems, he adds that health care executives are skeptical that networks or systems will achieve significant cost savings from integration. A national survey by Deloitte & Touche in 2000 revealed that more than 50% of the surveyed hospitals in systems or networks reported they had not eliminated or reduced any patient services (Coile, 2001). This is reflective of findings reported earlier by Conrad and Shortell (1996). They found that "the greatest challenge remaining for system integration is to build *clinical integration:* the coordination of health services across providers, functions, activities, processes, and settings in order to realize maximum value for persons for whom the system has assumed responsibility."

TABLE 1.1 Network/System Characteristics

Type of network/system	Hospital organization	Physician organization	Insurance product	Hospital characteristics
Centralized health networks/systems	Service delivery organized centrally	Organized centrally at the network/system level	Organized centrally at the network/system level	Located in urban areas with hospitals in close geographic proximity to one another
Centralized physician/insurance health systems	Services decentralized and dispersed widely across individual affiliated hospitals	Organized centrally at network/system level	Organized centrally at network/system level	Hospitals located in close proximity to each other
Moderately centralized health networks/systems	Individual hospitals have great autonomy in organizing service delivery	Physician/hospital organizations both at the local hospital and the system level	Contracts and products both at the local hospital and system level	Moderate number of hospitals more geographically dispersed
Decentralized health networks/systems	Organized at individual hospital level, highly differentiated services	Organized at the local level only	Local contracts	Large number of hospitals spread over broad geographic area
Independent hospital networks/systems	Aggregation of horizontally affiliated hospitals each with substantial autonomy	Organized at the local level only	Local contracts only	Small numbers of hospitals primarily in rural areas

Source: Shortell, Bazzoli, Dubbs, & Kralovec, "Classifying Health Networks and Systems: Managerial and Policy Implications," 2000, *Healthcare Management Review,* 25(4), 9–17.

As noted earlier, horizontal integration results from the aggregation of organizations delivering similar services, such as hospitals. Many networks/systems are horizontally integrated and are comprised of only hospitals. There have been similar initiatives in certain markets among nursing homes. Vertical integration, on the other hand, results from different levels of providers coming together, that is, hospitals, nursing homes, physician groups, home health care agencies, and others. Conrad and Shortell (1996) make a critical distinction between horizontal and vertical integration. They argue that the two goals of achieving economies of scale and increased market power that have driven hospitals to horizontal integration are not necessarily collinear. Although scale economies imply reduced average costs due to consolidation of services, increased market power can result in higher prices due to monopolistic behavior. The authors take the position that vertical integration, on the other hand, is unlikely to yield "increased prices or reduced output." In other words, although horizontal integration may result in higher prices, vertical integration need not, because it brings a range of organizations that deliver different levels of care under single management. The components of such an organizational structure would encompass ambulatory care, acute care, subacute care, home care, and long-term care, and its goals would include "increasing efficiency, enhancing coordination of care along the continuum, and providing 'one-stop shopping' for managed care purchasers and payers" (Conrad & Shortell, 1996).

In 1996, when Conrad and Shortell published their findings, evidence about the performance of networks/systems was only beginning to emerge. They reported, however, that more integrated systems were found to perform better financially relative to their competitors. They also stated that "greater physician-system integration was significantly related to higher inpatient productivity and to higher levels of clinical integration" (Conrad & Shortell, 1996). Yet the authors concluded that the track record of horizontally integrated hospital systems was one of "unfulfilled promises" and that these systems had failed to demonstrate a competitive advantage or deliver "added value." The authors added that creating a continuum of care is extremely difficult due to barriers such as the lack of "well-developed, flexible, and timely information systems" and the failure of individual medical disciplines and other groups of health professionals to see the "connections outside of their own immediate roles in the care process" (Conrad & Shortell, 1996).

Results of a national survey on the level of integration of IDSs (Burns et al., 2001) clearly shed light on the inability of IDSs to achieve true integration and the failure of systems to deliver added value. The most progressive systems had created integrated *structures,* but they had failed to integrate the *processes* of patient care. Therefore, even the most advanced systems that had developed beyond the narrow acute-care mind-set were unable to deliver coordinated clinical care across the different care settings experienced during a given episode of illness. Burns et al. (2001) concluded that "integrative structures do not automatically imply a given set of integrative processes."

Given the importance of coordinating care across all care settings, the business concept of *virtual integration* has been proposed to substitute for *vertical integration* (Pallarito, 1996; Robinson & Casalino, 1996). Virtual integration would have different providers of care structurally integrate by collaborating through contractual arrangements, even in the absence of common ownership, using information systems as the vehicle to achieve functional integration. The electronic medical record is one illustration of this concept. Although virtual integration has been applied successfully in the business world, with different companies aligning virtually to develop and market a product, application to health care has definite limitations. First, health care is local. Therefore, the different care settings required (i.e., hospital, nursing home, doctor's office, etc.) need to be relatively close to where the patient resides. Yet facilities within a given geographic area are often affiliated not with one another, but with competing networks/systems. Second, in environments where provider oversupply leads to intense competition locally, it is unlikely that organizationally unrelated providers will share data. The competition is further aggravated by the blurring of distinctions between settings such as hospitals and nursing homes that historically have provided different levels of care; for example, settings other than hospitals are providing acute care, resulting in competition even among dissimilar institutions. In the absence of common ownership, it is unlikely that these providers will achieve well-coordinated patient care through virtual integration. Nevertheless, experimentation has yielded some success stories where impeding factors do not exist. The small town of Winona, Minnesota, has become a "wired community" where the local 99-bed hospital, patients, physicians, and other health care entities are connected via the Internet (Innovations in Technology, 2000).

THE QUALITY QUESTION

Driven by the concern of health care systems about possible payment denials by managed care plans, quality initiatives of hospital systems in the era of managed care have focused principally on utilization review. Furthermore, lack of processes and the necessary infrastructure have prevented systems from measuring the true clinical consequences of controlled utilization or engaging in clinical outcomes studies. Because recovery from a single episode of illness now stretches across multiple care settings as the duration of care within hospital walls is diminishing, true outcomes analysis is not possible unless the cases are followed through the entire continuum of care.

The recommendations of the Committee on Quality in Healthcare in America (Institute of Medicine, 2001) are pertinent to the measurement of quality throughout the continuum of care. The committee was formed by the Institute of Medicine (IOM) in 1998 and has most recently issued its report and recommendations on "Crossing the Quality Chasm: A New Health System for the 21st Century" (IOM, 2001). Included among the ten rules formulated by the committee to guide the patient-clinician relationship are the following: "care should be continuous, responsive and customized to the patient's needs; the system should anticipate needs rather than simply react to events; the system should not waste resources or the patient's time; there should be increased cooperation among clinicians for exchange of information and coordination of care." These recommendations reinforce the importance of extending quality improvement across the entire continuum of care. The committee further recommends that health care organizations, clinicians, and patients work together to redesign how care is delivered and suggests that information technology and care teams be used to coordinate care for patients who may have multiple conditions and who may therefore use a variety of services in different settings over time.

WHAT LIES AHEAD

The recommendations of the IOM Committee (IOM, 2001) to use information technology and teams to coordinate chronic care appears to be a most effective way to reduce health care costs while at the same time improving clinical quality of care, when one considers the following factors. Many studies, such as that of the IOM, have noted that approximately 15 to 25 conditions, nearly all of which are chronic in nature, account for the majority of health care services consumed by Americans. Further, these chronic conditions are most highly prevalent in the older population; 79 million baby boomers will reach the age of 65 starting in the year 2011 (Coile, 2001). Implementing the recommendations of the IOM, however, requires a perspective much broader than the narrow acute-care focus of hospital-dominated systems. Implementation requires attention to prevention and health maintenance, the availability of the full continuum of care settings, and effective clinical and administrative integration of the different care settings.

It is important to note that, as illustrated in this chapter, the name acquired by an organization—for example, network, system, integrated delivery system, and others—may not accurately reflect the operation of the organization, nor does it mean that two different organizations using the same term necessarily function in identical ways. In other words, the degree and effectiveness of clinical and administrative integration will vary even among organizations that present themselves as networks or systems, or even those that purport to be integrated delivery systems.

Given all this, the effectiveness and success of hospitals in the twenty-first century will be a function of the degree to which they are capable of affecting the clinical care of each acute episode of illness from onset to full recovery across different care settings. Furthermore, hospitals must be part of an enterprise that can manage the chronic conditions of the older population, as this population has always been an important source of hospital admissions.

Although economic incentives built into new insurance products will diminish the rate of hospitalization of the older population, and components of care that traditionally took place in the hospital will now occur in other care settings, hospitals will always be a very important component of health care delivery. They will continue to provide the most sophisticated, highly intensive care and will therefore remain as the most costly care setting. Their future viability will be strengthened by membership in an effectively integrated system.

REFERENCES

Bazzoli, G. J., Shortell, S. M., Dubbs, N., Chan, C., & Kralovec, P. (1999). A taxonomy of health networks and systems: Bringing order out of chaos. *Health Services Research, 33, 6,* 1683–1717.

Burns, L. R., Walston, S. L., Alexander, J. A., Zuckerman, H. S., Anderson, R. M., Torrens, P. R., & Hilberman, D. (2001). Just how integrated are integrated delivery systems? Results from a national survey. *Health Management Review, 26, 1,* 20–39.

Coile, R. C. Jr. (2001). A millennium mindset: The long boom. *Journal of Healthcare Management, 6, 2,* 86–90.

Conrad, D. A., & Shortell, S. M. (1996). Integrated health systems: Promise and performance. *Frontiers of Health Services Management, 13, 1,* 3–40.

Innovations in technology, from promises to performance (2000). *Hospitals and Health Networks, 74*(12), 4–7.

Institute of Medicine. (2001). *Crossing the quality chasm: A new health system for the 21st century.* Washington, D.C.: National Academy Press.

Luke, R. D., & Begun, J. W. (1996). Permitting organizational boundaries: The challenge of integration in healthcare. *Frontiers in Health Services Management, 13, 1,* 46–49.

Pallarito, K. (1996). Virtual healthcare—Linking firms to form all-star teams. *Modern Healthcare, 26, 12,* 42–47.

Robinson, J. C., & Casalino, L. P. (1996). Vertical integration and organizational networks in healthcare. *Health Affairs, 15, 1,* 7–22.

Shortell, S. M., Bazzoli, G. J., Dubbs, N. L., & Kralovec, P. (2000). Classifying health networks and systems: Managerial and policy implications. *Health Care Management Review, 4,* 9–17.

Stevens, R. (1989). *In sickness and in wealth: American hospitals in the twentieth century.* New York: Basic Books.

■ 2
Paying for Hospital Care

Kyle L. Grazier

Although physicians and other health care providers dedicate their lives to the prevention, alleviation, and cure of illness, their position at the core of health care delivery mandates a comprehension of the health care payment and reimbursement system. Until a few decades ago, payment for services provided by institutions and practitioners was a relatively straightforward process. A simpler mix of economics and service provision reflected subjective, nearly regulation-free judgements of the monetary value of a visit with the doctor or a night in the hospital. Few consumers had medical insurance, and those who did seldom had a choice about the extent of coverage or the fees paid to their providers. This simple schema no longer exists. The recent dramatic advances in clinical medicine, communications, and general technology have revolutionized the underlying assumptions of the worth of medical care and the rights of American citizens.

One of the consequences of these changes is the mix of intentional and unintentional incentives generated from payment policies specific to institutions and individual providers. Partly as a result of piecemeal planning and partly as a consequence of targeted action, mechanisms and formulas are in place that concurrently reward and penalize different behaviors. Although all are interested in quality, the interests of payers intent on controlling costs are often at odds with the interests of clinicians intent on providing state-of-the art care. Many times the choice between quantity and quality is unnecessary; nonetheless, the production of high quality, moderate cost, and most effective care is hard to achieve.

PAYMENT SYSTEMS: A BRIEF HISTORY

The history of health care payments systems is a complex puzzle of serendipity, politics, and financial management. Well before the development of a large-scale health care system, employers recognized that maintaining the

16

health of their workers, whether sailors on merchant ships, railroad builders, or laborers on automobile assembly lines, was in their financial interest. Salaried and capitated physicians provided care for groups of employees and contract workers, leading to the development of health plans such as Kaiser Permanente and the Mayo Clinic that combined insurance coverage with delivery of health care. During and after the Second World War, when the government froze wages, health benefits were used to entice workers to large manufacturers and assembly plants. Once in place, health insurance coverage would remain on the bargaining table for years to come. Despite its widespread use in recruiting and maintaining workers, coverage was tied to active employment; it ended for those who retired, were disabled, or became unemployed.

Several presidents, starting with Dwight D. Eisenhower, sought to meet the needs of some constituents without insurance coverage. To better understand the environment, Eisenhower ordered a national survey to determine the types of plans available to citizens (Rayburn, 1992). The survey documented that few had coverage, and benefits were sparse for those who did. Although his attempt to establish a national business-controlled health insurance plan failed, he introduced health care coverage as an item for the national agenda. John F. Kennedy also attempted to promote a program for national health insurance, at least for the aged, but met opposition from national trade organizations. It was not until 1965 that Lyndon B. Johnson kept a campaign promise and signed legislation creating Medicare and Medicaid, transforming the health care payment system.

Medicare is a health insurance program for U.S. citizens 65 years of age or older (depending upon prior qualifying employment) and some younger persons with a qualifying disability or end-stage renal disease. The Medicare program is divided into two main components: Part A and Part B. Part A is an entitlement program of hospital insurance (HI) whose benefits are automatically provided at no charge on the basis of work history. The program generally covers inpatient hospital services, subacute care in a rehabilitation or skilled nursing facility, and hospice care. Part B is a voluntary program of supplementary medical insurance (SMI) whose benefits are available only if individuals choose to pay a monthly premium (Employee Benefits Research Institute, 1997). This program covers both inpatient and outpatient physicians' services, emergency room visits, ambulatory surgery diagnostic tests, laboratory services, and some medical equipment. Most individuals in the program enroll in both Part A and B (Iglehart, 1999a). Individuals entitled to benefits under Part A and enrolled in Part B may have the option to enroll in a Medicare + Choice plan. These plans can offer coverage arrangements that include some features of managed care, possible access to a medical savings account, or coverage under a traditional fee-for-service arrangement (Medicare, 1965a).

Payment for services received by a Medicare enrollee can be made solely by Medicare or, if the person is covered under another plan, can be shared between Medicare and the health plan or other insurer. Which payer is the primary or secondary payer and the terms under which each pays are prescribed by the federal government. The distribution of payment, or coordination of benefits, depends on such factors as the types of services, size of employer, health plan coverage, involvement of Workers' Compensation claims, and other very specific features (Medicare, 1965b).

Medicaid is an entitlement program that covers health services for many people of limited means, including individuals with low-income who are receiving public assistance, the working poor, and those who are disabled and blind (Iglehart, 1999b). In 1965, Title XVII of the Social Security Act, known as Grants to States for Medical Assistance Programs, established this jointly funded cooperative program to aid states in the provision of adequate medical care to eligible persons who are needy. It has since become the largest program providing medical and health-related services to America's poorest people (Health Care Financing Administration [HCFA], 2001). Medicaid is funded though a combination of federal and state monies, the formula for which is based on state income levels. Under broad guidelines specified by the federal government, states administer the program, determine who is eligible, decide the scope and duration of services, and set payment levels to providers. Thus, some benefits vary from state to state. To receive matching federal funds, states must provide some services to those who are eligible by virtue of their participation in other government programs; these individuals are known as the "categorically needy." States that wish to provide services to the "medically needy" must also include a minimum scope and duration of services defined by the federal program. Recently, other optional services can be offered by states under the aegis of the Medicaid program, the costs of which are also shared between the states and the federal government.

Part of the political calculus for passage of this federal support for those who are aged and poor involved the recognition that hospitals and other providers would be unwilling to participate in such plans unless their financial viability were guaranteed. Thus, the pricing system for Medicare and Medicaid was based on the hospitals' recovery of their reported costs (Rayburn, 1992), essentially allowing hospitals and physicians to set their own prices. Although generous cost-based reimbursement protected hospitals and physicians financially, it also led to the escalation of health care costs, as it lacked incentives to economize on care or improve efficiency.

Congress revisited the legislation that created Medicare and Medicaid several times in an attempt to deal with the cost inflation. Section 223 of the amended act imposed restrictions on the growth in costs that would be compensated by the programs. The amendments set target limits on reimbursement levels and attempted to modify the behavior of hospitals by changing the manner in which ancillary and labor costs were reported and reimbursed. In 1982, the Tax Equity and Fiscal Responsibility Act (TEFRA) (1982) imposed further constraints. Congress instructed the Department of Health and Human Services (HSS) to recommend a plan for paying for care on the basis of an entire admission, rather than per day. Within months of the passage of TEFRA, the secretary of HHS presented a plan for a prospective payment system (PPS) in which hospitals would be reimbursed a fixed predetermined amount of dollars for each Medicare admission based on its classification into a diagnosis related group (DRG) (Schweiker, 1982). The payment a hospital receives for each admission is based on average resource use for that particular diagnosis. These averages were generated by government-sponsored research that supported the design and pilot testing of DRGs (Fetter, Thompson, Freeman, & Vertrees, 1980). As opposed to the prior cost-based strategy in which hospitals were reimbursed based on their reported costs, it was felt that the PPS would create incentives for hospitals to decrease unnecessary costs, as they would lose money if costs per case exceeded the DRG payment. The application of the DRG formula within the prospective payment system also recognized the possibility of cases outside the norm, or outliers. When a hospital had cases with extraordinarily high lengths of stay and/or costs, those cases used a different formula for payment (Ellis & McGuire, 1988). Because the research did not include data for some specialty services, such as for children, psychiatry, and rehabilitation, prospective payment by Medicare excluded those admissions. Payment for those cases instead fell within the more cost-based formula originally set under TEFRA. This dual formula for Medicare payment still exists to a limited extent in most hospitals today.

In many states, the Medicare formula for hospital payment was also used for Medicaid programs, and the cost escalation seen in the Medicare program was mirrored in the Medicaid program. As state budgets suffered under the weight of their Medicaid expenditures, innovations in payment systems were encouraged.

MEDICARE'S PAYMENT TO HOSPITALS

Because Medicare pays for more than 36% of all hospital care, making it the largest single purchaser of inpatient care, it is important to understand its payment mechanisms. Since implementation of prospective payment in 1984, hospitals have seen a major shift in the characteristics of inpatients, the type and amount of clinical care delivered, and the nature of financial incentives for physician and hospital.

Under Medicare's PPS program, hospitals receive a prospectively determined amount for each admission that has at least one Medicare billable day. This amount reflects Medicare's assessment of the operating and capital (property, plant, and equipment) costs per case attributable to Medicare. Hospitals also receive funds for graduate medical education to cover the costs of educating interns and residents, and other funding from Medicare beneficiary copayments.

The operating and capital payments are based on a similarly structured payment formula. (Medicare Payment Advisory Commission, 2001) This formula consists of three major factors: (a) a per-case base payment rate, (b) case mix, and (c) a disproportionate share adjustment and/or indirect medical allowance. The per-case base payment rate reflects the average cost of a Medicare case across the country. The base payment rate is modified from the national rate by the differences in input prices in the hospital's market area. A wage index that reflects the cost of hospital wages in a metropolitan or a statewide rural area is applied to the standard case rate to adjust for local labor costs. An average national rate for PPS capital costs is now used, following a 10-year phase-in period in which the rate was proportioned between national and local costs.

The intent of the second piece of the formula is to reflect the differing case mix of a particular hospital relative to other hospitals. *Case mix* is the scheme used to characterize the clinical complexity and expected resource utilization of each diagnostic category. Each DRG is assigned a separate weight. The product of the DRG weight per case seen in the hospital and the base payment rate is the hospital's payment per case. The facility's case mix index (CMI) is the weighted average of the DRG weights for the mix of Medicare patients seen in that hospital. An increase in a hospital's CMI reflects a higher proportion of cases with more highly weighted DRGs. A higher CMI results in a higher operating and capital PPS payments to the hospital.

The third component of the formula is Medicare's attempt to reimburse hospitals for other costs out of their control. This includes an amount for those hospitals that treat a large proportion of poor and indigent people, called a disproportionate share adjustment. An indirect medical education amount is added for the added costs associated with additional services ordered by interns and residents. Extremely costly cases can qualify for an additional outlier case amount. These payments, added to the per case PPS amount, promote societal policy objectives and help hospitals achieve their own goals, such as improving Medicare beneficiaries' access to care (Cone & Dranove, 1986; Hadley & Swartz, 1989; Keeler, Carter, & Trude, 1988).

THE EFFECT OF MEDICARE PPS ON HOSPITALS

Hospital operations have felt a significant impact from DRGs. Fixed payments per DRG created incentives for hospitals to shorten inpatient lengths of stay as a means of controlling costs and increasing profitability. Pressure to control costs increased further, as private insurers also switched to a similar prospective payment system. Hospitals instituted policies and processes to review ongoing inpatient care, strengthen discharge planning, and substitute ambulatory services where feasible. Many hospitals diversified into home care, rehabilitative care, and long-term care for patients in the convalescent phases of their illnesses (Burda, 1993). As a result, length of stay declined between 1970 and 1998 from 13.2 to 6.3 days for persons aged 75 to 84, and 13.7 to 6.4 days for persons age 85 and older (Bernstein, Hing, Burt, & Hall, 2001).

Although DRGs were found to have some positive effects in controlling inpatient Medicare expenditures, they did not significantly slow increases in total Medicare spending, as costs were often shifted to outpatient departments and post-acute-care services, which were still not affected by prospective payment financing. The Center for Medicare and Medicaid Services (CMS, formerly the Health Care Financing Administration) has since instituted prospective payment for home care and long term care; similar systems for other facilities are under consideration.

Over the past 10 years, many analysts have monitored the adequacy of Medicare's inpatient rates (Bray, Carter, Dobson, Watt, & Shortell, 1994; Ellis & McGuire, 1986, 1988; Manton, Woodbury, Vertrees, & Stallard, 1993; McCarthy, 1988). As measured by their operating margins, hospitals have had good and bad years. Several pieces of recent legislation have had significant negative impacts on Medicare payments to hospitals. These include the Balanced Budget Act of 1997, the Balanced Budget Refinement Act of 1999, and the Medicare, Medicaid and SCHIP Benefits Improvement and Protection Act of 2000.

Some of the most profound consequences to hospitals of this legislation derived from the effect on coverage of the cost of training medical providers, most specifically, physicians. The amount the hospital is reimbursed directly, for salaries, and indirectly, through reimbursement for services ordered, is dependent on the Medicare formula (Schoenman, 1999). Indirectly, the availability of internships and residencies may be partially dependent upon the reimbursement levels received by hospitals for graduate medical education. Academic medical centers and other teaching hospitals petitioned the government to readjust the new formula to retain education subsidies. More legislation is likely as society grapples with the responsibilities for educating clinically competent providers.

THE EFFECT OF MEDICARE PAYMENTS ON PHYSICIANS

Although much of the effort in the early 1980s was directed at controlling inpatient costs, policymakers also began to focus their attention on the way

Medicare reimburses physicians. Although physician services accounted for less than one quarter of all spending, physicians potentially influence more than 70% of all health care spending (Thorpe & Knickman, 1998). Medicare had continued to reimburse physicians generously through fee-for-service arrangements that were based on the usual, customary, and reasonable charges for the service in the providers' own or similar communities. Under this payment system, the physician was reimbursed for services based on the lowest of three factors:

> the actual charge for the service; the physician's usual charge for the service the previous year; or the customary charge by physicians in that area and specialty for that service in the previous year. As this was still a fee-for-service method of payment, it was felt that this payment method still financially rewarded physicians for increasing volume of services. It was also felt to be inflationary, as physicians were able to increase their income by raising their usual charges. (Rice, 1997)

Continued escalation of costs stimulated an attempt to understand better the economic and noneconomic components that drive the cost of physician services (Greco & Eisenberg, 1994).

The Consolidated Omnibus Reconciliation Act of 1985 authorized funding for research that was to become the basis for Medicare's Resource Based Relative Value Scale (RBRVS) and the Medicare Fee Schedule (MFS). The Omnibus Budget Reconciliation Act of 1989 mandated the phase-in of the methodologies prescribed by that research. During the transition, the fees paid by Medicare for physicians' services were a blend of resource-based values and historical charges.

The philosophy of the RBRVS is similar to that underlying the DRGs and PPS: that indemnity, or compensation for loss, should reflect the resources consumed in the process of delivering services (Iglehart, 1991; Ogrod, 1997). This perspective led to a model for physician payment that identified components of resource use. These included a *physician work* relative value component: the time, skill, and technical effort needed to perform the procedure, the mental effort, and the psychological stress concerning the risk to the patient. The *practice cost* included practice overhead, such as rent, salaries for staff, medical equipment, and supplies. The third component was a *malpractice* value measure, to incorporate the expense of carrying liability insurance. Data for the second and third components came from the Medical Group Management Association and the American Medical Association surveys, and in some cases from government-supplied averages from accounting data sets. Although the RBRVS attempts to recognize the resources that are expended in providing care, it is only a piece of a broader formula that retains many of the negative aspects of the retrospective fee-for-service system infrastructure (Glickman & Noether 1997; Gold, Hurley, & Lake, 2001). Despite mandated volume controls, RBRVS was still a payment scheme that reimbursed physicians for higher volumes of services and increased charges, resulting in the continued escalation of health care costs.

CONFLICTING INCENTIVES

Although modifications to the original Medicare legislation have attempted to control costs incurred by both hospitals and physicians, success has been limited for the following reasons:

• Depending on the procedure or diagnosis, physicians can bill Medicare for in-hospital visits to their patients; hospitals can only receive the average costs for the average patient with this diagnosis. Physicians may have a financial incentive to maximize length of stay; hospitals have a financial incentive to minimize it.

• Patients demand the best quality care and the latest technology. They and their physicians are concerned about the effectiveness of care. Hospital managers, however, must also be concerned with efficiency; costs that exceed reimbursement reduce financial viability in the short and long run.

MANAGED CARE

Despite the many voluntary and involuntary changes, health care and hospital costs have continued to escalate. Concurrent attempts to control cost and behavior have included the use of managed care. Although variously defined, components of managed care usually include financial or behavioral incentives to manage the utilization of services for a designated group of enrollees or patients. The focus often is on the primary care gatekeeper, the physician who manages a group of patients over time to ensure that care is appropriate, coordinated, and cost-effective.

Managed care models differ in their methods and extent of control over the quantity and cost of services provided to enrollees who may or may not have had a choice in where to access care. These managed care organizations, or MCOs, differ in their governance, relationships with providers, cost-sharing, and extent to which incentives lead to controls over the quantity and price of services. Some plans offer limited services only at their facilities, using salaried providers. Other models offer networks of providers from which members can select when services are required. These preferred provider organizations (PPOs), with and without point-of-service options, substitute control over providers with consumer choice. This freedom to choose, as well as lower start-up costs for PPOs, has led to a rapid market expansion. In these scenarios, payment to hospitals for care of members is most often negotiated, not regulated, and usually is based on the DRG metric. In most cases, payment to physicians is on a fee-for-service/RBRVS formula, but with restricted volumes (Stearns, Wolfe, & Kindig, 1992; Schoenman, Hayes, & Cheng, 2001). In both cases, hospitals and physicians are faced with considerable responsibility for costs, but little control.

The consumer appeal and early cost controls of managed care caught the attention of the Medicaid and Medicare programs. Medicare proposed regulations that would allow health plans that met certain criteria to enroll Medicare clients. CMS introduced the Medicare + Choice program as an option to the traditional Medicare program. Under Medicare + Choice, Medicare pays managed care plans to provide all health services for the enrolled Medicare beneficiaries, on the assumption that traditional cost controls implemented by managed care as well as the greater emphasis on prevention would be an effective way of controlling health care costs in these populations. Managed care plans often provided incentives for enrollment by offering extra benefits beyond the traditional Part A and Part B services. Medicaid also followed suit by establishing mandatory enrollment into managed care plans for some beneficiaries. Medicare and Medicaid's managed care programs devised payment mechanisms that were intended to recognize the likely added costs of serving these populations and removed penalties that might arise from attracting sicker patients. Complex formulas have been in place to adjust the payment levels to plans that care for Medicare and, in many states, Medicaid, clients. These government payment policies have imposed a downward pressure on the fees paid to physicians and hospitals that serve the public sector managed-care clients.

Although managed care has not lived up to its original intent, most believe that the managed care movement has provided benefit. Preventive health services have received considerably more attention, for example, because of a greater emphasis on health maintenance. However, capitating providers—a process in which physicians or practices are given a fixed price to cover all the costs of inpatient and outpatient services for a fixed time for a fixed number of patients—has proven less acceptable to providers and may be unsustainable. This level of risk-sharing, in which the provider is responsible for utilization outside of his or her control, has often led to patient distrust and the appearance of inappropriate constraints on care.

THE FUTURE

In spite of the recognized flaws, many state Medicaid programs and most private insurers have adopted the federal formulae for paying facilities and physicians (Fossett et al., 2000; Rosenbaum, 1997). Currently, researchers and policy makers are exploring the feasibility of using mixed models of payment for services (Grazier, 1999; Newhouse, Buntin, & Chapman, 1997). These models rely on the combination of a prospectively paid predetermined amount and a retrospectively paid fee for services. The goal is to hold providers accountable for those aspects of care that are controllable, but also to pay them for utilization of services not under their direct control. The capitated amount would cover the costs of preventive and illness care, for instance, but the formula would also allow a provider to recover the costs of care given to a particularly ill individual who requires high intensity, acute care (Gabel, Ginsburg, Whitmore, & Pickreign, 2000; Hornbrook, 1999). A payment formula that includes a mix of payment types should create multiple incentives that would meet institutional and individual provider payment system goals.

CONCLUSION

The history of payment system regulation is a relatively short one. Despite that, we have learned a considerable amount about what is effective and what remains uncertain. In light of the unintended consequences of fixed formulas and single methods, future policies are much more likely to consider the conundrum clinicians generally face when confronted with separate institutional and individual payment methodologies. Discussions are underway to reexamine the original Medicare legislation for its separate regulations of practitioners and institutions. As service delivery becomes even more integrated across settings and providers, reimbursement formulas must consider a more global approach to payment. Perhaps the only way to align incentives is to align methodologies. Although the incremental approach to this effort has been only partially successful, we know more now about what needs to be changed and how best to implement the change. Perhaps in the foreseeable future, the delivery of the highest quality, most efficient and reasonable cost care will be available in concert with, rather than in spite of, the methods for payment.

REFERENCES

Balanced Budget Act of 1997 (Pub. L. No. 105–133).
Balanced Budget Refinement Act of 1999. (Pub. L. No. 106–113).
Bernstein, A. B., Hing, E., Burt, C. W., & Hall, M. J. (2001). Trend data on medical encounters: Tracking a moving target. *Health Affairs, 20*(2), 58–72.

Bray, N., Carter, C., Dobson, A., Watt, J. M., & Shortell, S. (1994). An examination of winners and losers under Medicare's Prospective Payment System. *Health Care Management Review, 19*(1), 44–55.

Burda, D. (1993, October 4). What we've learned from DRG's. *Modern Healthcare*, 42–44.

Cone, K. R., & Dranove, D. (1986). Why did states enact hospital rate-setting laws? *Journal of Law and Economics 29*, 287–302.

Consolidated Omnibus Budget Reconciliation Act of 1985. (Pub. L. No. 99–272).

Ellis, R. P., & McGuire, T. G. (1986). Provider behavior under prospective reimbursement. *Journal of Health Economics 5*, 129–151.

Ellis, R. P., & McGuire, T. G. (1988). Insurance principles and the design of prospective payment systems. *Journal of Health Economics 7*, 215–223.

Employee Benefits Research Institute. (1997). Social Security and Medicare. In *Fundamentals of employee benefit programs* (5th ed., pp. 15–33). Washington, DC: Author.

Fetter, R. A., Thompson, J. D., Freeman, J., & Vertrees, R. (1980). Case mix definition by diagnosis related groups. *Medical Care, 18*(Suppl.), 1–53.

Fossett, J. W., Goggin, M., Hall, J. S., Johnston, J., Plein, C., Roper, R., & Weissert, C. (2000). Managing Medicaid managed care: Are states becoming prudent purchasers? *Health Affairs, 19(4)*, 36–49.

Gabel, J. R., Ginsburg, P. B., Whitmore, H. H., & Pickreign, J. D. (2000). Withering on the vine: The decline of indemnity health insurance. *Health Affairs, 19*, 152–157.

Glickman, M. E., & Noether, M. (1997). An examination of cross-specialty linkage applied to the Resource-Based Relative Value Scale. *Medical Care, 35*, 843–866.

Gold, M. R., Hurley, R., & Lake, T. (2001). Provider organizations at risk: A profile of major risk-bearing intermediaries, 1999. *Health Affairs, 20*, 175–185.

Grazier, K. L. (1999). Managing risks in managed care. In *Managed Care Essentials* (pp. 65–83). Chicago: Health Administration Press.

Greco, P. J., & Eisenberg, J. M. (1994). Changing physicians' practices. *New England Journal of Medicine, 329*, 1271–1274.

Hadley, J., & Swartz, K. (1989). The impacts on hospital costs between 1980 and 1984 of hospital rate regulation, competition, and changes in health insurance coverage. *Inquiry, 26*, 35–47.

Health Care Financing Administration. (2001). CMS Data and Statistics [Online]. Available at www.hcfa.gov/stats

Hornbrook, M. (1999). Commentary: Improving risk-adjusted models for capitation payment and global budgeting. *Health Services Research, 33*, 1745–1751.

Iglehart, J. K. (1991). The struggle over physician-payment reform. *New England Journal of Medicine, 325*, 823–828.

Iglehart, J. K. (1999a). The American health care system: Medicare. *New England Journal of Medicine, 340*, 327–332.

Iglehart, J. K. (1999b). The American health care system: Medicaid. *New England Journal of Medicine, 340,* 403–408.

Keeler, E. B., Carter, G. M., & Trude, S. (1988). Insurance aspects of DRG outlier payments. *Journal of Health Economics, 7,* 193–214.

Manton, K. G., Woodbury, M. A., Vertrees, J. C., & Stallard, E. (1993). Use of Medicare services before and after the introduction of PPS. *Health Services Research, 28,* 269–292.

McCarthy, C. M. (1988). DRG's—Five years later. *New England Journal of Medicine, 318,* 1683–1686.

Medicare. (1965a). Social Security Act, Title XVIII, § 1851. (42 U.S.C. 1395w-21).

Medicare. (1965b). Social Security Act, Title XVIII, § 1862. (42 U.S.C. 1395y; 42 CFR 411.46).

Medicare, Medicaid, and SCHIP Benefits Improvement and Protection Act of 2000. (Pub. L. No. 106–554).

Medicare Payment Advisory Commission. (2001, March). Report to the Congress: Medicare payment policy. Washington, D. C.: MedPAC.

Newhouse J. P., Buntin, M. B., & Chapman J. D. (1997). Risk adjustment and Medicare: Taking a closer look. *Health Affairs, 16,* 26–43.

Ogrod, E. S. (1997) Compensation and quality: A physician's view. *Health Affairs, 16 (3),* 82–86.

Omnibus Budget Reconciliation Act of 1989 (Pub. L. No. 101–239).

Rayburn, J. M. (1992). History and process of the Medicare reimbursement programs. *Health Marketing Quarterly, 9*(3/4), 115–131.

Rice, T. (1997). Recent changes in physician payment policies: Impacts and implications. *Annual Review of Public Health, 18,* 549–565.

Rosenbaum, S. (1997). A look inside Medicaid Managed Care. *Health Affairs, 16,* 266–271.

Schoenman, J. (1999). Impact of the BBA on Medicare HMO payments for rural areas. *Health Affairs, 18,* 244–254.

Schoenman, J. A., Hayes, K. J., & Cheng, C. M. (2001). Medicare physician payment changes: Impact on physicians and beneficiaries. *Health Affairs, 20*(2), 263–273.

Schweiker, R. J. (1982 December). Report to Congress: Hospital Prospective Reimbursement. Washington, DC: Department of Health and Human Services.

State Children's Health Insurance Program (SCHIP). Social Security Act (Title XXI). Available at www.cms.hss.gov/schip.

Stearns, S. C., Wolfe, B. L., & Kindig, D. A. (1992). Physician responses to fee-for-service and capitation payment. *Inquiry, 29,* 416–425.

Thorpe, K. E., & Knickman, J. R. (1998). Financing for health care. In A. R. Kovner et al. (eds), *Health Care Delivery in the United States* (6th ed., pp. 32–63). New York: Springer Publishing.

Tax Equity and Fiscal Responsibility Act of 1982. (Pub. L. No. 97–248).

■ 3
Working in Teams

Eugenia L. Siegler

Hospitals are full of teams. House staff work in teams; patient care units may have wound-care teams and discharge planning teams; and committees that implement quality improvement measures and other administrative functions may be modeled as teams. Despite the omnipresence and importance of teams, clinicians have little training in team skills. This chapter will introduce teams and the factors that promote and discourage their effectiveness in the hospital setting.

TEAM FUNDAMENTALS

In its simplest form, a team is a group of individuals who work together for a shared purpose. Katzenbach and Smith (1993) define a team as "a small number of people with complementary skills who are committed to a common purpose, set of performance goals, and approach for which they hold themselves mutually accountable." The defining outcome of teamwork is the "collective work product." This distinguishes the team from the task force or other kind of group whose output reflects a primary focus on individual accomplishment.

Teams are not built in a day. Drinka and Clark (2000) describe in detail how teams form and develop. The authors divide team evolution into five phases (pp. 18–27):

1. *Forming:* In this stage, the team members come together and begin their work, falling into familiar, comfortable role patterns and suppressing conflict in order to "get started."

2. *Norming:* In this phase, participants try to develop goals and a sense of purpose for the team. Drinka and Clark suggest that in this phase, conflict

28

("storming") is suppressed because of avoidance and time pressures unique to the health care environment; needless to say, conflicts do not stay dormant forever.

3. *Confronting:* In this phase the team acknowledges and addresses conflicts that have arisen over power and decision-making. Here, members establish "the right to individual power as a norm" (p. 26) and begin to confront one another and debate constructively.

4. *Performing:* In this phase the team is functioning well; differences lead to creative solutions, not unresolved personal conflicts. Rapid turnover in team membership can limit the opportunities to enter this phase.

5. *Leaving:* This phase usually refers to the effect of loss of individual members on the team's functioning as a whole—how the team copes with both the absence of an important contributor and the changes in relationships that follow. Teams themselves can be dissolved when they no longer have a purpose or institutional support.

Health care teams can move back and forth between phases, and individual participants, especially newcomers or those with little prior team experience, may be out of phase with the rest of the team.

THE MEDICAL PHYSICIAN TEAM: A CLASSIC HIERARCHY

A clinician trainee's first and most frequent exposure to teams is through participation in a group that consists of an attending physician, one or two residents, interns, medical students, and occasionally others (i.e., nurse practitioners or physician assistants). The overt function of this team is patient care; it oversees a patient's hospital course, determining the diagnosis and effecting appropriate treatment. Nonetheless, the medical physician team actually serves multiple purposes, some of which may be conflicting. Patient care may be the primary goal, but the team is also the locus of house staff and student training and evaluation. In some settings, implementation of research protocols may conflict with patient care goals and lead to confusion about roles and responsibilities. These other functions are rarely as obvious to team members as the clinical focus, and yet failure to understand how these secondary goals determine the team's purpose and behavior may undermine its primary patient-care mission. (Chapter 5 describes the conflicts between teaching and patient-care missions in more detail; chapter 23 is devoted to the ethical conflicts between patient care and research.)

When evaluating how teams function, it is useful to examine the impact of the team's structure on its effectiveness (Siegler & Whitney, 1994). The structure of a classic medical physician team is strictly hierarchical; that is, a clear chain of command begins at the top with an attending physician and proceeds downward by rank: resident, intern (PA or NP), student. Certain things are noteworthy about this hierarchy. First, the most powerful and experienced tend to spend the least amount of time with the patient. Attending physicians, especially those who rotate 1 or 2 months a year on teaching services, know the least about the patient and are dependent on the medical students and house staff to provide fundamental information (Christensen & Larson, 1993). Second, many others who play crucial roles in the patient's care (e.g., the staff nurse, the social worker, and the patient) are rarely thought of, or treated as, members of the team. The staff nurse receives orders via chart or computer; in hospitals verbal communication is secondary because the need for documentation takes precedence over personal communication. Thus, although the staff nurse and medical physician team may have important information to exchange about the patient's status, such communications usually must take place outside the formal times set aside for discussion (medical team rounds and nursing report). The social worker may also be viewed as an outsider, important for discharge planning or accessing of services but rarely recruited to assist the patient in coping with illness and even more rarely brought into the medical team's inner circle. Nor is the patient usually considered a member of the team; in the inpatient setting the patient is considered the object of care.

The acuity of the patient's illness, the hierarchical nature of classic inpatient-care teams, and their exclusivity promote efficiency of care but may also reduce the team's overall effectiveness. Discrepancies in power and status often influence communication patterns (Christensen & Larson, 1993), and this may prevent the most experienced members of the team from finding out information essential to decision-making. Lower-status members of the team such as medical students or interns spend the greatest amount of time with the patient and may know the most details of the history, but may be the most reluctant to speak up. The structure of rounds overcomes this to some degree, as the intern or student is often the first to present the case, but team discussions about patient care tend to revert to a more deferential decision-making system, and other members of the team may be much less likely to talk, even if they can contribute. In particular, one study suggests that an individual team member may not discuss details he or she alone knows (Christensen et al., 2000); instead, the team members tend to talk about the aspects of patient history that they share. Thus, the hierarchical power structure undermines one of the great benefits of working in teams—sharing knowledge and experience to create plans of care that are better than what any individual could accomplish.

A second important characteristic of inpatient-care teams, the transience of their membership, is also harmful to team effectiveness. Here, the team's secondary educational function takes precedence; house staff and medical students rotate every 2 to 6 weeks in order to obtain experience in different venues and learn from different residents and attending physicians. Despite the importance of team members' awareness of their colleagues' knowledge and interests to overall team functioning and decision-making (Christensen & Larson, 1993), the frequent reshuffling of team members impedes this kind of understanding, and medical teams rarely have the opportunity to mature and develop a deep sense of trust that allows individuals to rely on their colleagues' special interests or talents.

OTHER TEAM MODELS

It is hard to imagine a nonhierarchical team in a hospital setting; someone must write orders, and someone else must carry them out. In acute care, where diagnostic tests, medications, and procedures dominate the agenda, hierarchies would seem to be the most efficient structures. It has been argued that even in settings where collaboration across disciplines is essential—the intensive care unit, for example—policies and regulations mandate a hierarchical chain of command. Nonetheless, it is important to separate the legal formalities from the behaviors and interactions of professionals (Siegler & Whitney, 1994). Even in highly acute settings, one can have some flexibility of roles, bidirectional communication, and a more equitable responsibility for decision-making.

Just as teams need not be hierarchical, they need not be unidisciplinary (that is, composed of members all from the same discipline), as are most hospital patient-care teams. Although the term "unidisciplinary" is self-explanatory, team theorists often distinguish between the terms "multidisciplinary" and "interdisciplinary." Multidisciplinary teams need fulfill only one requirement: that they be composed of individuals from different disciplines. Exactly what those disciplines may be is subject to some interpretation. Specialty teams may consist of individuals from multiple fields within the same profession (oncologist, radiation oncologist, and surgeon, for example), but more often a team is considered multidisciplinary when its members are from different professions (e.g., nurse, physician, social worker, physical therapist, nutritionist). Interdisciplinary teams, a subset of multidisciplinary teams, by definition must fulfill more than these structural requirements; they collaborate—their members work together in ways that enhance one another's contributions. These kinds of teams are rarely found on general medical-surgical floors but have been implemented in specialty areas—rehabilitation units, acute care for the elderly (ACE) units, intensive care units (ICUs), and inpatient psychiatry floors, for example.

By definition, interdisciplinary teams cannot be hierarchical. Team leadership may shift, depending on the patient and the nature of the problems under discussion. The advantages of interdisciplinary teams are clear: management of complex cases requires input from multiple disciplines who feel free to speak up, disagree, and advocate in a way that unidisciplinary and even multidisciplinary teams tend to stifle. Interdisciplinary teams have disadvantages, too. They can be unwieldy and time-consuming; they require months of practice before they work well and time devoted to ongoing team maintenance. Figure 3.1 illustrates a model interdisciplinary team.

ICUs and ACE units appear to have improved clinical outcomes through this kind of teamwork. In the ICU, whether research has focused on the collaborative process and perceptions of collaboration (Baggs et al., 1999) or on continuous quality improvement (CQI) initiatives with collaboration as a tool taught to perform CQI (Clemmer, Spuhler, Oniki, & Horn, 1999), interdisciplinary care has been shown to improve outcomes such as cost control, antibiotic use, and transfer decisions.

ACE units, first subjected to rigorous studies in the mid-1990s, have been designed to provide acute care to older patients in a setting less likely to result in functional decline. ACE units require four components: a prepared environment, patient-centered care, interdisciplinary team rounds and discharge planning, and medical director review and oversight of patient care (Palmer, Counsell, & Landefeld, 1998). Thus, although the team is only one requirement of an ACE unit, team care is central to its effectiveness. ACE units have been shown to improve short-term patient functional outcomes in some studies (Landefeld, Palmer, Kresevic, Fortinsky, & Kowal, 1995; White et al., 1994) but not all (Counsell et al., 2000; Harris et al., 1991).

TRAINING TO WORK IN TEAMS

Few would argue that health care professionals must be taught team skills (Boaden & Leaviss, 2000; Counsell, Kennedy, Szwabo, Wadsworth, & Wohlgemuth, 1999; Drinka & Clark, 2000). Nonetheless, when to teach these skills and how to use them remain serious questions. This dilemma largely stems from our unidisciplinary training. Doctors, nurses, social workers, physical therapists, and all of the other professions spend their first, formative years isolated from other disciplines. Moreover, even when completing their training in a hospital setting, they rarely experience formal opportunities to work with other disciplines. As a result, they do not think to question the prevailing culture when they are finally in practice.

Although it can be argued that educational initiatives such as problem-based learning (PBL) are introducing concepts of teamwork into health

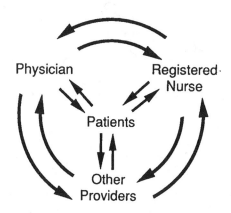

FIGURE 3.1 Model interdisciplinary team.

care education, it is unlikely that this kind of change will increase health professionals' sophistication about teamwork. In PBL, where students teach themselves under the guidance of a faculty mentor, students are all of one discipline, at the same level of training, and have no sense of role identity. Moreover, teamwork skills are rarely an explicit goal of PBL, and little work has been done to describe and analyze the team group process that occurs (Hak & Maguire, 2000).

In the clinical setting, interdisciplinary teams have been showcased for decades, and teamwork training has been available, usually through special programs such as the Interdisciplinary Team Training Program (ITTP) of the Veterans Affairs System or courses offered by federally funded centers such as area health education centers or geriatric education centers (Tsukuda, 2000). Foundation-sponsored team training programs include the John A. Hartford Foundation Geriatric Interdisciplinary Team Training (GITT) initiative (Siegler, Hyer, Fulmer, & Mezey, 1998).

Those interested in learning team skills in such a formal setting should seek out opportunities that are available through such programs. Needless to say, such training is costly, logistically cumbersome, and not universally available. Equally important, these courses tend to be brief and fail to provide opportunities to give the participant a sense of membership in a mature team.

In light of the dearth of formal opportunities for team training, there are a few opportunities to learn about teams on the job:

1. *Look around.* Most hospitals have some interdisciplinary care teams. Acute rehabilitation, ACE, and psychiatry units may offer rotations. Some hospitals have disease-based wards (heart failure, fracture, stroke, traumatic

brain injury) or consultation services (wound care, palliative care) that provide experience working in well-established teams. Ambulatory rotations in geriatrics or home care may also be available for physicians and nursing or medical students.

2. *Read up.* Although theory is no substitute for experience, learning about group process and the history of teams can enhance the clinical exposure, however brief. References provided at the end of the chapter offer background material.

3. *Join a nonclinical team.* Hospital service lines can provide opportunities to work on teams that integrate services over multiple sites (Parker, Charns, & Young, 2001). Clinicians are welcome on CQI teams, which often tackle clinical issues but have difficulty convincing health care providers to commit the time and energy. Chapter 28 offers ideas for working with quality improvement teams.

4. *Step back and observe your own team.* Think about how your teams (mal)function. How might you improve them? Inviting the unit's nurse manager or social worker to join medical physician team rounds, even if only once a week, can provide insights into not only the patients' problems but also the team's thought processes and assumptions; inviting the hospitalist to nursing report at change of shift may offer similar advantages.

5. *Change the way things are done.* If the present structure does not facilitate communication between disciplines, find a way to exchange ideas and information. Try rounds at a different time. Move out of the conference room and spend more time at the bedside, where you may provide opportunities for others to join you. Create a discharge planning team that meets consistently and frequently to discuss problem patients.

CONCLUSION

Good hospital care requires teamwork, and teams function well only when they have good team members. These skills are not intuitive; like clinical skills, they must be acquired through reading, observation, and practice. Learn how to work on teams. Learn from others how they want to work with you, and you will find that your patient care will be more effective and gratifying.

REFERENCES

Baggs, J. G., Schmitt, M. H., Mushlin, A. I., Mitchell, P. H., Eldredge, D. H., Oakes, D., & Hutson, A. D. (1999). Association between nurse-physician collaboration and patient outcomes in three intensive care units. *Critical Care Medicine, 27,* 1991–1998.

Boaden, N., & Leaviss, J. (2000). Putting teamwork in context. *Medical Education, 34,* 921–927.

Christensen, C., & Larson, J. R. (1993). Collaborative medical decision making. *Medical Decision Making, 13,* 339–346.

Christensen, C., Larson, J. R., Abbott, A., Ardolino, A., Franz, T., & Pfeiffer, C. (2000). Decision making of clinical teams: Communication patterns and diagnostic error. *Medical Decision Making, 20,* 45–50.

Clemmer, T. P., Spuhler, V. J., Oniki, T. A., & Horn, S. D. (1999). Results of a collaborative quality improvement program on outcomes and costs in a tertiary critical care unit. *Critical Care Medicine, 27,* 1768–1774.

Counsell, S. R., Holder, C. M., Liebenauer, L. L., Palmer, R. M., Fortinsky, R. H., Kresevic, D. M., Quinn, L. M., Allen, K. R., Covinsky, K. E., & Landefeld, C. S. (2000). Effects of a multicomponent intervention on functional outcomes and process of care in hospitalized older patients: A randomized controlled trial of acute care for elders (ACE) in a community hospital. *Journal of the American Geriatrics Society, 48,* 1572–1581.

Counsell, S. T., Kennedy, R. D., Szwabo, R., Wadsworth, N. S., & Wohlgemuth, C. (1999). Curriculum recommendations for resident training in geriatric interdisciplinary team care. *Journal of the American Geriatrics Society, 47,* 1145–1148.

Drinka, T. J. K., & Clark, P. G. (2000). *Health care teamwork: Interdisciplinary practice and teaching.* Westport, CT: Auburn House.

Hak, T., & Maguire, P. (2000). Group process: The black box of studies on problem-based learning. *Academic Medicine, 75,* 769–772.

Harris, R. D., Henschke, P. J., Popplewell, P. Y., Radford, A. J., Bond, M. J., Turnbull, R. J., Hobbin, E. R., Chalmers, J. P., Tonkin, A., Stewart, A. M., O'Brien, K. P., Harris, M. G., Champion, G., & Andrews, G. R. (1991). A randomized study of outcomes in a defined group of acutely ill elderly patients managed in a geriatric assessment unit or a general medical unit. *Australian and New Zealand Journal of Medicine, 21,* 230–234.

Katzenbach, J. R., & Smith, D. K. (1993, March-April). The discipline of teams. *Harvard Business Review,* 111–120.

Landefeld, C. S., Palmer, R. M., Kresevic, D. M., Fortinsky, R. H., & Kowal, J. (1995). A randomized trial of care in a hospital medical unit especially designed to improve the functional outcomes of acutely ill older patients. *New England Journal of Medicine, 332,* 1338–1344.

Palmer, R. M., Counsell, S., & Landefeld, C. S. (1998). Clinical intervention trials: The ACE unit. *Clinics in Geriatric Medicine, 14,* 831–849.

Parker, V. A., Charns, M. P., & Young, G. J. (2001). Clinical service lines in integrated delivery systems: An initial framework and exploration. *Journal of Healthcare Management, 46,* 261–275.

Siegler, E. L., Hyer, K., Fulmer, T., & Mezey, M. (1998). *Geriatric interdisciplinary team training.* New York: Springer.

Siegler, E. L., & Whitney, F. W. (1994). What is collaboration? In E. L. Siegler & F. W. Whitney (Eds.), *Nurse-physician collaboration: Care of adults and the elderly* (pp. 3–10). New York: Springer.

Tsukuda, R. A. (2000). A perspective on health care teams and team training. In E. L. Siegler, K. Hyer, T. Fulmer, & M. Mezey (Eds.). (1998). *Geriatric interdisciplinary team training* (pp. 21–37). New York: Springer.

White, S. J., Powers, J. S., Knight, J. R., Harrell, D., Varnell, L., Vaughn, C., Brawner, D., & Burger, M. C. (1994). Effectiveness of an inpatient geriatric service in a university hospital. *Journal of the Tennessee Medical Association, 87,* 425–428.

4
Nurses and Nursing Care

Christine T. Kovner

This chapter presents an overview of the nursing profession and its role in the hospital. "Nurse" is a generic term that is applied to a variety of practitioners from nurses' aides and assistants to nurse researchers with PhDs. The focus of this section will be the professional registered nurse and the licensed practical nurse.

Approximately 2.7 million people had licenses to practice as registered nurses in the United States in 2000 (Health Resources and Services Administration [HRSA], 2001). Most nurses were women, although the percentage of men employed in nursing was almost 6%, a slight increase from 1996. About 10% were minorities (defined as non-Whites). The percentage of minority RNs is inconsistent with their representation in the general population and has been a concern of nursing and government for many years.

The 2.2 million employed registered nurses were prepared in a variety of educational programs, with 55% having less than a baccalaureate degree. The number of graduates from associate degree programs exceeded those from baccalaureate programs. Although fewer nurses are now prepared at the diploma level, about 22% of employed RNs had a diploma as their highest level of education; 33% had a baccalaureate degree.

Most registered nurses continue to work in hospitals. In 2000, about 1.3 million (59.1%) of RNs worked in hospitals, while only 151,900 (6.9%) worked in nursing homes. About 9.5% of RNs worked in ambulatory care settings. Staff nurses in hospitals typically work in direct patient care, where they provide nursing care to individuals who are acutely ill (HRSA, 2001).

The American Nurses Association (ANA) is the national professional organization for registered nurses. Founded in 1897, its members are not nurses but are state or territorial nurses' *associations*. The so-called trilevel system is composed of individual nurses who may join local or district nurses associations. City or county associations are organized into state associations. Delegates from the state associations meet annually at a national convention to set policy for the ANA.

Licenses practical nurses (LPNs)/Licensed vocation nurses (LVNs) work under the supervision of RNs or physicians and perform care-giving tasks such as medication administration and wound dressing changes. LPNs/LVNs must pass a national examination and are licensed in each state.

Like other states, New York differentiates professional nursing from practical nursing, defining the latter as "performing tasks and responsibilities . . . under the direction of a registered, professional nurse or licensed or otherwise legally authorized physician or dentist (New York Education Law, 1989).

Other nursing personnel include a variety of unlicensed assistive personnel (UAP) such as nurses' aides, assistants, orderlies, and technicians. These personnel also work under the supervision of registered nurses and perform such simple tasks as temperature taking and comfort measures such as bathing and linen change. These occupations are not licensed by the states, although federal regulations require that nurses' aides who work in long-term care facilities that are reimbursed by Medicare and Medicaid must complete a specified educational program and pass a written and practical test. In addition, Medicare-certified home health agencies have to hire certified home-health aides. More than half of the states have regulations or guidelines for RNs who supervise UAPs. Some states have specific educational requirements for some of these workers (Thomas, Barter, & McLaughlin, 2000).

DEFINITION OF NURSING

A classic definition of nursing is that of Virginia Henderson (1966), who states

> The unique function of the nurse is to assist the individual (sick or well), in the performance of those activities contributing to health or its recovery (or peaceful death) that he would perform unaided if he had the necessary strength, will, or knowledge. And to do this in such a way as to help him gain independence as rapidly as possible.

The American Nurses Association (1995) suggests that authority for nursing is based on a social contract between society and the profession. The regulation of health professionals is a state responsibility. As such, each state has its own legal definition of the practice of nursing. Each state board of nursing defines and interprets the authority and scope of practice of registered nurses although it is usually defined as the diagnosis and treatment of human responses. By 1923 legislation was enacted in all states for voluntary registration (Bullough, 1975). The first mandatory licensing law went into effect in New York State in 1947. It required that, with certain exceptions, only licensed professional nurses could legally use the title of registered nurse.

All states require that prospective registered nurses attend an approved nursing program and take a national licensing exam—the National Council Licensure Examination for RN (NCLEX-RN)—developed by the National Council of State Boards of Nursing. In some states, nurses (or certain categories of nurses) may prescribe pharmacologic agents or deliver a baby; in other states they may not. In addition, some states require continuing education for license renewal.

EDUCATION OF NURSES

One of the most confusing aspects of nursing is the variety of programs for educating nurses. Unlike medicine, which has consistent educational requirements, nursing offers the student a number of options. Although the ANA recommends that states require a baccalaureate degree to become a registered nurse, students can attend a 2-year college program, a 3-year hospital-based (diploma) program, a 4-year college program, a 2-year master's degree program, or a nursing doctoral (ND) program. North Dakota requires a baccalaureate degree, while all other state boards of nursing accept any of these programs as appropriate preparation for the registered nurse licensing exam. Practical-nurse education occurs in high schools, hospitals, junior colleges, or vocational schools.

Registered Professional Nursing

The first associate's degree program was started in 1952 (Anastas, 1984). The typical associate's degree program requires basic liberal arts courses such as English and sociology. In addition, science courses such as anatomy and physiology are required. Nursing courses usually include fundamentals of nursing (clinical skills), maternal and child health, and care of acutely ill hospitalized adult patients. Experience is gained by practicing skills in the campus laboratory and by care of patients in institutional settings such as hospitals. The nurses enrolled in associate's degree programs are educated to be direct providers of care at the patient bedside. The programs are from 2 academic years to 2 calendar years in length.

The typical diploma program is similar to the associate's degree program, though usually under the auspices of a hospital. The practical-experience sessions are usually longer than in the associate's program, and the entire course takes about 3 years, with an emphasis on acute care (hospital-based) nursing. Often students are required to take liberal arts courses at a local college, and they receive college credit that can later be transferred to other colleges. However, diploma graduates who attend college often are not able to transfer the credits earned in the diploma program because until recently most of these programs were not degree-granting institutions.

The curriculum of the baccalaureate program is similar to that of liberal arts programs in other fields. Because the program is at least eight semesters long, the student takes more nonnursing courses than in either the associate's or the diploma program. Students take liberal arts courses such as English, math, and psychology and are required to take science courses such as microbiology, anatomy, and physiology. In addition, approximately half of the credits are usually in nursing courses. The organization of these courses varies from school to school. Some schools organize curricula developmentally and have courses devoted to care of infants, children, adults, and older people. Others base the curriculum on the relative health of populations and offer courses on prevention, episodic care, continuous care, and critical care. In addition, students learn to read and interpret research. Baccalaureate nurses are prepared to work in community settings and leadership positions as well as in acute-care settings. They are generalists who can provide care to individuals, groups, families, and communities. Graduates are also prepared for advanced education in nursing.

Another opportunity for education in nursing is the external degree program, such as that offered by the Board of Regents of New York State. In 1971 an external associate's degree program was begun, followed by a baccalaureate degree program in 1976. Students obtain either degree by completing equivalency testing in liberal arts, sciences, and nursing. Students also must complete a practical exam. The program's philosophy centers on a person's knowledge and skills, rather than how the information and these skills were acquired. Graduates of these programs are eligible for state licensure.

Licensed Practical Nursing (LPN/LVN)

Licensed practical nurses are educated in one of approximately 1,100 state-approved programs in the U.S. (National League for Nursing Accrediting Committee, 2000). More than half of these programs are in trade, technical, or vocational schools, while the remainder are in colleges, community colleges, high schools, and hospitals. Many of those who take the LPN licensing examination are actually students in professional nursing programs. They take the examination to become LPNs prior to taking the RN examination. The typical LPN program takes about 1 year and includes basic courses in physical and social sciences and simple nursing procedures.

Other Nursing Personnel

Educational requirements for other nursing personnel, such as nurses' aides, vary by employment setting. Some are educated in the setting in which they work, some in programs in high schools, and others in not-for-profit or for-profit vocational schools. Training takes from a few hours to 6 months or more.

GRADUATE NURSING EDUCATION

Nursing degree programs at the master's and doctoral level concentrate on nursing courses, with the assumption that the nurse baccalaureate graduate has had the basic liberal arts and science courses. Historically, specialists in nursing were educated in specialized hospitals or became specialists based on clinical practice with a particular type of patient. In the 1950s, colleges and universities began offering academic programs for specialty education. By the 1960s, postgraduate education for clinical practice specialization was concentrated in universities.

Registered nurses with baccalaureate degrees can earn master's degrees in advanced clinical practice, teaching, and nursing administration management. Within these three broad areas, students usually focus on a nursing content area such as adult health, maternal-child health, psychiatric-mental health, or community health. Specific programs include everything from nursing informatics (computers), home health-care management, geriatrics, and pediatric nurse practitioners. Most students choose to focus on advanced clinical practice. In a few programs people with a baccalaureate in another field can earn a master's degree to prepare them for professional practice.

Within the generic category of advanced practice nurses, those with a clinical practice focus include: clinical nurse specialists (CNSs), nurse practitioners (NPs), nurse midwives, and nurse anesthetists. Clinical nurse specialists have advanced degrees with expert skills in a particular area, such as mental health, cancer, or women's health. Nurse practitioners are educated to perform an expanded nursing role and diagnose and manage most common and many chronic health problems, often in primary care. They are also found in small numbers in the hospital setting. In most states they can prescribe medicines. However, their scope of practice, including whether they must have a collaborating relationship with a physician, varies from state to state. Nurse midwives are educated to provide pre-, intra-, and postpartum care; provide family planning services; and routine gynecological care, as well as caring for newborns. Nurse anesthetists are educated to administer anesthetics. (More information on nurse practitioners is provided in chapter 6.)

Doctoral Programs

Nurses can also earn doctoral degrees in nursing. There are three types of degrees offered. The ND (doctor of nursing) is similar to the MD; that is, it is the first professional degree, building on the earlier liberal arts or scientific education and preparing the student to take the state licensing exam to practice as a registered nurse. The DSN and DNSc are professional doctorates that prepare the nurse for advanced clinical practice. The PhD is a research degree, with requirements similar to the PhD in other fields; it requires extensive preparation in a narrow field and a dissertation. In 1999 there were 74 doctoral programs in nursing in the U.S., having grown from five programs in 1967 (American Association of Colleges of Nursing, 2000).

HOW NURSING CARE IS ORGANIZED IN THE HOSPITAL

There are many variations in the way nursing departments are set up in hospitals, often depending on size, location (urban or rural), and whether the hospital is a teaching hospital. However, a typical nursing department is headed by a director of nursing or vice president for nursing, who oversees all of the nurses in the hospital. This executive typically reports directly to the administrator of the hospital. Nursing can represent more than 50% of a hospital's operating budget (Caroselli, 2001, p. 222).

Nurse managers, often prepared with a master's degree, oversee all the nursing care on a particular service. They have responsibility for the overall nursing care in this area, which often involves hiring, budgetary accountability, and responsibility for quality and performance. Assistant nurse managers or head nurses are responsible for the staff nurses on the particular unit on which they work and have similar responsibilities to the nurse manager within the specific unit, and often during a specific time period (e.g., day or night). Staff nurses work directly with the patient. Nursing shifts usually overlap for about a half hour, so that the outgoing shift can give a report on their patients to the incoming shift.

Although nurses in direct patient care make up the majority of nursing positions in the hospital, some nurses may work in a more specialized capacity. A staff developer is responsible for orienting new nursing staff and providing continuing education for current nursing staff. A nurse recruiter is responsible for attracting qualified new nursing candidates. A clinical nurse specialist has a master's degree in a clinical specialty, and both teaches staff nurses more advanced clinical skills and provides specialized care to patients. An acute-care nurse practitioner may manage the medical care of patients in the absence of the patient's personal physician who is not based in the hospital. This involves keeping the physician's medical plan going smoothly in the hospital, under the direction of the physician.

CONCLUSION

This chapter demonstrates that nurses come to their work with a variety of educational backgrounds and degrees of specialization. The lack of a common educational pathway for nurses may cause some confusion among colleagues from other disciplines, who may assume that "a nurse, is a nurse, is a nurse" or the lowest common denominator in terms of educational preparation. Nevertheless, nurses as a group are the professionals who spend the most time with patients in the hospital, and patient satisfaction with care is probably more dependent on good nursing care than on anything else.

REFERENCES

American Association of Colleges of Nursing. (2000). *1999–2000 Enrollment and graduations in baccalaureate and graduate programs in nursing.* Washington, DC: Author.

American Nurses Association. (1995). *Nursing social policy statement.* Washington, DC: Author.

Anastas, L. (1984). *Your career in nursing.* New York: National League for Nursing.

Bullough, N. (1975). Barriers to the nurse practitioner movement: Problems of women in a women's field. *International Journal of Health Sciences, 5,* 225.

Caroselli, C. (2001). Cost control heroism: Strategies to reduce operating expenses. In H. Feldman (Ed.), *Strategies for nursing leadership* (pp. 222–238). New York: Springer.

Health Resources and Services Administration (HRSA). (2001, February). *The Registered Nurse Population National Sample Survey of Registered Nurses, March 2000.* Rockville, MD: Author.

Henderson, V. (1966). *The nature of nursing.* New York: Macmillan.

National League for Nursing Accrediting Committee. (October 15, 2000). [Online]. Available: www.nlnac.org

New York Education Law, Article 139 § 6902 (1989).

Thomas, S. A., Barter, M., & McLaughlin, F. E. (2000). State and territorial boards of nursing approaches to the use of unlicensed assistive personnel. *JONA's Healthcare Law, Ethics, and Regulation, 2*(1), 13–31.

■ 5
Training Physicians in the Hospital

Mark S. Pecker and Eugenia L. Siegler

A key element of the reforms of medical education in the late nineteenth and early twentieth centuries, first epitomized and then directed by the Flexner report, was the development of teaching hospitals as the prime site for the clinical training of medical students (Flexner, 1910). The initial model was the Johns Hopkins University Hospital, and by the 1930s every medical school had its teaching hospital. Postgraduate training, that is, internship and residency, became commonplace by the 1930s. Initially required only for academic careers, it subsequently became mandatory for specialty certification and eventually for state licensure.

The Flexnerian revolution in medical education followed a scientific revolution based on the achievements in pathology and the "germ theory" of disease. As scientific understanding of disease increased exponentially, it became clear that medicine could no longer be viewed as received knowledge. The ideal of medical education shifted from a focus on what was known, to an emphasis on skills that would allow the physician to learn and implement new knowledge throughout an entire career: lifelong learning. The principles of progressive education—active learning and the key role of the experiences of the learner—became the paradigm for medical education, well before John Dewey (Field, 2001) developed and proposed these same concepts for more general educational settings. These ideals came to fruition through hospital-based training. Readers who wish more in-depth discussion of these changes can consult the works of Kenneth Ludmerer (1985, 1999), who brilliantly details the history of medical education in the United States.

ADVANTAGES OF THE HOSPITAL SETTING

When compared to the outpatient setting, the hospital has several distinct characteristics that make it well suited for training doctors.

- *Volume.* A large volume of patients allows for the rapid accumulation of an extensive experience.
- *Acuity.* Patients are sick, often with multiple illnesses. Interns become comfortable dealing with severely ill patients. They learn to recognize and treat crises.
- *Intensity.* Inpatients tend to be severely ill and especially vulnerable. Involvement with each patient is intense, and individual encounters can be frequent during the day (and night!) and of relatively long duration, allowing an intern to get to know a patient as a person and observe the course of an acute illness.
- *Variety.* House staff are exposed to a large number of illnesses, many of them rare, requiring them to think broadly and thoroughly and to expand their diagnostic and therapeutic abilities.
- *Convenience.* The patient is continuously available. Errors of omission by a trainee—a question unasked or a maneuver of the physical exam not performed—can be remedied by walking down the hall to the patient's room, a situation very unlike that in the outpatient clinic. In addition, training hospital settings are also replete with specialists, allowing for easy access to consultants who are not only expert but also often on the cutting edge of medicine, especially at academic medical centers.
- *System redundancy.* As team members (see chapter 3), house staff work with, and learn about, all patients that the team cares for—rounding on them in the morning, discussing them on attending rounds, and covering them at night. Thus, a house officer's experience is amplified beyond his or her direct caseload. In addition, overlapping coverage of patients by medical students, interns, residents, fellows, and attending physicians provides a safety net for patients. Responsibility can be assigned to junior members of the team, but the oversight helps catch many mistakes, regardless of cause. It also means that roles are defined, adding a sense of security. From a pedagogical standpoint, everyone is responsible for teaching someone—a valuable learning situation for those doing the teaching as well as those receiving it. One of the unstated consequences of this hierarchy is that most teaching is not done by faculty. Rather, given the intensity and amount of time the house staff spend together, they are, after their patients, one another's most important teachers.
- *Accountability.* Caring for patients on a teaching service is a "social" process. A house officer is accountable not only to the patient him or herself and a preceptor for medical decisions, as is the case in most outpatient

settings, but implicitly and explicitly to the medical students, fellow interns, supervising residents, and other members of the team. An intern will go over a newly admitted patient with a 3rd year medical student, then with the junior resident on call, and with the team on work rounds. The resident will present the case at morning report. The patient will be discussed on attending rounds and then with appropriate consultants. This creates a learning environment that is both rich and open. The house officer's work and decisions are always on display; he or she has constant explicit and implicit accountability for them.

EFFECTS OF CHANGES IN HEALTH CARE DELIVERY ON THE HOSPITAL'S TEACHING FUNCTION

During the past 10 to 20 years, hospital-based physician training has changed. Advances in medical care have allowed a shift in the treatment of a variety of diseases to the outpatient realm and shortened the duration of hospital care for most others. As the first two chapters in this book describe in detail, modifications in reimbursement for patient care and pressures to cut costs have placed efficiency at the top of the hospital agenda and shortened the duration of hospital admissions. Despite these changes, however, census has not decreased in most teaching hospitals.

Because hospitals have become a location in which patients are cared for only during the crisis phase of an acute illness, physician training is under dual pressures. On the one hand, outpatient skills are more important and residency programs have incorporated more time in outpatient settings. Outpatient experience is now necessary for the resident to achieve a broad clinical exposure and to see the entire course, including convalescence, of an acute illness.

On the other hand, these changes have increased the stress on residents caring for inpatients. House staff are, in general, responsible for the day-to-day details of patient management in teaching hospitals. Most of the work of caring for an inpatient occurs during the first few days after admission and at the time of discharge; shortened lengths of stay have augmented the intensity of work for each patient. This increase is amplified further on each end of the admission. On the admitting end, patients enter a hospital sicker and in the midst of a long, complicated illness, increasing the need for communication and coordination with prior physicians. On discharge, patients are often still sick, and much effort must be devoted to ensuring that the transition from inpatient to outpatient care goes smoothly. The net result is that for a given census or even a given number of admissions, the workload of a house officer has increased (Dellit et al., 2001).

Impact of New Technologies

The explosion of medical knowledge and technology has been dramatic and has created additional pressure on house staff. Not only must residents master new and expanding areas of knowledge (such as genomics, virology, and immunology), but they must also develop complex skills in areas that until recently were not part of the standard curriculum such as ethics, end-of-life care, health care economics, home care, and cultural competence.

Diagnostic technology has also changed dramatically. Sonography, computed tomographic scanning, positron emission tomography, and magnetic resonance imaging, all used routinely today, were in their infancy or were nonexistent just a quarter century ago. These techniques are critical to the care of patients, but their use is highly specialized and remote from the average physician.

Contemporary medicine has changed the relationship between house officer and tests. House staff rarely perform simple, older tests like gram stains because of quality control concerns, and a trip to the laboratory (often far away) to view a slide or spin a urine specimen is time-consuming and increasingly rare. Interventional radiologists often perform diagnostic procedures; high-technology diagnostic tests all require interpretation, and the trainee is dependent upon others to interpret the findings. Information technology has improved access to images—radiologic studies are now available on computer terminals on the wards of many hospitals. Although enhancing access to imaging studies, this creates another disincentive to spend time in the radiology department and understand how tests are done and interpreted. As a result, test results have become more abstract, those who perform them have become more remote and less collegial, and the diagnostic process has diminished somewhat in satisfaction.

Paying for Education

Graduate Medical Education (GME) is not free. Medicare has long assumed, albeit without much evidence, that trainees add to the cost of medical care. It seems logical: They work less efficiently than seasoned physicians, they know less and therefore take longer to arrive at diagnoses and order more tests. In one study examining 1993 data, costs of care in academic medical centers were 44% greater than in nonteaching hospitals, and 14% greater in nonacademic teaching hospitals than in nonteaching hospitals (Mechanic, Coleman, & Dobson, 1998). Despite this, training doctors is generally viewed as a public good and in the public interest—both because house officers provide care to individuals who might not otherwise receive medical care, and because the training of highly skilled physicians is presumed to have a positive effect on the health of the citizenry.

Medicare is the primary source of funding for GME. In 1998, Medicare spent $5.9 billion on GME, supplementing teaching hospitals $71,000 on average per resident (Nicholson & Song, 2001). Medicare's payments are divided into two types: Direct Medical Education (DME) payments, which "reimburse a teaching hospital for Medicare's share of the direct costs of training residents" and support resident, faculty, and administrative salaries (Nicholson & Song, 2001); and Indirect Medical Education (IME) payments, which were instituted in 1983 at the time of enactment of the Prospective Payment System as a means of subsidizing losses to hospitals due to failure of Diagnosis Related Groups (DRGs) to fully account for illness severity. They are related in part to the resident-to-bed ratio (Fryer, Green, Dovey, & Phillips, 2001; Nicholson & Song, 2001), and the presence of residents in a hospital is used as a proxy for unreimbursed care, the use of high-technology, as well as uncaptured "severity of illness." There is also a disproportionate share hospital (DSH) policy that subsidizes hospitals to provide care to the indigent (Fryer et al., 2001). These subsidies are calculated through use of complex formulae.

Not surprisingly, the federal government has attempted to shape hiring and care policies through these subsidies. As an example, Medicare pays higher GME subsidies for primary care residents than for other specialties (Fryer et al., 2001). Although the original effect of GME was to encourage hospitals to hire more residents, recent attempts to change hospital hiring patterns through GME payments has met with only mixed success (Fryer et al., 2001; Nicholson & Song, 2001). Despite the apparent inefficiencies associated with the presence of house staff, their energy, stamina, and intelligence—not to mention their relatively low salaries compared with other clinicians, including nurse practitioners, physician assistants, or attending level physicians—make them difficult to replace in a cost-effective manner.

In addition to the GME subsidies for education, Medicare also provides payments from Part B for "medical direction of residents" when resident teaching occurs in the context of providing care to a patient whom the physician later bills (American Association of Medical Colleges [AAMC], 1997). How much physicians must be involved in patient care while supervising residents is a subject of several regulations and significant controversy.

In 1996, the Office of Inspector General (OIG) at the Department of Health and Human Services (HHS) initiated a series of audits in a program called Physicians at Teaching Hospitals, or PATH. Through these audits, OIG sued hospitals for millions of dollars under the Federal False Claims Act for failing to comply with rules established under Intermediary letter 372 (IL-372) in 1967, which governed the degree of physician supervision that was necessary in order to be able to bill. PATH audits also examined the accuracy of physician coding for services. The Health Care Financing Administration (now Centers for Medicare and Medicaid Services, or CMS) issued new regulations clarifying the rules in December 1995, and these went into effect in July 1996 (AAMC, 1997). The new rules explicitly state that the physician must perform or be present while a resident performs the "key portion" of the service billed to Medicare (AAMC, 1997). Needless to say, PATH audits have been quite controversial; hospitals, AAMC, and the American Medical Association (AMA) have argued that before 1996 the regulations were unclear and inconsistently applied. As of October 2001, audits in progress were still continuing, but no new audits were taking place (AAMC, 2001a).

The PATH audits caused a considerable stir in teaching hospitals in the late 1990s, and the specter of multimillion dollar fines has led to the initiation of programs that ensure compliance with Medicare regulations. The implications are clearest for medical and surgical procedures, where attending physicians must be present and must document their presence clearly in the chart in order to bill. Resident supervision cannot be over the phone or from the next suite. Perhaps for all its controversies, PATH has enhanced the quality of resident education by ensuring more active attending supervision of house staff.

In general, hospitals are having a more difficult time paying for medical education. Cuts in Medicare and the reluctance of managed care organizations to pay for education have added to hospitals' fiscal burdens (Kuttner, 1999), and faculty must generate more income, which leaves less time to teach. Faculty practice revenues contributed only 5% of teaching hospital income in the 1960s. This rose to 30% in the early 1980s and is now approximately 50% (Kuttner, 1999).

Concerns about supervision of residents and adequate documentation have also changed the role of the "teaching attending" and the attending/resident relationship. Teaching attendings are obliged to balance a number of competing demands in order to train house staff effectively. They must

- generate income
- ensure their patients' safety
- make the hospital administration happy by limiting patient length of stay
- serve as compassionate, intellectual, role models who make clinical decisions on the basis of evidence and inculcate a love of lifelong learning
- give the house staff enough freedom to exercise clinical judgment, make and learn from mistakes, and develop a sense of professionalism.

Under these conditions, it should come as no surprise that the hospital has lost some of its cachet as an ideal environment for training physicians.

THE RESIDENT'S EXPERIENCE: MAKING THE TRANSITION FROM STUDENT TO PHYSICIAN

Becoming a doctor after graduating from medical school invokes the cliché, nonetheless true, of the transition from "a medical student to a student of medicine." There are many aspects of this metamorphosis for which residents have had little preparation.

Most house officers enter residency with little life experience outside of school. As medical students they were among the elite, doing well in school, rarely having opportunities to make and recover from serious mistakes or live with failure. In addition, years of schooling have made them comfortable with the didactic and, except during clinical clerkships, responsible only to themselves, not to teams or to patients.

Residency changes all this. House staff become responsible not just for themselves and their patients but for others, too. They must quickly learn to coordinate and lead (under the aegis of an attending physician). Residents, now in their first meaningful job, may suddenly feel responsible for everything, even things beyond any control. And they will experience failures—many of them. Patients refuse to follow advice, become angry, sicken, even die, despite the best of care and intentions. Residents will also make mistakes and must learn to acknowledge and learn from them (Bosk, 1979). These phenomena create enormous emotional stress that can overwhelm a house officer who may be physically exhausted.

Implicit Learning

Some of the conflicts and confusion that a house officer experiences relate to the new roles and to old expectations of a learning environment. Although residency is clearly educational, *learning* takes place in a different context, includes different content, and occurs via processes that are often implicit:

> *In early October, after three months of internship, Dr. Z. came to my office for a routine visit to discuss how her year is going. I began with a few pleasantries.*
>
> *"Are you learning anything?"*
>
> *"Not really. . ." A bit embarrassed. "I mean I'm learning how to micromanage."*
>
> *A bit later in the conversation, I asked, "What floors have you rotated on?"*
>
> *"Oncology, HIV–general medicine, pulmonary."*
>
> *"How did you find them?"*
>
> *"All good. A lot of work. The residents are wonderful. Pulmonary was the hardest. I was really frightened when I started."*

"There is something immediate about not being able to breathe!"

"Yes, but now I can handle it. I know how to evaluate it and what to do!"

"But you haven't really learned anything?"

"Well . . . I guess."

Residency training is not didactic and this can be very disconcerting to the former medical student. For many house officers, the overt learning is in some sense intellectually trivial, involving mundane procedures, working the system, whom to call for what. The day seems to be spent documenting in charts and making phone calls, rather than caring for patients or acquiring knowledge. In reality, residents are translating theory into practice: They learned about diabetic ketoacidosis in medical school; as house officers they learn how to take care of a patient who is ill with it. Because house officers are revisiting previously encountered concepts that in the hospital have greater immediacy, they learn to understand nuance. They develop a basic competence in their specialty, but they also learn to acknowledge limits, to find answers, and to ask for help. Despite this, unless they are given the opportunity to understand what they are mastering and how, they often feel they are not learning anything new. This feeling of dissatisfaction contributes to the stress of residency.

Threats to Professionalism

Time pressures, increasing acceptance of house staff unionization, and social changes have contributed to a sense of residency as "less of a calling, more of a job." Trainees have greater expectations of life outside of medicine, and residency must be humane while at the same time providing the intense exposure to illness and hospital care that is necessary to create talented physicians.

Control of residency training is no longer the purview only of the medical establishment. The death of 18-year-old Libby Zion in 1984 at a New York City hospital catalyzed a series of changes in residency work regulations in New York State. These include (a) limitations on the number of hours a resident can work (maximum 80 hours per week, 24 hours in a row); (b) one 24-hour period of time off each week; (c) on-site supervision by PGY-4 resident or superior at all times; and (d) direct attending supervision of all procedures performed by residents (Wallack & Chao, 2001). The regulations have had nationwide implications, and hospitals throughout the country are also under pressure to modify resident work hours (Wallack & Chao, 2001). Federal legislation (HR 3236) to limit residents' work hours (AAMC, 2001b) has also been introduced.

These rules were intended to improve patient safety and care by reducing residents' sleep deprivation and increasing oversight. Although these rules clearly have improved the quality of life for house staff, there is little evidence that the potential benefits to patients of shortened work hours exceed the costs of the disruptions in continuity (Laine, Goldman, Soukup, & Hayes, 1993). A British study suggests that the availability of adequate support and supervision is far more important than limitation of work hours in reducing mistakes by house staff (Baldwin, Dodd, & Wrate, 1998).

Medical educators have expressed concern that these changes in work hours may come at the cost of professionalism, continuity of care, and in-depth understanding of the course of disease (Holzman & Barnett, 2000; Wallack & Chao, 2001). This is not a merely theoretical concern. It is very difficult to teach a house officer to take personal, intense responsibility for ill patients and simultaneously to watch the clock. A resident who is required by law to leave the hospital after 24 hours cannot possibly develop, or have reinforced, the same sense of duty as the house officer who stays until the work is done regardless of hour. How to instill in residents the sense of responsibility without endangering their health and their patients' may be the biggest challenge that residency training programs must now face.

CONCLUSION

Medical schools graduate doctors, but only residencies can prepare them for practice. Although it was once thought to be completely aligned with the health care system, residency training is now often in overt conflict with it. Many of the features that make the hospital the prime location for training physicians appear to be eroding under the pressures of technological advances and the demands for efficiency in our current system. As Ludmerer (1999) has suggested, the time for a house officer to think and digest what he or she is seeing is at a premium, and the cost appears too high. Nevertheless, until outpatient education can be structured to include those components that promote the implicit curriculum and subtext of medical training as well as a high density of pathology, hospital-based training will remain the location critical to the creation of superior physicians. The future of medical education depends on achieving the right balance between inpatient and outpatient medicine, between supervision and responsibility and autonomy, between practice and teaching. The production of humane professionals lies in the balance.

REFERENCES

American Association of Medical Colleges. (1997). *Background paper: Physicians at Teaching Hospitals (PATH) Initiative.* [on-line]. Available: www.aamc.org/ hlthcare/path/bckgrnd.htm. Accessed 1/9/02.

American Association of Medical Colleges. (2001a). *Issue Briefs: Physicians at Teaching Hospital (PATH) audits.* [on-line]. Available: www.aamc.org/advocacy/issues/medicare/path.htm. Accessed 1/9/02.

American Association of Medical Colleges. (2001b). Washington Highlights. *Bill focuses on resident work hours and resident supervision.* [on-line]. Available: www.aamc.org/advocacy/washhigh/01nov16/_3.htm. November 26, 2001. Accessed 01/25/02.

Baldwin, P. J., Dodd M., & Wrate, R. M. (1998). Junior doctors making mistakes. *Lancet, 351,* 804.

Bosk, C. (1979). *Forgive and remember: Managing medical failure.* Chicago: The University of Chicago Press.

Dellit, T. H., Armas-Loughran, B., Bosl, G. J., Sepkowitz, K. A., Thaler, H., & Blaskovich, J. (2001). A method for assessing house staff workload as a function of length of stay. *Journal of the American Medical Association, 286,* 1023–1024.

Field, R. (2001). John Dewey. *The Internet Encyclopedia of Philosophy.* [on-line]. Available: www.utm.edu/research/iep/d/dewey.htm. Accessed 01/08/02.

Flexner, A. (1910). *Medical education in the United States and Canada.* New York: Carnegie Foundation for the Advancement of Teaching.

Fryer, G. E., Green, L. A., Dovey, S., & Phillips, R. L. (2001). Direct graduate medical education payments to teaching hospitals by Medicare: Unexplained variation and public policy contradictions. *Academic Medicine, 76,* 439–445.

Holzman, I. R., & Barnett, S. H. (2000). The Bell Commission: Ethical implications for the training of physicians. *Mount Sinai Journal of Medicine, 67,* 136–139.

Kuttner, R. (1999). Managed care and medical education. *New England Journal of Medicine, 342,* 1092–1096.

Laine C., Goldman L., Soukup, J. R., & Hayes J. G. (1993). The impact of a regulation restricting medical house staff working hours on the quality of patient care. *Journal of the American Medical Association, 269,* 374–378.

Ludmerer, K. M. (1985). *Learning to heal: The development of American medical education.* New York: Basic Books.

Ludmerer, K. M. (1999). *Time to heal: American medical education from the turn of the century to the era of managed care.* New York: Oxford University Press.

Mechanic, R., Coleman, K., & Dobson, A. (1998). Teaching hospital costs: Implications for academic missions in a competitive market. *Journal of the American Medical Association, 280,* 1015–1019.

Nicholson, S. & Song, D. (2001). The incentive effects of the Medicare indirect medical education policy. *Journal of Health Economics, 20,* 909–923.

Wallack, M. K., & Chao, L. (2001). Resident work hours: The evolution of a revolution. *Archives of Surgery, 136,* 1426–1431.

■ 6
Physician Assistants and Nurse Practitioners

Freddi I. Segal-Gidan

Current economic pressures and changes in the health care system have promoted the increased use and an expanded scope of practice for physician assistants (PAs), nurse practitioners (NPs), and other nonphysician clinicians (NPCs). The American College of Physicians-American Society of Internal Medicine (ACP-ASIM) (ACP, 1999) and the American Academy of Pediatrics (1999) have endorsed an expanded role for PAs and NPs in the hospital. To work effectively, provide optimal patient care, and ensure high quality outcomes, physicians and other health care professionals working in the hospital must understand the increasing and varied roles of PAs and NPs.

HISTORY AND DEFINITIONS

The PA and NP professions developed simultaneously and independently during the mid-1960s in response to a perceived shortage of physicians, especially in medically underserved communities (rural and urban). Both professions were originally envisioned as primary health care providers who would work under the supervision of physicians, extending the ability of the physician to provide services to a greater number of patients. The PA profession began in 1965 at Duke University with the retraining of a small group of medical corpsmen recently returned from Viet Nam. The first nurse practitioner program was developed around the same time at the University of Colorado School of Nursing. PAs and NPs are currently authorized to practice in all 50 states and the District of Columbia.

A nurse practitioner (NP) is one form of advanced practice nurse, a term that includes NPs, clinical specialists, certified nurse midwives (CNMW), and nurse anesthetists. Nurse practitioners are registered nurses with advanced education and clinical training that enables them to diagnose and manage most common and many chronic illnesses (American College of Nurse Practitioners [ACNP], 2001). Nurse practitioners are educated through programs of varying length (9 months to 3 years) that grant either a certificate or a master's degree. Nurse practitioners must be registered professional nurses, authorized to perform services in the state they practice, certified, and as of January 2003, required to hold a master's degree in nursing for reimbursement under federal health programs (Balanced Budget Amendments, 1997). Nurse practitioners work by collaborative agreement with a physician, but in 21 states and the District of Columbia are allowed to practice independently of physicians (ACNP, 2001). The majority of NPs in most states continue to work as part of physician-NP teams, although a small but growing number are establishing independent NP practices alone or in groups. Nurse practitioners have prescriptive authority in all 50 states. In 12 states and the District of Columbia they have independent prescriptive authority, including controlled substances, and in the 38 remaining states they have prescriptive authority in collaboration with a physician. Nationally, the number of nurse practitioners has increased from 30,000 in 1990 to more than 65,000 in 2001, with a projection of 120,000 NPs by 2010.

Physician assistants (PAs) are trained in programs that combine didactic and clinical instruction in medicine over 2 to 3 years after a minimum of 2 years' undergraduate education. Programs may offer a certificate, baccalaureate, or master's degree. Upon completion of training, PAs must take a national certifying examination and then are licensed or registered individually by each state. PAs are trained to provide medical care under the supervision of a physician who retains ultimate responsibility for the patient's care. Supervision need not take place in person but is often provided indirectly or by electronic communication. PAs have prescriptive authority in 47 states, and 41 states allow delegated prescribing of controlled substances. There are now more than 40,000 PAs in clinical practice nationally, with an expected growth to 70,000 by 2010. About 25% of PAs work in rural areas, including rural hospitals, and 12% work in inner city areas.

Over the past three decades since the inception of the PA and NP professions, the health care system has changed, and the roles for PAs and NPs have evolved and expanded beyond that of primary care to include care of patients in all settings and medical specialties. Since the early years of the profession, a small and growing number of PAs have worked in the hospital setting, primarily in surgical specialties. Only recently have NPs been venturing away from primary care and outpatient settings to find jobs in the inpatient hospital, both in medicine and surgery. Today, 40% of PAs identify the hospital as their primary practice setting, and 18% report that they work in general surgery or a surgical subspecialty (American Academy of Physician Assistants [AAPA], 2000). On the other hand, only 15% of NPs list the hospital as their practice site, and fewer than 5% report working in surgery (ACNP, 2001).

Although NPs work in a collaborative relationship with physicians and PAs work by delegated authority of a supervising physician, they make many autonomous medical decisions. Both provide physician services and have a high level of responsibility for patient care.

CREDENTIALING

Hospitals should have in place, or develop, a detailed credentialing process for NPs and PAs, just as they do for physician medical staff and others. This is usually accomplished by an amendment to the hospital's staff bylaws and should include a clear delineation of privileges and lines of responsibility. The Joint Commission for Accreditation of Healthcare Organizations (2000) standards for hospital accreditation state that medical staffs include "fully licensed physicians" and may include other "licensed independent practitioners" (LIPs) credentialed and privileged through the medical staff. PAs work under the direct supervision of a physician and should be credentialed through the medical staff process. Because NPs are nurses, they can be credentialed either through the established nursing channels with delineation of privileges for inpatient care in collaboration with the medical staff, or, as is more commonly the case, they may be credentialed through the medical staff office. Some hospitals form an interdisciplinary practice committee within the medical staff charged specifically with credentialing of nonphysician staff, including PAs and NPs.

PAs and NPs should be recredentialed regularly, usually every 2 years, consistent with the hospital's practices. The supervising physician(s), the unit medical director, and PA colleagues working in similar roles in the hospital should evaluate PAs. Nursing supervisory personnel, the collaborating physician(s), and unit medical director should jointly perform evaluations of NPs working in the hospital.

ROLES AND RESPONSIBILITIES

Within the hospital setting, PAs and NPs work in medical and surgical inpatient units, intensive care units, acute rehabilitation and step-down units, as part of the emergency room staff, in radiology, and in outpatient care. Their duties are often similar, but vary according to the individual's training, the type of patient, the scope of practice of the collaborating and supervising physician(s), and the hospital's practice and history. PAs and NPs can do most tasks previously performed only by physicians. Unless either federal or state regulation or hospital policy designates a task as "physician only," then with proper training and authorization a PA or NP can perform it.

The scope of practice for PAs and NPs is defined by each state in statutes that are usually quite broad in their language. The state nursing board usually sets the scope of practice for NPs, and state medical boards usually, but not always, set the scope of practice for PAs. The state scope of practice provides specific requirements for the physician's supervisory role in relation to PAs and guidance for the collaborative agreement between the NP and physician. It is therefore imperative that physicians, as well as PAs and NPs, be familiar with the specific statutes and requirements for supervision or collaboration in the state where they are practicing.

As funding for house staff positions is reduced and states enact regulations that limit residents' work hours (see chapter 5), PAs and NPs are filling these roles. Only 20% of a house officer's activities have been found to require a physician's attention (Knickman, Lipkin, Finkler, Thompson, & Kiel, 1992). Outcomes of similar inpatients cared for by PAs or NPs and house staff have been found to be comparable (Pioro et al., 2001; Ruby et al., 1998). Employment of PAs and NPs within a teaching hospital can also free up time for residents and attending physicians to attend to more complicated cases or to devote to teaching.

On a medical inpatient unit, the duties of a PA or NP encompass the wide range of tasks normally performed by the patient's physician or house staff. These might include performance and dictation of the admission history and physical examination, daily patient evaluation, charting of patient's status and progress, ordering of laboratory and radiologic testing, ordering of medications and medication dose adjustment, requests for consultation from specialists, and discussions with the patient and family. PAs and NPs might also perform or assist with bedside procedures such as wound debridement, lumbar puncture, joint injection, and paracentesis. In some hospitals, NPs are responsible for case management and discharge planning from the inpatient unit.

PAs and NPs perform a variety of roles in surgery. PAs have had a longer and greater presence in the operating room and perioperative areas than have NPs. In the operating room, a PA or NP may serve as the first or second assistant, perform a technician's role, or if the NP is a nurse anesthetist, function as the anesthesiology provider for the procedure. In different regions of the country, PAs and NPs are members of coronary bypass and cardiothoracic surgery teams, transplant teams (renal, cardiac, liver, pancreatic, heart), and orthopedic surgery teams. PAs and NPs frequently are responsible for both the preoperative and postoperative evaluation (history and physical) and orders and may perform daily rounds and follow-up of the postoperative patient. They are also highly involved in patient education, having the time to prepare the patient and family before the operation and afterwards to answer questions about postoperative care, discharge, and follow-up care.

Emergency room staff may also include PAs and NPs, as hospitals attempt to find ways to serve a growing ER population. The PA or NP may be part of the hospital's ER staff or a member of a physician medical group contracted by the hospital to provide emergency room services or coverage. They might provide the full range of medical services commonly associated with an ER physician, handle less acute cases, or function in technical roles doing suturing, intubation, and other procedures. Some hospital emergency rooms are creating fast-track programs or other specially designated units within the ER, where patients who meet specific criteria are cared for exclusively by PAs or NPs, thus freeing up the emergency room physicians for trauma victims and the more acutely ill patients (Hooker & McCaig, 1996). PAs and NPs are also incorporated into special teams that have developed within the ER and hospital to improve care and outcomes of patients with specific diagnoses such as myocardial infarction, acute stroke, and hip fracture.

Radiology departments are hiring PAs and NPs to assist the radiologist with technical aspects of interventional radiologic examinations (Van Valkenburg, Lopatofsy, Campbell, & Brown, 2000).

PAs and NPs offer an innovative staffing solution for small rural hospitals that lack adequate physician staffing to meet federal or state regulations. The Federal Essential Access Community Hospital/Rural Primary Care Hospital (EACH/RPCH) program has been implemented in seven states (Wright, Gelt, Wellever, Lake, & Sweetland, 1995). In this program limited-service rural hospitals are linked with larger referral hospitals. PAs or NPs are allowed to provide short-term (average of 72 hours) inpatient and emergency room services as long as a physician is available by telephone or radio. A similar program in Montana (Medical Assistance Facility, or MAF) allows PAs or NPs to staff small, isolated rural hospitals. Under this program a physician must review all admissions by telephone within 24 hours and must visit the facility every 30 days.

EMPLOYMENT AND PHYSICIAN RELATIONSHIP

The PA or NP working in a hospital setting might be employed by the hospital itself, the organization that owns or operates the hospital, or by a physician or physician group that is part of the hospital's medical staff. When the PA and NP are employed by the hospital or the corporation that owns or manages the hospital, the PA's supervising physician(s) or the NP's collaborating physician(s) are also usually an employee of the hospital or the same corporation. In this situation, the employer usually determines which PA or NP will work with which physician(s) and where. When the PA or NP is associated with a physician or medical group that is part of the hospital medical staff but a private entity, then the PA's or NP's role in the hospital is under the supervision of, or in collaboration with, only the physician or physicians of the medical group within the policies allowed by the hospital.

The relationship between a PA and the supervising physician(s) or an NP and the collaborating physician is one of trust that must be nurtured and cultivated over time. There should be a shared sense of values and approach to patient care. It takes time, commitment, and work for these relationships to develop and mature. Scheduled time on a regular basis (weekly, monthly) to review patient cases, clarify practice management styles, and openly discuss differences is essential. As the relationship between the PA/NP and physician matures over time, less oversight is necessary. The vast majority of physicians who work with PAs or NPs report that they find it to be professionally fulfilling and a good way to provide quality patient care (Burl & Bonner, 1991; Greene, 2001; Office of Technology Assessment, 1986).

REIMBURSEMENT

Services provided by a PA or NP in the hospital are reimbursed in much the same way as those of any physician provider. The Current Procedural Terminology (CPT) code book, which most payers consult to determine reimbursement rates, uses the word physician in many of its descriptors, and this terminology has led to confusion about whether such services provided by a PA or NP can be reimbursed (American Medical Association [AMA], 2001). To clarify that the book describes medical and surgical services and is not meant to determine which health care providers can or cannot perform specific services, the 2002 CPT book will include the statement that "Any procedure or service in any section of this book may be used to designate the services rendered by any qualified physician or other qualified health care professional" (AAPA, 2001).

Payment for services provided by a PA or NP differs, depending on the reimbursement source and the employment arrangement. Services provided by a PA are generally reimbursed to the physician, medical practice, health care organization, or hospital that employs the PA. Nurse practitioners can be reimbursed directly for their services, but this rarely occurs for hospital-based care. Hospital services provided by an NP are usually reimbursed to the hospital, medical practice, or health care organization in a manner similar to that of PAs.

Medicare and Medicaid both explicitly permit reimbursement for services provided by PAs or NPs. Like physicians and other health care providers whose services are reimbursable under Medicare, PAs and NPs are required to have their own billing number (UPIN). Under Part B Medicare, all services that would be reimbursed if provided by a physician in the hospital setting (inpatient, first-assist, ER, outpatient) are also reimbursable if provided by a PA or NP. The Balanced Budget Act of 1997 established that any service provided by a PA is reimbursed at 85% of the Medicare physician fee schedule, regardless of setting (Balanced Budget Amendments, 1997). If the physician is directly involved in seeing the patient at the same time in the hospital, either in the inpatient or ER setting, then Medicare is only billed for the physician's service, and not the PA's. In the outpatient or clinic setting when the PA and physician are both directly involved in seeing a patient during a single visit, the PA's services are billed under Part B Medicare as "incident to" the physician. Payment under Part B Medicare for services provided by an NP under the Balanced Budget Act of 1997 now equals "80 percent of the lesser of either the actual charge or 85 percent of the physician fee schedule amount" (Balanced Budget Amendments, 1997). When the PA or NP is functioning as hospital house staff, the reimbursement for services may be indirect and included in negotiated bundled rates. If the salary of the PA or NP is paid by the hospital from Medicare Part A funds, then the provider cannot bill separately for these services.

Federal statutes permit reimbursement within the Medicaid system for services provided by a PA or NP, but leaves the specifics up to each state. Federal law mandates direct reimbursement to pediatric nurse practitioners (PNP) and family nurse practitioners (FNP) for services provided to children. Currently, most state Medicaid programs reimburse for services provided by PAs and NPs. The reimbursement rate is set by each state, as it is for physician services, and varies between 75% and 100% of the physician rate.

Private health insurance carriers each have their own policy regarding reimbursement for services provided by a PA or NP. Most, but not all, reimburse for services provided in the hospital setting by a PA or NP, including first-assist and emergency room care. The reimbursement rate and requirements (physician presence, etc.) are also set individually.

CURRENT AND FUTURE ISSUES

PAs and NPs working in hospital settings across the country report encountering similar issues as institutions adjust to these "new" clinicians in ever-expanding and changing roles. These problems often have to do with resistance to change within the institution and concern about areas of professional and legal responsibility.

1. *Orders.* A recurring issue in the hospital setting has to do with the execution of orders. This has been, and will probably continue to be, an issue between PAs and nursing, more so than between NPs and nursing. Laws in many states often list explicitly whom nurses may accept and act upon orders from. Rarely are PAs or NPs named in these statutes, because most were written long before the development of these professions. Most state statutes do include nurse-to-nurse orders, which have been interpreted to include NPs. Clarification that nurses can act on orders written by PAs has required the legal opinion of the attorney general in a number of states. In almost all these cases, it has been determined that the PA acts as the agent of the supervising physician, and in that capacity an order written by a PA is the same as if the order was written by the physician. When acting on an order written by a PA or NP, nurses and other health professionals should perform their duties in the same manner as if a physician had written the order. If the order seems incorrect or inappropriate, the PA or NP who is writing the order should be questioned for clarification of the order. If concerns remain, the supervising or collaborating physician should then be consulted.

2. *Independence.* It remains unclear how hospitals will deal with the growing role of the independent practice of nonphysician clinicians, particularly NPs. The AMA, along with most regional and local medical societies, is resistant to the growing independence among NPs. At the present time, most hospitals continue to require that NPs have physician collaboration and PAs have physician supervision. Without the requirement for physician collaboration or supervision, a hospital is unlikely to allow independent NPs onto its medical staff or to function independently of any physician relationship as part of the nursing staff. At present, NPs in independent practice have been confined to the outpatient setting. When under the care of an independently practicing NP, a patient who requires hospitalization is either referred to a physician colleague in the community with medical staff privileges, or directly to the hospital ER.

3. *Expanding roles.* The clinical roles and responsibilities of PAs and NPs in hospital settings will continue to expand and change, just as they have over the last three decades. They

- may provide care for patients with simpler illnesses, leaving the more complicated and complex cases for physicians;
- will serve on the growing number of specialized disease management teams (i.e., CHF, stroke, asthma) under the direction of a physician leader;
- will become technical specialists for specific procedures or services under the supervision of physicians;
- may serve as generalist clinicians working with physician specialists, providing basic clinical services and patient education.

How and where PAs and NPs work in the hospital in the future will depend upon changes in federal and state policies (health professional education, reimbursement, scope of practice), advances in medical technology (proliferation and adoption of new equipment and techniques), and local or regional factors (employment, population demographics).

The number and size of training programs for both PAs and NPs has grown dramatically in the past decade, introducing many more of these clinicians into the health care work force. As the health care marketplace continues to shift, it is difficult to predict how and where PAs and NPs will be used, but after three and half decades it is clear that PAs and NPs will flourish in the hospital setting.

REFERENCES

American Academy of Pediatrics, Committee on Hospital Care. (1999). The role of the nurse practitioner and physician assistant in the care of hospitalized children. *Pediatrics 103*, 1050–1052.

American Academy of Physician Assistants. (2000). *AAPA physician assistant census report (10/6/01)*. Alexandria, VA: Author.

American Academy of Physician Assistants. (2001). *Reimbursement watch (4/6/01)*. Alexandria, VA: Author.

American College of Nurse Practitioners. (2001). *What is a nurse practitioner?* [on-line]. Available: www.nurse.org/acnp

American College of Physicians, ACP Task Force on Physician Supply, 1994. Physician assistants and nurse practitioners. *Annals of Internal Medicine, 121*, 714–716.

American Medical Association. (2001). *Current procedural terminology, 2001*. Chicago: Author.

Balanced Budget Amendments. (1997). Pub. L. 105–33. [on-line]. Available: hcfa.gov/regs/bbupdat

Burl, J. B., & Bonner, A. F. (1991). A geriatric nurse practitioner/physician team in a long-term care setting. *HMO Practice, 5*, 139–142.

Greene, J. (2001, July 30). Multiplying efforts: Expanding the health care team. *American Medical News.*

Hooker, R. S., & McCaig, L. (1996). Emergency department uses of physician assistants and nurse practitioners: A national survey. *American Journal of Emergency Medicine, 14*, 245–249.

Joint Commission on Accreditation of Hospitals and Healthcare Organizations. (2000). Standard Medical Staff. 1.1.1. in *Comprehensive accreditation manual for hospitals: The official handbook*. Oakbrook Terrace, IL: Author.

Knickman, J. R., Lipkin, M., Finkler, S. A., Thompson, W. G., & Kiel, J. (1992). The potential for using non-physicians to compensate for the reduced availability of residents. *Academic Medicine, 67*, 429–438.

Office of Technology Assessment. (1986). *Nurse practitioners, physician assistants, and certified nurse-midwives: A policy analysis (Health technology case study 37)*, OTA-HCS-37. Washington, DC: U.S. Government Printing Office.

Pioro, N. H., Landefeld, C. S., Brennan, P. F., Daly B., Fortinsky, R. H., Kum, U., & Rosenthal, G. E. (2001). Outcomes-based trial of inpatient nurse practitioner service for general medicine patients. *Journal of Evaluation in Clinical Practice, 7,* 21–33.

Ruby, E. B., Davidson, L. J., Daly, B., Clochesy, J. M., Serelika, S., Baldisseri, M., Hravnak, M., Ross, T., & Ryan, C. (1998). Care activities and outcomes of patients cared for by acute nurse practitioners, physician assistants, and resident physicians: A comparison. *American Journal of Critical Care, 7,* 267–281.

Van Valkenburg, J., Lopatofsy, L., Campbell, M., & Brown, D. (2000). The role of the physician extender in radiology. *Radiology Technology, 7,* 45–50.

Wright, G., Gelt, S., Wellever, A. L., Lake, T., & Sweetland, S. (1995). *Limited service hospital pioneers: Challenges and successes of the Essential Access Community/Rural Primary Care Hospitals (EACH-RPCH) Program and Medical Assistance Facility (MAF) Demonstration.* Washington, DC: Mathematica Policy Research, Inc.

■ 7
Medical Informatics

David A. Campbell and Peter D. Stetson

"*Medical informatics* is the scientific field that deals with biomedical information, data, and knowledge—their storage, retrieval and optimal use for problem-solving and decision-making" (Shortliffe, 2001). In other words, *medical informatics* is the academic field that covers the relationship between medicine and information. The term originated in Europe in the 1970s and has supplanted the American term *medical information science.*

Concurrent advances in computer science, cognitive science, and public health have fostered the growth of medical informatics. These advances have provided a better understanding of how humans and computers relate to information, how humans interact and acquire information from each other and computers, and how we can optimize the use of information; such advances can enhance the information-rich science of medicine.

Although heavily involved with computing technology, medical informatics is a discipline distinct from computer science. The primary tool of the informatician is the computer, but the use of a tool does not define the field. Most informatics research focuses on practical computer-based solutions in different domains of medicine. Nonetheless, the ties between medical informatics and the science and art of medicine are equally important. The goal of informatics is not to design computers to "do medicine." Medical informatics is a discipline parallel to medicine, augmenting and enhancing its practice. Trained medical informaticians must have an understanding of the practice of medicine and the goal of continually improving the practice of medicine.

This chapter will illustrate the dependence of high-quality medical care on the effective management of information. It is our hope that the reader will understand the promise and limitations of medical computing technology.

UNDERLYING THEMES OF MEDICAL INFORMATICS

To understand medical informatics as a field, it is important to discuss the basic concepts. As stated, medical informatics draws on several scientific fields, including medicine, computer science, public health, biostatistics, cognitive science, biomedical engineering, and genetics. The basic concepts of medical informatics combine themes from all these disciplines.

Data, Knowledge, and Information

When describing medical informatics as the science of medical information, it is necessary to describe what information is. Although everyone has an intuitive sense of the word, there are three distinct concepts: data, information, and knowledge. *Data* are a single or series of measurements on a phenomenon. Data are collected everywhere in medicine, from blood pressures to lab reports to radiology images. In and of themselves, data have little medical value. Only after the application of reasoning and interpretation do data become *information*. For example, a trained radiologist can extract a great deal of information from chest X-ray data (the image). *Knowledge* is achieved through the inductive interpretation of information and allows one to describe behavior, draw conclusions, and make predictions about the future. All three concepts are crucial to the practice of medicine and medical informatics. Data must be collected accurately and in a timely manner. Correct information must be interpreted from those data. Finally, that information must be saved as knowledge to improve the level of understanding in the future.

In a sense, medical informatics is a discipline as old as medicine. The earliest records of physicians relate how data, in the form of observations, were recorded and conclusions drawn to attempt a treatment. The outcomes were recorded on paper, in a book or medical record for posterity, and medical knowledge was passed to the next reader. This is the goal of medical informatics: maximizing the human ability to use medical data, information, and knowledge correctly.

Biomedical Data and Their Storage

Without methods to acquire and store medical data, informed medical decisions cannot be made. Medical data include clinical observations and tests like vital signs, physical findings, laboratory data, and diagnostic test results. Data are represented in narrative text of daily SOAP notes and discharge summaries and are collected from the signals of patient monitoring devices like EKGs or Swan-Ganz catheters. Diagrams, photographs, and bioimaging techniques (X-rays, CT scans, MRIs, etc.) generate enormous amounts of data critical to patient care. Even traditionally nonmedical data, such as billing and charge data, have been the basis for medical study. New types of data, such as whether a patient has a specific genetic risk factor, will be seen in the medical record of the future. The paper chart is no longer an adequate storage device for the data generated by a single patient. For these reasons, medical computer databases—computer applications designed to store data—play a significant role in the management of patient care and clinical research.

Standards for Data and Information—Technologies and Terminologies

Standards improve communication and reduce confusion and ambiguity. All technologies require compliance with standards in order to interoperate correctly. Medical informatics has been heavily involved in developing and implementing standards in the medical community. Meaningful, efficient, and accurate exchange of data and information requires a common language (terminology) and rules for how the information is exchanged and processed.

The development of standards is a long, difficult process requiring the consensus of many stakeholders. Stakeholders in the health care field include health care providers, hospital information technology staff, product vendors, and patients. The government has also played a critical role in standards development. The Health Insurance Portability and Accountability Act of 1996 (HIPAA) (Office for Civil Rights, 2001) requires that the Department of Health and Human Services adopt standards regarding the privacy, security, and transfer of health-related data. Medical institutions will require information systems that comply with these standards or face legal consequences. One specific recommendation of the law is the development of a "universal, unique health identifier," a critical first step in providing a standard for exchanging data between two health care facilities.

There are a few common terminology standards and data exchange standards that all health care providers should recognize. Many clinicians have encountered the International Classification of Diseases system (ICD-9-CM), which is a standard terminology for pathologies and is used for coding billing and reimbursement claims (National Center for Health Statistics, 2002). Many other standards are in use throughout the hospital. The Systematized Nomenclature of Human and Veterinary Medicine (SNOMED) and the Unified Medical Language System (UMLS) are two terminologies that cover broad areas of medicine (American College of Pathologists, 1982; Humphreys, 1990). The Logical Observation Identifiers Names and Codes (LOINC) is the standard terminology used by most hospital laboratory systems (Huff et al., 1998), and Health Level Seven (HL7) is the most common medical data exchange standard. This standard was designed to handle data exchange over a number of software and hardware configurations and is widely supported by hospitals and application vendors. Digital Imaging and Communications in Medicine (DICOM) is the National Electrical Manufacturers Association standard for the storage, transmission, and display of radiographic images and information.

Knowledge Acquisition and Representation

Knowledge acquisition describes the process of gathering knowledge to make it sharable. Determining the best format to represent acquired knowledge is the study of *knowledge representation*. Both concepts are central to medical informatics. Traditionally, medical knowledge has been captured in textbooks, in research literature, and in the minds of experts. Cognitive science plays an important role in knowledge acquisition, providing methods for interviewing experts and judging the quality of knowledge sources. A *knowledge base* is the product of acquiring and representing knowledge in an electronic format.

The categories of medical knowledge and their uses are too broad to be fully listed, and the methods that have been developed to represent knowledge electronically are equally broad. Choosing the best representation format is crucial for the success of a knowledge base. Some more common forms of knowledge representation are logical rules, probabilistic systems, frames, and heuristics. Knowledge bases have been used in medical computer systems that predict drug-drug interactions, provide diagnostic assistance, suggest guidelines, and determine patient risk factors from their history.

MEDICAL DECISION-MAKING

Medical computer-system designers must understand the processes of medicine to help health care providers make good medical decisions. Medical decision-making is a complex cognitive process, fraught with risk for patients and considerable uncertainty for providers. The process of differential diagnosis and treatment is an iterative one, often requiring reevaluation and assistance from colleagues. For this reason, modeling medical decision-making means modeling uncertainty. Humans are adept at reasoning under uncertainty; this is very difficult for computers, which rely on logic and probability. An example of how computers can help with decision making is *decision analysis,* a popular strategy for modeling uncertainty because it incorporates both the medical evidence and patient preferences as determined by any of several established methods (Sox, Blatt, Higgins, & Marton, 1988).

OVERVIEW OF DISCIPLINES WITHIN MEDICAL INFORMATICS

Most professionals who work in informatics develop a particular area of interest or expertise. As the field has developed over the last few decades, a few general "tracks" or "application domains" have evolved. There are four general areas of focus.

Clinical Informatics

This is the branch of medical informatics that is directly involved in patient care. Clinical informatics contains subdomains such as nursing, dental, and veterinary informatics. Clinical informaticians often design and implement information systems within hospitals. They also act as mediators between stakeholders in the hospital on technology issues. A deep understanding of human-human and human-computer interactions is critical for the adoption of novel computer-based clinical systems. People drawn to this track commonly have training in medicine, nursing, dentistry, computer science, psychology, and cognitive science.

Bioimaging

This domain within medical informatics is concerned with the analysis and storage of medical images and the development and enhancement of image modalities. Imaging affects diagnosis, assessment and planning, guidance of procedures, communication, education and training, and research. Some common imaging applications that overlap with clinical informatics will be discussed later in this chapter. People drawn to this subdiscipline commonly have backgrounds in radiology, biomedical engineering, computer science, or physics.

Public Health Informatics

This subdiscipline is concerned with using information technology to manage the health of communities and populations. Areas of focus in public health informatics include the development of health surveillance systems, national reporting of infectious diseases, immunization registries, and tracking preventive medical care usage. Public health informatics is also concerned with evaluating the performance of managed care companies against measures such as the Health Plan Employer Data and Information Set (HEDIS) (Mainous & Talbert, 1998).

More recently, public health informaticians have been interested in using health technology to empower patients and improve the health of communities. One strategy under investigation is to provide patients with access to their own medical data and answer questions they may have about their care through self-help information resources. The major challenges in providing these information resources are maintaining privacy and confidentiality, developing standards for assessing the quality, and credentialing the content of, the information provided to the patients. Public health informaticians usually have backgrounds in public health, epidemiology, nursing, and clinical medicine.

Bioinformatics

Bioinformatics is the study of how information is represented and transmitted in biological systems, starting at the molecular level. Many bioinformaticians are involved in the processing of genetic information from the Human Genome Project. Another area of interest is the prediction of three-dimensional structure information of proteins from sequence data. This area of informatics has grown rapidly in the academic community and in private industry. Pharmaceutical companies are developing targeted therapies based on genetic sequence and protein structure data. Bioinformaticians often have training in mathematics, computer science, molecular biology, and genetics.

APPLICATIONS OF MEDICAL INFORMATICS

It is impossible to practice medicine in a modern hospital today without using medical computing systems. These systems are designed to assist health care professionals directly with the care of their patients. The goal of these systems is to provide accurate, legible, appropriate, and reliable information to the right person at the right time. This section will describe some medical computing applications found in *clinical information systems* (CIS) and touch briefly on other informatics systems.

Computer-Based Patient Records and Patient Care Systems

The computer-based patient record (CPR) is perhaps the most visible medical computing application in the hospital. The CPR, also known as electronic medical record or EMR, is a computer system for collecting, storing, analyzing, and viewing a patient's medical history. However, many CPRs still contain only a fraction of a patient's history. Many hospitals have not yet implemented rudimentary CPRs.

CPRs serve the same purpose as paper-based medical records: providing the health care professional with the information needed to diagnose, treat, and care for a patient. However, it is a mistake to think that a CPR is simply an electronic duplication of the paper record. To do so would underestimate the power and flexibility of the computer. There are many limitations to the paper-based medical record that CPRs are designed to eliminate.

Paper-based medical records have limited *accessibility.* Only one copy of a paper-based medical record exists, and that copy must be physically moved from one location to another. This constant movement increases the chances that a chart may be misplaced, lost, or damaged. The paper-based medical record has also only one *view,* or way, to search and review the information. Legibility of the record may be poor in some parts, making information questionable or unreliable. Multiple records on the same patients may be created if observations must be recorded and the existing record is not available.

In contrast, a CPR is available to all users at all times and can be accessed by more than one person simultaneously. A CPR offers multiple views of the data. Information appropriate for different users (physicians, nurses, physical therapists) can be displayed and customized. It may provide additional functions, ranging from simple tools like spell checking to complex diagnostic decision support. CPRs can provide extra services, including the computerized ordering of drugs, lab tests, or referrals. They may be made available remotely by transmitting the record over a network or traditional phone lines using a modem. CPRs give more flexibility to researchers by allowing them to aggregate data from different patients more easily.

CPRs generally consist of at least three basic components. The user interacts with the *interface.* This includes information display, usually on a monitor, and data input, usually from a keyboard or mouse. The *patient database* is the actual storage device that contains and organizes all the patient data. The database must be large enough and fast enough to deal with the number of patients and users for the institution. The third component is the *network,* which links the interface to the database.

In an effort to improve sharability, new CPRs may use an established protocol such as the Internet, which allows any computer with an Internet browser to access the database. Some CPRs have access to outside databases such as pharmacy or laboratory systems, guideline support systems, and information retrieval systems.

There are a number of reasons why successful implementation of CPRs is difficult. The interface may be confusing or difficult to use. Oftentimes this problem can be attributed to a lack of understanding of the practice of medicine by the developers of the system. It can also result from insufficient training or general resistance to using computers. CPRs must be extremely reliable because down time, where records are unavailable, is not acceptable. From an institutional standpoint, a CPR can be very expensive, especially when a network is not in place to support one. The security of CPRs is crucial to protect the privacy of the medical data contained. Many CPRs require users to enter passwords before accessing information, are protected against attacks and hacking, and encrypt the data on the network to prevent medical data from being compromised. Security in CPRs can be improved over paper-based records by allowing access only to authorized users. For example, a CPR could limit access to highly confidential information, such as HIV status, to physicians and nurses, while blocking that information from other users who have no need for it.

Patient Monitoring Systems

Patient monitoring systems are designed to make repeated measurements of a patient's physiological status without direct continuous observation by the health care provider. Patient monitoring systems are now ubiquitous in most hospitals and range from telemetric heart monitors to sophisticated implantable devices. Monitors commonly measure patient vital signs such as blood pressure, heart and respiratory rates, and chemistries. Recent advances in monitoring technology have made units smaller, more reliable, and portable, making home monitoring of vital signs realistic in the near future.

Imaging Systems

Imaging systems are systems that generate, manipulate, and store data in the form of an image or picture of a patient. Image data are generated using radiographic modalities like X-rays, MRI, and ultrasound. Medical informatics and biomedical engineering research is involved in discovering new image modalities and creating new software and hardware to improve the production of these images. Imaging systems also allow users to manipulate images to improve diagnostic decisions. Managing the images is another informatics challenge. Image files are difficult to store on a computer because they are often large. Transmitting these files over a network or a phone line can take a prohibitively long time.

Picture-archiving and communication (PACS) are designed for the practical storage, transmission, and display of high-resolution images. Currently, PACS are rarely integrated into CPRs because of the expensive technology required for PACS. As it becomes less expensive and difficult to store large images and as high-speed networks become more common, the integration of PACs and CPRs will become a focus of informatics research.

Information Retrieval Systems

Information retrieval (IR) systems are designed to retrieve text documents that are relevant to some question. Until recently, IR has concentrated on literature documents, such as journal articles and reference texts. By far the most popular IR system used in medicine is MEDLINE/PubMed. MEDLINE was developed by the National Library of Medicine and includes more than 11,000,000 citations from 4,000 medical journals back to the 1960s.

Information retrieval has expanded to clinical documents, such as radiology reports or patient notes. *Digital libraries* are more complicated IR systems that are designed specifically for answering questions or pointing users toward resources that can answer them. The usefulness of IR systems is often measured in terms of *precision* and *recall.* Systems that retrieve most of the relevant documents have good recall. Systems that do not retrieve many irrelevant documents have good precision. High precision allows the user to view only relevant documents without wasting time looking at irrelevant ones. Systems with high recall give the user confidence that all of the best documents were found.

Decision Support Systems

Some of the first medical informatics applications were decision support (DS) systems. As the name implies, these systems are designed to assist medical professionals in making medical decisions. DS systems offer suggestions, focus attention, or help manage information about many aspects of medical practice ranging from diagnosis, creating appropriate care plans, guiding and planning radio-surgery, and prescribing drugs. A few DS systems, like Quick Medical Reference (QMR) and DXplain, are commercially available, although their use is still not widespread (Barnett, Cimino, Hupp, & Hopper, 1987; Miller, McNeil, Challinor, Masarie, & Myers, 1986). At the core of every DS system is a knowledge base captured from professionals. There are many different ways in which computers can arrive at their decisions using this knowledge. A common method is to base decisions on the probability of events and the likelihood of a positive outcome. Other systems are *rule-based,* where the knowledge is represented as "if-then" rules provided by the system designer. *Case-based* systems try to find a historical case similar to the one seen currently and then extrapolate decisions based on the similarities and differences between the two. Many DS systems are interactive and have the ability to ask for more information when needed.

MEDICAL INFORMATICS APPLICATIONS BEYOND CLINICAL CARE

Medical Networks and Enterprise Systems

The business of running a hospital often extends beyond the practice of medicine. Hospitals require information to flow readily among the nonmedical staff. With the increasingly competitive medical market, standardizing financial and patient information at an institutional level can reduce costs and improve overall service.

Medical Education

The current generation of medical students grew up with computers and are comfortable using them as educational tools in medical school. Advances in multimedia technology and biological modeling will give the doctors of the future entirely new ways to learn medicine.

Public and Community Health

Computer applications that inform and educate patients directly will help them make intelligent decisions about their health. These systems allow patients to review their own medical data, explore educational resources, and communicate with health care professionals.

THE FUTURE OF MEDICAL INFORMATICS

Medical informatics has an exciting and challenging future. For clinical practitioners, medical applications such as CPRs, patient monitors, and decision support systems will become faster, more powerful, and more reliable. Informatics advances outside of the clinical realm will give rise to new imaging modalities and drugs based on computational genetics and bioinformatics. Medical informatics will be heavily involved in some of the most exciting advances in medical practice, including the following:

- Telemedicine and remote practice. Telemedicine will allow professionals who are separated geographically to work together by having access to the same patient data. Many of these technologies are already being implemented on a small scale in remote areas and in military situations, where trained health care professionals are not available. Eventually, "telepresence" may allow physicians to conduct physical examinations and perform surgery remotely.
- Lifelong medical records. Patients often have as many medical records as doctors encountered. Medical informatics will lead in making "one-person, one-record" a reality. Health care practitioners will have a complete view of a patient's health, saving time and improving overall patient care.
- Virtual reality (VR). Virtual reality is the coupling of advanced computer graphics and simulations to allow users to experience artificial environments realistically. In the future, medical students will explore the

human body through immersive simulations. VR will also allow surgeons to practice surgeries based on a patient's imaging data before conducting the surgery.

TRAINING AND CAREER OPPORTUNITIES IN MEDICAL INFORMATICS

The principal professional organization of Medical Informatics in America is the American Medical Informatics Association (AMIA). AMIA was formed in 1990 by the merger of three informatics organizations—the American Association for Medical Systems and Informatics (AAMSI), the American College of Medical Informatics (ACMI), and the Symposium on Computer Applications in Medical Care (SCAMC). AMIA is the official United States representative organization to the International Medical Informatics Association. AMIA publishes the *Journal of the American Medical Informatics Association (JAMIA)*. Other clinically oriented medical informatics journals include the *Journal of Biomedical Informatics* and *Methods of Information in Medicine*. Popular journals with bioinformatics themes are the *Journal of Computational Biology* and *Bioinformatics*.

Opportunities for training, research, and full-time careers in medical informatics abound. For health care professionals, informatics offers a unique way of applying their health care expertise. The American Medical Informatics Association Web site contains a list of more than 40 training programs for those interested in pursuing a career in medical informatics. Most programs offer a combination of tracks that may include master and doctoral degrees, fellowships, certificate programs, and short courses. Trainees in informatics have many career paths available, including academic medical informatics, industrial research, clinical practice with informatics activities, hospital information technology, and work for the government.

REFERENCES

Ball, M. J., Douglas, J. V., & Garets, D. E. (Eds.) (2000). *Nursing informatics: Where caring and technology meet* (3rd ed.). New York: Springer-Verlag.

Barnett, G. O., Cimino, J. J., Hupp, J. A., & Hopper, E. P. (1987). DXplain. An evolving diagnostic decision-support system. *Journal of the American Medical Association*, 258(1), 67–74.

College of American Pathologists. (1982). SNOMED. Skokie, IL.

Huff, S. M., Rocha, R. A., McDonald, C. J., De Moor, G. J., Fiers, T., Bidgood, W. D., Jr., Forrey, A. W., Francis, W. G., Tracy, W. R., Leavelle, D., Stalling, F.,

Griffin, B., Maloney, P., Leland, D., Charles, L., Hutchins, K., & Baenziger, J. (1998) Development of the logical observation identifier names and codes (LOINC) vocabulary. *Journal of the American Medical Informatics Association, 5*(3), 276–292.

Humphreys, B. L. (Ed.). (1990). *UMLS knowledge sources—First experimental edition documentation.* Bethesda, MD: National Library of Medicine.

Kohane, I. (2000, September-October). Bioinformatics and clinical informatics: The imperative to collaborate. *Journal of the American Medical Informatics Association, 7*(5), 512–516.

Mainous, A. G. III., & Talbert, J. (1998). Assessing quality of care via HEDIS 3.0. Is there a better way? *Archives of Family Medicine, 7*(5), 410–413.

Miller, R. A., McNeil, M. A., Challinor, S. M., Masarie, F. E., Jr., & Myers, J. D. (1986). The Internist-1/quick medical reference project: Status report. *Western Journal of Medicine, 145*(6), 816–822.

National Center for Health Statistics (2002). *International Classification of Diseases, Ninth Revision* (ICD-9) www.cdc.gov/nchs/about/major/dvs/icd9des/htm

Office for Civil Rights. (2001). National standards to protect the privacy of personal health information. [on-line]. Available: www.hhs.gov/ocr/hipaa/

Shortliffe, E. H., & Perreault, L. (Eds.). (2000). *Medical informatics, computer applications in health care and biomedicine.* New York: Springer-Verlag.

Sox, H. C., Blatt, M. A., Higgins, M. C., & Marton, K. I. (1988). *Medical decision making.* Boston: Butterworths.

OTHER RESOURCES

Sowa, J. F. (1999). *Knowledge Representation: Logical, philosophical, and computational foundations.* New York: Brooks/Cole.

Van Bemmel, J. H., & Musen, M. A. (Eds.). (1997). *Handbook of medical informatics.* Bonn, Germany: Houten/Diegem.

WEB SITE INFORMATION

American Medical Informatics Association. www.amia.org
Health Level Seven. www.hl7.org
National Center for Biotechnology Information. www.ncbi.nlm.nih.gov/PubMed
National Electronics Manufacturers Association. www.medical.nema.org/dicom
National Library of Medicine. www.nlm.nih.gov

Part II
Caring for Patients in the Hospital

■ 8
Hospitalization Can Be Dangerous

Barrie G. Raik

Your college roommate calls from out of state to ask you to look in on his previously independent grandmother, who has been a patient in your hospital for the last 4 days. She was admitted with abdominal pain, which resolved. Without her glasses, she tried to go to the bathroom in the middle of the night, slipped and fell. Now, she is restrained, confused, and agitated. Her medication makes her groggy and nauseated, and she is refusing to eat or participate in physical therapy. She also has a urinary tract infection from an indwelling catheter. The team is recommending nursing home placement. What are you going to tell your friend? How did this happen in your hospital, one of the best in the state?

When we care for hospitalized patients, we seek to cure or ameliorate their medical conditions. But first we must realize that although the hospital may be the best place to treat patients with serious and acute problems, it can be a dangerous place, and some of our own behaviors and assumptions are contributing to those dangers.

Many of our actions are based on myths about how to care best for patients in the hospital. Often when we look at these beliefs carefully we can see that they are based on habit, not evidence. By examining the myths in some detail we can see how to fight our own instincts, and instead provide the best care for our patients. A recent report for the Agency for Healthcare Research and Quality (AHRQ) (Shojania, Duncan, McDonald, & Wachter, 2001), reviews evidence about the effectiveness of practices to improve safety of patients in hospitals. (This report is available on the Web at www.ahrq.gov/clinic/ptsafety/).

MYTH 1: THE HOSPITAL IS THE BEST PLACE FOR A SICK PATIENT, SO THE PATIENT SHOULD FEEL SAFE AND SECURE

We hospitalize patients to administer—to order—round-the-clock monitoring, high technology investigations or treatments, and therapies that would be too complex to provide elsewhere. We like being in control, but that is exactly what patients dislike about the hospital.

People usually prefer to be at home in familiar surroundings, especially when they are ill. Think of what happens when a person enters the completely unfamiliar environment of the hospital. Not only has he left his spouse, bedroom, and comfortable chair, he also may have left a pet, a child, or even a neighbor who relies on him. He cannot pay his bills, go to church, or visit the community center. He cannot do his work, and perhaps his job is in jeopardy. The active, independent person suddenly loses autonomy. The system schedules his tests and treatments for its own convenience; often he is taken away for such treatments just as his visitors arrive. He wears a hospital gown that is designed for the convenience of the whole array of examiners but is uncomfortable and embarrassing for him, and certainly discourages him from getting out of bed. The schedule is not his own, and this affects his sleeping, eating, and bathing. The adult patient may regress. If the patient has functional limitations on admission, it is likely that he will deteriorate further, even if the specific medical reason for hospitalization is appropriately treated.

Hospital rooms and corridors can be under- or overstimulating. Rooms that are undecorated, without a clock, and with curtains drawn around the bed can isolate the patient and cause her to become disoriented, particularly if there is any degree of preexisting cognitive impairment. Hearing-impaired patients may not understand plans for their care, especially if health care workers become frustrated with their failed attempts to communicate. Even systems as basic as call bells may not help. Visually impaired patients may be unable to find the call bell, the telephone, or the way to the toilet. Sensory deprivation may lead to misperceptions and distorted views that are interpreted as hallucinations and evidence of psychiatric illness.

Excessive noise can cause overstimulation. Beepers, intercoms, and pill crushers are loud and disturbing. The patient in the next bed may keep the television on at loud volumes, may have noisy visitors, or may be crying or moaning. The lights are turned on at 5 a.m. and sleep is disrupted. In fact, sleep disturbances are a major complication of hospitalization and can lead to disorientation, confusion, and depressed mood.

Programs to maintain functional status and prevent delirium promote a good night's sleep not with sedative-hypnotic medication, but rather through the use of massage, warm drinks, soothing music, and noise reduction

(McDowell, Mion, Lydon, & Inouye, 1998). Nonpharmacologic approaches to insomnia avoid the complications associated with sedatives. This is another example of how we must resist the instincts—in this case, to give a *prn* sleeping pill. Rarely is it truly "needed."

Cultural factors such as language and diet can also isolate patients. The food in the hospital may be totally unfamiliar to someone from a minority ethnic group, who may refuse to eat. Religious observances, dietary and otherwise, are often unaddressed in the rush to care for the acute illness. Failure to appreciate the role of culture in patient care may lead to withdrawal, depression, anger, or even medical mishaps and nonadherence to therapy. These topics and techniques for achieving cultural competence are described in chapter 21.

Other patients at risk in hospitals are those with psychiatric or psychosocial problems. Such patients are frequently admitted to medical and surgical units and require special attention. Depression is present in 40% to 50% of medical inpatients and is underdiagnosed (Katon & Schulberg, 1992). It is even harder for patients with emotional problems to adjust to the demands of the hospital routine. Ignoring the depression or attributing it to the medical illness may lead to a prolonged hospitalization. Suicide risk needs to be assessed and treated promptly.

MYTH 2: A SICK PATIENT SHOULD STAY IN BED

It is convenient for us to place the patient at bed rest, but it is not healthy for the patient. Patients recover more quickly when they are out of bed and are certainly less likely to develop skin breakdown. Bed rest often results in loss of muscle tone, loss of bone mineralization, and increases in pressure on soft tissue (Creditor, 1993). These changes develop very quickly. Young men at bed rest lose 10% of muscle strength per week, particularly in the lower extremities (Muller, 1970). Lack of activity also leads to muscle shortening, and then limitation of motion (Harper & Lyles, 1988). Immobility thus leads to deconditioning and the inability to perform activities of daily living; 16% of older adults in a recent study were newly dependent in walking after a hospital stay (Mahoney, Sager, & Jalaluddin, 1998).

With bed rest, fluid shifts and limited access to fluids cause a loss of plasma volume. This increases the likelihood of orthostatic hypotension and syncope. Bed rest also leads to venous thromboembolism. Ventilation decreases with bed rest, increasing the risk for respiratory and cognitive difficulties. The bed-bound patient is more likely to become constipated and to have episodes of urinary incontinence. Unrelieved pressure on skin can lead to pressure ulcers. Lying in bed without any stimulation or interaction can contribute to delirium or acute confusion as well as to depression. In many ways, almost all the dangers of hospitalization start with bed rest.

Fortunately, many hospital staff now understand the importance of increasing the activity of patients. It may seem more convenient to have the patient in bed, but he will recover more quickly and avoid functional decline if exercise is part of the treatment plan. Chapter 9 discusses in greater detail how to prevent functional decline, but the message can be expressed in simple terms: GET THE PATIENT OUT OF BED.

MYTH 3: RESTRAINTS PROTECT PATIENTS FROM INJURY

This is rarely the case. Patients pull out endotracheal tubes despite wrist restraints. Vest restraints do not prevent patients from getting out of bed. Side rails can be climbed over, under, or through. Restraint use necessitates increased, not decreased, patient monitoring.

Measures to prevent falls and fall-related injury are discussed in the next chapter. The chapter on avoiding restraints also addresses solutions to some of these problems. The AHRQ report recommends decreasing use of physical restraints, increasing use of hip protectors, and further study of bed alarms and specialized flooring (Shojania et al., 2001).

MYTH 4: WE ARE HIGHLY TRAINED PROFESSIONALS. WE DON'T MAKE MISTAKES

Chapter 25 disproves the myth of the infallible health professional. Errors are frequent unless there are systems in place to help prevent them. Even when no error has been made, therapies or tests can have unintended consequences. Recognizing and reducing risk is one way to make hospital care safer. We all need to be alert to the consequences of decisions we make, even basic choices about medications or diagnostic tests. Many treatments can lead to unintended consequences. In preparation for radiologic studies, a patient may become fluid depleted. Intravenous contrast agents can precipitate acute renal failure (as can medications). Skin ecchymoses and hematomas are common results of phlebotomy. Ventilator-associated pneumonias, procedure-related complications such as pneumothorax, anesthesia-related complications, and transfusion reactions are among the many risks of hospitalization.

When errors are made, the typical response is to place blame (Reinertsen, 2000). A more successful approach is to direct attention to the error and for health care leaders to take personal responsibility. Then, individual practitioners would be less intimidated and would acknowledge their errors; systems could then be analyzed and redesigned to prevent errors.

MYTH 5: MEDICATIONS ARE AN EFFICIENT WAY TO CALM AN ANXIOUS OR AGITATED PATIENT

Adverse drug events are a major risk of hospitalization. A meta-analysis (Lazarou, Pomeranz, & Corey, 1998) found that 6.7% of hospital admissions had an adverse drug reaction. Another recent study found that the incidence of fatal adverse drug events on the medical service was 9.5 per 1000 hospitalized patients (Ebbesen et al., 2001). Older patients are at higher risk. The more medications prescribed, the more likely a drug-drug reaction will take place. In addition, dosing errors and transcription errors are common.

Adverse drug reactions can occur without error. Known side effects such as nausea, somnolence, or GI bleeding can occur with appropriate doses. Drugs can cause fevers, rashes, confusion, weakness, and many other symptoms. Interactions between drugs can cause unexpected toxicity, and always need to be reviewed.

Whenever a patient's condition worsens, look for a medication as a possible explanation. Drug allergy histories should be documented clearly in the chart, ideally in a computerized prescribing system. A particularly dangerous cascade is when one drug is given to treat a condition caused by another drug, leading to more polypharmacy and more adverse effects. For example, an agitated patient is given a neuroleptic that causes extrapyramidal symptoms and is then given anti-Parkinsonian medications that make him hallucinate. Active patient involvement may reduce the risk of adverse effects. In one study, patient self-management of medication use was shown to reduce the rate of complications in anticoagulation treatment (Sawicki, 1999).

MYTH 6: CATHETERS ARE THE BEST TREATMENT FOR INCONTINENCE; DIAPERS ARE USEFUL, TOO, SINCE THEY REDUCE THE NEED TO VISIT AND TOILET THE PATIENT

Urinary incontinence alone is not an indication for indwelling catheter use. Urinary tract infections in the setting of indwelling catheter use are responsible for 40% of nosocomial hospital infections and lead to bacteremia 2% to 4% of the time (Stamm, 1991). Because of the high rate of infection, a catheter should never be placed routinely on admission, and it should be removed as soon as possible.

Although it is easier to change a diaper than the entire bed, use of diapers is associated with increased frequency of skin damage because patients are allowed to remain wet for longer periods, especially when they are not able to communicate. Helping the patient to the toilet or bringing the bedpan encourages continence. A quick response to a call for assistance can help a patient maintain continence and avoid the shame and guilt associated with urinary or fecal incontinence. Between 5% and 15% of community-dwelling older adults are incontinent of urine (Resnick & Yalla, 1985). Most of these individuals are able to maintain continence through a variety of strategies, but when they are admitted to the hospital, these strategies are much less successful or impossible to implement. The patient doesn't have the same control over access to the toilet, the amount of fluid intake, activities during the day, or new medications (e.g., diuretics). Thus, 40% to 50% of hospitalized patients over the age of 65 develop functional incontinence.

Previously continent patients develop incontinence when hospitalized for many reasons. Intravenous fluid treatment and diuretic use will cause increased urine production and increased frequency of urination. The tethers mentioned earlier (IVs, oxygen tubing, bed rails) will make it harder for the patient to get to the toilet. She may call for help, but be unable to wait. Sometimes the staff will use diapers to minimize the calls, but this obviously encourages incontinence. The patient who is disoriented may not find the call bell to summon the nurse. Even the nontethered patient may find it difficult to find the toilet because of poor lighting or obstructed pathways.

Once incontinent, the patient is at higher risk for developing skin breakdown. New onset of incontinence is a major reason for admission to a nursing home. Maintaining continence should be a high priority during a hospital stay. Chapter 12 addresses ways to protect skin, and chapter 9 describes methods for maintaining continence by enhancing overall function.

MYTH 7: SPENDING TIME WITH FAMILIES KEEPS US FROM GETTING OUR "REAL" WORK DONE

Just as the patient is easily traumatized during a hospital stay, his family also experiences significant stress. Family members are often key helpers during the hospital stay, performing some basic nursing functions and keeping track of medical issues, but they need clear information from the health care team. Patients and family members may not understand the diagnostic uncertainties, the treatment plan, or the course of the illness. Communication between staff and families can break down for many reasons. Families are emotionally upset over the illness of a loved one, especially if it is unexpected and serious. Family members may worry over the loss of support from the patient, and relationships suddenly change, as when adult children become caregivers to their parents. Unresolved conflicts between family members are revived as everyone gathers in Grandfather's hospital room. Although the hospital staff members are not charged with solving these problems, it does help to be aware that they exist. Health care providers who keep in mind these adjustment difficulties, for both patients and families, associated with hospitalization will be better able to predict and prevent some of the adverse outcomes of the hospital stay. Chapter 20 explores in detail the role of families in the care of hospitalized patients.

MYTH 8: GLOVES ARE SUFFICIENT TO CONTROL INFECTION

Most nosocomial infection is transmitted from one patient to another via the hands or clothing of a health care worker. Preventing infections in hospitals has been an active area of concern since Semmelweis showed that infection-related mortality could be reduced when health care workers washed their hands. Nosocomial infections occur in 7% to 10% of hospitalized patients (Haley et al., 1985) and cause about 80,000 deaths in the United States (Jarvis, 1996). Health care workers understand the need for hand-washing, but overestimate their adherence to guidelines. Most studies show compliance with hand-washing to be very low; in one study average compliance was only 48% (Pittet, Mourouga, & Perneger, 1999). Studies to improve compliance have shown short-term benefits at best.

Hand-washing remains the key to infection control, but other factors contribute to the development of nosocomial infections. More than half of all hospitalized patients are treated with antibiotics (Pestotnik, Classen, & Evans, 1996). Antibiotics are often prescribed at the wrong dose, for the wrong indication, or for the wrong duration, and this is the main reason for the dramatic increase in antibiotic-resistant infections. Patients with resistant infections are more likely to have prolonged hospital stays and have an increased risk of death.

Urinary catheters and intravascular catheters, particularly central venous catheters, also cause hospital-acquired infections. Whether increased mortality associated with these catheter-related bloodstream infections is a marker of severe underlying disease or of the catheter itself is a matter of controversy. Increased length of stay and increased costs are clearly associated with these infections.

The AHRQ report (Shojania et al., 2001) highlights three evidence-based strategies to prevent infections: use of maximum sterile barriers while placing central intravenous catheters, use of antibiotic-impregnated central venous catheters to prevent catheter-related infection, and use of antibiotic prophylaxis in surgical patients to prevent postoperative infections. Systems to improve hand-washing compliance may not yet have proven effective, but each of us must know that we need to wash our hands before and after each patient encounter.

MYTH 9: IT IS BETTER TO WITHHOLD NARCOTICS; THEY WILL MASK THE PATIENT'S PAIN, KEEPING US FROM FOLLOWING THE CLINICAL COURSE

Both the Joint Commission on Accreditation of Healthcare Organizations (JCAHO) and AHRQ (under its previous name, Agency for Health Care Policy and Research [AHCPR]) have published pain management guidelines (AHCPR, 1992). Nonetheless, at least 40% to 50% of postoperative patients report inadequate pain relief, despite pharmacologic interventions (Wolfe, Lein, Lenkoski, & Smithline, 2000). The AHRQ report maintains that "postoperative pain can have deleterious psychological and physiologic consequences that contribute to patient discomfort and longer recovery periods, and may compromise outcomes. It also consumes greater healthcare resources" (Shojania et al., 2001). Patients with chronic pain are also frequently inadequately treated.

CONCLUSION

Admission to a hospital is necessary but has multiple risks. Awareness of the unpleasantness, the complications, and the real risks faced by patients will help health care workers reduce these risks. These hazards range from minor frustrations to "misadventures" to serious life-threatening errors. Doctors and nurses working in hospitals need to be aware of these risks. We need to refocus our frame of reference and see the patient first, the disease second. The patient must get out of bed, have a good night's sleep, and participate in his own care. Systems to reduce errors, assess and treat pain, and avoid infection will help us achieve our goals of optimal care for our patients.

Looking back to your roommate's grandmother, we can see a much happier outcome. When she was admitted to the hospital, the staff made sure that she had access to her eyeglasses, that the path to the toilet was clear, and that the call bell was easily located. If she had trouble sleeping, she would get a warm drink and a massage, leading to a comfortable night without grogginess the next morning. She would be out of bed and not lose muscle tone. And your friend would congratulate you for working at such a well-run hospital.

REFERENCES

Agency for Health Care Policy and Research. (1992). Acute pain management: Operative or medical procedures and trauma. *Clinical Pharmacology, 11(Pt. 1),* 309–331.

Creditor, M. C. (1993). Hazards of hospitalization of the elderly. *Annals of Internal Medicine, 118*, 219–223.

Ebbesen, J., Buajordet, I., Erikssen, J., Brørs, O., Hilberg, T., Svaar, H., & Sandvik, L. (2001). Drug-related deaths in a department of internal medicine. *Archives of Internal Medicine, 161*, 2317–2323.

Haley, R. W., Culver, D. H., White, J. W., Morgan, W. M., Emori, T. G., & Munn, V. P. (1985). The efficacy of infection surveillance and control programs in preventing nosocomial infection in US hospitals. *American Journal of Epidemiology, 121*, 182–205.

Harper, C. M., & Lyles, Y. M. (1988). Physiology and complications of bed rest. *Journal of the American Geriatrics Society, 36*, 1047–1054.

Jarvis, W. R. (1996). Selected aspects of the socioeconomic impact of nosocomial infections: morbidity, mortality, cost, and prevention. *Infection Control Hospital Epidemiology, 17*, 552–557.

Katon, W., & Schulberg, H. (1992). Epidemiology of depression in primary care. *General Hospital Psychiatry, 14*, 237–247.

Lazarou, J., Pomeranz, B. H., & Corey, P. N. (1998). Incidence of adverse drug reactions in hospitalized patients. *Journal of the American Medical Association, 279*, 1200–1205.

Mahoney, J. E., Sager, M. A., & Jalaluddin, M. (1998). New walking dependence associated with hospitalization for acute medical illness: Incidence and significance. *Journals of Gerontology: Biological and Medical Sciences, 53A*, M307–M312.

McDowell, J. A., Mion, L. C., Lydon, T. J., & Inouye, S. K. (1998). A nonpharmacologic sleep protocol for hospitalized older patients. *Journal of the American Geriatrics Society, 46*, 700–705.

Muller, E. A. (1970). Influence of training and of inactivity on muscle strength. *Archives of Physical Medicine and Rehabilitation, 51*(8), 449–462.

Pestotnik, S. L., Classen, D. C., & Evans, R. S. (1996). Implementing antibiotic practice guidelines through computer-assisted decision support: Clinical and financial outcomes. *Annals of Internal Medicine, 124*, 884–890.

Pittet, D., Mourouga, P., & Perneger, T. V. (1999). Compliance with handwashing in a teaching hospital. *Annals of Internal Medicine, 130*, 126–130.

Reinertsen, J. L. (2000). Let's talk about error. *British Medical Journal, 320*, 730.

Resnick, N. M., & Yalla, S. V. (1985). Management of urinary incontinence in the elderly. *New England Journal of Medicine, 313*, 800–805.

Sawicki, P. T. (1999). A structured teaching and self-management program for patients receiving oral anticoagulation: A randomized controlled trial. Working group for the study of patient self-management of oral anticoagulation. *Journal of the American Medical Association, 281*, 145–150.

Shojania, K. G., Duncan, B. W., McDonald, K. M., & Wachter, R. M. (Eds.). (2001). *Making health care safer: A critical analysis of patient safety practices.* Evidence report/technology assessment no. 43 (prepared by the University of California at San Francisco-Stanford Evidence-Based Practice Center under Contract No. 290-97-0013), AHRQ Publication No. 01-E058. Rockville, MD: Agency for Healthcare Research and Quality.

Stamm, W. E. (1991). Catheter-associated urinary tract infections: Epidemiology, pathogenesis, and prevention. *American Journal of Medicine, 91*(Suppl. 3b), 65s–71s.

Wolfe, J. M., Lein, D. Y., Lenkoski, K., & Smithline, H. A. (2000). Analgesic administration to patients with an acute abdomen: A survey of emergency medicine physicians. *American Journal of Emergency Medicine, 18,* 250–253.

■ 9
Preventing Functional Decline

Sandy B. Ganz

Function is multifactorial and encompasses a patient's physical, emotional, cognitive, and psychological well-being. The components of function are interrelated; a deficit in one component may affect the integrity of another. Failure to prevent functional decline may lead to prolonged hospitalization, institutionalization, or death, and optimizing function should be a priority for hospitalized patients. Unfortunately, functional status rarely receives sufficient attention, usually because treatment of acute illness is given a higher priority. The purpose of this chapter is to discuss methods commonly used to assess function and prevent physical functional decline in the hospitalized patient (Guccione, 2000).

Physical function may be defined as the ability to perform basic activities of daily living (BADLs) and instrumental activities of daily living (IADLs). Basic ADLs include fundamental tasks (self-care activities) such as eating, dressing, toileting, bathing, grooming, bed mobility, transfers, and walking. Instrumental ADLs consist of more complex tasks such as managing medications, cooking, housekeeping, shopping, ability to use public transportation or drive a car, and banking (Guccione, 2000).

Preventing functional decline of the hospitalized patient is a daunting task, even for the experienced clinician. Although a myriad of factors such as acute illness, isolation, sedating medications, and psychiatric illness can cause functional decline, the process often begins with bed rest, which can lead to cardiac and muscular deconditioning within a few days (Creditor, 1993; Hoenig & Rubenstein, 1991). Older persons are at higher risk, as they often have a dangerous combination of decreased physiologic reserve and multiple coexisting comorbidities (Fretwell, 1993; Palmer, 1995; Sager et al., 1996). Between 25% and 60% of hospitalized older patients experience a loss of independent physical function when undergoing treatment for an acute illness (Palmer, 1995). This high rate of functional decline leads to an increased dependence in ADLs (Hirsch, Sommers, Olsen, Mullen, & Winograd, 1990).

The key to preventing functional decline of the hospitalized patient is the continuous and systematic assessment of risk factors and timely intervention for those at risk. Iatrogenic functional decline is preventable if the team can foresee a potential problem and resolve it early.

SELF-CARE: THEORY IN PRACTICE

Preventing functional decline in the hospitalized patient poses quite a challenge to clinicians, who tend to view patients as recipients of care. It may be helpful to look outside the standard biomedical model and glean some insights from nursing theory. Orem's theory of self-care (Orem & Vardiman, 1995) provides a conceptual framework for encouraging and maximizing patient function. Patients are human beings "attending to and dealing with themselves" (Orem, 2001). The individual is both the *agent* and *object* of action. When individuals are unable to independently engage in self-care, a self-care deficit then exists. Just as with organ-based diagnoses, the diagnosis of a self-care deficit requires a treatment plan and an outcome assessment. By viewing functional impairment as a problem that requires assessment, diagnosis, and management, the team is less likely to allow a functional decline to occur.

PREVENTING AND CORRECTING FUNCTIONAL DECLINE THROUGH OCCUPATIONAL AND PHYSICAL THERAPY

Occupational and physical therapists play an important role in the prevention of functional decline of hospitalized patients. In each hospital setting, the policies for obtaining a referral for physical or occupational therapy are unique. In some facilities, the first step is a referral to the rehabilitation medicine department; a physiatrist sees the patient initially, and then refers the patient for physical therapy (PT) or occupational therapy (OT). In other facilities, PT or OT departments may accept direct referrals. Regardless of facility, occupational and physical therapists work together to diagnose and manage movement dysfunction and enhance physical and functional abilities.

The primary goals of both occupational and physical therapists are to restore, maintain, and promote not only physical function, but also optimal wellness, fitness, and quality of life. The secondary goals are to prevent the onset, symptoms, and progression of impairments, functional limitations, and disabilities that may result from diseases, disorders, injuries, or hospitalization itself.

Occupational therapy is "the art and science of helping people do the day-to-day activities despite impairment, disability or handicap" (Niestadt & Crepeau, 1998, p. 5). OTs evaluate and treat patients with a wide variety of diagnoses, including neurological, cardiopulmonary, or musculoskeletal disorders that result in cognitive and sensorimotor deficits (Niestadt & Crepeau, 1998). In the hospital setting, the occupational therapist addresses the patient's impairments by focusing on activities of daily living. Difficulty performing self-care tasks such as grooming, dressing, bathing, toileting, and eating would necessitate a referral to occupational therapy.

Physical therapists evaluate and treat patients with a myriad of clinical manifestations resulting from neurological, musculoskeletal, cardiopulmonary, and skin disorders. Their focus of treatment addresses functional strength deficits, functional activity intolerance, balance and gait impairments, and wound management.

Whether to refer to PT or OT (or both) is institution-dependent. At some facilities, upper extremity impairments are referred to OT, and lower extremity impairments are referred to PT. For example, a patient whose sole problem is a torn rotator cuff may be referred to OT, and a patient who has undergone an ankle reconstruction may be referred to PT. A patient who sustains a cerebrovascular accident that results in an upper and lower extremity hemiparesis would most likely be referred to both. In this case, the occupational therapist may work on muscle reeducation of the upper extremity, wheelchair mobility, and self-care deficits. The physical therapist may concentrate on lower extremity-strengthening, gait, and balance retraining. Together they might work on transfer and balance training.

PERFORMING FUNCTIONAL ASSESSMENT

As part of the initial patient evaluation, clinicians should perform a comprehensive functional assessment to obtain a baseline level of physical performance and identify impairments. A simple bedside assessment can be performed in a relatively short amount of time.

The following is an example of a simple observational bedside functional assessment: *The patient is lying supine in bed. The examiner asks the patient to roll onto his side, sit up over the side of the bed, and put his slippers on.*

By asking the patient to roll in bed, sit up, and don his slippers, you are simultaneously addressing cognitive and physical function. What you have asked the patient to do is a three-step command. If the patient has difficulty with this task, try a two-step command such as, "Roll onto your right side and sit up over the bed." If the patient is unable to do this, try a one-step command. Always assess hearing loss and language ability if the patient is unable to follow directions. If the patient has difficulty following commands and you have ruled out a physical impairment and hearing loss, assess cognitive status and consider a referral for formal cognitive testing.

These tasks encompass the following areas of physical function: bed mobility, sitting balance, transfer ability, and range of motion in the lower extremities. The patient who is unable to roll onto his side without physical assistance or has difficulty and requires a side rail to turn is exhibiting impaired bed mobility, which places the patient at risk for developing pressure ulcers because he is unable to reposition himself independently in bed. OT or PT may be able to reduce this risk by evaluating the patient's ability to use an enabler for bed repositioning.

A patient who is unable to transfer from the supine position to a sitting position (requiring manual assistance from the examiner) or has difficulty performing the activity is at risk for falls. PT or OT may reduce the patient's risk of falling out of bed by incorporating bed mobility and transfer training techniques utilizing a side rail, overhead trapeze, or another type of device that can enable safe transfers in and out of bed.

If the patient can slide his foot into the slipper on the floor, ask him to bend down and pick the slipper up from the floor and hand it to you. If he is able to perform this task without using his contralateral upper extremity to support himself, there is no deficit in sitting balance. A patient who is unable to maintain an upright sitting position, that is, who uses his upper extremities to sit, requires manual assistance from the examiner to maintain a sitting position, uses one arm to hold onto the bed for support, or loses balance while bending down to don the slippers, is at increased risk for falls; OT or PT should be consulted for balance retraining.

A baseline assessment would not be complete without addressing transfer status, static and dynamic standing balance, and ambulation. The basic task of balance is to position the body's center of gravity (COG) over some portion of the support base (i.e., the feet while standing or the buttocks while seated) (Nashner, 1989).

Before attempting to stand and ambulate a patient, evaluate sitting balance. If the patient is unable to sit unsupported and requires manual assistance to maintain an upright sitting posture, it is inadvisable to attempt standing. A patient with poor postural control when sitting will most likely have poor postural control when standing, as standing is a higher level activity.

This simple examination demonstrates how much information can be obtained merely by asking the patient to sit up over the side of the bed: *A chair should be positioned next to the patient's bed. The patient is asked to move from the bed and sit in the chair. The examiner observes the patient's ability to perform this transfer.*

If the patient requires manual assistance to transfer from the bed to the chair, this may be indicative of trunk or lower extremity strength deficit, and the patient is at risk for falls. If the patient has difficulty transferring, it is likely that standing balance and walking ability are impaired. If she requires some form of external support to stand or walk (the examiner's hand, a piece of furniture, or an assistive device like a walker or cane), a referral to PT is indicated for gait instability. If the patient is able to stand without external support, perform a sternal push test to assess static standing balance (Ropper, 1985).

Observe the following:

- Is the patient's base of support narrow (less than 4 inches)?
- Is the patient able to stand with her feet together with eyes closed without loss of balance?
- Is the patient able to weight shift adequately and march in place without loss of balance?
- Can the patient remove her hands from the walker and stand unsupported?

If the answer to any of these questions is no, a referral to PT for balance dysfunction and gait instability is recommended. Normal standing posture consists of a narrow base of support (< 4″) with arms at sides (Guccione, 2000).

When observing a patient walk, note step height, step length, gait speed, and ambulatory posture (i.e., is there reciprocal arm and leg swing?). If the patient demonstrates a gait impairment such as decreased step height, inability to clear the floor when ambulating, increased or decreased hip or knee flexion, pronounced trunk sway, or an antalgic (painful) gait, a referral to PT for gait instability is appropriate.

These simple assessments are brief and easy to perform at the bedside. They enable the clinician to make informed and specific consultation requests to PT and OT. If a functional assessment is included in the initial evaluation, early intervention can prevent functional decline and iatrogenic complications. Moreover, getting the patient out of bed changes both the patient's and the clinician's perspective about why the patient is in the hospital and the nature of the care the patient will receive.

FALLS

Falls and immobility are common and serious problems facing the hospitalized patient; falls account for a large proportion of injuries (Janken, Reynolds, & Swiech, 1986). The definition of a fall is "a sudden unintentional change in position causing an individual to land at a lower level, on an object, the floor, or the ground other than as a consequence of sudden onset of paralysis, epileptic seizure or overwhelming external force" (Tinetti, Baker, Dutcher, Vincent, & Rozeti, 1997).

Unintentional injuries are the fifth leading cause of death in older adults, and falls are responsible for two thirds of these deaths. In the United States 75% of deaths due to falls occur in the 13% of the population who are over age 65 (Josephson, Fabacher, & Rubinstein, 1991). Impaired gait and balance rank among the most significant underlying causes of falls. Older persons who demonstrate a functional impairment are at risk for falls; conversely, older persons who fall are at risk for functional impairment. The important interaction between mobility disorders and falls is highlighted by numerous epidemiological case-control studies. These studies indicate that lower extremity weakness, gait and balance disorders, functional impairment, visual deficits, cognitive impairment, and polypharmacy (defined as taken five or more prescription medications) are the most important intrinsic risk factors for falls (Leipzig, Cumming, & Tinetti, 1999; Robbins, Rubenstein, & Josephson, 1989; Schlict, Camaione, & Owen, 2001).

Approximately 6% of all hospital falls result in serious injury (Catchen, 1983). Incidence rates for falls in hospitals are almost 3 times greater than the community rates (1.5 falls per bed annually) (Rubenstein, Powers, & MacLean, 2001). Studies have shown that intrinsic risk factors for falling in the hospital setting are decreased mobility, poor balance, impaired vision, dizziness, neurologic deficits, and confusion (Robbins et al., 1989; Rubenstein et al., 2001).

The hospital surroundings themselves increase the risk of falls. The environment is unfamiliar to a newly admitted patient; unlike home—where the bed is low, there is carpeting on the floor, and the bathroom is in a familiar location—hospital rooms have shiny slippery floors, beds that are at a different height, and controls that are not within reach.

Basic environmental changes can reduce fall risk. Nonskid strips should be placed on the floor by both sides of the bed (St. Pierre, 1998) and in front of the toilet and the customary bedside chair. Patients should be provided with nonskid slipper socks (Palmer, 1995). Essential bedside items such as call light, water, and telephone should be within easy reach. Assistive devices should be easily accessible, and wheelchairs should be placed next to the bed with the brakes locked. Patients who have functional lower-extremity strength deficits may have difficulty rising from a low toilet. To avoid a bathroom fall and facilitate a safe toilet transfer, an elevated toilet seat or a commode placed over the standard toilet to increase the seat height is recommended.

Many clinical approaches have been advocated for ameliorating serious falls in the older population (Tinetti, 1986), but this requires identification of high-risk patients. A falls risk assessment can determine objectively whether a patient is at risk for falls (Edelberg, 2001). Based on the assessment, staff can then develop a care plan that addresses fall prevention for the patient at risk (Edelberg, 2001). A basic fall evaluation consists of

- history of fall circumstances
- vision examination
- medications (number and type)
- examination of gait and balance
- comorbidities
- lower extremity joint function
- basic neurological function
- mental status
- muscle strength
- reflexes
- cerebellar function
- cortical and extrapyramidal function
- basic cardiovascular status and, if appropriate, heart rate and blood pressure responses to carotid sinus stimulation (American Geriatrics Society, British Geriatrics Society, and American Academy of Orthopaedic Surgeons, 2001).

Tinetti (1986) developed a simple assessment tool that is valid and reliable. It specifically addresses impairments of balance and gait, requires no special equipment, is easily done in any setting, and takes 3 to 4 minutes to complete (see Table 9.1). The test is divided into two sections, balance and gait. Scoring is ranked from 0 to 2, where 0 = unable, 1 = able but requires assistance or more than one attempt, and 2 = able to complete activity without assistance. Balance consists of nine activities comprised of sitting and standing. The maximum score is 16. The gait section addresses initiation of gait, step length, step height, step symmetry, walking stance, amount of trunk sway, and path deviations. The highest score is 12. Together a score of < 19/28 indicates that the patient is at high risk for falling (Tinetti, 1986). Any patient who has a Tinetti gait and balance score < 19/28 should be referred to physical therapy for gait instability and balance dysfunction.

Another very simple test to determine fall risk is the Timed Up and Go Test (TUG) developed by Podsiadlo (1991). The TUG test requires a 46 cm armchair and a stopwatch. The TUG measures in seconds the time it takes for an individual to stand up from a standard armchair, walk 3 meters, turn, walk back to the chair and sit down again. For scores greater than 20 seconds, further evaluation of balance and gait is recommended (Podsiadlo, 1991).

PREVENTING FALLS AND INJURIES

- Remove clutter in the patient's room and hallway.
- Ensure that the bed is at a safe height. It is difficult for patients with trunk weakness or functional strength deficits in the lower extremities to transfer into excessively high beds or out of excessively low beds.

TABLE 9.1   Tinetti's Balance and Mobility Assessment

I. Balance Tests

Initial Instructions: Subject is seated in a hard, armless chair. The following maneuvers are tested.

1. Sitting balance _____
    0 = Leans or slides in chair
    1 = Steady, safe
2. Arises _____
    0 = Unable without help
    1 = Able, uses arms to help
    2 = Able without using arms
3. Attempts to arise _____
    0 = Unable without help
    1 = Able, requires > 1 attempt
    2 = Able to rise, 1 attempt
4. Immediate standing balance (first five seconds) _____
    0 = Unsteady (swaggers, moves feet, trunk sway)
    1 = Steady but uses walker or other support
    2 = Steady without walker or other support
5. Standing balance _____
    0 = Unsteady
    1 = Steady but wide stance (medial heels > 4″ apart) and
    uses cane or other support
    2 = Narrow stance without support
6. Nudged _____
    Subject is at maximum stance position with feet as close together as possible; examiner pushes lightly on subject's sternum with palm of hand 3 times.
    0 = Begins to fall
    1 = Staggers, grabs, catches self
    2 = Steady
7. Eyes closed _____
    (at maximum position, feet together)
    0 = Unsteady
    1 = Steady
8. Turning 360 degrees _____
    0 = Discontinuous steps
    1 = Unsteady (grabs, staggers)
    2 = Continuous
9. Sitting down _____
    0 = Unsafe (misjudged distance, falls into chair)
    1 = Uses arms or not a smooth motion
    2 = Safe, smooth motion

BALANCE SCORE: _____ /16

TABLE 9.1 **(Continued)**

II. Gait Tests

Initial Instructions: Subject stands with the examiner, walks down hallway or across room, first at usual pace, then back at rapid, but safe pace (usual walking aids).

10. Initiation of gait (immediately after told to go) _____
  0 = Any hesitancy or multiple attempts to start
  1 = No hesitancy
11. Step length and height
  a. Right swing foot _____
    0 = Does not pass left stance foot with step
    1 = Passes left stance foot
    0 = Right foot does not clear floor completely with step
    1 = Right foot completely clears floor
  b. Left swing foot _____
    0 = Does not pass right stance foot with step
    1 = Passes right stance foot
    0 = Left foot does not clear floor completely with step
    1 = Left foot completely clears floor
12. Step symmetry _____
  0 = Right and left step length not equal (estimate)
  1 = Right and left step appear equal
13. Step continuity _____
  0 = Stopping or discontinuity between steps
  1 = Steps appear continuous
14. Path _____
  (Estimated in relation to floor tiles, 12″ diameter; observe excursion of one foot over about 10′ of the course)
  0 = Marked deviation
  1 = Mild/moderate deviation or uses walking aid
  2 = Straight without walking aid
15. Trunk _____
  0 = Marked sway or uses walking aid
  1 = No sway but flexion of knees or back pain or spreads arms out while walking
  2 = No sway, no flexion, no use of arms, and no use of walking aid
16. Walking stance _____
  0 = Heels apart wide base
  1 = Heels almost touching while walking.

GAIT SCORE:____/12

BALANCE AND GAIT SCORE:____/16

The maximum total score on the test is 28 points. Patients who score less than 19 are probably at a high risk for falls.

Note: Reprinted from Encyclopedia of Elder Care, M. Mezey, Ed. (2000) Springer Publishing Co., with permission from M. Tinetti.

- Provide proper footwear (Palmer, 1995). Most hospitals dispense non-skid socks.
- Place nonskid strips on the floor beside the bed and in front of the toilet to decrease the "slip factor."
- Avoid psychotropic medications whenever possible; minimize number of medications.
- Offer hip protectors to patients at risk.
- Consider the use of one-on-one observation, bed alarms, or other devices to alert staff when impaired patients start to move without assistance.
- Avoid restraint use (see chapter 10).
- Offer bedside commodes and other equipment to minimize unsupervised trips to the bathroom.
- Keep assistive devices within reach of patients who need them.
- Provide raised toilet seats for patients who have functional strength deficits in the lower extremities or who have recently undergone hip surgery.

CONCLUSION

The health care team must actively promote function in the hospitalized patient. This necessitates identification of risk factors for falls, injuries, and functional decline, maintenance of a philosophy of health promotion, and creation of a safe hospital environment for the patient.

REFERENCES

American Geriatrics Society, British Geriatrics Society, & American Academy of Orthopaedic Surgeons Panel on Falls Prevention. (2001). Guideline for the prevention of falls in older persons. *Journal of the American Geriatrics Society, 49,* 664–672.

Catchen, H. (1983). Repeaters: Inpatient accidents among the hospitalized elderly. *Gerontologist, 23*(3), 273–276.

Creditor, M. C. (1993). Hazards of hospitalization of the elderly. *Annals of Internal Medicine, 118*(3), 219–223.

Edelberg, H. K. (2001). Falls and function. How to prevent falls and injuries in patients with impaired mobility. *Geriatrics, 56*(3), 41–45, 49.

Fretwell, M. D. (1993). Prevention of functional decline in older hospitalized patients. *Rhode Island Medicine, 76*(1), 13–18.

Guccione, A. (Ed.). (2000). *Geriatric physical therapy* (2nd ed.). St. Louis, MO: Mosby.

Hirsch, C. H., Sommers. K., Olsen, A., Mullen, L., & Winograd, C. H. (1990). The natural history of functional morbidity in hospitalized older patients. *Journal of the American Geriatrics Society, 38*(12), 1296–1303.

Hoenig, H. M., & Rubenstein, L. Z. (1991). Hospital-associated deconditioning and dysfunction. *Journal of the American Geriatrics Society, 39*(2), 220-222.

Janken, J. K., Reynolds, B. A., & Swiech, K. (1986). Patient falls in the acute care setting: Identifying risk factors. *Nursing Research, 35*(4), 215–219.

Josephson, K. R., Fabacher, D. D., & Rubenstein, L. Z. (1991). Home safety and fall prevention. *Clinics in Geriatric Medicine, 7,* 701–731.

Leipzig, R. M., Cumming, R. G., & Tinetti, M. E. (1999). Drugs and falls in older people: A systematic review and meta-analysis: Psychotropic drugs. *Journal of the American Geriatrics Society, 47,* 30–39.

Nashner, L. (1989). *Sensory, neuromuscular, and biomechanical contributions to human balance.* Paper presented at the American Physical Therapy Association Annual Meeting, Nashville, TN.

Niestadt, M., & Crepeau, E. (Eds.). (1998). *Willard and Spackman's occupational therapy.* New York: Lippincott.

Orem, D. E. (2001). Response to W. Lauder (2001). The utility of self-care theory as a theoretical basis for self-neglect. *Journal of Advanced Nursing, 34*(4), 552–553.

Orem, D. E., & Vardiman, E. M. (1995). Orem's nursing theory and positive mental health: Practical considerations. *Nursing Science Quarterly, 8*(4), 165–173.

Palmer, R. (1995). Acute hospital care of the elderly: Minimizing the risk of functional decline. *Cleveland Clinic Journal of Medicine, 62*(2), 117–128.

Podsiadlo, D. R. S. (1991). The timed 'up and go': A test of basic functional mobility for frail elderly persons. *Journal of the American Geriatrics Society, 39,* 142–148.

Robbins, A. S., Rubenstein, L. Z., & Josephson, K. R. (1989). Predictors of falls among elderly people. Results of two population-based studies. *Archives of Internal Medicine, 149,* 1628–1633.

Ropper, A. (1985). Refined Romberg test. *Canadian Journal of Neurological Science, 12,* 282.

Rubenstein, L. Z., Powers, C. M., & MacLean, C. H. (2001). Quality indicators for the management and prevention of falls and mobility problems in vulnerable elders. *Annals of Internal Medicine, 135,* (8, P. 2), 686–693.

Sager, M. A., Franke, T., Inouye, S. K., Landefeld, C. S., Morgan, T. M., Rudberg, M. A., Siebens, H., & Winograd, C. H. (1996). Functional outcomes of acute medical illness and hospitalization in older persons. *Archives of Internal Medicine, 156*(6), 645–652.

Schlict, J., Camaione, D., & Owen, S. (2001). Effect of intense strength training on standing balance, walking speed and sit to stand performance in older adults. *Journal of Gerontology, 56a*(5), M281–M286.

St. Pierre, J. (1998). Functional decline in hospitalized elders: Preventive nursing measures. *American Association of Colleges of Nursing Clinical Issues, 9*(1), 109–118.

Tinetti, M. E. (1986). Performance-oriented assessment of mobility problems in elderly patients. *Journal of the American Geriatrics Society, 34*(2), 119–126.

Tinetti, M. E., Baker, D. I., Dutcher, J., Vincent, J. E., & Rozeti, R. T. (1997). *Reducing the risk of falls among older adults in the community.* Berkeley, CA: Peaceable Kingdom Press.

■ 10
Choosing Alternatives to Restraints

Elizabeth Capezuti and Sharon Stahl Wexler

Physical and cognitive impairments increase a patient's risk for falls, and fall-related injuries and behavioral symptoms interfere with treatment. For this reason, maintaining patients' physical safety and life-sustaining treatments are major concerns among health care providers who may elect to restrain patients as an immediate solution. Yet restraining the patient does not address the underlying problem and may worsen it. This chapter will describe these patient problems and offer practical solutions that decrease the use of restrictive measures such as physical restraints and side rails. This perspective is consistent with a "mobility-enhancing" or a "functional recovery" approach to care (Hamilton & Lyon, 1995) and is supported by federal regulations (Capezuti & Braun, 2001).

TREATMENT INTERFERENCE AND BEHAVIORAL SYMPTOMS

A common reason for using restrictive devices is to manage treatment interference or behavioral symptoms that interfere with care and treatment. Treatment interference refers to both removal and manipulation of a monitoring or treatment device (Evans, Strumpf, & Williams, 1992). It is especially important when the treatment or device fulfills a lifesaving or life-maintaining function such as mechanical ventilatory support. Behavioral symptoms, such as anxiety, agitation, verbal and physical aggression, and delirium, interfere with treatment and may have possible physical, psychological, and environmental etiologies. Alternatively, treatment interference may include the way a patient communicates a choice to limit life-maintaining treatments; a patient's decision may challenge the clinician to explore the futility of painful or uncomfortable treatments with the patient, or in cases of patient incompetence, with a family member or other surrogate decision-maker.

RESTRAINTS AND SIDE RAILS

Physical restraint is defined according to its functional application in acute medical and postsurgical care as any device, material, or equipment that inhibits mobility or change in position and is not easily removed by the person who is being restrained (Stillwell, 1988). Examples include, but are not limited to, limb restraints, vest, chest, or jacket restraints, hand mitts, waist or belt restraints, pelvic restraints, and chest/pelvic combination restraints, commonly referred to as Houdini suits (Braun & Capezuti, 2000). Side rails are adjustable metal or rigid plastic bars that attach to the bed and come in assorted sizes (full-length rail, three-quarter-length rail, half-length rail, quarter-length rail, split-rail configuration, and alternate split-rail configuration) and shapes (Capezuti & Lawson, 1999). Side rails are defined as restraints or "restrictive" when used to prevent a patient's voluntary movement (Capezuti, 2000).

Restraints and restrictive side rails are frequently employed to prevent falls and injuries and treatment interference. Use of these devices without an appropriate workup for underlying causes or without consideration of nonrestrictive measures is inadequate care from both a professional and legal standard (Braun & Capezuti, 2000). Unfortunately, the routine use of restraints and restrictive side rails has become an embedded practice, because for decades each has been linked to safety and protection (Brush & Capezuti, 2001; Strumpf & Tomes, 1993). For example, permanent side rails on beds were first introduced in the 1940s because the fixed "nursing height" of approximately 26 inches was too high for most adults to transfer out of bed without a footstool (Brush & Capezuti, 2001). Despite the introduction of variable height beds in the 1950s, side rail use persisted as a "common sense" intervention to prevent falls (Brush & Capezuti, 2001). The perception that failure to restrain patients or raise side rails puts clinicians and facilities at risk for legal liability reinforces the belief in the effectiveness of restraints (Capezuti & Braun, 2001; Kapp, 1999).

Side rails and other forms of restraints can cause patient death and injury. Positional asphyxiation is the most common mechanism of restraint-related death; the patient is fully or partially suspended by a restraint from a bed or chair or between the side rail and mattress, unable to inhale because of gravitational chest compression (Miles, 1996; Miles & Irvine, 1992). Numerous accounts of restraint and side rail-related injuries and deaths in the print and electronic media, professional literature, sentinel event reports to the Joint Commission on Accreditation of Healthcare Organizations (JCAHO) (1998), and reports to the Food and Drug Administration (FDA) (1995; Todd, Ruhl, & Gross, 1997) have led to changes in regulatory, professional, and liability standards in the last decade. On November 16, 1991, the FDA issued a medical bulletin entitled "Potential Hazards with Restraint Devices" and reissued it on July 15, 1992, as an FDA Safety Alert, warning of the hazards associated with restraint use (FDA, 1991, 1992).

The FDA received 371 incident reports between 1985 and 1999 involving patients caught, trapped, entangled, or strangled in beds with rails, representing 228 deaths, 87 persons with nonfatal injury, and 56 who avoided injury because staff intervened (FDA, 1995, 2000; Todd et al., 1997). Parker and Miles (1997) categorized 74 side-rail-related deaths and injuries contained in the files of the U.S. Consumer Product Safety Commission into three types: asphyxiation; rail and in-bed entrapment; and rail and off-bed entrapment.

Restraint standards developed by JCAHO (1996) have led to reductions in overall physical restraint use and changes in restraint use patterns (Capezuti, Bourbonniere, Strumpf, & Maislin, 2000; Minnick, Mion, Leipzig, Lamb, & Palmer, 1998; Sullivan-Marx & Strumpf, 1996). The Centers for Medicare and Medicaid (CMS, formerly named the Health Care Financing Administration) have specific rules for side rails that mimic physical restraint standards. In July 1999, CMS issued an interim final rule describing hospital Conditions of Participation (CoP) necessary for continued participation in the Medicare and Medicaid programs (Capezuti & Braun, 2001; Moyers, 2000; U.S. Department of Health and Human Services [DHHS], 2000). The ruling classifies objects as restraints by functional definition: "any manual method or physical or mechanical device, material, or equipment attached or adjacent to the patient's body that he or she cannot easily remove that restricts freedom of movement or normal access to one's body" (Moyers, 2000). Thus, side rails that inhibit a patient's ability to voluntarily get out of bed (e.g., four raised half rails) constitute a restraint (Kahn-Kothmann, 1999). JCAHO's accreditation requirements must, at a minimum, meet applicable federal law and regulation; thus, it is expected that JCAHO standards regarding side rails will be updated soon.

Restraint and rail use must be based on a thorough assessment that examines the patient's medical symptoms and builds or modifies a treatment plan to meet patient needs (DHHS, 2000). Physical restraints and side rails present an inherent safety risk even when assessment indicates the presence of a medical symptom that may warrant restrictive rail use; a risk-benefit analysis should be undertaken before ordering these devices (DHHS, 2000).

Although physical restraints should always be considered restrictive measures, side rails also serve a variety of additional functions. An upper rail usually contains controls that adjust bed position, over-the-bed light, and television (Letizia, 1999a). It is often the favored location for call bell placement and a holder for personal care items such as urinals (Letizia, 1999a). Upper rails without raised lower rails can assist patients with moving in bed or transferring in and out of bed (Capezuti, Talerico, Strumpf, & Evans, 1998; Capezuti et al., 1999). Upper rails and other nonrestrictive measures should be considered before initiating any physical restraint or restrictive side rail use.

LEAST RESTRICTIVE MEASURES

Efforts toward restraint reduction begin with decreasing the time a patient is restrained. For example, orders for wrist restraints can be limited to particular situations, for example, only during infusion of intravenous medications. Devices like mittens, mitts (without ties), and digit extenders that restrict movement less than physical restraints can reduce the patient's ability to manipulate or disrupt treatments without decreasing range of motion. Air splints reduce hand or arm movement but not trunk mobility. A recliner or a very low chair (less than 13 inches from the floor) decreases the patient's ability to stand but does not affect other types of body movement.

JCAHO and CMS standards emphasize that alternatives to restrictive devices should be implemented and evaluated prior to initiating restraints. Alternatives and resources describing their application are readily available (Bochino, Capezuti, Driscoll, & Strumpf, 1999; Mion, 1996; Rader, Jones, & Miller, 1999; Strumpf, Robinson, Wagner, & Evans, 1998). The clinician should do the following:

1. *Assess behavioral and functional changes.* Behavioral symptoms (e.g., physical aggression) and functional changes (e.g., new gait disturbance) should first trigger a comprehensive evaluation of potential physical causes prior to initiating any physical or chemical restraint (see chapter 13). Referral to physical and occupational therapists may be necessary to evaluate functional consequences of medical problems or to prevent deconditioning (see chapter 9) that can contribute to fall risk. Periodically assess the need for any treatment like bladder catheterization or intravenous fluids; determine if it can be discontinued or if a less invasive treatment can replace it (Strumpf et al., 1998).

2. *Evaluate fall risk.* If a patient has been deemed at risk of falls or has fallen, then a thorough evaluation of amenable risk factors contributing to

future risk should be conducted. Falls, especially sudden onset of repeated falls, may indicate underlying acute pathology, such as infection, hypoglycemia, or dehydration (Miceli, Waxman, Cavalieri, & Lage, 1994). Also, a thorough pharmacologic review should check for appropriateness, usage, and dose. A general rule of geriatric pharmacology is to minimize the number of medications, assess the risk and benefit of each medication, and use those medications with the shortest half life, least centrally acting or least associated with hypotension, and at the lowest effective dose (Rizzo, Baker, McAvay, & Tinetti, 1996).

3. *Orient and inform.* In addition to medical and functional changes, the hospital environment (physical setting and staff practices) can affect behavior. Increase social contact and provide signs and other cues to increase orientation. Provide clocks and calendars in each room as well as an orientation board on each unit. Staff should offer frequent explanations and reminders of the patient's condition, physical environment, and treatments.

4. *Facilitate observation.* Move at-risk patients to rooms closer to the nurses' station to facilitate observation. Increase time spent out of rooms in hallways, at the nurses' station, or in day rooms with other patients to facilitate surveillance. Encourage family and friends to visit, especially during mealtimes and treatments, and at night to provide both meaningful distraction and assistance to staff. Providing communal dining when possible serves both this purpose and an opportunity for socialization. Volunteer or paid "companions" can be an alternative when families are unable to stay with the patient (Mahoney, 1998). This, however, can incur significant cost and must be evaluated in a cost-benefit analysis. An open intercom or nursery or baby monitor will promote contact between staff and patients. Devices such as alarms and video monitoring are useful; however, staff must be available to respond quickly.

5. *Distract.* Camouflage devices by hiding them under cloth (e.g., abdominal binder), undergarments or clothing, sheets, or blankets to divert the patient's attention from a treatment. Cover infusion sites with commercial holders, bandages, or stockinettes. For confused patients who "pick" or who are seeking tactile stimulation, provide fabric, stuffed animals, or an activity apron.

6. *Offer activities.* It is not surprising that patients will attempt to ambulate without assistance or remove tubes when isolated in a room without meaningful activities. Television is not the solution; it may be overstimulating and worsen confusion. Recreation therapy, if available, can be very helpful. Encourage the family to bring in favorite music or videotapes, hobby materials (e.g., knitting), or other items that the patient may enjoy. Staff can also provide activities based on the patient's interest and cognitive level, for example, towels to fold, magazines to read, and stuffed animals to hold. Activities also serve to distract patients from investigating or disturbing tubes, monitor, leads, and dressings (Happ, 2000).

7. *Promote mobility.* Certain activities promote mobility, such as encouraging or assisting patients with changing position in bed, transferring out of bed to chair, and ambulating. These also serve to prevent iatrogenic complication of functional decline that can result from bed rest, immobilizing devices (such as catheters), physical restraint use (a vest restraint, for example), and lack of encouragement of independence in self-care (Inouye, Bogardus, Baker, Leo-Summers, & Cooney, 2000). Organized group walks around the nursing unit at specific times during the day promote mobility, provide diversion, and involve the patient in his or her recovery.

Assistive devices such as walkers and canes will assist with transferring and ambulating. Place them in an easily accessible location to promote use. Transfer devices to enable or assist in safe transfer and promote stability when standing include a trapeze, transfer pole or bar, or raised quarter- or half-length side rail directly attached to or adjacent to the top of the bed. These may also serve as assistive bed mobility devices. Other interventions to prevent falls from bed include adjusting bed height to the patient's lower leg height, a nonskid rubber-backed rug at bedside, and raised-tread socks to be worn to bed.

8. *Maintain continence.* Traveling to the bathroom is the activity most likely to result in falls. Nocturia especially increases fall risk due to a sudden change in position, a need to locate the bathroom quickly, and low or absent lighting. "Elimination rounds," intended to anticipate patients' bathroom needs, can reduce falls. (Another suggestion: administering diuretics early in the day.) Also, use of urinal and bedpans may reduce frequent trips to the bathroom. Reduce the distance to the toilet by placement of a bedside commode (without wheels) specific to the patient's size on the patient's strongest side (Capezuti et al., 1999). Reevaluate the need for intravenous fluids daily.

9. *Promote comfort.* The patient's comfort in bed can be improved with an overlay mattress cushion, air mattress, or sheepskin mattress pads. Specific positions may promote comfort, for example, side-lying with bent knees for those with back pain (Capezuti et al., 1999). Pillows and leg-separator cushions can be used to facilitate positioning. Heel pads or bed cradles are good choices for those with significant peripheral vascular disease or pressure ulcers.

In the critical care unit, although sedation and analgesics can improve tolerance of invasive technologies, there is a dearth of research guiding such practice (Happ, 1998). Moreover, excessive sedation may extend the need for assisted ventilation (Happ, 1998; Robinson, Sucholeiki, & Schocken, 1993). To reduce the likelihood of injuries (e.g., skin tears) in those with involuntary movements during sleep or those who choose to use side rails but are prone to injury, position the patient in the center of bed and use body-length pillows, side-rail pads, or bumpers. Meet basic comfort needs with frequent (at least every 2 hours) changes in position, appropriate pain management, and individualized attention to elimination. Discomfort caused by unstable tube placement can increase the chances of self-removal or disruption of tube performance. Use commercial tube holders to stabilize Foley catheters, intravenous lines, and feeding, drainage, and endotracheal tubes. Apply waterproof tape to decrease accidental extubation (Tominaga, Rudzwick, Scannell, & Waxman, 1995).

When the patient is seated, the chair should be comfortable; recliners are better choices than geri-chairs. Wheelchairs are designed for transport, not continuous seating; sling seats do not provide adequate support for long periods of sitting. Occupational therapists can provide inserts that increase the support of the chair or pressure-relieving seat cushions (Rader et al., 1999).

10. *Provide reminders.* For those patients who are unable to stand safely but who may accidentally roll out of or unsafely exit from bed, bed bumpers on mattress edges, concave mattresses, pillows, swimming-pool "noodles," or rolled blankets under the mattress edge demarcate bed perimeters. Some alarms provide a verbal message to call or wait for assistance instead of a sound that may potentially frighten or increase the patient's confusion.

11. *Reduce injury risk.* Because falling onto hard surfaces may increase the likelihood of fractures (Nevitt & Cummings, 1993), a bedside cushion such as an exercise mat or an egg-crate foam mattress may be used to reduce impact (Capezuti et al., 1999; Letizia, 1999b). Hip pad protectors have also been found to reduce the risk of hip fracture among fallers (Kannus et al., 2000; Lauritzen, Petersen, & Lund, 1993; Robinovitch, Hayes, & McMahon, 1995).

12. *Diminish entrapment risk.* When using restraints and restrictive side rails, make every effort to reduce the likelihood of entrapment injuries. Since restraint-related deaths can occur in less than a few minutes, these devices necessitate increased, not decreased, staff observation. Inspect bed frames, side rails, and mattresses to identify possible entrapment areas (Parker & Miles, 1997).

CLINICAL EXAMPLE: THE MOUNT SINAI ACE UNIT

Acute Care for the Elderly (ACE) units developed in the 1990s as a systematic approach toward prevention of iatrogenic complications among hospitalized older adults (Covinsky, 1998; Landefeld, Palmer, Kresevic, Fortinsky, & Kowal, 1995; Smyth, Dubin, Restrepo, Nueva-Espana, & Capezuti, 2001). For example, the ACE unit at the Mount Sinai Hospital in New York City noted that all bed-related fall injuries occurred when four half rails were raised (Wexler, Brennan, & Cortes, 2000). This led to the development of an innovative program to prevent falls and injuries while reducing physical restraint and restrictive side-rail use (Wexler et al., 2000).

Before reducing restrictive side-rail use, staff initiated several fall-prevention measures. The initial interventions were simple and included two changes in practice. First, toileting rounds were instituted every 2 hours for all patients on the unit. Second, data concerning falls were shared at all staff meetings on a monthly basis. Falls decreased 50% in a 1-month period.

The second phase of the project addressed other issues identified in the initial review of fall occurrences and were implemented a month after the first phase. Lack of footwear or inadequate or inappropriate footwear had been identified in 43% of the falls reviewed. Before the fall program, the hospital slippers were foam and available in only two sizes. Nonskid slipper socks replaced the foam slippers. Although these socks cost approximately twice as much as the foam slippers, the benefit was significant.

Approximately 25% of the falls on the Mount Sinai Hospital ACE unit occurred in areas other than the patients' rooms. All patients on the ACE unit have medical orders to be out of bed unless contraindicated, and the unit has an ongoing activities program in congregate space. The patients go for many diagnostic tests. Many of the falls took place in areas where the primary care team was not with the patient and therefore could not alert others of the patient's risk status for falls. Neon pink wristbands stating "fall precautions" were implemented for all patients identified on the admission fall-risk assessment. Neon pink signs were placed above the beds of these patients as well. It was felt that this would be helpful to the ancillary personnel on the unit, as they played an important role in fall prevention. An indicator on the electronic nursing assignment was added to identify those patients at risk for falls. In this manner the staff would know a patient's risk status when answering call lights from the nurses' station.

Side-rail reduction was the major intervention and was introduced in the third phase of the project. Before this project, the routine practice was to raise all four half-rails. This practice was supported by policy and included in all of the standards of care related to safety and fall prevention. The policy further stated that four half-rails were indicated for the patient who was cognitively impaired. The policy was changed to state that only the top two half-rails were to be routinely raised. In the circumstance that the registered nurse, physician, patient, or family felt that four half-rails were appropriate, a note was required in the patient's medical record explaining the rationale. Injuries declined significantly following the change in side-rail usage.

A major portion of phases two and three was education. Staff education was conducted for all levels of staff, addressing their role in fall prevention. The nurse manager taught the support staff, who learned their role in eliminating environmental hazards. They also had significant contact with family and were able to teach them about the initiative. The unit-based education specialist conducted the education of the nursing staff, who attended classes on the anatomy and physiology associated with increased fall risk in older persons, identifying those patients at risk for falls, choosing appropriate interventions and patient education techniques.

The medical codirectors of the Mount Sinai Hospital ACE unit were instrumental in educating the medical staff about the fall program. It is one of the topics included in the welcome orientation that is conducted monthly on the ACE unit. The other members of the team learned about the fall-prevention program in the interdisciplinary staff meetings on the ACE unit, where fall data are routinely shared. Falls are discussed in daily interdisciplinary rounds on the unit as well.

Finally, patient and family education was addressed in phases two and three. Before the implementation of the fall-prevention program, most education occurred at time of discharge and focused on fall prevention in the community. Little was addressed in the inpatient setting. We developed a patient-family education brochure that describes the hazards of side rails while emphasizing more effective fall-prevention strategies.

After its success on the ACE unit, the fall-prevention program was expanded to the remaining acute medical units, with similar results. Side-rail reduction efforts are being implemented throughout the hospital. Similar fall-prevention interventions are being implemented in other populations in the medical center and across the health system.

The program is in its fourth phase, which involves a redesign of the fall risk-assessment tool, as well as the electronic charting pathways for this information. We are attempting to store the patient's risk assessment at time of discharge as universal data so that it will automatically appear on the medical record at the time of readmission. Other areas of evaluation include the role of medications in falls and the effectiveness of beds that are lower to the ground than the standard hospital bed.

CONCLUSION

Although the nonrestrictive measures described in this chapter promote mobility and functional recovery, family members may not always be receptive to their use, especially when prior hospital experiences have encouraged physical restraint or restrictive side rail use to promote "safety." It is important to educate the patient and family about the potential hazards associated with immobility in general and restraints in particular, and encourage them to promote mobility throughout the hospitalization (Kanski, Janelli, Jones, & Kennedy 1996; Mahoney, 1998). Choosing least restrictive measures can reduce the risk of liability (Braun & Capezuti, 2000; Capezuti & Braun, 2001). Most crucially, use of nonrestrictive measures promotes positive patient outcomes and represents care that is dignified and safe.

REFERENCES

Bochino, N., Capezuti, E., Driscoll, G., & Strumpf, N. (1999). *Restraint reduction and fall prevention* [video]. Available from Envision, Inc., Nashville, TN.

Braun, J. A., & Capezuti, E. (2000). The legal and medical aspects of physical restraints and bed side rails and their relationship to falls and fall-related injuries in nursing homes. *DePaul Journal of Healthcare Law, 3,* 1–72.

Brush, B. L., & Capezuti, E. (2001). A historical analysis of side rail use in American hospitals. *Journal of Nursing Scholarship, 33,* 381–385.

Capezuti, E. (2000). Preventing falls and injuries while reducing side rail use. *Annals of Long-Term Care, 8,* 57–63.

Capezuti, E., Bourbonniere, M., Strumpf, N., & Maislin, G. (2000). Side rail use in a large urban medical center [Abstract]. [Special Issue I]. *Gerontologist, 40,* 117.

Capezuti, E., & Braun, J. A. (2001). Medico-legal aspects of hospital side rail use. In M. B. Kapp (Ed.), *Ethics, law, and aging review* (vol. 7, pp. 25–57). New York: Springer.

Capezuti, E., & Lawson, W. T., III. (1999). Falls and restraint liability issues. In P. Iyer (Ed.), *Nursing home litigation: Investigation and case preparation* (pp. 205–249). Tucson, AZ: Lawyers and Judges.

Capezuti, E., Talerico, K. A., Strumpf, N., & Evans, L. (1998). Individualized assessment and intervention in bilateral side rail use. *Geriatric Nursing, 19*(6), 322–330.

Capezuti, E., Talerico, K. A., Cochran, I., Becker, H., Strumpf, N., & Evans, L. (1999). Individualized interventions to prevent bed-related falls and reduce side rail use. *Journal of Gerontological Nursing, 25,* 26–34.

Covinsky, K. E. (1998). Improving functional outcomes in older patients: Lessons from an acute care for elders unit. *Joint Commission Journal on Quality Improvement, 24,* 63–76.

Evans, L. K., Strumpf, N. E., & Williams, C. C. (1992). Limiting restraints: A prerequisite for independent functioning. In E. Calkins, A. Ford, & P. Katz (Eds.), *Practice of geriatrics* (2nd ed., pp. 204–210). Philadelphia: Saunders.

Food and Drug Administration (1991, November 16). Medical Alert: *Potential hazards with restraint devices.* Rockville, MD: Author.

Food and Drug Administration. (1992, July 15). Safety Alert: *Potential hazards with restraint devices.* Rockville, MD: Author.

Food and Drug Administration (1995, August 23). Safety Alert: *Entrapment hazards with hospital bed side rails.* Rockville, MD: Author.

Food and Drug Administration, Hospital Bed Safety Workgroup. (2000). *A guide to bed safety* [Brochure]. Washington, DC: Author.

Hamilton, L., & Lyon, P. S. (1995). A nursing-driven program to preserve and restore functional ability in hospitalized elderly patients. *Journal of Nursing Administration, 25*(4), 30–37.

Happ, M. B. (1998). Treatment interference in acutely and critically ill adults. *American Journal of Critical Care, 7,* 224–235.

Happ, M. B. (2000). Preventing treatment interference: The nurse's role in maintaining technologic devices. *Heart and Lung: Journal of Acute and Critical Care, 29,* 60–69.

Inouye, S. K., Bogardus, S. T., Jr., Baker, D. I., Leo-Summers, L., Cooney, L. M., Jr. (2000). The hospital elder life program: A model of care to prevent cognitive and functional decline in older hospitalized patients. *Journal of the American Geriatrics Society, 48,* 1697–1706.

Joint Commission on Accreditation of Healthcare Organizations. (1996). *Comprehensive accreditation manual for hospitals* (Restraint and seclusion standards plus scoring: Standards TX7.1-TX7.1.3.3, 191–193j). Oakbrook Terrace, IL: Author.

Joint Commission on Accreditation of Healthcare Organizations. (1998, November 18). *Issue 8 sentinel event alert: Preventing restraint deaths.* [Online]. Available: wwwb.jcaho.org/pub/sealert/sea8.html

Kahn-Kothmann, A. M. (1999, August). HCFA interim final rules on patients' rights under Medicare hospital conditions of participation. *Health Lawyer, 11*(6), 18.

Kanski, G. W., Janelli, L. M., Jones, H. M., & Kennedy, M. C. (1996). Family reactions to restraints in an acute care setting. *Journal of Gerontological Nursing, 22*(6), 17–22.

Kannus, P., Parkkari, J., Niemi, S., Pasanen, M., Palvanen, M., Järvinen, M., & Vuori, I. (2000). Prevention of hip fracture in elderly people with use of a hip protector. *New England Journal of Medicine, 343,* 1506–1513.

Kapp, M. B. (1999). Restraint reduction and legal risk management. *Journal of the American Geriatrics Society, 47,* 375.

Landefeld, C. S., Palmer, R. M., Kresevic, D. M., Fortinsky, R. H., & Kowal, J. (1995). A randomized trial of care in a hospital medical unit especially designed to improve the functional outcomes of acutely ill older patients. *New England Journal of Medicine, 332,* 1338–1344.

Lauritzen, J. B., Petersen, M. M., & Lund, B. (1993). Effect of external hip protectors on hip fractures. *Lancet, 341*(8836), 11–13.

Letizia, B. (1999a). Brackets attach this phone to bed rails. *RN, 62*(3), 76.

Letizia, B. (1999b). When bed rails aren't used, consider these mats. *RN, 62*(5), 84.

Mahoney, J. E. (1998). Immobility and falls. *Clinics in Geriatric Medicine, 14,* 699–726.

Medicare and Medicaid Programs: Hospital Conditions of Participation; Patients' Rights; Interim Final Rule, 64 Fed. Reg. 36,070 (July 2, 1999). [on-line]. Available: www.access.gpo.gov/su_docs/fedreg/a990702c.html

Miceli, D. L. G., Waxman, H., Cavalieri, T., & Lage, S. (1994). Prodromal falls among older nursing home residents. *Applied Nursing Research, 7,* 18–26.

Miles, S. H. (1996). A case of death by physical restraint: New lessons from a photograph. *Journal of the American Geriatrics Society, 44,* 291–292.

Miles, S. H., & Irvine, P. I. (1992). Deaths caused by physical restraints. *Gerontologist, 32,* 762–766.

Minnick, A. F., Mion, L. C., Leipzig, R., Lamb, K., & Palmer, R. M. (1998). Prevalence and patterns of physical restraint use in the acute care setting. *Journal of Nursing Administration, 28,* 19–24.

Mion, L. C. (1996). Establishing alternatives to physical restraints in the acute care setting: A conceptual framework to assist nurses' decision making. *AACN Clinical Issues, 7,* 592–602.

Moyers, J., U.S. Department of Health and Human Services, Health Care Finance Administration. *Questions and answers: Hospital conditions of participation for patients' rights.* [on-line]. Available: www.hcfa.gov/quality/4b1.htm (updated May 23, 2000).

Nevitt, M. C., Cummings, S. R., & the Study of Osteoporotic Fractures Research Group. (1993). Type of fall and risk of hip and wrist fractures: The study of osteoporotic fractures. *Journal of the American Geriatrics Society, 41,* 1226–1234.

Parker, K., & Miles, S. H. (1997). Deaths caused by bedrails. *Journal of the American Geriatrics Society, 45,* 797–802.

Rader, J., Jones, D., & Miller, L. L. (1999). Individualized wheelchair seating: Reducing restraints and improving comfort and function. *Topics in Geriatric Rehabilitation, 15,* 34–47.

Rizzo, J. A., Baker, D. I., McAvay, G., & Tinetti, M. E. (1996). The cost-effectiveness of a multifactorial targeted prevention program for falls among community elderly persons. *Medical Care, 34,* 954–969.

Robinson, B. E., Sucholeiki, R., & Schocken, D. D. (1993). Sudden death and resisted mechanical restraint: A case report. *Journal of the American Geriatrics Society, 41,* 424–425.

Robinovitch, S. N., Hayes, W. C., & McMahon, T. A. (1995). Energy-shunting hip padding system attenuates femoral impact force in a simulated fall. *Journal of Biomechanical Engineering, 117,* 409–413.

Stillwell, E. (1988). Use of physical restraints in older adults. *Journal of Gerontological Nursing, 14,* 42–43.

Smyth, C., Dubin, S., Restrepo, A., Nueva-Espana, H., & Capezuti, E. (2001). Creating order out of chaos: Models of GNP practice with hospitalized older adults. *Clinical Excellence for Nurse Practitioners, 5,* 88–95.

Strumpf, N. E., Robinson, J. P., Wagner, J. S., & Evans, L. E. (1998). *Restraint-free care: Individualized approaches for frail elders.* New York: Springer.

Strumpf, N. E., & Tomes, N. (1993). Restraining the troublesome patient: An historical perspective on a contemporary debate. *Nursing History Review, 1,* 3–24.

Sullivan-Marx, E., & Strumpf, N. E. (1996). Restraint-free care for acutely ill patients in the hospital. *AACN Clinical Issues, 7,* 572–578.

Todd, J. F., Ruhl, C. E., & Gross, T. P. (1997). Injury and death associated with hospital bed side-rails: Reports to the US Food and Drug Administration from 1985 to 1995. *American Journal of Public Health, 87,* 1675–1677.

Tominaga, G. T., Rudzwick, H., Scannell, G., & Waxman, K. (1995). Decreasing unplanned extubations in the surgical intensive care unit. *American Journal of Surgery, 170,* 586–590.

U.S. Department of Health and Human Services, Centers for Medicare and Medicaid. (2000, June). *Guidance to surveyors—Hospital conditions of participation for patients' rights* (Rev. 17). [on-line]. Available: www.hcfa.gov/quality/4b.htm

Wexler, S., Brennan, N., & Cortes, T. (2000). Side rail reduction in an acute care setting. [Abstract]. [Special Issue, 1]. *Gerontologist, 40,* 117.

■ 11
Deciding About Diets

Bruce Kinosian, Rebecca Berlin, Charlene Compher, and Robert Cato

Clinicians have been cognizant of the impact of malnutrition since Studley's report of increased mortality with gastric surgery after a 10% weight loss (Studley, 1936). The links between protein deficiency, infection, and wound healing (Rhoads, Fliegelman, & Panzer, 1942) stem from the same era. Forty years ago, malnutrition was labeled as the skeleton in the closet of American hospitals. Since that time, more clinicians have become aware of the prevalence of protein-energy malnutrition (PEM), the consequences of PEM, and of the means to avoid it. Malnutrition in frail, chronically ill populations is associated with poor clinical outcomes and is an indicator of risk for increased mortality in a variety of settings—acute surgical, acute medical, rehabilitative services, and long-term care (Sullivan, 1995; Sullivan & Walls, 1995).

Malnutrition develops through four main physiologic pathways: (a) increased metabolism (e.g., from Parkinson's disease, advanced COPD and CHF, tuberculosis, hyperthyroidism, various cancers); (b) anorexia (a protean and common response to illness from infections to depression); (c) swallowing difficulties; and (d) malabsorption. Patients with severe malnutrition are at higher risk for a variety of complications, and a number of chronic medical conditions are associated with an increased risk of malnutrition. The complications frequently associated with malnutrition include delayed wound healing, increased nosocomial infections, pressure ulcers, poorer response to therapy for a primary condition (e.g., pneumonia), death (up to eightfold higher risk), and decreased functional status (particularly mobility and cognition) (Akner & Cederholm, 2001; Kinosian & Jeejeebhoy, 1995; Sullivan & Walls, 1998).

THE INFLUENCE OF THE HOSPITAL SETTING

The hospital setting potentiates the risk of malnutrition. A great portion of time is spent in bed; various patient attachments (intravenous lines, catheters, oxygen tubing) can all limit mobility from the bedside. Bed attachments and adjustment modes for the bed may make sitting difficult or uncomfortable. The upright position in electric beds is generally inadequate to provide a safe means of swallowing for an older patient with dysphagia. Common diagnostic evaluations necessitate "nothing per os" (NPO) from the night before, even if performed late in the day. Up to one quarter of patients admitted to acute medical services may have markedly inadequate intakes during their hospital stay (due in large part to frequent NPO orders without alternate nutritional repletion), which results in substantially worse clinical outcomes (Sullivan, Sun, & Walls, 1999). Increased workloads on hospital floors and division of the nutritional mission between dietary (getting the food to the bedside) and nursing (getting the food from the bedside into the patient) can leave trays sitting on a table, out of reach. For many frail, older patients with impaired cognition, the time available for staff to help the patient eat (from encouraging to actual feeding) is the primary factor determining the amount of calories and fluid consumed (Kayser-Jones, 1996).

Time is an increasingly scarce commodity in hospital units that have adopted industrial production methods (such as the division of labor into specialized tasks) to improve efficiency. Such a division between dietary and nursing has led to an unfortunate perception that diet is part of the "hotel services" offered at a hospital, and not a focus of medical concern. For this reason, malnutrition is often addressed too late, after it has become quite apparent, and given too low a priority. As a result, some aspects of nutrition that would benefit from a hotel-service perspective—things like tastes and preferences that make eating enjoyable—are often ignored. A recent nutritional guideline highlights some of these issues: "Unpalatability due to overly restricted diets may cause decreased intake. Consideration of food preferences, food consistency, food temperature and snacks should be included. Provision of pleasant, well-lighted, unhurried mealtimes in a social environment can increase intake" (Thomas, Ashmen, Morley, & Evans, 2000). Another high-risk group, patients with advanced Alzheimer's disease, have a circadian shift in their eating patterns and consume the preponderance of their calories during the morning; food delivery patterns in institutions have not adapted to this change (Young & Greenwood, 2001). Patients who have had recent limited food intake prefer lighter foods and often take greater portions of the morning meal than they are able to ingest at lunch and dinner. They may be aided by the use of liquid formula supplements or milkshakes later in the day.

Because an episode of illness may take place across several sites of care (e.g., hospital, subacute facility, nursing facility, home) hospital-based clinicians may fail to diagnose developing nutritional deficiencies. In the past, when more of the therapy and recovery were monitored in the hospital, lengths of stay were longer and impact of inadequate intake could be observed. With shorter in-hospital times, the consequences of inadequate nutrition are often only apparent in the subsequent setting (e.g., subacute nursing facility or home) or upon readmission.

A patient can become malnourished even when the length of stay is brief. In one study, the prevalence of PEM for patients admitted with an acute stroke increased from 16% at admission to 26% at discharge (Davalos et al., 1996). It is important to be aware of when during the episode of illness a hospitalization occurs and to keep a high awareness of nutritional risk.

EPIDEMIOLOGY

Although illness itself may lead to malnutrition, certain populations are at special risk, including those residing in long-term-care facilities (the prevalence of PEM ranges from 10% to 50% in nursing homes), frail older patients with multiple, chronic illnesses, and recently hospitalized patients. High-risk conditions include chronic obstructive pulmonary disease (COPD), congestive heart failure (CHF), prior stroke, chronic liver disease, chronic renal failure, rheumatoid arthritis, hip fracture, advanced HIV disease, various cancers, and short bowel syndromes, whether anatomic (e.g., a patient with Crohn's disease who has had multiple small-bowel resections) or functional (e.g., a patient with radiation enteritis) (Potter, Langhorne, & Roberts, 1998).

Other risk factors have been defined over the past 2 decades: polypharmacy (both prescribed and over-the-counter medications), cognitive impairment (depression, delirium, and dementia), social isolation, poverty, inappropriate food intake (both inadequacy and intake of substances that replace food calories such as alcohol), impaired basic activities of daily living (BADL), and instrumental activities of daily living (IADL). A useful mnemonic for reversible causes of protein energy malnutrition is "MEALS-ON-WHEELS" (Morley & Silver, 1995).

*M*edications
*E*motional problems (depression)
*A*norexia, alcoholism
*L*ate-life paranoia
*S*wallowing disorders
*O*ral problems (dentures, thrush, gingivitis, atrophy)
*N*osocomial infections (*Clostridium difficile, Helicobacter pylori*)

Wandering (and other dementia-related behaviors)
Hyperthyroidism, hypercalcemia, hypoadrenalism
Enteric problems (malabsorption)
Eating problems (from acquiring food to feeding)
Low-salt, low-fat diets
Stones (cholelithiasis)

ASSESSMENT

Screening tools have been developed to integrate these various risk factors. Of these, the Mini-Nutritional Assessment (MNA) has had the most extensive validation in acute- and long-term-care settings (Garry & Vellas, 1999). A shortened version that uses 6 items from the full MNA has recently been developed and validated (MNA-SF; see Appendix A): decreased food intake due to loss of appetite; digestive problems, chewing, or swallowing difficulties; weight loss; immobility; neuropsychological problems; acute illnesses; and the person's body-mass index (Rubenstein, Harker, Salva, Guigoz, & Vellas, 2001). The MNA-SF has a sensitivity of .96 for identifying those who are clinically judged to be undernourished. When the MNA-SF is used as the first step in a two-step process (those who score above 12 on the MNA-SF are then evaluated with the full MNA), there is a 14% false-positive rate, but a 3.4% false-negative rate. To emphasize the importance of the relationship between cognitive function and nutritional risk, both the clinical guideline (Thomas et al., 2000) and the MNA require assessment of cognitive function, BADLs, and mood. (The MNA can be accessed on-line at www.mna-elderly.com)

An alternative approach is the clinical technique termed "subjective global assessment" (SGA) of nutritional status (Detsky, Smalley, & Chang, 1994). The method is designed to assign the *risk* of malnutrition-associated complications, not to identify a specific state of malnutrition. The underlying assumption is that the risk of complications is principally related to fluctuations of nutrients, rather than to the total body supply of nutrients. This has been supported by refeeding studies in anorexic patients where organ function (heart, skeletal muscle, immune cells) normalizes within 10 to 14 days, well before there are substantial increases in lean body mass (Lopes, Russel, Whitwell, & Jeejeebhoy, 1982).

The SGA consists of three components: history, physical, and an overall assessment of the patient's nutritional status. In the history, loss of weight and the pattern of weight loss are assigned primary importance. An individual who loses substantial weight but then starts to regain some weight is assigned less risk than an individual who is still losing weight. History must take into account the presence of edema or ascites, which may mask weight loss.

SGA history also includes gastrointestinal symptoms such as anorexia or nausea, functional capacity, and changes in dietary intake. When making assessments, the clinician should note the duration of the dietary change and the current diet type. These are (a) suboptimal solid diet, (b) full liquid diet, (c) hypocaloric liquids, and (d) starvation. SGA physical findings include presence of muscle wasting and loss of subcutaneous fat, in addition to evidence of fluid overload. In the final step, the clinician makes a subjective estimate of the patient's nutrition-related risk, approximating (a) well nourished, (b) moderately malnourished, or (c) severely malnourished.

SGA uses a three-level classification system of risk that is based on the history and physical. Depending on the pattern of change, a patient is classified as being (a) low risk for malnutrition-associated complications (MACs) (less than 5% weight loss, or more than 5% total loss, but recent weight gain and increased appetite); (b) moderate risk for MACs (those with 5% to 10% weight loss without recent stabilization or gain, poor dietary intake, and slight loss of subcutaneous tissue); or (c) at severe risk of MACs (ongoing weight loss of more than 10% with severe subcutaneous tissue loss and muscle wasting).

The central common element of any nutrition assessment is the amount and pattern of weight loss. SGA uses weight loss and has slightly improved specificity with the addition of an albumin level. The subjective components in SGA incorporate the other elements of the MNA—functional level, mobility, cognitive state, appetite. Knowing the prior weight and current weight is crucial. A good historian may give the correct estimate of change for purposes of SGA classification, but obtaining reliable historical data may be difficult. Nonetheless, those who have had recent contact with the medical system or who reside in institutional settings (e.g., nursing homes) may well have a prior weight in the record, which should be obtained. All patients should be weighed on admission to the hospital.

LABORATORY STUDIES

Serum albumin has a long tradition as a nutritional marker of protein status. Although albumin reflects visceral protein status, however, extravascular fluid shifts and inflammatory states can affect its serum level. The depressed albumin levels of patients admitted with acute, inflammatory conditions often reflect acute illness, rather than diminished visceral protein stores.

Prealbumin has become more widely used as a marker of nutritional status, because of its shorter half-life (3 to 4 days compared to 3 weeks for albumin); however, like albumin it is a negative acute phase reactant.

Thus, although a low prealbumin in an individual without any other inflammatory condition may indicate inadequate protein intake, low levels in acutely ill individuals usually represent active inflammation (Bernstein & Pleban, 1996).

Despite this, the *direction of change* in prealbumin over 5 to 7 days is closely related to the *sign* of the patient's nitrogen balance (that is, whether the person is anabolic or catabolic). Although the direction of change takes into account both inflammatory and nutritional causes of catabolism (a positive change may be due to resolving inflammation rather than correct nutritional prescription), the goal of nutritional repletion is to maintain or increase lean body mass, making the change in prealbumin level a useful marker. Prealbumin is distorted in those with chronic liver disease (decreased synthetic function) and chronic renal failure (elevated because of reduced renal clearance). Shortened hospital stays often require that a follow-up prealbumin (which is necessary to complete the measure) be performed in a subsequent setting. This requires communication and integration of care across sites.

PRESCRIBING DIETS

The goal of assessment is to help guide a nutrient prescription. Both protein and nonprotein energy (as fat and carbohydrates) are important. They are not distinguished in oral diets, and some guides include protein calories in the total calories provided when discussing enteral tube or parenteral feedings. Unfortunately, this confuses the two specific purposes of the prescription, because protein and caloric needs may vary considerably.

Distinguishing between protein and nonprotein kilocalories (Kcals) assists with the management of obesity and its sequelae. Calories that are stored in the body as fat are available for use by the body to meet its energy needs, with the exception of the brain and certain cell types (e.g., immune system and fibroblasts). Those exceptions necessitate a minimal daily carbohydrate (i.e., glucose) requirement of 400 to 600 Kcals. If glucose is not provided, the body will catabolize protein in order to generate it. Thus, only this minimal amount of calories need be supplied to overweight patients. However, protein requirements (e.g., tissue repair) must be considered separately; the protein prescription should not be limited by an oversupply of calories on the body.

A second dilemma relates to specific nutrients that can exacerbate specific diseases. For example, sodium can promote fluid retention; vitamin K can reduce the effectiveness of anticoagulation; protein can increase azotemia in patients with reduced renal function; potassium-rich foods can potentiate hyperkalemia; high-oxalate foods and high levels of vitamin C can promote kidney stone formation in susceptible patients; simple carbohydrates can exacerbate glucose fluctuations in diabetics; and saturated fats can promote atherosclerosis. At times a prescription for protein and energy involves a trade-off between restricting specific nutrients that adversely affect the course of a disease and meeting an individual's macronutrient needs. For many frail, older individuals, medically dictated dietary restrictions can exacerbate sarcopenia (muscle wasting) (Rosenberg, 1997).

The need for NPO and clear liquid diets influences decisions about diet orders and increases the risk of iatrogenic malnutrition. Most hospital nutrition departments have screening systems in place to detect the number of days a patient receives such diets. Because a clear liquid diet typically provides < 700 Kcals daily, low-residue meal replacement formulas may sometimes be used in addition to clear liquids to provide greater nutrient intake.

A major philosophical switch during the past decade has been the deemphasis of medical restrictions that reduce taste and desirability of food in favor of a liberalized diet that ensures adequate intake of macronutrients; medical management of underlying diseases is adjusted accordingly. Examples include additional diuresis rather than severe sodium restriction for patients with protein-energy malnutrition; lipid-lowering medications rather than fat restrictions; and additional hypoglycemics rather than calorie restriction for diabetics. Similarly, the concept of providing patients on warfarin with a *stable* intake of vitamin K–rich foods that they enjoy and adjusting the warfarin dose to it has replaced the prior practice of teaching avoidance of all vitamin K–rich foods.

Patients may also require adjustment of food texture. Those with dysphagia may benefit from soft (chopped) or pureed foods; thickened liquids may also be desirable. Patients who are without their dentures may also benefit from changes in food texture.

Other considerations include the following:

1. *Acidity.* Those with oral/esophogeal candidiasis or chemotherapy-induced mucositis may benefit from an individualized food plan that limits acidity and seasoning while enhancing moisture content.

2. *Bacterial content.* Patients with HIV or malignancies (especially after bone marrow transplantation) may require special foods and education about safe food handling upon discharge.

3. *Food intolerance or allergy.* Dietitians should address these because prepared foods may be hidden sources of the offending item.

4. *Ethnic or religious dietary considerations.*

CALORIC PRESCRIPTION

The primary considerations in estimating the calories a person needs are the activity level and the amount of metabolically active tissue. Lean body mass (skeletal muscle) uses most of the energy consumed by a body, hence most methods of calculating caloric need use a measure of lean body mass. Fat mass tends to be much less metabolically active; additional caloric requirements are due to food ingestion and processing (generally representing 10% of caloric requirements). Most equations used to predict energy requirements in older persons are based on a medically stable, healthy population and may not be appropriate for hospitalized, stressed older patients. Direct measurement of caloric use is more accurate than any of the available predictive equations, but this may not be an option in many hospital settings.

The equations most typically used by hospital dieticians are the Harris-Benedict equations, which predict resting energy expenditure (REE)—the energy requirements for an individual who has had at least 20 minutes to equilibrate at rest. These equations were derived from 239 men (aged 16 to 63) and women (aged 15 to 74) (Benedict, 1928). They were later supplemented with data from 33 men (aged 21 to 92) and 66 women (aged 18 to 88); in this population, nearly 20% of the predictions deviated from measured REEs. These equations have been supplemented by disease-specific factors and an activity factor. For example, Long and colleagues documented an increase in REE of 120% due to surgery, 135% for trauma, 160% for severe sepsis, and 210% for severe burns (Long, Schaffel, & Geiger, 1979). The equations and correction factors are listed in Appendix B.

More recent studies that have used indirect calorimetry to measure energy requirements precisely have shown a wider distribution of energy needs among hospitalized patients that the Harris-Benedict equations do not accurately predict. These studies have shown that from 25% to 70% of hospitalized critically ill or oncology patients have metabolic needs greater than 110% of what the Harris-Benedict equations estimate (Foster, Know, Dempsey, & Mullen, 1987). We have found in an expanded set of 108 older patients that the mean REE was 122% of the Harris-Benedict BEE (basal energy expenditure), with a skewed distribution to the right, suggesting that many patients are hypermetabolic (see Figure 11.1).

It appears that weight-based predictions can be accurate, with adjustment for the different proportion of lean body mass to total weight into four categories: desirable (BMI > 20, < 26), overweight (BMI 26–30), obese (BMI > 30), and thin (BMI < 20). These are the same weight-based measures found by others (Ahmad, Duerksen, Munroe, & Bistrian, 1999) in a limited population (*N* = 14). We favor using either the weight-based measure

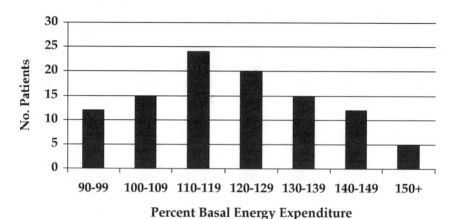

FIGURE 11.1 Many older patients are hypermetabolic. Mean resting energy expenditure measured in 108 patients was more than 20% greater than basal energy expediture calculated from the Harris-Benedict equation.

or an adjusted Harris-Benedict measure for desirable weight patients, and the weight-based measure for thin patients. These equations are included in Table 11.1.

Although overfeeding has both acute (e.g., excess CO_2 production and hyperglycemia) and chronic (e.g., hepatic steatosis) effects, in the noncritical care setting these are of less concern than underfeeding and subsequent muscle (and functional) losses. For individuals who fail to attain their therapeutic objective (whether it be weight gain or wound healing), direct measurement of REE may be helpful.

PROTEIN PRESCRIPTION

Acute illness frequently places an individual in a catabolic state that mobilizes body protein stores. Physical inactivity potentiates this loss of lean body mass. For individuals with sarcopenia and marginal functional reserves, the loss of lean mass can have severe functional consequences. Although younger patients can regain muscle mass rather quickly after an acute illness, it is often more difficult for older patients who are frail to regain lean body mass. It is essential to prevent tissue losses during hospitalization.

Estimated protein requirements for healthy older patients vary from 0.7 to 1.1 g/kg/d; during acute stresses 1.3 to 1.5 gm/kg/d may be necessary to meet most nitrogen needs. For patients who require repletion of lean body mass or have large wounds (such as with pressure ulcers), a higher protein prescription is desirable (1.75 to 2 gm/kg/d) (Breslow, Hallfrisch, Guy, Crawley, & Goldberg, 1993).

TABLE 11.1   Summary of Recommendations

Assessment: Mini-Nutritional Assessment-SF or Subjective Global Assessment + serum albumin

Caloric needs based on weight:

For maintenance:

BMI < 20 kg/m^2	30 Kcal/kg
BMI 20–26 kg/m^2	25 Kcal/kg
BMI > 27 kg/m^2	20 Kcal/kg

For repletion (BMI < 20 kg/m^2):
35 Kcal/kg

Disease-specific modifications:

Diabetes: complex carbohydrates, increased soluble fiber to delay gastric emptying

Short bowel syndromes: high-carbohydrate, low-fat diet (if colon in continuity), separate liquids from solid foods, pectin to thicken stool; glutamine for villous growth

CO_2 retention: caloric supply limited to total energy expenditure

Renal failure: appropriate protein intake, restrictions on potassium, phosphorus

Hepatic failure: appropriate protein intake, restriction on sodium and fluid intake

Protein requirements:
RDA: 0.8 g/kg
Basal: 1.3 g/kg
Stressed: 1.5 g/kg
Repletion/wound healing: 1.7–2 g/kg
Impaired protein handling (severe liver disease, chronic renal failure): 0.4–0.8 g/kg *Consult RD

It is important to emphasize the substantial role of physical activity in maintaining and restoring muscle mass. Resistance training, implemented at the bedside by provision of a theraband, can reverse negative nitrogen balance at lower levels of protein supplementation and can enhance positive nitrogen balance in those who are fed larger quantities of protein (Campbell & Evans, 1996).

Two conditions that impair protein-handling require limitation of the protein prescription and should trigger a full nutritional assessment to target protein intake appropriately. In chronic, severe liver disease, provision of nonbranched chain amino acids in excess of the liver's ability to use the protein can result in potentiation of hepatic encephalopathy. In chronic renal failure patients who are not undergoing dialysis, the extra protein load can result in worsening acidosis and uremia. In both conditions, the protein prescription may be limited to 0.4–0.8 g/kg/d, and should be addressed on an individual basis with consideration for protein losses. For example, a patient with nephrotic syndrome who excretes 6 gm/protein/day would have that amount added back into his diet. Anabolic agents, such as testosterone or oxandralone, have successfully promoted anabolism at lower protein intakes in these patients (Johansen, Mulligan, & Schambelan, 1999; Mendenhall et al., 1995).

Meeting adequate protein intake in ill patients who are anorexic can be challenging. Food preferences are important, as is flexibility on the part of the food preparers to include protein enrichment when possible. This includes protein powder that can be added to soups and other foods, as well as foodstuffs (e.g., pasta) and drinks (e.g., juices) that are made with higher protein content. In many hospitals, dieticians can order nutrient-, protein-, and calorically dense foods, making it possible meet nutrient requirements with a limited overall intake.

Supplements are commonly provided as a means to address inadequate intake of protein and calories from regular meals. The various supplements have similar nutrient compositions and are often selected by hospitals based on cost. Each supplement, however, has its own taste and consistency, and a patient may have to try several before finding one that is palatable. We conducted an informal single-blind taste test of four supplements by eight house officers at the University of Pennsylvania and found that each brand of supplement was preferred by two house officers, with professed moderately strong dislike of the other supplements. If patients don't like the taste of supplements, they will refuse them. A prescription is no guarantee of consumption.

NON-ORAL FEEDING

Non-oral feeding can take place in three ways: peripheral parenteral, central parenteral, or enteric, via tube. Each route has limitations and costs to the patient; the oral route is preferable to all of them, as it maintains the GI tract and avoids iatrogenic complications from parenterally supplied nutrition. Currently, provision of fluids and electrolytes are treated independently of protein and energy, the latter two being linked in the route they are administered.

Certain routes (i.e., peripheral parenteral nutrition) are too limited by osmotic load to provide sufficient calories and protein. When the GI tract is not functional, use of a central venous catheter allows provision of an adequate feeding regimen for most patients, and should be tailored to nutritional goals and clinical realities. Caloric supply can be set for weight loss, maintenance, or gain, and the protein goal can be adjusted, based on nutritional status, catabolism, and level of organ dysfunction. Glucose content can be adjusted for patients with hyperglycemia, and the electrolyte mix adjusted as needed. The complexity of total parenteral nutrition (TPN) and its associated risks (catheter sepsis, hyperglycemia, hypertriglyceridemia, electrolyte imbalance, and hepatic steatosis) justify consultation with a nutrition support.

For individuals with adequate body fat but marginal muscle mass, peripheral supplementation of protein and the minimally required glucose as part of an integrated therapeutic approach (including physical activity) may preserve lean body mass, while avoiding the complications of TPN or tube feeding.

Optimal enteral feeding necessitates attention to the access and formula. Enteral tubes can be temporary (naso-gastric, -duodenal, or -jejunal) or long term (surgically placed or percutaneous endoscopic gastrostomy or jejunostomy), with the decision based on estimated duration of support (≤ 2 weeks for temporary tubes). Postpyloric (duodenal or jejunal tube tip sites) tubes are often advocated in patients with a high risk of aspiration of gastric contents and for those with altered consciousness, even though the data supporting this practice are inconclusive. Feeding can begin once the tube position is confirmed radiographically; the choice of formula depends on the patient's nutritional goals. Clinical dietitians are required to evaluate these patients (and those who receive TPN) in a timely fashion, due to their risk of complications, which include aspiration pneumonia, diarrhea, hyperglycemia, electrolyte imbalance, and fluid overload.

Numerous trials of non-oral feeding by different routes have been conducted over the past 20 years, with mixed results. These studies have had the problem of separating effects of the route chosen from the effects of the nutritional repletion on the underlying conditions. A recent review found that the preponderance of trials of oral supplementation of protein and calories demonstrated positive effects in frail older patients and those with COPD, CHF, hip fracture, or chronic renal failure (Akner & Cederholm, 2001; Potter et al., 1998). Limited randomized trials of tube feeding have found striking functional improvements in hip fracture recovery in frail, older women (Bastow, Rawlings, & Allison, 1983; Sullivan, Nelson, Bopp, Puskarich-May, & Walls, 1998). Trials in aspiration pneumonia have demonstrated a slightly increased mortality in patients where the aspiration is related to severe cognitive impairment, but modest success where aspiration is related to discrete, fixed neurologic deficits (e.g., stroke) (Finucane, Christmas, & Travis, 1999; Gillick, 2000; Mitchell, Kiely, & Lipsitz, 1997). TPN is effective in reducing perioperative complications in severely malnourished patients (SGA class C), but not in those moderately malnourished (SGA classes A or B) (Buzby et al., 1988). Comparative trials of TPN and TEN (total enteral nutrition via tube) have found TEN consistently superior in reduction in infections and mortality (Moore & Moore, 1991).

We favor aggressive oral supplementation when possible, including the use of orexigenic drugs. These include anabolic steroids, dronabinol, megace, and, when psychopharmacologic agents are necessary, preference for those with marked effects on appetite—olanzepine (Zyprexa) as an antipsychotic, and mirtazapine (Remeron) as an antidepressant (Morley, Thomas, & Wilson, 2001). None of these agents can substitute for adequate time spent assisting, encouraging, and adapting environments and foods to improve oral intake.

Refeeding syndromes can occur any time intake is suddenly increased after a period or starvation or semistarvation. In the hospital setting, this usually occurs when non-oral feedings (TPN or tube feedings) are instituted in a patient who had previously undergone a substantial period of starvation. The physiologic issues are present regardless of route. Thus, for individuals who are severely malnourished due to inadequate access to protein and calories, rapid provision of calories, particularly as carbohydrates, can result in increased fluid retention and rapid intracellular shifts in potassium, magnesium, and phosphorous. The intracellular shifts occur during periods of starvation or semistarvation primarily because in the setting of reduced metabolic demands, the body maintains adequate serum levels by depleting intracellular stores. When caloric restraints are relaxed, the higher metabolic demand causes cellular uptake of those elements, precipitating a fall in serum levels. In order to guard against sequelae of severe hypophosphatemia (rhabdomyolysis, respiratory depression, hemolysis), hypokalemia (arrhythmias, decreased muscle contractility), or hypomagnesemia and hypocalcemia (myoclonus, tetany, seizures), phosphorus, potassium and magnesium must be closely monitored during refeeding and aggressively supplemented, usually by the intravenous route, if serum levels decline.

Fluid retention appears to be promoted through an insulin-linked, angiotensin-mediated increase in aldosterone, which causes sodium and fluid retention and further loss of potassium. Use of high concentration, low-volume glucose regimens for initial refeeding of the seriously malnourished tends to diminish the fluid accumulation. Spironolactone or triamterene is generally effective in both reversing the fluid accumulation and reducing potassium losses. Populations where the fluid retention can have more severe consequences include patients with CHF or COPD, where the underlying malnutrition may have been relatively unnoticed (due either to masking edema in the case of CHF or to morphologic changes found with pulmonary cachexia).

CONCLUSION: DIETICIANS AND DIETS

The clinician should be able to provide an initial estimate of energy and protein needs; the most important aspects of the initial assessment are to determine the history of weight change, obtain relevant serum measures, ensure that the patient is weighed, establish the patient's functional ability and cognitive capacity, and set the goals of treatment. A full assessment by the dietitian will also include an estimate of recent food intake with assessment of macro- and micronutrient adequacy, screening for diet-drug interactions, nutritional history, individualized nutritional goals based on current clinical process and body composition data, and nutritional education, as needed. The dietician may recommend referrals for further consideration of swallowing dysfunction or for home-based meal delivery or nutritional supplements.

Setting the goals of treatment is a central role of the primary care provider. As a review of tube feeding in patients with advanced dementia suggests (Gillick, 2000), nutrition in itself is inadequate to reverse or even improve the underlying course of progressive cognitive impairment. Although nutritional support may be important for healing of pressure ulcers, and lack of nutrition certainly reduces the chances of successful management, use of particular nutritional technologies should be consistent with an overall strategy of care. From the assembled data, the hospital dietician can provide reasonable estimates of protein and caloric needs if the physician chooses not to do so. Conversely, if the goal is functional improvement in a frail, older patient, not only is provision of nutrients important, but also conversion of those nutrients to lean body mass. This requires coordination with physical therapists and nursing, in order to provide exercise to maintain lean mass (Sullivan, Walls, Bariola, Bopp, & Frost, 2001).

More important is to direct the dietician to those patients where intake is a problem, in order to individualize the provision of nutrients, their timing, composition, and delivery. Advocacy for the patient to individualize foods and have the hospital provide adequate help for those who require assistance eating will help to prevent subsequent functional losses due to PEM.

REFERENCES

Ahmad, A., Duerksen, D. R., Munroe, S., & Bistrian, B. B. (1999). An evaluation of resting energy expenditure in hospitalized, severely underweight patients. *Nutrition, 15,* 384–388.

Akner, G., & Cederholm, T. (2001). Treatment of protein-energy malnutrition in chronic non-malignant disorders. *American Journal of Clinical Nutrition, 74,* 6–24.

Bastow M. D., Rawlings J., & Allison, S. P. (1983). Benefits of supplementary tube feeding after fractured neck of femur: A randomized controlled trial. *British Medical Journal, 287,* 1589–1592.

Benedict, F. G. (1928). Basal metabolism data on normal men and women (series II) with some considerations on the use of prediction standards. *American Journal of Physiology, 85,* 607–620.

Bernstein, L., & Pleban, W. (1996). Prealbumin in nutrition evaluation. *Nutrition, 12,* 255–259.

Breslow, R. A., Hallfrisch, J., Guy, D. G., Crawley, B., & Goldberg, A. P. (1993). The importance of dietary protein in healing pressure ulcers. *Journal of the American Geriatrics Society, 41,* 357–362.

Buzby, G. P., Williford, W. O., Peterson, O. L., Crosby, L. O., Page, C. P., Reinhardt, G. F., & Mullen, J. L. (1988). A randomized clinical trial of total parenteral nutrition in malnourished surgical patients: The rationale and impact of previous clinical trials and pilot study on protocol design. *American Journal of Clinical Nutrition, 47*(Suppl. 2), 357–365.

Campbell, W. W., & Evans, W. J. (1996). Protein requirements of elderly people. *European Journal of Clinical Nutrition, 50,* S180–S185.

Davalos, A., Ricart, W., Gonzalez-Huix, F., Soler, S., Marrugat, J., Molins, A., Suner, R., & Genis, D. (1996). Effect of malnutrition after acute stroke on clinical outcome. *Stroke, 27,* 1028–1032.

Detsky, A., Smalley, P. S., & Chang, J. (1994). Is this patient malnourished? *Journal of the American Medical Association, 271,* 54–58.

Finucane, T. E., Christmas, C., & Travis, K. (1999). Tube feeding in patients with advanced dementia: A review of the evidence. *Journal of the American Medical Association, 282,* 1365–1370.

Foster, G. D., Know, L. S., Dempsey, D. T., & Mullen, J. L. (1987). Caloric requirements in total parenteral nutrition. *Journal of the American College of Nutrition, 6,* 231–253.

Garry, P. J., & Vellas, B. (1999). Practical and validated use of the Mini-Nutritional Assessment in geriatric evaluation. *Nutrition and Clinical Care, 2,* 146–154.

Gillick, M. R. (2000). Rethinking the role of tube feeding in patients with advanced dementia. *New England Journal of Medicine, 342,* 206–210.

Johansen, K. L., Mulligan, K., & Schambelan, M. (1999). Anabolic effects of nandrolone decanoate in patients receiving dialysis: A randomized controlled trial. *Journal of the American Medical Association, 281,* 1275–1281.

Kayser-Jones, J. (1996). Mealtime in nursing homes: The importance of individualized care. *Journal of Gerontological Nursing, 22,* 26–31.

Kinosian, B., & Jeejeebhoy, K. N. (1995). What is malnutrition? Does it matter? *Nutrition, 11*(Suppl. 2), 196–197.

Long, C. L., Schaffel, N., & Geiger, J. W. (1979). Metabolic response to injury and illness: Estimation of energy and protein needs from indirect calorimetry and nitrogen balance. *Journal of Parenteral and Enteral Nutrition, 3,* 452–456.

Lopes, J., Russel, D., Whitwell, J., & Jeejeebhoy, K. N. (1982). Skeletal muscle function in malnutrition. *American Journal of Clinical Nutrition, 36,* 602–610.

Mendenhall, C. L., Moritz, T. E., Roselle, G. A., Morgan, T. R., Nemchausky, B. A., Tamburro, C. H., Schiff, E. R., McClain, C. J., Marsano, L. S., & Allen, J. I. (1995). Protein energy malnutrition in severe alcoholic hepatitis: Diagnosis and response to treatment. *Journal of Parenteral and Enteral Nutrition, 19,* 258–265.

Mitchell, S., Kiely, D., & Lipsitz, L. (1997). The risk factors and impact on survival of feeding tube placement in nursing home residents with severe cognitive impairment. *Archives of Internal Medicine, 157,* 327–332.

Moore, E. E., & Moore, F. A. (1991). Immediate enteral nutrition following multisystem trauma: A decade perspective. *Journal of the American College of Nutrition, 10,* 633–648.

Morley, J. E., & Silver, A. J. (1995). Nutrition issues in nursing home care. *Annals of Internal Medicine, 123,* 850–859.

Morley, J. E., Thomas, D. R., & Wilson, M. M. (2001). Appetite and orexigenic drugs. *Annals of Long Term Care, 9*(10 Supplement), 1–12.

Potter, J., Langhorne, P., & Roberts, M. (1998). Routine protein energy supplementation in adults: Systematic review. *British Medical Journal, 317,* 495–501.

Rhoads, J. E., Fliegelman, M. T., & Panzer, L. M. (1942). The mechanism of delayed wound healing in the presence of hypoproteinemia. *Journal of the American Medical Association, 118,* 21–25.

Rosenberg, I. H. (1997). Sarcopenia: Origins and clinical relevance. *Journal of Nutrition, 127,* 990S–991S.

Rubenstein, L. Z., Harker, J. O., Salva, A., Guigoz, Y., & Vellas, B. (2001). Screening for undernutrition in geriatric practice: Developing the Short-Form Mini-Nutritional Assessment. *Journals of Gerontology A: Biological Sciences and Medical Sciences, 56,* M366–M372.

Studley, H. O. (1936) Percentage of weight loss: A basic indicator of surgical risk in patients with chronic peptic ulcer. *Journal of the American Medical Association, 106,* 458–460.

Sullivan, D. H. (1995) The role of nutrition in increased morbidity and mortality. *Clinics in Geriatric Medicine, 11*(4), 661–674.

Sullivan, D. H., Nelson, C. L., Bopp, M. M., Puskarich-May, C. L., & Walls, R. C. (1998). Nightly enteral nutrition support of elderly hip fracture patients: A phase I trial. *Journal of the American College of Nutrition, 17,* 155–161.

Sullivan, D. H., Sun, S., & Walls, R. C. (1999). Protein-energy undernutrition among elderly hospitalized patients: A prospective study. *Journal of the American Medical Association, 281,* 2013–2019.

Sullivan, D. H., & Walls, R. C. (1995). The risk of life-threatening complications in a select population of geriatric patients: the impact of nutritional status. *Journal of the American College of Nutrition, 14*(1), 29–36.

Sullivan, D. H., & Walls, R. C. (1998). Protein-energy undernutrition and the risk of mortality within six years of hospital discharge. *Journal of the American College of Nutrition, 17,* 571–578.

Sullivan, D. H., Walls, R. C., Bariola, J. R., Bopp, M. M., & Frost, Y. M. (2001). Progressive resistance muscle strength training of hospitalized frail elderly. *American Journal of Physical Medicine and Rehabilitation, 80,* 503–509.

Thomas, D. R., Ashmen, W., Morley, J. E., & Evans, W. J. (2000). Nutritional management in long term care: Development of a clinical guideline. *Journals of Gerontology A: Biological Sciences and Medical Sciences, 55,* M725–M734.

Young, K. W., & Greenwood, C. E. (2001). Shift in diurnal feeding patterns in nursing home residents with Alzheimer's disease. *Journals of Gerontology A: Biological Sciences and Medical Sciences, 56,* M700–M706.

APPENDIX A

Components of the Mini-Nutrition Assessment (Short form)

A. Loss of appetite over past 3 months:
   0 = severe   1 = moderate   2 = none

B. Weight loss during the last 3 months:
   0 = > 3 kg   1 = between 1–3 kg   2 = none

C. Mobility:
   0 = bed/chair bound   1 = able to get out of bed/chair but does not go out
   2 = goes out

D. Has suffered psychological stress or acute disease in the past 3 months:
   0 = yes   2 = no

E. Neuropsychological problems:
   0 = severe dementia or depression (MMSE < 18, GDS > 5/15)
   1 = mild dementia (MMSE < 24, > 18)
   2 = neither demented nor depressed

F. BMI
   0 = < 19   1 = 19–21   2 = 21–< 23   3 = 23+

Scores ≥ 12 indicate low risk for "undernutrition."

Scores < 12 require a full assessment.

Note: Based on "Screening for Undernutrition in Geriatric Practice," by L. Z. Rubenstein et al., 2001. *Journals of Gerontology A: Biological and Medical Sciences, 56,* M366–M372.

Complete MNA can be found at www.mna-elderly.com/practice/forms\MNA_english.pdf

APPENDIX B

Formulae

Body Mass Index
   BMI = weight (kilograms) / height (meters)^2
   BMI = [weight (lbs) x 705] / height (inches)^2

Basal Energy Expenditure (BEE) in kilocalories calculated by the Harris-Benedict method (Benedict, 1928):

   BEE (male) = 66 + [13.7 x weight (kg)] + [5 x height (cm)] – [6.8 x age]
   BEE (female) = 655 + [9.6 x weight (kg)] + [1.9 x height (cm)] – [4.7 x age]

   Multiply by the following correction factors:
      Adjustment for activity/disease alteration in metabolism: 1.3
      Adjustment for weight gain (repletion): 1.5

■ 12
Wound Care

Elizabeth A. Ayello and Eugenia L. Siegler

All too often in the rush to cure an acute illness, we neglect the skin. Auscultation and phlebotomy take precedence over visual inspection, and early, easily treatable wounds are missed. Enforced bed rest, restraint use, lack of physical and mental stimulation, and improper bed positioning may also lead to skin breakdown in a patient who arrived at the hospital without wounds, or may worsen a preexisting wound. Because so much of what happens to the skin of acutely ill patients may be preventable and treatable, the clinician is in an excellent position to improve overall patient care merely by paying attention to the skin.

Prevention of wounds is much easier than treatment. It is a joint effort, involving all members of the staff. Hess (2000) has suggested following these steps to preserve skin integrity:

- Inspect the skin, especially over bony prominences, at least daily.
- Clean the skin using warm water and a mild, pH balanced agent using minimal force and then apply moisturizers.
- Don't massage bony prominences or reddened skin areas.
- Clean the skin of incontinent patients immediately. Use barrier creams or ointments to protect the skin.
- Minimize environmental factors such as low humidity (less than 40%) or coldness, which can dry the skin.
- Use proper positioning, transferring, and turning techniques.

WOUND ETIOLOGY

Even in the setting of preventive care, wounds are found in all health care settings. One of the most important questions that health care professionals should ask first is, "What kind of wound am I treating?" Identification of the correct etiology of the wound is imperative because the individual characteristics of the wound must be considered when selecting the appropriate wound cleansing and dressing. Decisions about appropriate supportive care of the individual, which may include education, medical management, mattress or other support services, and nutrition, also depend on the etiology of the wound.

Wounds can be classified as acute or chronic. A surgical incision is an acute wound; in the absence of infection, it heals rapidly and predictably. On the other hand, chronic wounds "have failed to proceed though an orderly and timely process to produce an anatomic and functional integrity, or proceed through the repair process without establishing a sustained and functional result" (Lazarus et al., 1994).

In addition to skin tears, wound etiologies include pressure, diabetic (neuropathic), arterial, and venous ulcers. These wounds can also have multiple causes. Proper care requires identification of all of the etiologic factors.

SKIN TEARS

Skin tears are traumatic wounds that result when the epidermis is separated from the dermis (Malone, Rozario, Gavinski, & Goodwin, 1991). Skin changes that occur with aging, such as thinning of the epidermis, flattening of the epidermis and dermis junction, and a decrease in the ridges of the epidermal rete pegs, make older patients more susceptible to skin injury from mechanical trauma (Baranoski, 2000). Skin tears are common in the older persons; more than 1.5 million occur in institutionalized adults annually (Thomas, Goode, LaMaster, Tennyson, & Parnell, 1999). Skin tears commonly occur at areas of age-related purpura (Malone et al., 1991).

Clinicians should use the Payne & Martin (1993) Classification System to document the type of skin tear. The three categories in this classification system are

- Category I—a skin tear without tissue loss
- Category II—a skin tear with partial tissue loss
- Category III—a skin tear with complete tissue loss, where the epidermal flap is absent

In one study, the number of skin tears was reduced (although not to statistical significance) when emollient soap rather than nonemollient soap was used for the routine, thrice weekly bathing of older patients in a long-term-care facility (Mason, 1997). Baranoski (2000) suggests the following prevention measures for patients at risk for skin tears:

- Use a lift sheet to move and turn patients.
- Use transfer techniques that prevent friction or shear.
- Pad bed rails, wheelchair arms, and leg supports.
- Support dangling arms and legs with pillows or blankets.
- Have patients wear long sleeves or pants to protect their extremities.
- Use and gently remove paper tape or nonadherent dressings on frail skin.
- Use gauze wraps, stockinettes, or other wraps to secure dressings rather than tape.
- Use moisturizers on dry skin.
- Provide adequate light to reduce the risk of bumping into furniture or equipment.
- Educate staff or family caregivers in the correct way of handling patients to prevent skin tears.

With little published about how to treat skin tears, the management of skin tears varies among agencies. Some clinicians use transparent film dressings to treat skin tears. Baranoski (2000) recommends the following protocol for treating skin tears:

- Gently clean the skin tear with normal saline.
- Let the area air dry or pat dry carefully.
- Approximate the skin tear flap.
- Apply petroleum-based ointment, steri-strips or a moist wound dressing.

PRESSURE ULCERS

Pressure ulcers are "localized areas of tissue necrosis that develop when soft tissue is compressed between a bony prominence and an external surface for a prolonged period of time" (Cuddigan, Ayello, & Sussman, 2001). The most common site for pressure ulcers is the sacrum, with the heels second (Cuddigan et al., 2001). NPUAP reports that the best current estimate of pressure ulcer prevalence in acute care in adults is 15%. Pressure ulcer incidence ranges from 0.4% to 38%, with 7% the current "best" estimate (Cuddigan et al., 2001).

Risk Assessment

The Agency for Healthcare Research and Quality (AHRQ, formerly the Agency for Healthcare Policy and Research [AHCPR]) Clinical Practice Guideline #3 (U.S. Department of Health and Human Services [DHHS], 1992) recommends that patients be assessed for risk of pressure ulcer development upon admission to an acute care hospital and reassessed at periodic intervals. A suggested frequency for pressure-ulcer risk assessment in acute care (Ayello & Braden, 2001) is on admission, every 48 hours, and when the patient's condition changes.

The Norton Scale (Norton, 1989) and the Braden Scale (Braden & Bergstrom, 1987) are two tools that the guidelines recommend to assess for pressure ulcer risk in adults. The Braden Scale for Predicting Pressure Sore Risk is widely used clinically for adults in the United States. A new scale, the Braden Q, is used for infants and children (Quigley & Curley, 1996).

The Braden Scale has six categories, which are evaluated to give a numerical score. Sensory perception, mobility, and activity address clinical situations that predispose the patient to intense and prolonged pressure; and moisture, nutrition, and friction/shear address clinical situations that affect tissue tolerance for pressure. The scores from each of the six categories are summed to provide the Braden Scale score. These scores can range from a high of 23 to a low of 6. Low numerical scores on the Braden Scale mean that a patient is at risk for developing a pressure ulcer. The onset of risk or "cutoff score" for the general population is 16. Further research of older (Braden, 2001) and Black and Latino patients (Lyder et al., 1998, 1999) suggests that a cutoff score of 18 be used for these specific populations. (The Braden Scale is available at www.bradenscale.com/braden.pdf).

Pressure Ulcer Staging and Healing

The pressure ulcer staging system developed by the National Pressure Ulcer Advisory Panel classifies the ulcer based on the visual inspection of the depth of the wound. The NPUAP pressure ulcer staging definitions are as follows:

Stage I: A stage I pressure ulcer is an observable pressure-related alteration of intact skin whose indicators as compared to an adjacent or opposite area on the body may include changes in one or more of the following:

- skin temperature (warmth or coolness)
- tissue consistency (firm or boggy feel)
- sensation (pain, itching)

The ulcer appears as defined area of persistent redness in lightly pigmented skin, whereas in darker skin tones, the ulcer may appear with persistent red, blue, or purple hues. Although most pressure ulcers in the United States are stage I, higher-staged pressure ulcers are more commonly seen among patients with darkly pigmented skin (Cuddigan et al., 2001).

Stage II: Partial thickness skin loss involving epidermis and/or dermis. The ulcer is superficial and presents clinically as an abrasion, blister, or shallow crater.

Stage III: Full-thickness skin loss involving damage or necrosis of subcutaneous tissue that may extend down to, but not through underlying fascia. The ulcer presents clinically as a deep crater with or without undermining of adjacent tissue.

Stage IV: Full thickness skin loss with extensive destruction, tissue necrosis or damage to muscle, bone, or supporting structure (e.g., tendon, joint capsules, etc.).

Pressure ulcers are only staged after debridement removes the necrotic tissue. Pressure ulcers can worsen to a higher stage, but they cannot revert to an earlier stage. A stage III ulcer that is improving is not a stage II ulcer, but a healing stage III ulcer (NPUAP, 2000). Validated tools such as the Pressure Ulcer Scale for Healing (PUSH) (NPUAP, 1997) or the Pressure Sore Status Tool (PSST) (Bates-Jensen, 1997) are available to measure healing. Similarly, if a healed ulcer reopens, it reverts back to its former stage (NPUAP, 2000).

The PUSH Tool (NPUAP, 1997) has three subscores of pressure ulcer characteristics (length times width, exudate amount, and tissue type), which are summed to give a total score. Comparison of the total scores over time can provide an indicator of improvement or deterioration in ulcer healing. (See www.npuap.org/push3.pdf for a copy of the PUSH Tool).

Pressure Ulcer Care

The four principles of local pressure ulcer care are debride the wound; clean the wound; cover the wound with appropriate dressing(s); relieve the pressure.

Debridement

Necrotic tissue must be removed from the pressure ulcer, because it impedes wound healing and can serve as a source of infection. Necrotic heel ulcers are an exception and should not be debrided but instead monitored daily for signs of complications (edema, erythema, fluctuance, or drainage) that signal that debridement is now required.

The appropriate method of debridement depends on the pressure ulcer characteristics, the goals of patient care, urgency of need for debridement (for example, sepsis), degree of selectivity desired to avoid injury to healthy tissue, skill of the clinician, and the amount of time available for debridement (Sibbald et al., 2000). Debridement and wound care can be painful, and it is essential to assess and treat pain aggressively (DHHS, 1994).

Sharp and surgical debridement involves using a scalpel or scissors to cut away the moist yellow, tan, or gray nonviable slough tissue or the dry, black, leathery eschar tissue. It is quickest and is the method of choice when there is an urgent need for debridement such as for patients with advancing cellulitis or sepsis (DHHS, 1994). Use a clean, dry dressing for 8 to 24 hours immediately after doing sharp debridement with bleeding, and then change to moist dressings (DHHS, 1994).

Enzymatic debriding agents are applied topically to the wound bed to cause the breakdown of the necrotic tissue. An example of a selective enzymatic topical agent is collagenase; papain/urea is a nonselective enzymatic debridement agent. Correct use of these drugs requires understanding the frequency of application, the type of cleaning solutions that can be used, and the appropriate secondary dressing. Crosshatching of the eschar may be required when using enzymatic agents.

Autolytic debridement is a selective method by which the wound bed utilizes phagocytic cells and proteolytic enzymes to remove the necrotic debris. The dressings that promote autolytic debridement are easy to use and typically cause little or no discomfort to patients. This method of debridement may take longer than the other methods and is contraindicated in the presence of infection.

Mechanical debridement is the removal of foreign material and dead or damaged tissue by physical forces. Common ways of achieving this nonselective method of debridement are wet-to-dry dressings, irrigation, and whirlpool (hydrotherapy). Wet-to-dry dressings may be painful, cause skin maceration, and can be time-consuming.

Wound Cleaning

Clean the wound at each dressing change (DHHS, 1994). The AHCPR Clinical Practice Guidelines (DHHS, 1994) recommend that normal saline (not skin cleansers or antiseptic agents such as povidone iodine, sodium hypochlorite [Dakin's solution], hydrogen peroxide, or acetic acid) be used for most pressure ulcers. A safe and effective irrigation system (such as a 35-cc syringe and 19-gauge angiocatheter) that has an irrigation pressure from 4 to 15 psi will cleanse the ulcer without causing trauma to the wound bed. Use quantitative bacterial cultures rather than swab cultures, as pressure ulcers are considered colonized wounds (DHHS, 1994).

Dressings

Choose a dressing that will keep the ulcer bed moist while keeping the peri-wound skin intact and dry (DHHS, 1994). Wet-to-dry dressings should only be used for debridement and should *not* be used for healing clean, granulating wounds. Some important considerations when selecting a wound dressing are control of wound exudate, wound characteristics, location of wound, frequency of dressing change, caregiver time, and cost. A description of commonly used dressings can be found in Table 12.1. Research has provided support for the use of newer products such as normothermic dressings (Kloth et al., 2000) or negative pressure dressings (Chua Patel, Kinsey, Koperski-Moen, & Bungum, 2000) in treating pressure ulcers.

TABLE 12.1   Wound Dressings—Selected Examples*

Gauze

 Can be used on draining wounds and wounds with tunnels

 Use as a secondary dressing over other dressings

 MOIST to DAMP gauze dressings are used to heal clean, granulating
 wounds. *Never let the gauze dry out!*

 Wet-to-dry gauze dressings may only be used for mechanical debridement of
 necrotic wounds

Transparent films

 Use with superficial wounds

 Good for wounds with little or no drainage

 Acts by softening dry eschar by moisture (autolysis)

 Don't use on infected wounds

Foam

 Nonadherent, absorptive wound dressing

 Requires a secondary dressing

 Can absorb moderate to heavy wound drainage

 Not recommended for use in dry wounds

Hydrocolloid

 "Melt" or "swell" when exposed to moisture and wound fluid

 Can absorb minimal to moderate wound drainage

 Don't adhere to the wound bed, but to surrounding skin

 Can stay on wound for 3–4 days; require change if there is leakage

Hydrogel

 Two forms are available—sheets or amorphous gels

 Cooling property makes it useful for thermal burns and painful wounds

 Will add moisture to dry eschar

 Fills the empty wound space

 Requires a secondary dressing to hold sheet or gel in the wound

Calcium Alginate

 Highly absorptive dressing useful for wounds with heavy amounts of
 drainage

 Available as sheets or ropes

 Requires a secondary dressing

 Has a "seaweed" odor

 May desiccate wounds with little or no drainage

Collagens

 Stimulates cellular migration and new tissue growth

 Absorbent dressing

 Conformable, nonadherent dressing

(continued)

TABLE 12.1   Wound Dressings—Selected Examples* *(Continued)*

Silver-coated antimicrobial
   Sustained release of silver in a layered dressing material
   Requires a secondary dressing
   Dressing can remain for 7 days depending upon amount of drainage
   Contraindicated for patients sensitive to silver or having MRI procedures

Topical negative pressure therapy
   Specialized dressing consisting of foam, cover dressing, tubing and pump
      attachment, positioned in the wound or over a flap or graft
   Pressure in this dressing system helps remove fluids from the wound and
      stimulate the growth of healthy granulation tissue
   Requires experience to apply correctly
   Not for use in infected, malignant, or fistula wounds
   Different pressures are required for different types of wounds
   If pump off for more than 2 hours, remove dressing and then reapply

Normothermic therapy—noncontact thermal wound therapy
   A specialized wound management system consisting of a foam frame,
      a noncontact transparent wound cover, and a warming device (100.4°F
      or 38°C).
   Uses warmth to enhance wound healing

* This is not an all-inclusive list.

Pressure Relief

Because the primary etiology of pressure ulcers is pressure, the redistribution of pressure is vital to prevention and to treatment of pressure ulcers. A variety of support surfaces (bed, mattresses or chair cushions) can be used. Static support surfaces (constant low pressure) include products made of foam (minimum height of 3 to 4 inches, a density of 1.3 to 1.6 pounds per cubic foot). Some static overlays are filled with water or air. Dynamic support surfaces include alternating-pressure air mattresses and air-fluidized or low-air-loss specialty beds.

The AHCPR Clinical Guidelines (DHHS, 1994) provide a useful algorithm for support surfaces. (The guidelines can be accessed on-line at www.ahcpr.gov/clinic/cpgonline.htm) Static support surfaces are used for patients who can change positions and who don't "bottom out" on the surface; dynamic support surfaces are needed for patients who cannot assume a variety of positions, or who do bottom out on the support surface.

Peripheral Vascular Ulcers

Lower leg ulcers can be of arterial, venous, neuropathic (patient with diabetes mellitus), or mixed etiology. Table 12.2 compares assessment findings in each of these ulcers and a summary of management strategies. Correct identification of the wound etiology, which includes evaluation of ankle/brachial index (ABI), is essential for these wounds, as the many aspects of care depend on the nature of wound. Local wound care will include the general wound principles of cleaning and dressing application described under the pressure ulcer section.

Arterial ulcers require both the correction of blood perfusion and local wound care using an appropriate dressing. Other measures include smoking cessation and teaching measures to prevent mechanical, thermal, and chemical trauma to the feet. Routine skin care is essential for patients with peripheral vascular disease (PVD) and includes the careful washing of the feet daily, drying between the toes, using lamb's wool to separate the toes and prevent pressure of friction injury, and application of emollients to unbroken areas on the feet.

Care of patients with venous ulcers includes use of an appropriate dressing and a compression layer bandage such as Unna's boot (a zinc-based paste bandage system, not an actual boot), or a layered bandage system (several 3- or 4-layered systems are available from dressing manufacturers). Some patients may also use dynamic compression pumps and devices to further reduce leg edema and aid in venous blood return. Research has shown that human skin replacements can heal difficult, long-standing venous leg ulcers (Schonfeld, Villa, Fastenau, Mazonson, & Falanga, 2000).

Neuropathic foot ulcers in patients with diabetes have recently been treated with platelet-derived growth factors such as becaplermin (Edmonds, Bates, Doxford, Gough, & Foster, 2000) or human skin equivalents (Brem, Balleduz, Bloom, Kerstein, & Hollier, 2000). Proper care of foot ulcers in patients with diabetes mellitus includes careful inspection and treatment of any infection, early aggressive debridement of the wound, determining blood supply to the feet, weight-shifting orthoses for the affected foot (contact casting, special shoes, or bed rest), and good control of the blood sugar (Steed, 1998). Patients should stop smoking and must be taught how to prevent injury from mechanical, thermal, and chemical trauma.

SUMMARY: WOUND CARE ESSENTIALS

- Assess patients who are dependent for their activities of daily living for skin tears.
- Assess ambulatory patients for skin tears on their lower extremities.

TABLE 12.2 Diagnosis and Treatment of Lower Extremity Ulcers

	Arterial	Venous	Diabetic
Pain	Sudden, very painful Intermittent claudication	Some minimal pain No claudication	Often painless due to neuropathy No claudication
Hair	Hair loss distal to occlusion	No hair loss	No hair loss
Location	Develop on or between toes	Ankle area Lower calf	Plantar surface of foot Metatarsal heads Heels
Skin color	Pale with dependent rubor	Brawny discoloration of lower extremity around ulcer	Pale
Skin temperature	Cool	Warm	Cool or warm
Skin texture	Thin, shiny, dry	Edema Stasis dermatitis Visible veins Skin mottling	
Pulses	Diminished or absent	Normal	Usually present
Treatment	Education–PVD Exercise program Invasive intervention Angioplasty/stent Surgical bypass Amputation Smoking cessation Weight loss *Never use compression*	Education–PVD Exercise—"Skin care aerobics" Weight loss Gravity drainage Elevate leg Drugs Discharge teaching *Always use compression*	Education—foot care Casting or orthosis to eliminate pressure on wound Control blood sugar Prevent infection

- Use the three categories of the Payne-Martin Classification system to describe skin tears.
- Use accepted tools to assess for pressure ulcer risk on admission and frequently thereafter.
- Cleanse wounds with normal saline, which is the best solution to use to clean wounds, not cytotoxic solutions.
- Use the method of debridement (sharp, enzymatic, mechanical, and/or autolytic) based on the patient's condition and care goals.
- Never treat a clean, granulating wound with wet-to-dry dressings.
- Use dressings that maintain a moist wound-healing environment and can absorb the amount of wound exudate expected.
- Monitor heel ulcers with dry eschar and debride only if there is edema, erythema, fluctuance, or drainage.
- Always compress venous stasis ulcers using a layered bandage system. Never compress arterial ulcers.

REFERENCES

Ayello, E. A., & Braden, B. (2001). Why is pressure ulcer risk assessment so important? *Nursing 2001, 31*(11), 74–79.

Baranoski, S. (2000). Skin tears: The enemy of frail skin. *Advances in Skin and Wound Care, 13*(3), 123–126.

Bates-Jensen, B. M. (1997) The pressure sore status tool: A few thousand assessments later. Proceedings of the 5th National NPUAP Conference. *Advances in Wound Care, 10*(5), 65–73.

Braden, B. J. (2001). Risk assessment in pressure ulcer prevention. In D. L. Krasner, G. T. Rodeheaver, & R. G. Sibbald (Eds). *Chronic wound care: A sourcebook for healthcare professionals* (3rd ed., pp. 641–651). Wayne, PA: HMP Communications.

Braden B. J., & Bergstrom, N. (1987). A conceptual schema for the study of the etiology of pressure sores. *Rehabilitation Nursing, 12*(1), 8–16.

Brem, H., Balledux, J., Bloom, T., Kerstein, M. D., & Hollier, L. (2000). Healing of diabetic foot ulcers and pressure ulcers with human skin equivalent—A new paradigm in wound healing. *Archives of Surgery, 135,* 627–634.

Chua Patel, C. T., Kinsey, G. C., Koperski-Moen, K. J., & Bungum, L. D. (2000). Vacuum-assisted wound closure. *American Journal of Nursing, 100*(12), 45–48.

Cuddigan, J., Ayello, E. A., & Sussman, C. (Eds.). (2001). *Pressure ulcers in America: Prevalence, incidence, and implications for the future.* Reston, VA: NPUAP.

Edmonds, M., Bates, M., Doxford, M., Gough, A., & Foster, A. (2000). New treatments in ulcer healing and wound infection. *Diabetes and Metabolism Research Reviews, 16,*(Suppl. 1), S51–S54.

Hess, C. T. (2000). Skin care basics. *Advances in Skin and Wound Care,* *13*(3),127–128.

Kloth, L. C., Berman, J. E., Dumit-Minkel, S., Sutton, C. H., Panek, P. E., & Wurzel, J. (2000). Effects of a normothermic dressing on pressure ulcer healing. *Advances in Skin and Wound Care, 13*(2), 69–74.

Lazarus, G. S., Cooper, D. M., Knighton, D. R., Margolis, D. J., Pecoraro, R. E., Rodeheaver, G., & Robson, M. C. (1994). Definition and guidelines for assessment of wounds and evaluation of healing. *Archives of Dermatology, 130,* 489.

Lyder, C. H., Yu, C., Emerling, J., Mangat, R., Stevenson, D., Empleo-Frazier, O., & McKay, J. (1999). The Braden scale for pressure ulcer risk: Evaluating the predictive validity in Black and Latino/Hispanic elders. *Applied Nursing Research, 12*(2), 60–68.

Lyder, C. H., Yu, C., Stevenson, D., Mangat, R., Empleo-Frazier, O., Emerling, J., & McKay, J. (1998). Validating the Braden scale for the prediction of pressure ulcer risk in Blacks and Latino/Hispanic elders: A pilot study. *Ostomy/Wound Management, 44*(3A) (Suppl.), 42S–50S.

Malone, M. L., Rozario, N., Gavinski, M., & Goodwin, J. (1991). The epidemiology of skin tears in the institutionalized elderly. *Journal of the American Geriatrics Society, 39,* 591–595.

Mason, S. R. (1997). Type of soap and the incidence of skin tears among residents of a long-term care facility. *Ostomy/Wound Management, 43*(8), 26–30.

National Pressure Ulcer Advisory Panel. (2000). Position statement on reverse staging: The facts about reverse staging in 2000. [on-line]. Available: www.npuap.org/positn5.htm

National Pressure Ulcer Advisory Panel. (1997). The pressure ulcer scale for healing. [on-line]. Available: www.npuap.org/pushins.htm

Norton, D. (1989). Calculating the risk: Reflections on the Norton scale. *Decubitus, 2*(3), 24–31.

Payne, R. L., & Martin, M. L. (1993). Defining and classifying skin tears: Need for a common language. *Ostomy/Wound Management, 39,* 16–19, 22–24, 26.

Quigley, S. M., & Curley, M. A. (1996). Skin integrity in the pediatric population: Preventing and managing pressure ulcers. *Journal of the Society of Pediatric Nursing, 1*(1), 7–18.

Schonfeld, W. H., Villa, K. F., Fastenau, J. M., Mazonaon, P. D., & Falanga, V. (2000). An economic assessment of Apligraf (Graftskin) for the treatment of hard-to-heal venous ulcers. *Wound Repair and Regeneration, 8*(4), 251–257.

Sibbald, R. G., Williamson, D., Orsted, H. L., Campbell, K., Least, D., Krasner, D., & Sibbald, D. (2000). Preparing the wound bed—Debridement, bacterial balance, and moisture balance. *Ostomy/Wound Management, 46*(11), 14–35.

Steed, D. L. (1998). Foundations of good ulcer care. *American Journal of Surgery, 176*(Suppl. 2A), 20S–25S.

Thomas, D. R., Goode, P. S., LaMaster, K., Tennyson, T., & Parnell, L. K. S. (1999). A comparison of an opaque foam dressing versus a transparent film dressing in the management of skin tears in institutionalized subjects. *Ostomy/Wound Management, 45*(6), 22–28.

U.S. Department of Health and Human Services. (1992). *Pressure ulcers in adults: Prediction and prevention.* (AHCPR Publication No. 92-0047). Rockville, MD: Author.

U.S. Department of Health and Human Services. (1994). *Treatment of pressure ulcers* (AHCPR Publication No. 93-0652). Rockville, MD: Author.

■ 13
The Delirious Patient

Lisa Honkanen and Bharathi Raman

Case #1: A highly functional 82-year-old woman with hypertension, coronary artery disease, osteoporosis and Parkinson's disease fell at home and is admitted for repair of a left hip fracture. She is receiving one Tylenol with codeine every 8 hours for pain but complains that this is inadequate. However, the intern is concerned that excess opioid use in an older patient might "cloud her thinking." Overnight, her vital signs are recorded twice and she seems more confused each time when disturbed from her sleep. In the morning, the intern is alarmed when he enters the room and finds that the patient is halfway out of the bed with the vest restraint tangled around her arms, the IV is pulled out, and she spits at him.

Case #2: A 74-year-old man has severe chronic obstructive pulmonary disease (COPD), and he requires oxygen at home. Yesterday he refused dinner and seemed more quiet than usual through the evening. This morning he was found by his home attendant to be lethargic and incontinent but without any other symptoms. He is brought to the emergency room for evaluation where he is found to be afebrile and in no acute distress but drowsy, incoherent, and uncooperative. Although he has no cough or fever, there is an infiltrate on chest X ray consistent with a new pneumonia.

A BRIEF OVERVIEW OF DELIRIUM

Delirium is acute in onset and marked by fluctuating attention and disorganized thinking that often lead to behavioral changes. Usually, it resolves gradually with the elimination of underlying precipitants, although some

146

individuals never fully recover to previous cognitive function (American Psychiatric Association, *Diagnostic and statistical manual of mental disorders [DSM-IV-TR]*, 2000; Francis, 1992). The prevalence of delirium in older persons on admission to the hospital is 10% to 16%, and as the most frequent complication of hospitalization in older patients, it develops in up to 31% during the hospital stay (Francis, 1992).

Delirium may be the first and only indicator of serious illness; hence, its onset warrants immediate attention so that correctable causes are detected early (Inouye, Schlesinger, & Lydon, 1999; Meagher, 2001). However, because patients may have periods of lucidity between hypoactive symptoms, the change in mental status may go completely unrecognized (Inouye, Schlesinger, et al., 1999). Moreover, delirium may be misdiagnosed as dementia, depression, or other psychiatric conditions (Rummans, Evans, Krahn, & Fleming, 1995; Meagher, 2001). The distinguishing features of these diagnoses can be reviewed in Table 13.1.

Delirium is associated with prolonged length of stay, a higher frequency of complications, increased likelihood of institutionalization, and increased mortality before and after discharge from an acute hospitalization (Cole, Primeau, & Elie, 1998; Francis, 1992). These adverse events are not necessarily a direct result of the delirium itself, but instead may be consequences of advanced age, frailty, and severity of illness. The factors that increase risk of delirium probably serve as markers for impaired physiological reserve (Rummans et al., 1995). Unfortunately, the problem is amplified when patients who are demented or from nursing homes receive less time and attention from hospital staff, and this is associated with poorer outcomes (Inouye, Schlesinger, et al., 1999).

RECOGNIZING DELIRIUM

Patients will present with clouded consciousness and confusion about routine tasks and familiar roles. As changes in behavior may range from hyperactive qualities of irritability, physical agitation, and frank psychosis to more hypoactive symptoms of apathy, lethargy, and withdrawal, delirium has many different names, such as change in mental status or acute confusional state. Nonetheless, the hallmarks of either subtype are the same: acute onset and fluctuation in consciousness and cognition. Even if premorbid elements of cognitive function are impaired because of dementia or depression, a superimposed delirium is distinguished by an abrupt and rapidly fluctuating deterioration (Meagher, 2001; Rummans et al., 1995).

In older patients, somatic features such as impairments in speech, eating, sleeping, continence, and ambulation mark delirium. Emotional liability is common. Frank psychosis with delusions or hallucinations can occur

TABLE 13.1 Differential Diagnosis of Altered Mental Status

	Delirium	Dementia	Depression +/- Psychosis	Schizophrenia	Acute Anxiety
Onset	Acute	Insidious	Relatively rapid; psychosis must occur exclusively during mood disturbance	Variable; generally younger at initial presentation	Abrupt +/- cues
Course (over 24 hours)	Fluctuating; may be worse at night	Stable; may be worse at night	Diurnal variation (mood may be worse in morning)	Variable	Discrete intensity
Duration	Days to months	Persistent with progressive decline over time	Variable, > 2 weeks by definition	Chronic or relapse/remitting over lifetime	Minutes to hours; panic peaks in less than 10 minutes
Consciousness	Clouded	Clear until late in course	Clear	Clear	Clear
Cognition	Globally disordered	Globally impaired	May be selectively impaired	Intact	Intact
Psychomotor Activity	Hypo- or hyperactive	Stable over short term (declines over time)	Decreased	Variable (ranges from agitation to catatonia)	Hyperactive; somatic features (activation of peripheral autonomic nervous system)
Orientation	Decreased, at least part of the time	Decreased	May be decreased	Intact	Intact

TABLE 13.1 (*Continued*)

	Delirium	Dementia	Depression +/− Psychosis	Schizophrenia	Acute Anxiety
Attention and Memory	Disordered attention; immediate and recent memory decreased; remote memory intact	Attention intact until later; decreased short-term memory; long-term memory impairments later	Decreased attention; memory intact but short-term memory may be impaired	Decreased attention; intact memory	Decreased attention possible; intact memory
Hallucinations and Delusions	Simple psychotic symptoms; visual or audio-visual hallucinations; poorly systematized, paranoid delusions are fleeting	Less common; paranoid delusion in moderate to severe cases	Less common; complex psychotic features if present; auditory hallucinations, mood congruent delusions are sustained	Complex psychotic symptoms; auditory hallucinations; systematized delusions	Feelings of de-realization or de-personalization
Thinking Patterns	Disorganized and incoherent	Impoverished, vague; perseveration	Impoverished, lacking spontaneity	Bizarre, disorganized	Temporarily irrational (imminent doom without danger)
Insight	New disability appears suddenly	Conceals disabilities	Recognizes disabilities	Poor recognition	Appropriate acknowledgement
Responses to Questions	Incoherent	"Near misses"	"I don't know"; apathy	Flattened, empty	Pressured

From: American Psychiatric Association, 2000; Bair, 1998; Lipowski, 1989; Meagher, 2001.

in both hyper- and hypoactive forms but are less common in older patients than in younger delirious patients. When present, delusions are usually paranoid or persecutional in nature, and hallucinations are typically visual (Rummans et al., 1995).

Patients with hyperactive delirium tend to experience better outcomes. This better prognosis may be due to a more treatable cause such as anticholinergic medications, drug intoxication, and withdrawal states (Rummans et al., 1995), better health at baseline, or receiving more attention because of the behavioral disturbances (Liptzin & Levkoff, 1992; Meagher, 2001). Although anxiety may resemble hyperactive delirium and both may be exaggerated by the same precipitants, delirium involves clouded awareness and a fluctuating course; anxiety does not (Rummans et al., 1995). Likewise, psychotic behaviors in delirium are differentiated from schizophrenia, which is characterized by unimpaired consciousness, orientation, and memory, and by more systematized perceptual disturbances (DSM-IV-TR, 2000).

Although patients may commonly exhibit both hyperactive and hypoactive symptoms (Liptzin & Levkoff, 1992), older patients are more likely to present with hypoactive symptoms (Rummans et al., 1995). This decreased psychomotor activity can be distinguished from dozing or the sleep state; delirious patients are difficult to rouse, and sleeping patients are not (Rummans et al., 1995). One study confirmed previous findings that physicians often mistake the mood disturbances in delirium for depression, requesting psychiatric consultation without having considered delirium in the differential diagnosis (Farrell & Ganzini, 1995). Hypoactive symptoms of depression may mimic delirium, but depression is distinctive because its features are stable and the patients are alert (Lipowski, 1989; Meagher, 2001).

Delirium is not "sundowning," which describes increased agitation strongly associated with darkness at the end of the day in demented patients (Bliwise, 1994). It is not entirely clear what mechanism is implicated or why sundown appears to be a more vulnerable period of the day, but fatigue and reduced sensory input may be involved (Rummans et al., 1995). In addition, there is some evidence that bright light exposure may help (Bliwise, 1994). Although disruptive behavior at sundown may be a benign phenomenon as a feature of dementia, it also may be caused by toxic, metabolic, and infectious encephalopathies. It should not be casually disregarded (Bliwise, 1994).

MAKING THE DIAGNOSIS OF DELIRIUM

Delirium is a clinical diagnosis, defined by DSM-IV-TR criteria (Table 13.2) as an acute and fluctuating change in consciousness and cognition induced

TABLE 13.2 *DSM-IV-TR* **Criteria for Delirium**

---

1. Disturbance of consciousness exhibited as a decreased ability to focus, sustain or shift attention

2. Change in cognition (memory, orientation, and language) or in the incidence of a perceptual disturbance that cannot be attributed to a premorbid or evolving dementia

3. Acute onset over hours or days and a fluctuating course throughout the day

4. Evidence from the history, physical examination, or laboratory results that the disturbance is a direct physiologic result of a specific medical condition, substance intoxication, or withdrawal; multiple causes; or an otherwise unspecified etiology (e.g., sensory deprivation or medication side effect).

American Psychiatric Association, 2000.

by a medical or environmental insult. To determine the rapidity of onset, family members or caregivers can provide information regarding baseline cognitive and functional status and the course of deterioration, if the clinician is unaware of previous cognitive function (Martin & Haynes, 2000).

Although several screening tests are available, the Confusion Assessment Method (CAM) which is based on *DSM-III-R* criteria, has the best combination of sensitivity and specificity (0.94–100% and 90–95%, respectively) (Inouye, van Dyck, Alessi, Balkin, Siegal, & Horwitz, 1990). From a brief patient interview, mental status exam, and family or nursing assessments, the interviewer determines whether these features have been met:

Feature 1: Acute change in mental status from baseline or changes in severity of behaviors.
Feature 2: Inattention or difficulty focusing on the content of the interaction.
Feature 3: Disorganized or incoherent speech and ideas.
Feature 4: Altered level of consciousness.

Delirium is present if Features 1 and 2 are present with either Feature 3 or 4 (Inouye et al., 1990).

A single poor score on any screening test may help to detect a state of delirium in patients who are not cognitively impaired under normal circumstances. However, pre-existing dementia, uncooperativeness, or inability to communicate can impair the diagnostic value of any single score; fluctuation in serial measurements will be more helpful than any single result.

CAUSES OF DELIRIUM

The etiologies of delirium can be broadly classified as internal, or patient related, and external, or environmentally related. Internal causes include primary organic brain disease (for example, cerebrovascular accidents and tumors or abscesses of the brain) and toxic or metabolic derangements that subsequently impair brain function. Medications, substance withdrawal, dehydration, electrolyte disturbances, and infections of the central nervous system and other organ systems fall into this latter category. Urinary tract infections and pneumonia are particularly common infectious causes of delirium (Liptzin, 1995; Rummans et al., 1995). Advanced age, preexisting cognitive impairment, serious comorbidity (including Alzheimer's disease, Parkinson's disease, history of cerebrovascular events, bone fractures on admission, and surgical procedures, among others) and polypharmacy are considered very strong *predisposing* risk factors for the development of delirium (Rummans et al., 1995). In a study by Inouye, Viscoli, Horwitz, Hurst, and Tinetti (1993), the most vulnerable patients were those with poor vision, severe illness, cognitive impairments, and elevated BUN.

In the hospital setting, delirium is often iatrogenic, due to environmental or external factors imposed on a patient. These *precipitating* factors include the initiation of psychoactive medications, immobilization, sleep deprivation, extremes of sensory input, physical restraints, indwelling catheters, complications of procedures, and inadequate hydration and nutrition (Liptzin, 1995; Inouye & Charpentier, 1996; Inouye et al., 1999). These factors may be used to stratify patients at risk.

Susceptibility to the development of delirium is related to both intrinsic and extrinsic factors, and these risks are cumulative (Cole et al., 1998; Francis, 1992; Meagher, 2001). Therefore, high-risk patients—that is, those with multiple intrinsic and extrinsic factors—should be screened frequently when hospitalized (Meagher, 2001). In contrast, patients with no predisposing factors are at very low risk of developing delirium regardless of the number of precipitants (Bair, 1998; Cole et al., 1998).

INVESTIGATING CORRECTABLE FACTORS

Once delirium has been diagnosed, an appropriate evaluation for potential etiologies should be tailored to the individual context. The suggestions that follow are grounded on some basic principles, for example, that the three most common causes of delirium are medications, metabolic disorders and infection in that order (Rudberg, Pompei, Foreman, Ross, & Cassel, 1997).

1. Obtain a good history, including a thorough review of the medication list.

2. Do a complete physical exam with emphasis on signs that indicate infection, cardiac etiologies, dehydration, malnutrition, urinary retention, and fecal impaction.

3. Remove potentially contributing medications, and consider substance withdrawal in the differential.

4. Initial laboratory tests should include electrolytes, glucose, and renal and hepatic function, complete blood count (CBC) with differential, urinalysis, and culture.

5. Thyroid tests, toxicology screen, arterial blood gas, and drug levels should be checked only if clinically appropriate. Include HIV in the differential diagnosis when risk factors are present.

6. A chest X ray may be warranted to diagnose pneumonia, a common infectious cause of delirium in the older patient, and an electrocardiogram (ECG) may indicate cardiac ischemia.

If these steps do not uncover a source:

7. A head CT or MRI should be performed if there are focal neurologic signs or a history of head trauma; otherwise the diagnostic yield is low.

8. An EEG is indicated if an undiagnosed seizure disorder is suspected, but in general it is not helpful.

9. A lumbar puncture should be performed only if there are meningeal signs or if infection is suspected without another obvious source (for example, pulmonary or bladder); otherwise this procedure is both difficult and of low yield in older patients (Meagher, 2001; Rummans et al., 1995).

Usually there are multiple simultaneous causes for an episode of delirium, often 2 to 6 factors in any single case (Inouye, Bogardus, et al., 1999; Meagher, 2001). Hence, identifying one cause for the delirium does not obviate continued investigation, reevaluation, or preventive measures. In addition, if the delirium is environmentally related, no test can precisely identify the problem source.

PREVENTING DELIRIUM

Heightened vigilance for cognitive and behavioral changes in high-risk patients and measures that minimize intrinsic and extrinsic factors have been effective in reducing the incidence and duration of in-hospital delirium and are probably cost effective (Inouye, Bogardus, et al., 1999). These rather simple interventions include early mobilization, vision and hearing aids, providing a serene environment, avoiding extremes in lighting, noise, and activity, frequent reassurance, review of orientation, explanations of all procedures, and attention to hydration and nutrition (Rummans et al., 1995;

Inouye, Schlesinger et al., 1999; Meagher, 2001). In addition, minimizing sleep disturbances and providing warm blankets, warm drinks to aid sleep, massage, and familiar comfort items from home also can help. A visible clock, a relative's presence, a room located near to the nursing station, and communication boards or writing instruments for intubated patients are also helpful (Rummans et al., 1995; Bair, 1998; Meagher, 2001). Furthermore, family members may be able to provide insight into cultural factors that may influence behaviors (Martin & Haynes, 2000).

It is best to avoid anticholinergic agents. Exposure to anticholinergic medications has been associated independently with the severity of delirium symptoms (Han et al., 2001). Tune, Carr, Hoag, and Cooper (1992) found that many commonly prescribed agents not typically identified as anti-cholinergic produced anticholinergic drug levels that have been shown to cause significant cognitive impairments in normal older individuals. This principle underscores the importance of discriminating accurately between delirium and depression, as the anticholinergic properties of many antide-pressants used to treat dysphoria may actually intensify the delirium (Farrell & Ganzini, 1995).

In general, the use of psychoactive substances should be minimized, but their use in appropriate circumstances actually may prevent delirium. For example, achieving optimal pain management might require the use of opioids (Inouye, Schlesinger, et al., 1999; Meagher, 2001). Although opi-oids can induce delirium if given nonjudiciously, doses just sufficient to control pain may prevent delirium, especially when pain causes agitation (Martin & Haynes, 2000). Patient-controlled analgesia has helped control pain and prevent delirium in postoperative patients (Cole et al., 1998; Meagher, 2001).

MANAGEMENT OF DELIRIUM

Interventions that treat an obvious medical cause for the delirium, such as antibiotics for infection or regimens for cardiac ischemia, should be initiat-ed as indicated. Nonpharmacologic interventions, such as staff education and special nursing attention, tend to address environmental causes of delirium. Physical restraints aggravate delirium, especially agitated behav-ior, and are unacceptable except under very limited situations to prevent harm (Liptzin, 1995; Martin & Haynes, 2000). Close supervision is prefer-able and more effective. Chapter 10 discusses restraint use and its alterna-tives in detail.

In postoperative patients, delirium seems to occur most commonly on or about the 3rd postoperative day, often with a prodromal onset of symptoms, before fully meeting delirium criteria (Liptzin, 1995). Cole and colleagues (1998) reviewed 13 studies of the prevention and therapy of postoperative delirium, finding that nonpharmacologic efforts appeared to have a larger beneficial effect (i.e., more rapid resolution, etc.) on older surgical patients than on older medical patients. However, they comment that these efforts actually may have been confounded by the fact that the medical causes of postoperative delirium tended to be more specific and amenable to (pharmacologic) treatment (e.g., hypoxia can be treated with supplemental oxygen). In another study, however, laboratory investigation for a specific underlying cause was usually unsuccessful, suggesting that iatrogenic and environmental factors played a large role in the delirium episodes in this particular group of patients (Brauer, Morrison, Silberzweig & Siu, 2000).

As the most common iatrogenic cause of delirium, medications are implicated in 20% to 40% of delirium cases; therefore, a careful review of medications with elimination of unnecessary agents should be the first step undertaken as both a preventive and therapeutic measure (Inouye, Schlesinger, et al., 1999; Meagher, 2001). Changes in body fat and water composition, renal and hepatic clearance, and albumin levels all contribute to the increased susceptibility of older patients to medications (Rummans et al., 1995). Even well-tolerated medications taken on a chronic basis may be metabolized differently in acute illness and may not be as well tolerated.

Pharmacologic intervention should be reserved for situations in which there are perceptual disturbances (even if hypoactive), when disruptive and uncooperative behavior threatens the well-being of the patient, caregiver, or staff, and when nonpharmacologic techniques have failed. In most situations the goal of pharmacologic intervention is to moderate unmanageable behaviors, *not* to sedate (Casarett & Inouye, 2001). Low-dose haloperidol remains the neuroleptic of choice; as little as 0.25–0.5 mg may be necessary, although some patients may require doses as high as 2–5 mg qd or divided through the day. For acute symptoms, haloperidol is often preferred over the atypical neuroleptics, such as olanzepine and risperidone. Haloperidol has few active metabolites, anticholinergic, sedative, and hypotensive side effects (Meagher, 2001; Rummans et al., 1995). Although it has higher risks for extrapyramidal symptoms, actual reported incidence is low, especially in the intravenous form (Meagher, 2001; Rummans et al., 1995). Parenteral forms are twice as potent as enteral forms (Bair, 1998). If administering frequent doses, blood pressure and ECGs for QT prolongation should be monitored (Bair, 1998). In patients with Parkinsonism, atypical neuroleptics may be more helpful. Quetiapine (brand name Seroquel) in doses of 12.5 mg qd to 50 mg bid is the drug of choice.

Dosing of the neuroleptics in older patients should start at half the recommended doses and can be carefully titrated upwards if needed. The larger doses included in the spectrum of general recommendations for these medications are based on treatment strategies for young schizophrenics and are in far excess of what is needed for control of agitation in a non-schizophrenic, geriatric patient.

In general, benzodiazepines are less effective than the neuroleptics in treating delirium. However, they can be used in small amounts in patients who otherwise are unable to tolerate neuroleptics, who are experiencing alcohol or sedative withdrawal, or who require some sedation (Meagher, 2001). Lorazepam is preferred in older patients because it has multiple routes of administration, rapid onset with short duration of action, no major active metabolites, and a low risk of accumulation except in patients with diminished hepatic metabolism (glucuronidation) or who are on other medications that undergo extensive hepatic oxidation (Bair, 1998; Meagher, 2001; Rummans et al., 1995). In addition, benzodiazepines can be quickly reversed with flumazenil if there is oversedation. Adequate initial dosing reduces the risk of paradoxical disinhibition (Meagher, 2001). Drug therapy should be carefully monitored and discontinued when no longer necessary.

Finally, it is important to be sensitive and compassionate with family members. Delirium itself is traumatic, but also may herald a terminal condition for which they need to prepare psychologically and emotionally. Gentle explanations of the underlying condition, prognosis, and future expectations can facilitate family understanding and cooperation. In addition, they should be informed that symptoms may endure for an extended period after discharge (Meagher, 2001).

DELIRIUM: LONG-TERM COURSE

Symptoms of delirium may persist beyond the acute phase of treatment, up to 6 to 12 months following hospitalization (Inouye, Schlesinger, et al., 1999; Meagher, 2001; Rummans et al., 1995). A prolonged course may be more likely in patients who experience the hypoactive subtype, have more comorbidities, or are prescribed more medications (Rudberg et al., 1997). Many of those who recover recall the episode of delirium and some may experience a posttraumatic syndrome following the psychological trauma of their psychotic experiences (Jacobson, 1997).

Dementia is a risk factor for developing delirium, and some propose that delirium can cause dementia; at the very least, and more likely, delirium can unmask previously unrecognized dementia. The diagnosis of dementia following an episode of delirium requires an appropriate recovery period (Rummans et al., 1995).

DELIRIUM AT THE END OF LIFE

Delirium frequently occurs at the end of life and can exaggerate the stressors already present by causing fear, precluding the opportunity to engage in decision-making and planning, and fostering regret at premature separation in family members (Casarett & Inouye, 2001). Terminal patients are often more susceptible because of cachexia, hepatic and renal dysfunction, impaired functional status, and other medical problems (Lawlor, Fainsinger, & Bruera, 2000).

Although strategies to prevent delirium should be implemented in all cases, treatment of delirium must be sensitive to the goals of the patient and family, focusing on preserving or improving quality of life. An aggressive evaluation in an actively dying patient may produce more harm than good and is more likely to discover causes that are not amenable to treatment (Casarett & Inouye, 2001).

At the end of life, treatment to ameliorate agitation is still appropriate. Opioids are often responsible for delirium in cancer patients, and this effect may be exacerbated by renal failure (Cassarett & Inouye, 2001). Although there are no randomized controlled trials, expert opinion suggests that "opioid rotation," rotating to a different opioid at a reduced equianalgesic dose, can improve both mental status and analgesia (Casarett & Inouye, 2001; Lawlor et al., 2000). Subcutaneous bisphosphonates can treat hypercalcemia-induced delirium (Lawlor et al., 2000). If fluid replacement is consistent with the patient's wishes regarding artificial hydration and nutrition, hypodermoclysis may be a more humane method to deliver fluids than nasogastric tubes or intravenous catheters (Casarett & Inouye, 2001; Lawlor et al., 2000). Finally, potentially offending medications can be switched (e.g., a proton pump inhibitor instead of an H2-blocker) or tapered (Casarett & Inouye, 2001).

COMMENTS ABOUT THE CASES

The 82-year-old woman with the hip fracture and hyperactive symptoms of delirium is probably undermedicated for pain control. However, there may have been other underlying causes that actually precipitated her fall and therefore a complete evaluation is indicated. Preventive measures should be taken, including discontinuation of restraints and all unnecessary catheters, as well as limiting overnight disruptions. Administering appropriate pain therapy is imperative. If these measures fail and pharmacologic intervention is needed, Quetiapine may be the preferred agent, given her history of Parkinson's disease.

The 74-year-old man with end-stage COPD has pneumonia as the likely cause of his delirium, which is characterized by more hypoactive symptoms. There also may be other exacerbating factors such as dehydration resulting from poor oral intake, hypoxia secondary to the pneumonia, and hypercarbia from the lung disease. A full evaluation is indicated within the goals of his end-stage care. Antibiotics and ventilatory support should be instituted as appropriate. If not already addressed, advanced directives should be reviewed with the health care agent, as the patient's wishes under the circumstances may preclude intubation. As always, measures to maximize comfort and limit distress should be implemented.

CONCLUSION

Delirium is a medical emergency. Because delirium may be the first sign of severe illness, it is essential to identify potentially life-threatening and reversible causes and to undertake appropriate interventions as quickly as possible. Then, treat correctable causes appropriately and implement measures to minimize disruptions, unpredictability, disorientation, and extremes of sensory stimulation. Avoid the use of restraints. When monitoring for improvements, remember that the more impaired a patient is at baseline, the more likely delirium may not resolve immediately with correction of the precipitating condition.

REFERENCES

American Psychiatric Association. (2000). *Diagnostic and statistical manual of mental disorders* (4th ed., text rev.). Washington, DC: Author.

Bair, B. D. (1998). Frequently missed diagnosis in geriatric psychiatry. *Psychiatric Clinics of North America, 21,* 941–971.

Bliwise, D. L. (1994). What is sundowning? *Journal of the American Geriatrics Society, 42,* 1009–1011.

Brauer, C., Morrison, S., Silberzweig, S. B., & Siu, A. L. (2000). The cause of delirium in patients with hip fracture. *Archives of Internal Medicine, 160,* 1856–1860.

Casarett, D. J., & Inouye, S. K. (2001). Diagnosis and management of delirium near the end of life. *Annals of Internal Medicine, 135,* 32–40.

Cole, M. G., Primeau, F. J., & Elie, M. (1998). Delirium: Prevention, treatment and outcome studies. *Journal of Geriatric Psychiatry and Neurology, 11,* 126–137.

Farrell, K. R., & Ganzini, L. (1995). Misdiagnosing delirium as depression in medically ill elderly patients. *Archives of Internal Medicine, 155,* 2459–2464.

Francis, J. (1992). Delirium in older patients. *Journal of the American Geriatrics Society, 40,* 829–838.

Han, L., McCusker, J., Cole, M., Abrahamowicz, M., Primeau, F., & Elie, M. (2001). Use of medications with anti-cholinergic effect predicts clinical severity of delirium symptoms in older medical inpatients. *Archives of Internal Medicine, 161,* 1099–1105.

Inouye, S. K., Bogardus, S. T., Charpentier, P. A., Leo-Summers, L., Acampora, D., Holford, T. R., & Cooney, L. M. (1999). A multicomponent intervention to prevent delirium in hospitalized older patients. *New England Journal of Medicine, 340,* 669–676.

Inouye, S. K., & Charpentier, P. A. (1996). Precipitating factors for delirium in hospitalized elderly persons. *Journal of the American Medical Association, 275,* 852–857.

Inouye, S. K., Schlesinger, M. J., & Lydon, T. J. (1999). Delirium: A symptom of how hospital care is failing older persons and a window to improve quality of hospital care. *American Journal of Medicine, 106,* 565–573.

Inouye, S. K., van Dyck, C. H., Alessi, C. A., Balkin, S., Siegal, A. P., & Horwitz, R. I. (1990). Clarifying confusion: The confusion assessment method. *Annals of Internal Medicine, 113,* 941–948.

Inouye, S. K., Viscoli, C. M., Horwitz, R. I., Hurst, L. D., & Tinetti, M. E. (1993). A predictive model for delirium in hospitalized elderly medical patients based on admission characteristics. *Annals of Internal Medicine, 119,* 474–481.

Jacobson, S. A. (1997). Delirium in the elderly. *Psychiatric Clinics of North America, 20,* 91–110.

Lawlor, P. G., Fainsinger, R. L., & Bruera, E. D. (2000). Delirium at the end of life. *Journal of the American Medical Association, 284,* 2427–2429.

Lipowski, Z. J. (1989). Delirium in the elderly patient. *New England Journal of Medicine, 320,* 578–582.

Liptzin, B. (1995). Delirium. *Archives of Family Medicine, 4,* 453–458.

Liptzin, B., & Levkoff, S. E. (1992). An empirical study of delirium subtypes. *British Journal of Psychiatry, 161,* 843–845.

Martin, J., & Haynes, L. C. (2000). Depression, delirium and dementia in the elderly patient. *American Operating Room Nurses Journal, 72,* 209–217.

Meagher, D. J. (2001). Delirium: Optimizing management. *British Medical Journal, 322,* 144–149.

Rudberg, M. A., Pompei, P., Foreman, M. D., Ross, R. E., & Cassel, C. K. (1997). The natural history of delirium in older hospitalized patients: A syndrome of heterogeneity. *Age and Ageing, 26,* 169–174.

Rummans, T. A., Evans, J. M., Krahn, L. E., & Fleming, K. C. (1995). Delirium in elderly patients: Evaluation and management. *Mayo Clinic Proceedings, 70,* 989–998.

Tune, L., Carr, S., Hoag, E., & Cooper, T. (1992). Anti-cholinergic effects of drugs commonly prescribed for the elderly: Potential means for assessing risk of delirium. *American Journal of Psychiatry, 149,* 1393–1394.

■ 14
Isolation

Barry Gallison

In 1900, 33% of all deaths in the United States were attributable to tuberculosis, diphtheria, pneumonia, and diarrhea enteritis. In 1997, only 4.5% of all deaths were due to the three most common infectious causes of death: influenza, HIV infection, and pneumonia (Centers for Disease Control and Prevention [CDC], 1999). However, despite the dramatic progress in combating infectious diseases, prevention of nosocomial (hospital-acquired) infections still remains an overwhelming challenge. Each year more than 2 million patients in the United States acquire nosocomial infections at a treatment cost exceeding $4.5 billion (Jordan, 2001).

Patients infected or colonized with certain microorganisms must be placed in isolation during hospitalization to prevent nosocomial transmission of these pathogens. Isolation systems enable health care workers to identify patients who require isolation and to institute the necessary precautions. Patient isolation prevents the transmission of microorganisms from infected or colonized patients to other patients, visitors, and health care workers. Appropriate use of isolation remains the cornerstone of infection control and is growing more important as the number of multiple antibiotic-resistant organisms increases. Isolation efforts may be costly, but the direct and indirect costs of nosocomial outbreaks can be more substantial.

Isolation can be defined as "placing apart or alone" and may be used in the hospital setting for noninfective reasons including privacy, patient choice, and severe or terminal illness. Uncooperative or disturbed patients may also be isolated, but this is usually termed "seclusion." Unfortunately, isolation for infection control purposes has detrimental psychological effects on the patient. The timely discontinuation of isolation can reduce a patient's length of stay, decrease cost of hospitalization, and contribute to the patient's overall mental health. This chapter will present an overview of isolation, the psychological implications these practices may pose for patients, and suggestions for alleviating the detrimental effects that isolation may have on a patient.

HISTORY

The first published recommendations for isolation precautions in the United States appeared as early as 1877, when a hospital handbook recommended placing patients with infectious disease in separate facilities (CDC, 1997). In the hospital setting, "isolation" came to mean quarantine, where a known infected patient was placed in a private room. In 1910, isolation practices were modified by the cubicle system, which placed patients in wards. Health care workers changed gowns and washed their hands with antiseptic solutions after each patient contact. This practice became known as "barrier nursing" (CDC, 1997).

The Centers for Disease Control and Prevention has led the effort to formalize guidelines for isolation. These guidelines, first published in 1970, were later revised in 1975. The CDC first recommended that hospitals use one of seven category-specific forms of isolation: strict isolation, respiratory isolation, protective isolation, enteric precautions, wound and skin precautions, discharge precautions, and blood precautions. Since then the CDC has modified and streamlined these guidelines several times. The changes addressed the emerging problems in infectious disease management and incorporated an increased understanding about the mechanisms of transmission for some diseases (CDC, 1997).

In 1996, the CDC and the Hospital Infection Control Practices Advisory Committee (HICPAC) issued the most recent guidelines for a new system of isolation. The revised guidelines contain two levels, *standard precautions* and *transmission-based precautions,* which replaced the system of universal precautions and category-specific precautions. The first and most important level contains the outline for the care of all patients in the hospital, regardless of their diagnosis or presumed infection status. Implementation of these standard precautions is the primary strategy for successful nosocomial infection control. Transmission-based precautions address the care of patients with specific clinical diagnoses and are used for patients known or suspected to be infected or colonized with epidemiologically important pathogens (CDC, 1997). In order to appreciate the rationale behind various isolation policies, it is important first to have a basic familiarity with the three elements required to transmit infections.

CHAIN OF INFECTION

Transmission of infection within a hospital requires three elements: a source of infecting microorganism, a susceptible host, and a means of transmission for the microorganism. Breaking the chain of infection is crucial in the prevention of nosocomial infections:

Source

Human sources of the infecting microorganisms in hospital may be patients, health care workers, or visitors. They may include persons with acute disease, persons in the incubation period of a disease, persons who are colonized by an infectious agent but have no apparent disease, or persons who are chronic carriers of a pathogen. Other sources of infecting microorganisms can be the patient's own endogenous flora, which may be difficult to control, and inanimate environmental objects that have become contaminated with the microorganism (Garner, 1996).

Host

Resistance to pathogenic microorganisms varies greatly. Some people may be immune to infection or may be able to resist colonization by an infectious agent. Other patients may become asymptomatic carriers, while others may develop clinical disease. Host factors such as age, underlying disease, certain treatments with antimicrobials, corticosteroids or other immunosuppressive agents, and irradiation may render patients more susceptible to infection (Garner, 1996).

Transmission

The most basic principle of infection control is to prevent the transmission of microorganisms from a source to a host. The most frequent mode of transmission of nosocomial infections is contact transmission. Droplet and airborne transmission can also occur (Garner, 1996).

STANDARD PRECAUTIONS

The first level of infection control is standard precautions. These apply to blood, nonintact skin, mucous membranes, all body fluids, secretions, and excretions, whether or not they are visibly bloody. The goal of the standard precautions is to reduce the risk of transmission of microorganisms from both recognized and unrecognized sources of infection in the health care setting.

A variety of infection-control measures can decrease the risks of transmission of microorganisms in hospitals. Handwashing, room placement, and the use of personal protective equipment are the key interventions that make up the fundamentals of isolation precautions. *Hand-washing is the single most important measure for reducing the risk of transmission of organisms from one person to another or from one site to another on the same patient.* Washing hands as promptly and thoroughly as possible between patient contacts and after contact with blood, body fluids, secretions, excretions, and equipment and articles contaminated by them is an important component of isolation precautions and infection control.

In addition to hand-washing, gloves play an important role in reducing the risks of transmission of microorganisms. Gloves are worn as a protective barrier and a prevention to gross contamination of the hands when touching blood, body fluids, secretions, excretions, mucous membranes, and nonintact skin. Gloves reduce the likelihood that organisms present on the hands of health care workers will be transmitted to the patient during invasive or other procedures that involve touching nonintact skin or mucous membranes. Wearing gloves does not replace the need for hand-washing. Gloves may have small defects or may rip during their use and the hands may become contaminated during their removal. The failure to change gloves between patient contacts is an infection-control hazard (CDC, 1997).

Various types of masks, goggles, and face shields worn alone or in combination can provide additional barrier protection. Health-care workers should wear eye protection and masks that cover both the nose and the mouth when performing tasks that are likely to generate splashes or sprays of bodily fluids. Gowns prevent contamination of health-care workers' clothing and protect the skin from blood and bodily fluids. Workers must remove gowns and thoroughly wash their hands before leaving the patient's area (CDC, 1997).

TRANSMISSION-BASED PRECAUTIONS

Transmission-based precautions are divided into three categories that reflect the major modes of transmission of infectious agents: airborne, droplet, and contact (see Table 14.1). Some diseases may require more than one isolation category.

Airborne precautions prevent diseases transmitted by droplet nuclei or contaminated dust particles. Droplet nuclei are less than 5 μm in size and may remain suspended in air, allowing them to migrate for long periods of time. Appropriate isolation requires a private room with negative air pressure and at least six air exchanges per hour. Air from the room should be exhausted directly to the outside or through a high-efficiency filter. The door to the room must be closed at all times (Edmond, 1997).

Any patient who must be transported outside of the isolation room should put on a mask before leaving the isolation area. All persons entering the room should wear masks, which must meet the following CDC performance criteria: (a) filter 1 μm particles with an efficiency of at least 95%;

TABLE 14.1 Transmission-based Precautions

	Airborne Precautions	Droplet Precautions	Contact Precautions
Known or suspected illness	Hemorrhagic fever Tuberculosis Rubeola	Adenovirus Diphtheria Meningitis Mumps	*Clostridium difficile* Scabies MRSA VREF
Room type	Single room, negative air pressure, door closed, patient not to leave room	Single room, door may remain open	Single room, door may remain open
Wash hands	Before and after contact	Before and after contact	Before and after contact
Gloves	Required for patient contact	Required for patient contact	Required for patient contact
Masks	Respiratory protection (PFR 95) worn by all entering room	Surgical masks worn by all entering room	Not required
Gowns	Not required	Required if clothing will touch patient or if patient has any type of drainage	Required for contact with patient or environment
Patient transport	Patient always wears surgical mask when leaving isolation room	Patient always wears surgical mask when leaving isolation room	Patient should wear gloves and gown when leaving isolation room
Patient-care equipment			Dedicated to one patient

(b) fit different facial sizes and characteristics; (c) be fit-tested to obtain a leakage of <10%; and (d) be checked for fit each time the health care provider puts on the mask (CDC, 1994).

Airborne precautions would be implemented for patients known or suspected to have serious illnesses transmitted by airborne droplet nuclei such as hemorrhagic fevers (Lassa, Ebola, & Marburg), tuberculosis, and rubeola.

Droplet precautions are designed to reduce the risk of droplet transmission of infectious agents. Droplet transmission involves contact of the conjunctivae or the mucous membranes of the nose or mouth of a susceptible person with large-particle droplets, larger than 5 µm in size, containing microorganisms generated from a person who has a clinical disease or who is a carrier of the microorganism. Droplets are generated from the source person primarily during coughing, sneezing, or talking and during certain procedures such as suctioning and bronchoscopy. Large-particle-droplet transmission requires close contact between the recipient and source. Droplets only travel less than 3 feet and do not remain suspended in the air for long periods of time. Special air handling and ventilation are not required.

Droplet precautions require patients to be placed in a private room or "cohorted" with another patient who is infected with the same organism. The door to the room may remain open. Health care workers should wear a mask when within 3 feet of the patient. The patient should wear a mask when transported out of the room (Edmond, 1997).

Droplet precautions would be implemented for patients known or suspected to have serious illnesses such as adenovirus, diphtheria (pharyngeal), meningitis, mumps, *Mycoplasma* pneumonia, pertussis, rubella, scarlet fever, and pneumonic plague.

Contact precautions are designed to reduce the risk of transmission of microorganisms by direct or indirect contact. Direct contact transmission involves skin-to-skin contact and physical transfer of microorganisms to a susceptible host from an infected or colonized person. This transmission can occur during physical assessment or while performing other patient-care activities that require physical contact. Indirect contact transmission involves contact of a susceptible host with a contaminated intermediate object in the patient's environment.

Contact precautions require patients to be placed in a private room or cohorted with another patient who is infected with the same organism. Health care providers should wear gloves when entering the room. When preparing to leave, providers should remove their gloves and wash their hands with a medicated hand-washing agent while still in the room. Gowns should be worn if workers may have substantial contact with the patient or the patient's environment. Noncritical patient-care items such as stethoscopes and bedside commodes that are used for patients on contact isolation should not be shared with other patients unless cleaned and disinfected between patient use (Edmond, 1997).

Contact precautions are implemented for patients known or suspected to have serious illnesses such as rotavirus, parainfluenza, skin infections that are contagious, including cutaneous diphtheria, *Clostridium difficile*, herpes simplex, impetigo, scabies, pediculosis, or infection or colonization with a multidrug-resistant bacteria.

PROTECTIVE ISOLATION

When the CDC revised its guidelines in 1996, it no longer supported protective isolation as an efficacious practice (CDC, 1997). The original goal of health care providers was to prevent infections during neutropenia by creating a "germ-free" patient in a "germ-free" environment. This placed much emphasis on the prevention of colonization of patients with extrinsic pathogens, rather than on the prevention of infection with antimicrobial prophylaxis once colonization had taken place. Methods used in the past for the protection of neutropenic patients were labor-intensive, expensive, and unpleasant for the patient (Fenelon, 1995). Therefore, the use of standard precautions and transmission-based precautions became the gold standard for hospital isolation practices. However, some cancer wards in hospitals still incorporate protective isolation for the care of immunocompromised patients.

ENDING ISOLATION

Although isolation serves an important purpose, it may cause undo stress and anxiety for some individuals. There is no reason for a patient to be in isolation any longer than absolutely necessary. Unfortunately, there are no literature-based or expert-based guidelines describing when isolation can end. The resolution of transmission-based isolation varies from institution to institution. Therefore, it is important for the care provider to become familiar with the hospital's policies and procedures involving the discontinuation of any isolation.

PSYCHOLOGICAL IMPLICATIONS OF ISOLATION

Although isolation may successfully contain microorganisms that are harmful to a patient, there are negative psychological implications to this practice. Health care providers recognize that dressing in protective clothing is a time-consuming activity that reduces the frequency of interactions, and staff feel that they do not get to know the patients in isolation as well as those patients on the general ward (Knowles, 1993). Studies have shown that some patients experience negative emotional effects when cared for in isolation for infection control purposes (Knowles, 1993; Lewis, Gammom, & Hosein, 1999; Oldman, 1998; Ward, 2000; Wilkins, Ellis, Dunbar, & Gibbs, 1988). Little information has been published that suggests what health care professionals can do to prevent or reduce these effects. Past research has been limited, because one patient's responses may not be representative of all isolated patients, and the experience of patients in protective isolation and those in transmission-based isolation cannot be assumed to be the same.

Transmission-based Isolation

The psychological care of patients who require isolation because of a transmittable disease remains an issue that is often discussed but not well researched (Gammon, 1999). The CDC (1997) briefly mentions that forced solitude deprives the patient of normal social relationships and may be psychologically harmful. Some patients who have been isolated have shared their experiences and feelings, both positive and negative.

Some studies have documented that isolation can have some benefits. Wilkins and colleagues (1988) found that most patients express a preference for a private room and that their anxiety is related to their current infectious illness rather than to their imposed isolation. Patients like being able to control their activities within the confines of their room despite not having any control over the decision for isolation (Knowles, 1993) and feel relief that their visitors will not disturb anyone else (Ward, 2000). They have reported feeling quiet, relaxed, and private (Ward, 2000) and have found moments of reflection and introspection to be therapeutic (Oldman, 1998).

However, patients have had many more negative experiences and feelings to report. Isolated patients experience more anxiety and depression than nonisolated patients (Gammon, 1999); they commonly feel confinement, loneliness, and boredom (Ward, 2000). Patients feel lonely and stigmatized because they perceive their infection could harm others (Oldman, 1998). Isolation can hamper rehabilitation and may increase hospital stay, lower morale, and worsen patient anxiety (Lewis et al., 1999; Prieto & Clark, 1999). Patients in isolation perceive that health care providers spend less time in their rooms than in other patients' rooms. Knowles (1993) noted that patients' experiences of having to wait for assistance left them feeling angry, neglected, and insignificant.

Patients have suggested ways to alleviate the negative aspects of isolation. They have expressed the desire for more information that would explain the reasons for being isolated, the rationale for infection-control precautions, and what activity limitations were imposed on them (Gammon, 1999; Ward, 2000). The lack of information and understanding of isolation made it difficult for them to explain to their visitors why they were isolated (Ward, 2000). The patients expressed that a written pamphlet, when supplemented by staff explanations, would help them understand the rationale for isolation.

Ward (2000) reported that visitors were seen by all the participants as vital for the prevention and alleviation of boredom and loneliness. For some patients the family was the primary support and coping aid. However, the lack of information regarding isolation caused many visitors to be afraid to stay for extended periods of time.

The patients also expressed opinions about the value of other patients in relieving boredom and loneliness and in helping them put their own condition into perspective. Knowles (1993) reported that patients in isolation saw other patients as a source of company and comfort. Ward (2000) noted there was an overwhelming agreement that a common room where isolated patients could meet and watch television together would be valuable.

Ward (2000) also reported that patients felt the doctors did not speak to them for very long and when they did, the patients could not always understand what was being said. Patients also expressed that there was a need for more nurses so more time could be spent in meaningful communication. Ward concluded that health care providers should explain their actions slowly and in an understanding manner and then check the patient's understanding of what has been discussed.

Protective Isolation

Patients in protective isolation are actively involved in the decision to be isolated and are able to prepare for the experience over a period of time. The research of Campbell (1999) suggests that the disease and treatment issues are of greater significance to the patient than the isolation conditions they have to undergo as a part of their treatment. Campbell's research confirms the perception that the experience of protective isolation induces psychological stress as a result of decreased social interaction and support. The patients who were studied coped with the experience of protective isolation well, while not necessarily enjoying it. The restrictions of the isolation were accepted with the understanding that it was a crucial protective function. Caring behaviors exhibited by the health care team mitigated the experience. Humor and touch were seen as key interpersonal interventions in making their experience of isolation more tolerable. The role of the nurse was seen as particularly important, with the emphasis on informational and emotional support, encouragement, and advocacy. Research also suggests that windows with a view of the outside world can provide a release from isolation and boredom (Baird & Bell, 1995; Gaskill, Henderson & Fraser, 1993; Knowles, 1993).

CONCLUSION

Infection control and isolation practices are common to all hospitals. Health care providers should become familiar with both the CDC guidelines and the policies and procedures of their home institution. Infectious disease practices are constantly evolving and necessitate annual reviews.

Health care providers often do not appreciate the emotional and psychological effects of isolation on their patients. In implementing isolation for infection-control purposes it is important to remember that not all patients may react the same. Research has shown that isolation has detrimental effects on the psychological well being of some individuals.

Infection-control procedures should be explained to reduce the feelings of stigmatization and frustration, and health care providers should make sure that patients understand the information that they receive. Development of informational pamphlets would help improve understanding and increase patient and visitor satisfaction. Cohorting appropriate patients instead of using private rooms can also help relieve boredom and loneliness. Further extensive research is needed to determine how to improve further the experience for patients in isolation.

REFERENCES

Baird, C. L., & Bell, P. L. (1995). Place attachment, isolation and the power of a window in a hospital environment: A case study. *Psychological Reports, 76,* 847–850.

Campbell, T. (1999). Feeling of oncology patients about being nursed in protective isolation as a consequence of cancer chemotherapy treatment. *Journal of Advanced Nursing, 30,* 439–447.

Centers for Disease Control and Prevention. (1994). Guidelines for preventing the transmission of *Mycobacterium* tuberculosis in health-care facilities. *Morbidity Mortality Weekly Report, 43, (RR-13),* 1–132. [On-line]. Available: www.cdc.gov./mmwr/preview/mmwrhtml/mm4313a1. Accessed June 18, 2001.

Centers for Disease Control and Prevention. (1997). Part I. Evolution of isolation practices. Part II. Recommendations for isolation precautions in hospitals. [On-line]. Available: www.cdc.gov/ncidod/hip/isolat. Accessed June 18, 2001.

Centers for Disease Control and Prevention. (1999). Achievements in public health, 1900–1999: Control of infectious diseases. *Morbidity Mortality Weekly Report, 48,* (RR-29), 621–629. [On-line]. Available: www.cdc.gov/mmwr/preview/mmwrhtml/mm4829a1. Retrieved June 18, 2001.

Edmond, M. (1997). Isolation. *Infection Control and Hospital Epidemiology, 18,* 58–65.

Fenelon, L. E. (1995). Protective isolation: Who needs it? *Journal of Hospital Infection, 30 (Suppl.),* 218–222.

Gammon, J. (1999). The psychological consequences of source isolation: A review of the literature. *Journal of Clinical Nursing, 8*(1), 13–21.

Garner, J. S. (1996). Hospital infection control practices advisory committee. Guideline for isolation precautions in hospitals. *Infection Control Hospital Epidemiology, 17,* 53–80.

Gaskill, D., Henderson, A., & Fraser, M. (1997). Exploring the everyday world of the patient in isolation. *Oncology Nursing Forum, 24,* 695–700.

Jordan, T. (2001). Infection control precautions. *Advance for Nurses, 1*(1), 32–33.

Knowles, H. (1993). The experience of infectious patients in isolation. *Nursing Times, 89*(30), 53–56.

Lewis, A.M., Gammon, J., & Hosein, I. (1999). The pros and cons of isolation and containment. *Journal of Hospital Infection, 43,* 19–23.

Oldman, T. (1998). Isolated cases. *Nursing Times, 94*(11), 67–69.

Prieto, J., & Clark, J. (1999). Dazed and confused: Isolation precaution problems. *Nursing Times, 95*(28), 49–50, 53.

Ward, D. (2000). Infection control: Reducing the psychological effects of isolation. *British Journal of Nursing, 9,* 162–170.

Wilkins, E. G. L., Ellis, M. E., Dunbar, E. M., & Gibbs, A. (1988). Does isolation of patients with infections induce mental illness? *Journal of Infection, 17,* 43–47.

■ 15
Care Management and Case Management

Barbara Doyle, Beryl C. Vallejo, Margaret Horgan, and Janice B. Foust

Care management and case management are two common strategies that clinicians and hospital administrators have developed to control increasing costs and improve clinical outcomes in the face of reduced reimbursement and intensified focus on quality of care. The varieties of programs and the lack of uniform terminology are confusing; care management, case management, disease management, medical management, clinical resource management, and utilization management all describe similar types of programs that aim to improve clinical and financial outcomes by attempting to reduce variation in length of stay, coordinate care, promote adherence to best practice standards, and control costs. However, the programs use different strategies to achieve these goals. This chapter provides an overview of two of these strategies, care management and case management.

CARE AND CASE MANAGEMENT: WHY NOW?

It is difficult to deliver quality care that is cost-effective, especially in light of the nursing shortage, an aging population, prospective payment systems, and managed competition; case management and care management can provide the appropriate structure. The Centers for Medicare and Medicaid Services (CMS) and accrediting bodies like the Joint Commission for the Accreditation of Healthcare Organizations (JCAHO) have recently mandated aspects of both care- and case-management programs; employer and purchaser groups and empowered consumers are also demanding programs to improve care and enhance clinical outcomes.

171

Effective management of clinical and financial outcomes is challenging, and programs that focus primarily on costs often alienate clinical staff. Health care systems are realizing the cost benefit of providing efficient, quality *clinical* management, and care management is an important strategy to examine systematically and refine clinical management. In fact, a paradox of care management is its use of standardized protocols or pathways to deliver individualized care and maintain the "art" of nursing and medicine. Successful organizations use care management programs to return the focus to individualized patient care, so that the best treatment choices are made for the right patient, in the right setting, at the right time. These organizations then extrapolate this information to study outcomes for larger populations of patients. Although management usually initiates these programs, engaging physicians and other clinicians to lead the change is essential to *any* clinical success.

CASE MANAGEMENT VERSUS CARE MANAGEMENT

Case Management

Case management started in public health in the 1860s (Kersbergen, 1996). Originally community-based, it has been recently adopted for use in hospitals to improve the quality and cost of care. To be successful, case management models must take into account the location of care (e.g., hospital, community) and the role of the case manager (e.g., patient advocate, coordinator of care) (Bedell, Cohen, & Sullivan, 2000; Lamb, 1992: Long & Marshall, 2000).

The role of case managers varies across institutions and settings (e.g., ambulatory) and may include a wide range of activities. Some of the most typical case management skills include case-finding and screening of high-risk patients, conducting comprehensive assessments, coordinating services, accessing community resources, and integrating patient and family resources (Bowers, 1992).

The many roles and competing priorities of case managers has caused confusion about their primary function. One role, that of discharge planner, is discussed in chapter 18. In some hospitals, case managers facilitate the plan of care (Silverstein, 1998), while in other institutions case managers are significantly involved with utilization review. Utilization reviewers monitor the clinical appropriateness and efficiency of inpatient care, using approved criteria. This necessitates communicating clinical and financial information to payers, physicians, and other clinicians and facilitating the resolution of system problems that result in payment denials.

Care Management

Although often used interchangeably, case management and care management are different concepts (Powell, 2000). Care management uses carefully developed algorithms to promote quality outcomes for all patients with a specific diagnosis or procedure. It addresses the overall process of care, relating patient treatment decisions to clinical and financial outcomes in order to manage care, improve outcomes, and improve operating efficiency (Brailer, 2001a; Newell, 1996). Care management focuses not on individual cases but on patient populations with similar diagnoses. The goal is to improve care for the majority of patients and decrease costs at the same time. Newell (1996) clearly delineates the distinctions between care- and case-management processes (See Table 15.1). Care management presumes that the majority of patients undergoing similar procedures or sharing similar diagnoses will have common treatment needs and will fit into a particular pattern or process (i.e., standard protocol, treatment algorithm, critical pathway). Higher-risk patients with unique characteristics and problems who do not "fit" the care management process may become candidates for case management in order to meet their individualized needs.

A key element of care management is the development and use of documentation systems that gather real-time clinical data (e.g., variance tracking systems) to study the impact that recommended interventions, and variance from them, have on clinical outcomes for the specific population of patients. Care management strategies most often rely on biological measures or clinical outcomes (i.e., lower mortality, fewer complications, improved laboratory findings; or reduced length of stay, fewer delays, etc.), as defined by health care providers. This focus is distinct from case management, which tends to focus on a patient's functional status and perception of well-being (Newell, 1996). Variances are also used to help identify the most effective and efficient methods to manage a specific patient population and to update guidelines as necessary. Data describing what is happening—both planned and unplanned events—provide the necessary information to drive improvements in the content and sequence of care management activities.

CARE MANAGEMENT TOOLS

Because the caregivers and disciplines fail to communicate, patients often may receive care that is fragmented, redundant, and costly. Care management systems provide continuity and foster cost reduction by establishing condition-specific schema or maps to facilitate a smooth transition through the health care system. Care management links the efforts of multiple

TABLE 15.1   Comparing Care and Case Management

Care Management	Case Management
Standardized processes for certain populations or diagnoses	Modified treatment plans to meet individual needs
Focused on diagnosis/process	Focused on patient/family
All patients eligible	Targets probable outliers
Clinician driven	Assists physicians and nurses
Uses documentation systems to track variances	Documentation system is focused on the individual patient needs
Outcomes measured by improvements in clinical indicators	Outcomes measured by improvement in functional status and perception of well-being
Needs information system and finance support	Needs information system and finance support

Note: From *Using Nursing Case Management to Improve Health Outcomes* (p. 180), by M. Newell, 1996, Gaithersburg, MD: Aspen. © by Aspen. Adapted with permission.

clinicians to orchestrate the clinical care of low- and moderate-risk patients with similar conditions. Common examples of care management tools include multidisciplinary guidelines and protocols for organ transplantation, rehabilitation, and chronic-disease-management programs (Michaels & Cohen, 2001). In actuality, most patients need some sort of care management, whereas only high-risk patients and outliers require individual case management (Rossi, 1999).

Determining exactly who in a hospital is responsible for managing and monitoring the care of specific diagnoses or populations is often difficult because of the many people and disciplines involved in providing clinical care. Hospitalists and other physicians play an important care-management role and frequently use condition-specific guidelines, pathways, and order sets when caring for patients. Nursing professionals may also use care management processes such as population- or diagnosis-specific guidelines and tools to monitor patient progress throughout the health system. Physicians and nurses also participate in quality improvement programs and projects. Usually nurses perform care management roles such as outcomes managers, clinical resource managers, clinical care coordinators, quality analysts, and advanced practice nurses. Unlike the roles and responsibilities of case managers, which tend to focus on individual patients and are usually well defined, care management roles and responsibilities relate to patient populations and are seldom clear. This lack of clarity often results in a blurring of care- and case-management activities. Physicians and nurses must understand that care managers play an important role on the patient care team, by communicating what care is needed for the majority of patients, providing the support systems to care for patients, and tracking clinical data to support decisions related to appropriate care interventions.

The objective of any care management program is to provide effective, efficient care to low- and moderate-risk patients in accordance with best practice information. Extending the process beyond the hospital setting may actually prevent some hospitalizations and reduce hospital readmissions. Michaels and Cohen (2001) describe three important tenets of a seamless, effective, interdisciplinary care management system. Care management

- must be *multidisciplinary* and establish clinical connections among services and programs across the continuum of care;
- uses approaches rooted in *best practice* for similar patient populations to serve as a template to address the typical needs of a defined population;
- *streamlines* the mechanics of health services, allowing care providers to spend more time with their patients.

A number of strategies used by health care systems to improve patient care are built around the common foundation of evidence-based practice and provision of feedback to clinicians involved with patients' care. Concrete examples of these strategies include call centers, clinical protocols, standardized orders, computer physician order entry, and education.

Call Centers

Medical call centers provide 24-hour information to patients in an effort to decrease unnecessary clinic and emergency room visits (Kastens, 1998). At first, call centers were outgrowths of emergency departments, where nurses used detailed protocols to address a patient's question. These protocols initiated follow-up clinic appointments or referral to an emergency department (Loeppke & Howell, 1999). Insurance companies have adapted call centers, or tele-health, for their disease management programs, initiating proactive calls to patients to monitor their illness and prevent additional outpatient or inpatient hospital visits. Physicians have expanded the use of call centers to provide information on a wider range of services such as smoking cessation programs.

The technological advances of the last decade, including the Internet, have enabled the storage and transfer of large amounts of detailed information necessary to medical call centers. When the appropriate technological systems are in place, patients can send detailed information such as vital signs, weights, and cardiac monitoring readings electronically to health centers. Information-technology support is critical to the ongoing success of these centers, because providers must have electronic access to individual patient information in order to offer appropriate advice and referrals (Kastens, 1998).

Clinical Protocols, Pathways, and Guidelines

Clinical protocols, pathways, and guidelines all describe patient-care algorithms, or paths, that outline the care of patients with specific diseases, conditions, or procedures. They are used in approximately 60% of U.S. hospitals and are often coupled with standardized order sets (Giffin & Giffin, 1994). Pathways, guidelines, or protocols can reduce variability and cost, increase efficiency with better communication between disciplines and departments, and ultimately improve patient care by decreasing the complication rate and improving patient satisfaction (Giffin & Giffin, 1994).

Usually a dedicated multidisciplinary committee develops clinical pathways, guidelines, or protocols in each institution. The multidisciplinary committee should complete the following steps:

1. benchmarking of best practice
2. analysis of national and local standards
3. comprehensive literature review (Forkner, 1999)

The committee can write these documents from scratch or can customize publicly available standard pathways. Standard pathways or guidelines are available from many professional organizations, from specialized web sites, and in books dedicated to the topic, which contain comprehensive collections (see Recommended Web Sites and Resources at end of chapter). However developed, they should be user-friendly, current, and reflect any change in standards (Forkner, 1996). Figure 15.1 is an example of a pathway.

Once completed, these documents are monitored to ensure that patients receive the predetermined standards of care. Some institutions elect to use them as documentation tools, where all providers can record care within the pathway or guideline and describe the patient's progress. Such tools can serve both educational and monitoring functions.

For example, a hospital may expect that patients admitted with a diagnosis of acute myocardial infarction (AMI) receive aspirin within 24 hours of admission. If a patient does not have either a record of receiving aspirin or an explanation of why the patient's care varied, then the care manager is alerted to resolve the issue. Monitoring can be done manually or via electronic alerts (depending on the sophistication of the hospital's

DIAGNOSIS: Femoral Popliteal Bypass Surgery

DRG: 478-479

(Printed with Permission, St. Luke's Episcopal, Houston, Texas)

Addressograph

Discharge Date: _____

History of: _____
Previous Vascular Surgery

DATE	Pre-Admit	Operative Day 0-4 hrs.	Operative Day 4-12 hrs.	Operative Day 12-24 hrs.	Day +1	Day +2	Day +3	Day +4
LOCATION	6 Tower Outpatient	CV Recovery	CV Recovery	CV Acute Care/Stepdown	CV Acute Care	CV Acute Care	CV Acute Care	CV Acute Care
CONSULTS	CV Surgery CV Anesthesia	Respiratory Care			Nutrition Consider PT	Care Coordinator (Social Worker & Home Care, if needed)		
DIAGNOSTIC	CBC, Chem 20 UA, PT/PTT, PTS CXR, ECG Duplex/ABI Arteriogram	ABGs, Hgb, Na, K+ on admission - glucose if diabetic			Hgb, Na, K+, and glucose if diabetic o	o			Hgb, K+ if needed o
TREATMENTS	Fleets enema hs Pre-op medications as ordered.	Wean mechanical ventilation according to protocol - extubate. IV Fluids Epidural protocol, if used.	IS every 1-2 hrs WA O₂ NC ___ L	IS every 1-2 hrs WA O₂ NC ___ L Consider telemetry DC art line, SPO₂	Remove Epidural, if used O₂ NC prn Saline lock IV when tolerated po fluids. Resume po meds DC telemetry if stable rhythm			
INTERVENTIONS	Soap / H₂O bath / shower hs. IS ___	Continuous monitoring art line, ECG, SPO₂. Vital signs per ICU routine. Pulse check w/Doppler with vital signs.	Pulse checks with Doppler every one hour.	Vital signs per routine. Pulse checks with Doppler every one hour. +	Pulse checks every 4 hours (with Doppler, if necessary) Change dressing	Pulse checks every shift (with Doppler, if necessary) Shower		+
ACTIVITY	Up ad lib	Bed rest	Progress activity as ordered / tolerated.	+	+	+		
NUTRITION	NPO after midnight. Meds with sips of H₂O as ordered by CV Anesthesia.	NPO	Ice chips after extubation - progress as tolerated to ordered diet					
TEACHING	Pre-op instruction by nursing staff IS instruction.	Orient patient/family to ICU, pain control, weaning process & safety measures.	Reinforce IS instruction, pain control.		DC instruction regarding medication, wound care, signs & symptoms of infection, early identification of graft failure.			Reinforce D/C instructions. Follow-up doctor appointment. Follow-up Duplex appointment (6 weeks). +
DRG SPECIFIC INFORMATION	PTS may be drawn up to 7 days before surgery.							

DATE OF LAST REVISION: December 14, 2001   Please return to Jackie Anderson, Outcomes Manager, Mail Code 4-278 when patient is discharged.

stdsrv/critical pathways/fem-pop.cp

FIGURE 15.1   Example of a pathway.

information-systems technology). Monitoring variances from set standards in real time allows care managers to intervene quickly in order to prevent a negative outcome. In this example, real-time monitoring would alert the team to the discrepancy and enable the patient to receive aspirin and benefit from its effects.

Variations in outcomes are expected in clinical health care and should be clearly documented in the patient record. In instances where variance from an expected outcome has become a question of liability, pathways, coupled with appropriate documentation in the patient record, have been beneficial to all providers. Variations from pathways should be monitored and evaluated by the performance improvement department and by the pathway committees and fed back to the clinical team to review performance and determine additional strategies for improvement (Hill, 1999).

Physician Orders

Standardized Physician Orders

Standardized physician (or provider) orders are usually developed by individual institutions to ensure that specific medications or interventions are ordered in specific clinical situations. Examples include orders as simple as vital signs every 15 minutes for an hour postprocedure, or as complicated as a chemotherapy protocol that incorporates multiple medication, laboratory, and vital-sign monitoring orders. These orders are either available on preprinted forms or as a special link in a computerized physician-order-entry system. Like clinical pathways, standardized orders must be reviewed and updated regularly to reflect changes in standards of practice.

Computer Physician Order Entry

Computer physician order entry (CPOE) systems are electronic prescribing systems that have been shown to reduce medication errors and can be used in inpatient and outpatient settings (Sittig & Kuperman, 1998). They not only ensure that the orders are legible, standardized, and complete, but can also be integrated with patient information such as allergies, laboratory, and other prescription data to alert providers to the possibility of drug interaction, allergy, or overdose (Kaushal & Bates, 2001). Other benefits associated with CPOE include specific information that eliminates confusion for drug names that sound alike, improved communication between clinicians and pharmacies, and reduced health care costs from improved efficiency. The Leapfrog Group for Patient Safety, "a voluntary program aimed at mobilizing large purchasers to alert the healthcare industry that big leaps in patient safety and customer value will be recognized and rewarded with preferential use and other intensified market reinforcements" (see

Recommended Web Sites and Resources) has endorsed CPOE systems as one strategy for reducing medical errors. The Institute of Medicine (1999) supports CPOE as well, and the state of California has passed legislation that requires hospitals as a condition of licensure to implement technology such as CPOE to reduce errors.

For all of their benefits, CPOEs also have a downside. They are cumbersome—it can take physicians up to three times longer to enter orders (Chin, 2001). They are also expensive, with costs in excess of $1 million, and the Leapfrog group reports that currently fewer than 2% of U.S. hospitals use them.

Education

Education and feedback are absolutely essential to any successful improvement strategy. Providers must learn new and best practices that are applicable to established pathways, standard orders, computer systems, and hospital policies. No matter how well designed, the effectiveness of a plan of care depends upon successful integration into current care processes. In addition to education, clinicians require feedback to keep them informed about their performance and how it compares to their peers and to their institution as a whole. Profiling of this type can be positive; clinicians can discover that they contributed to better outcomes and learn what they can do to improve personal performance.

MEASURING SUCCESS

A detailed analysis of the cost-effectiveness of care- and case-management programs is beyond the scope of this chapter. Nonetheless, it is worth discussing some of the factors that have been evaluated within care- and case-management models. Although case management tends to focus on high-risk outlier patients and care management focuses on clinical populations, both programs share the challenge of measuring their success in terms of clinical and financial outcomes. Despite the primary aim of providing quality care, any program must also be evaluated in terms of its cost-effectiveness. Measuring the success of these programs requires quantification of any or all of the following items:

- What are appropriate outcomes? What is the benchmark to strive for?
- Have we met the benchmark? Have clinical outcomes improved?
- Have clinical outcomes improved within an acceptable time?
- If outcomes improved, have they been sustainable over time?
- Have the improvements lead to a decreased cost burden?

FUTURE TRENDS

The technological advances that have occurred in other industries are slowly being incorporated into health care, as demand for information grows for practitioners and consumers. Care managers and management organizations will take advantage of this technology to help guide treatment decisions through the provision of improved and easily accessible information and by directing patients to care providers.

Evidence-Based Practice

There is a growing demand that evidence-based practice be built into standard pathways, guidelines, indicators, protocols, and order sets. Many clinicians have balked against a controlled pathway, protesting that they are being told what to do. Clinicians are far more receptive to interventions reported in the literature or generated from sound data analyses, however. Evidence-based protocols and guidelines are becoming more common, and the era of tightly controlled pathways is coming to a close.

Technology

The expanded use and accessibility of technology hold great potential to shape care management and other quality initiatives. Any mechanism that automates manual processes to facilitate communication and bring disparate pieces of information together will help to streamline work flow, prevent errors, and improve clinical and financial outcomes within the health care setting. The scope of technology and its influence are discussed in chapter 7.

PDAs

Personal digital assistants are now commonplace in the hospital—some academic institutions even give them to their interns as part of their orientation. PDAs can hold volumes of information, such as an entire *Physician's Desk Reference*, standard guides to medical practice, and downloaded information from the Internet. They help streamline workflow as well, maintaining "to do" lists that can be easily transferred to a covering physician's PDA, and can hold files of necessary information literally "in the palm" of the user's hand.

Electronic Medical Record

The electronic medical record (EMR) has met with some resistance from providers (Institute for the Future [IFTF], 1997). The combination of more computer-savvy physicians, friendlier user interfaces, and more sophisticated decision support systems should facilitate widespread adoption of the EMR within the next 10 years (IFTF, 1997).

Internet

Physician use of the Internet is also growing rapidly, as it provides quick and easy access to medical information affecting the physician-patient relationship. Some physicians correspond with patients via e-mail. Others utilize its technologic capabilities to facilitate outpatient monitoring—patients can send electronic information including vital signs, electrocardiogram tracings, and even daily weight directly to a physician's office. Community data exchanges allow physicians to interact directly with disparate facilities, such as independent laboratories, pharmacies, and other clinical sites, to compile recent patient information related to test results, ordered medications, and recent physician visits and hospitalizations (Brailer, 2001b).

HIPAA

Better access to disparate pieces of patient information has led to a growing concern for patient privacy. The Health Insurance and Portability and Accountability Act of 1996 (HIPAA) set federal privacy standards for identifiable health information and gives patients greater access to their own medical records and more control over how their personal health information is used. HIPAA has set standards for the security of the exchange of health information, and hospitals and other health care institutions have appointed compliance officers to ensure that the regulations are implemented correctly (see Recommended Web Sites).

CONCLUSION

Like all change, the adaptation of new technology, and of care management in general, will be a slow process. Perhaps because the nature of health care work revolves around people's lives, or perhaps because caring for patients combines science with art, change of this nature has traditionally been greeted somewhat skeptically within the health care environment. The ultimate goal of all of the strategies and trends discussed is to take better care of patients, and they will be adapted over time, when those involved in the day-to-day care of patients appreciate the value of these management tools.

The authors wish to acknowledge the contribution of Robin Bryant, BSN, RN, to the development of this chapter.

REFERENCES

Bedell, J. R., Cohen, N. L., & Sullivan, A. (2000). Case management: The current best practices and the next generation of innovation. *Community Mental Health Journal, 36,* 179–194.

Bowers, K. A. (1992). *Case management by nurses.* Washington, DC: American Nurses' Publishing.

Brailer, D. J. (2001a, November). Care-based management of cost. *Health Management Technology,* p. 60.

Brailer, D. J. (2001b, August). Connection tops collection. *Health Management Technology,* pp. 28–29.

Chin, T. (2001). Power steering: A push toward technology. *American Medical News, 44*(12). [On-line]. Available: www.ama-assn.org/sci-pubs/amnews/ pick_01/tesa0326.htm (March 26, 2001).

Forkner, D. J. (1996). Clinical pathways: Benefits and liabilities. *Nursing Management, 27*(11), 35–38.

Giffin, M., & Giffin, R. B. (1994). Critical pathways produce tangible results. *Health Care Strategic Management, 12*(7), 1, 17–23.

Hill, M. (1999). Outcomes measurement requires nursing to shift to outcome-based practice. *Nursing Administration Quarterly, 24*(1), 1–16.

Institute for the Future. (1997). *Health and healthcare 2010: The forecast the challenge.* [On-line]. Available: www.iftf.org/html/researchareas/private-work/healthcare_publicsector.html

Institute of Medicine. (1999). *To err is human: Building a safer health system.* L. T. Kohn, J. M. Corrigan, & M. S. Donaldson (Eds.). Washington, DC: National Academy Press.

Kastens, J. M. (1998). Integrated care management: Aligning medical call centers and nurse triage services. *Nursing Economics, 16,* 320–322, 329.

Kaushal, R., & Bates, D. W. (2001). Computerized physician order entry (CPOE) with clinical decision support systems(CDSSs). In A. J. Markowitz (Ed.), *Making health care safer: A critical analysis of patient safety practices.* San Francisco and Palo Alto, CA: Agency for Healthcare Policy and Research. www.ahrq.gov/clinic/ptsafety/chap6.htm

Kersbergen, A. L. (1996). Case management: A rich history of coordinating care to control costs. *Nursing Outlook, 44,* 169–172.

Lamb, G. S. (1992). Conceptual and methodological issues in nurse case management research. *Advances in Nursing Science, 15*(2), 16–24.

Loeppke, R., & Howell, J. W. (1999). Integrating clinical performance improvement across physician organizations: The PhyCor experience. *Joint Commission Journal on Quality Improvement, 25*(2), 55–67.

Long, M. J., & Marshall, B. S. (2000). What price an additional day of life? A cost-effectiveness study of case management. *American Journal of Managed Care, 6,* 881–886.

Michaels, C., & Cohen, E. (2001). Two strategies for managing care. In E. Cohen & T. Cesta (Eds.), *Nursing case management: From essentials to advanced practice applications* (pp. 31–35). St. Louis, MO: Mosby.

Newell, M. (1996). *Using nursing case management to improve health outcomes.* Gaithersburg, MD: Aspen.

Powell, S. K. (2000). *Case management: A practical guide to success in managed care.* Philadelphia: Lippincott.

Rossi, P. (1999). *Case management in health care: A practical guide.* Philadelphia: W. B. Saunders.

Silverstein, W. (1998). Care management: The right balance of care and management? *Nursing Administration Quarterly, 22*(4), 66–75.

Sittig, D. F., & Kuperman, G. J. (1998). Computer-based physician order entry system reduces medication errors. *Informatics-Review, 2*(1), 1.

RECOMMENDED WEB SITES AND RESOURCES

Web Sites:

www.aapmr.org/memphys/pracguid/clinpath.htm
www.pedsccm.wustl.edu/CLINICAL/pathways.html
www.leapfroggroup.org/about.htm
www.hhs.gov.ocr/hipaa

Books:

Birdsall, C., & Sperry, S. P. (1997). *Clinical Paths in Medical-Surgical Practice.* St. Louis, MO: Mosby.

Di Lima, S. N. (Ed.). Aspen Reference Group & S. Niemeyer (Ed.). (1997). *Chronic Disease Management: Clinical Pathways and Guidelines.* Gaithersburg, MD: Aspen.

Guinane, C. S. (1997). *Clinical Care Pathways: Tools and Methods for Designing, Implementing, and Analyzing Efficient Care Practices.* New York: McGraw-Hill.

Marcus, J. (Ed.). (1998). *Clinical Pathways for Medical Rehabilitation.* Gaithersburg, MD: Aspen.

Poirrier, G. P., & Oberleitner, M. G. (1999). *Clinical Pathways in Nursing: A Guide to Managing Care from Hospital to Home.* Springhouse, PA: Springhouse.

Cohen, E., & Cesta, T. (2001). *Nursing Case Management: From Essentials to Advanced Practice Applications* (3rd ed.). St. Louis, MO: Mosby.

Powell, S. (2000). *Case Management: A Practical Guide to Success in Managed Care.* Baltimore: Lippincott.

Part III
Facilitating Continuity
of Care

■ 16
Hospitalists

Saeid Mirafzali

Physicians whose main focus is inpatient care are a recent addition to the United States health care system. Although these hospital-based specialists have been part of the health care norm in Europe and Canada and a limited number of U.S. institutions in the 1980s and 1990s, the term "hospitalist" formally appeared in 1996, replacing such titles as house doctor, hospital rounder, and inpatient rounder (Goldmann, 1999; Wachter, 1999). The National Association of Inpatient Physicians (NAIP) defines a hospitalist as "a doctor whose primary professional focus is the general medical care of hospitalized patients. Their activities include patient care, teaching, research and leadership related to hospital care" (NAIP, 2000).

Many economic forces have precipitated the need for hospitalists. Personal health care expenditures increased an average of 10.4% annually in the 1980s (Letsch, 1993), largely as a result of hospital and physician services. With the introduction of Medicare's prospective payment system (PPS) by the Health Care Financing Administration (HCFA, now the Center for Medicare and Medicaid Services, or CMS) in 1983 and increased market penetration of managed care capitation plans in the 1990s, it actually became more profitable (or less costly) for hospitals to limit the inappropriate use of services and to deliver care more efficiently (see chapter 2). In addition, managed care companies created incentives for physicians to manage more of their patients' needs in the less costly outpatient setting.

This shift of emphasis to outpatient management encouraged physicians to reserve hospitalization for their sickest patients. Rates of hospitalization declined from 168 per 1,000 population in 1980 to 116 per 1,000 population in 1999 (Popovic & Hall, 2001). According to the AMA, the mean number of hospital-patient visits a physician conducts per week dropped from 22 in 1985 to 9.6 in 1996 (Chesanow, 1998), making it economically inefficient for many physicians to interrupt a busy office practice to manage a few complex and often time-consuming hospitalized patients. In addition, the difficulty of maintaining the necessary skills and knowledge base to manage today's inpatients and the added pressure on physicians by hospitals and managed care companies to decrease length of stay and resource utilization while improving quality of care have created further disincentives for office-based physicians to care for inpatients.

As a result, primary care providers, hospitals, and insurance plans are recognizing the utility of hospitalists. In 1999, the NAIP estimated that there were between 1,000 and 2,000 practicing hospitalists in the United States; these numbers are rapidly increasing (Lurie, Miller, Lindenauer, Wachter, & Sox, 1999). Some studies project that the number of American hospitalists will reach 19,000 in the future (Lurie et al., 1999). In the major medical journals, 10% of advertisements for internists are seeking hospitalists (Wachter & Goldman, 1999).

HOSPITALIST CHARACTERISTICS AND ROLES

The role of hospitalists is evolving. In 1997, a survey of 372 NAIP members was conducted to determine the characteristics and roles of hospitalists at that time. Some of these data are summarized in Table 16.1. Eighty-nine percent of the hospitalists surveyed had training in internal medicine. Of those, a majority (51.4%) were general internists while 37.6% were subspecialists, most commonly pulmonary and critical care. Family practice and pediatrics were the other most common specialties. The survey also delineated the clinical and nonclinical responsibilities of hospitalists at that time. Hospitalists serve as physicians of record and consultants on general medical wards, care for patients in intensive care units, perform preoperative evaluations, and play major roles in quality assurance, utilization review, and practice guideline development (Lindenauer, Pantilat, Katz, & Wachter, 1999).

The survey illustrates the great variety of clinical challenges a hospitalist may face; it also indicates the relevance of further training in management, health services delivery, and administration. The opportunities for hospitalists in both the clinical and nonclinical arenas, however, extend beyond what is captured in current surveys or definitions.

Clinical Responsibilities

Hospitalists are likely to see patients from a wide variety of backgrounds. A common misconception is that hospitalists only follow patients who are formally "handed off" by a primary care provider (PCP). This by no means reflects the scope of patients that many hospitalists care for. In addition to

TABLE 16.1   Hospitalist Training and Responsibilities

Training	
Internal medicine	89.0%
Generalist	51.4%
Specialist	37.6%
Critical care	7.2%
Pulmonary medicine	3.3%
Pulmonary medicine and critical care	7.2%
Infectious disease	3.3%
Family medicine	5.5%
Other	7.4%
Inpatient clinical responsibilities	
Medical ward	94.9%
Medical consultations	90.6%
Intensive care unit	83.1%
Preoperative evaluations	82.3%
Coordination of patient transfers	64.3%
Admission triage for emergency department	50.3%
Skilled nursing facility	45.7%
Supervision of nonmedical patients	43.8%
Other clinical responsibilities	
Outpatient general medical practice	23.1%
Medical consultation service	21.2%
Outpatient subspecialty practice	13.7%
Subspecialty consultation practice	13.4%
Nonclinical responsibilities	
Quality assurance and utilization review	52.7%
Practice guideline development	46.2%
Hospital administration	23.0%
Development of medical information system	22.3%

Note: Data from "Hospitalists and the Practice of Inpatient Medicine," by P. K. Lindenauer et al., 1999, *Annals of Internal Medicine, 130*(Suppl. 4), pp. 343–349.

caring for handed-off patients, hospitalists are often asked to serve as the attending of record for patients whose PCPs don't have admitting privileges to the institution. In these cases, the patient is not officially handed off to the hospitalist, but rather, is admitted through the emergency department without the PCP's knowledge.

Another role of hospitalists who are employed by hospitals is care of the indigent, Medicaid-insured, and uninsured populations. It is well accepted that poverty, general socioeconomic hardship, and lack of insurance are all associated with higher rates of many acute and chronic health problems. It also results in many patients' failing to access the health system until late in the course of their illness. In my experience, these patients often present with poor medical follow-up and no identifiable PCP. As such, they tend to pose a special challenge to inpatient physicians, as they often present with more advanced stages of disease and greater numbers of comorbidities. The intensity of services and the complexity of discharge planning for these populations often require higher levels of collaboration with consultants and discharge planning personnel. In many institutions, these patients are commonly placed on academic or teaching services (as opposed to private services), and their care is managed primarily by residents. Because ward attendings usually serve only brief rotations, the level of attending involvement can be quite variable. Hospitalists, on the other hand, can provide more consistent care and attend to the special needs created by lack of ready access to the health care system.

Nonclinical Responsibilities

Collaboration between hospitals and physician groups has been hampered by cultural clashes and conflicting financial incentives, often making it difficult to establish sustainable and effective hospital-physician partnerships. The hospitalist can be in a unique position to bridge clinical and administrative gaps that might otherwise impede efficient and effective patient care.

A hospitalist's clinical background and experience in the daily inpatient operations of a particular facility make the hospitalist the ideal medical professional to participate formally in hospital management and governance activities and to collaborate on salient issues such as quality assurance/medical errors, discharge planning, and patient satisfaction. Unique daily frontline exposure to many of these issues can give an important medical perspective to committees and task forces. This perspective can help to tighten linkages between the medical group and hospitals and, potentially, enhance quality improvement and cost containment activities.

STAGES OF HOSPITAL CARE

To understand better the various scenarios likely to be encountered in the inpatient setting, Wachter (1999) has divided hospital care into four stages.

Stage I, the PCP stage, is the traditional stage where patients are cared for by their own primary care providers. This is likely the most common stage in many regions in the country and was more viable when hospitalized patients were generally not as ill and when costs and efficiency were not particularly salient issues. Its main advantage is inpatient-outpatient continuity.

Stage II, the hospital rotation stage, has members of a medical group providing inpatient medical coverage in a rotational basis, allowing other members of the group to care for patients in the office without interruption. The inpatient primary care physician is responsible for admissions, discharges, and all inpatient management issues for the whole medical group. This scenario may not allow PCPs to gain enough experience in inpatient care. In addition, PCPs may not be interested in working on hospital operational issues.

Stage III, the voluntary hospitalist stage, describes a voluntary collaboration between PCPs and hospitalists. The PCP chooses whether or not to use the hospitalist. In this stage, the hospitalist is available to patients throughout the hospital day and is actively involved in inpatient operational issues within the institution. As with any hospitalist system, the potential for information loss during handoffs is present.

Stage IV, the mandatory hospitalist stage, describes a system that has fully committed to the hospitalist paradigm, requiring all PCPs to hand off their patients to hospitalists for inpatient care. Again, the value of having a dedicated hospitalist will be present as in stage III. However, the incentives to cooperate fully with outpatient providers is somewhat diminished, because handoffs are mandatory. In addition, this stage frequently engenders political problems if not fully supported by medical staff.

It seems logical that stage III will be the model adopted by most facilities, as it is based on voluntary collaboration, making political battles less likely. Wachter (1999) emphasized that the term "stage" does not imply progression or development. Rather, each hospital/PCP collaboration must determine which stage is appropriate for its particular medical, financial, and political climate. Nonetheless, it is likely that changes in the health care climate discussed earlier in this chapter have provided important incentives to adopt stage III and stage IV arrangements.

DEBATE

As with almost any new movement, the advent of hospitalists has engendered significant debate (Wolpaw & Bailey, 1998). Some question whether hospitalists are the answer to the quality and economic concerns of hospitals and primary care physicians (Chesanow, 1998). A thorough review of pro and con arguments is beyond the scope of this chapter. Instead, I will devote the following discussion to two questions that I find particularly important: (a) Is efficiency achieved at the expense of quality? and (b) Does communication suffer?

Efficiency versus Quality?

Some argue that the need for hospitalists is driven by desire for cost-cutting and efficiency at the expense of quality and continuity of care (Hundley, 1998). Although it is true that some studies have shown that hospitalists do decrease utilization of inpatient resources (Diamond, Goldberg, & Janine, 1998; Freese, 1999; Hackner et al., 2001), this is not synonymous with a decrease in quality. In fact, some clinical studies (vide infra) suggest that lengths of stay for some medical conditions can be shortened on average without adversely affecting patient outcomes. Much of the skepticism is predicated on policies implemented by some managed care companies and supported by CMS Medicare+Choice plans, which require primary care physicians to transfer the acute care of their patients to hospitalists, all in the name of significant cost savings (Maguire, 1999; Shepherd, 1997; Smith, 1997; Wilson, 2000). Physician organizations, including the American College of Physicians-American Society of Internal Medicine (ACP-ASIM) and NAIP, do not support these mandatory hospitalist programs. Rather, they support a voluntary and collaborative working relationship between hospitalists and primary care physicians that facilitates quality and continuity of care (Maguire, 1999). It is unlikely that these types of relationships will prosper under a mandatory program.

According to an NAIP survey, approximately 14.3% of physicians who identified themselves as hospitalists were employed by a managed care organization. Only 23% of the physicians surveyed reported mandatory hospitalist programs in their communities. Furthermore, the report indicated that 35% of medical groups were working with hospitalists, making them the largest employer (Lindenauer et al., 1999). A 1998 survey indicated that 62% of PCPs in California's largest urban counties had hospitalists available to them. Primary physicians employed in a group/staff model HMO or who had more than 75% of patients covered by capitated commercial HMO or private insurance were more likely to be required to use hospitalist services. Eighty-five percent believed that hospitalists increased or did not change the overall quality of care (Fernandez et al., 2000). According to a board member of the American Academy of Family Physicians, 20% of their members use hospitalists. Those physicians actually cited economic reasons for using hospitalists, including improvement in their office revenues as they could devote more of their time to their office practices. They did not cite quality as being a problem with using hospitalists (Jackson, 2001).

Studies comparing the quality of hospitalist and nonhospitalist care are particularly difficult, as they would require controlling for bias from unmeasured patient and hospital characteristics. They would also require a clear definition of what is considered quality and its measures. Some have defined quality of care as "whether individuals can access the health structures and processes of care which they need and whether the care received is effective" (Campbell, 2000). Others have added that needed care is not simply related to the accessing health care or the underuse of health care services, but the misuse and overuse of health services as well (Chassin & Galvin, 1998). Sparing patients unnecessary tests, procedures, medications, or even days in the hospital can add to the quality of patient care, as patients are not subjected to the associated risks.

Published experiences with hospitalist systems thus far, although not conclusive and clearly not controlling for all sources of bias, indicate that hospitalists may improve quality along these lines. For example, Stein and colleagues compared care of pneumonia patients within an institution and found that average length of stay was one day shorter on the hospitalist service compared to the non-hospitalist services, without significant differences in mortality, intensive unit transfers, and 30 day readmissions (Stein, Hanson, Tammaro, Hanna, & Most, 1998). Davis and colleagues found that patients cared for by hospitalists had lower costs and shorter lengths of stay; differences were most noticeable for the sickest patients. Mortality and readmission rates were similar between those cared for by hospitalists and those receiving care by PCPs (Davis et al., 2000).

Hospitalist proponents believe that these differences result from the hospitalist's inpatient clinical experience. Volume-outcome studies investigating specialist care of patients with acute myocardial infarction, coronary artery bypass graft surgery, percutaneous coronary interventions, and HIV have all shown that physician experience with these particular diagnoses or procedures correlates positively with improved outcomes (Jollis, Anstrom, Stafford, & Mark, 1998; Kitahata et al., 1996; McGrath et al., 2000; Showstack, Rosenfeld, & Garnick, 1987). As primary care physicians are seeing fewer hospitalized patients, their inpatient skills will naturally diminish. It is becoming less likely that an individual practitioner will see any one condition requiring hospitalization more than three times per year (Falk & Miller, 1998).

Other practical reasons why the hospitalist model can improve quality of care include

- on-site availability to respond rapidly to changes in patient condition or to results of important tests
- greater familiarity with the inpatient system to expedite care
- frequent communication with patients and families
- frequent communication with nursing staff

Hospitalists can also be an invaluable resource for identifying barriers to quality as they are on the frontlines of patient care. They can collaborate more effectively with various departments in the hospital to improve overall institutional quality of care.

COMMUNICATION

Many have voiced concerns about the potential loss of information that occurs as a result of transfers of care to and from hospitalist physicians. This is the most pressing quality and medical-legal challenge facing hospitalists and primary care providers. In a 1999 national survey (Lindenauer et al., 1999), 80% of the inpatient physicians reported that communication suffered "occasionally," while 1% reported that communication suffered "regularly" during the handoff. Potential mistakes include:

- an incomplete history of past medical problems
- inaccurate medication lists or doses
- duplication of diagnostic tests
- neglecting advanced directives
- failure to communicate to the PCP the necessity of prompt follow-up
- failure to communicate inpatient test results and pending laboratory and pathology results
- failure of the hospitalist to send, or the PCP to receive, a complete discharge summary

Seamless continuity of care between the hospitalist and PCP cannot occur without a reliable communication system. At the least, providers should exchange information for every inpatient upon admission and discharge. Ideally, hospitalists should update PCPs about their patients throughout the hospitalization. PCPs should also be encouraged to make social visits and phone calls to their inpatients. The nature and the frequency of communication, however, will vary based on the practice styles of the hospitalist and PCP and patient expectations.

In addition, it is important to recognize that no single method of communication is likely to be appropriate for all phases of hospitalization. Most hospitalists use a combination of methods, which may include telephone calls, faxes, e-mails, beepers, traditional mail, and electronic medical records. For example, a telephone call followed by a fax of office notes and previous test results might be the best way to ensure an accurate and complete admission history and physical. An e-mail or faxed message might efficiently update the primary care physician on a patient's course during hospitalization. A telephone call followed by a discharge summary, which can be sent by e-mail, fax, or traditional mail, would ensure more effective information transfer upon discharge. Despite the rapid dissemination of more sophisticated information technology, some communication problems will persist. The ultimate goal should be to avoid critical information lapses that would adversely affect care.

CONCLUSION

Having well-trained, dedicated inpatient physicians who care for acutely ill hospitalized patients is not only logical but also valuable to patients, hospitals, and PCPs. The goals of improved efficiency, outcomes, and quality of care are only possible within a collaborative framework between hospitalists, PCPs, and all other individuals involved with inpatient care.

The extent to which hospitalists provide added quality or value to patient care is dependent upon the experience of the hospitalist and the needs of both the primary care physicians and their patients. Many PCPs find that hospitalists enhance their ability to manage their patient panels effectively and efficiently. Others believe they can do just as well without a hospitalist. Whatever the case, health care providers should move beyond the question of whether using hospitalists is "right" or "wrong." Health care providers should also question the commonly held assumption that improved efficiency often provided by hospitalists will be at the expense of quality. Instead, physicians and institutions should investigate ways that hospitalists can improve the delivery of care to their patients. Patient care should be a collaborative endeavor whose primary goal is providing quality care with the appropriate use of resources. The voluntary use of hospitalist services will encourage collaboration and communication and promote the highest quality of care for inpatients.

REFERENCES

Campbell, S. M. (2000). Defining quality of care. *Social Science and Medicine, 51,* 1611–1625.

Chassin, M. R., & Galvin, R. W. (1998). The urgent need to improve health care quality. *Journal of the American Medical Association, 280,* 1000–1005.

Chesanow, N. (1998). When hospitals take over . . . Who wins? Who loses? *Medical Economics, 75,* 100–109.

Davis, K. M., Koch, K. E., Harvey, J. K., Wilson, R., Englert, J., & Gerard, P. D. (2000). Effects of hospitalists on cost, outcomes, and patient satisfaction in a rural health system. *American Journal of Medicine, 108,* 621–626.

Diamond, H. S., Goldberg, E., & Janine, E. (1998). The effect of full-time faculty hospitalists on the efficiency of care at a community teaching hospital. *Annals of Internal Medicine, 129,* 197–203.

Falk, C. T., & Miller, C. (1998). *Hospitalist programs: Towards a new practice of inpatient care.* Washington, DC: Advisory Board Company.

Fernandez, A., Grumbach, K., Goitein, L., Vranizan, K., Osmond, D. H., & Bindman, A. B. (2000). Friend or foe? How primary care physicians perceive hospitalists. *Archives of Internal Medicine, 160,* 2902–2908.

Freese, R. B. (1999). The Park Nicollet experience in establishing a hospitalist system. *Annals of Internal Medicine, 130*(Supplement 4), 350–354.

Goldmann, D. R. (1999). The hospitalist movement in the United States: What does it mean for internists? *Annals of Internal Medicine, 130*(Supplement 4), 326–327.

Hackner, D., Tu, G., Braunstein, G. D., Ault, M., Weingarten, S., & Mohsenifar, Z. (2001). The value of a hospitalist service. *Chest, 119,* 580–589.

Hundley, K. (1998, July 26). The inpatient physician. *St. Petersburg Times,* p. 1H.

Jackson, C. (2001, February 19). Doctors find hospitalists save time, money. *American Medical News* [On-line]. Available: www.ama-assn.org/sci-pubs/amnews/pick_01/bil20219.htm. Accessed 12/03/2001.

Jollis, J. G., Anstrom, K. J., Stafford, J. A., & Mark, D. B. (1998). Mortality following acute myocardial infarction according to physician experience, technical training, and specialty. *Journal of the American College of Cardiology, 31*(2) (Suppl. 1), 363A.

Kitahata, M. M., Koepsell, T. D., Deyo, R. A., Maxwell, C. L., Dodge, W. T., & Wagner, E. H. (1996). Physicians' experience with the acquired immunodeficiency syndrome as a factor in patients' survival. *New England Journal of Medicine, 333,* 701–706.

Letsch, S. W. (1993). National health care spending in 1991. *Health Affairs, 12*(1), 94–110.

Lindenauer, P. K., Pantilat, S. Z., Katz, P. P., & Wachter, R. M. (1999). Hospitalists and the practice of inpatient medicine: Results of a survey of the National Association of Inpatient Physicians. *Annals of Internal Medicine, 130*(Suppl. 4), 343–349.

Lurie, J. D., Miller, D. P., Lindenauer, P. K., Wachter, R. M., & Sox, H. C. (1999). The potential size of the hospitalist workforce in the United States. *American Journal of Medicine, 106,* 441–445.

Maguire, P. (1999, May). Use of mandatory hospitalists blasted. *ACP-ASIM Observer.* [On-line]. Available: www.acponline.org/journals/news/may99/hosps.htm. Accessed 01/17/02.

McGrath, P. D., Wennberg, D. E., Dickens, J. D., Jr., Siewers, A. E., Lee, L. F., Malenka, D. J., Kellett, M. A., Jr., & Ryan, T. J., Jr. (2000). Relation between operator and hospital volume and outcomes following percutaneous coronary interventions in the era of the coronary stent. *Journal of the American Medical Association, 284,* 3139–3144.

National Association of Inpatient Physicians. (2000). NAIP definition of a hospitalist. *Hospitalist, 4*(3), 4.

Popovic J. R., & Hall, M. J. (2001). 1999 National hospital discharge survey. *Advance Data, 319,* 1–18.

Shepherd, G. (1997, October 10). Humana "hospitalists" usher in a new era in medicine. *Business Journal of Tampa Bay.* [On-line]. Available: tampabay.bcentral.com/tampabay/stories/1997/10/13/story1.html. Accessed 12/03/02.

Showstack, J. A., Rosenfeld, K. E., & Garnick, D. W. (1987). Association of volume with outcome of coronary artery bypass graft surgery. Scheduled vs. nonscheduled operations. *Journal of the American Medical Association, 257,* 785–789.

Smith, B. (1997, March 7). "Hospitalists" challenge traditional care. *Denver Business Journal.* [On-line]. Available: denver.bcentral.com/denver/stories/1997/03/10/focus1.html. Accessed 12/03/01.

Stein, D. M., Hanson, S., Tammaro, D., Hanna, L., & Most, A. S. (1998). Economic effects of community versus hospital-based faculty pneumonia care. *Journal of General Internal Medicine, 13,* 774–777.

Wachter, R. M. (1999). An introduction to the hospitalist model. *Annals of Internal Medicine, 130* (Suppl. 4), 338–342.

Wachter, R. M., & Goldman, L. (1999). Implications of the hospitalist movement for academic departments of medicine: Lessons from the UCSF experience. *American Journal of Medicine, 106,* 127–133.

Wilson, C. B. (2000). Letter to HCFA on the use of hospitalists by Medicare+Choice organizations. [On-line]. Available: www.acponline.org/hpp/oplfinal.htm. Accessed 12/03/01.

Wolpaw, D. R., & Bailey, R. H. (1998). Old debate, new direction. *Journal of General Internal Medicine, 13,* 852–853.

■ 17
Easing the Transition Between Nursing Home and Hospital

Kenneth S. Boockvar and Maria Camargo

Movement through the health care system has become increasingly fragmented, as patients find themselves transferred to different levels of care within and between institutions. This is especially true for geriatric patients, who may be hospitalized for an acute medical problem, transferred to a nursing home for post-acute rehabilitation, and returned to the community to receive services from a home health program or to reside in an assisted-living facility. Along the way there is a good chance of readmission to the hospital. Although believed to be beneficial to the patient, each of these transitions causes discontinuity. Physicians, nurses, and environments change, disrupting care, jeopardizing patient health, and leading to patient dissatisfaction. Nowhere is the transition more strained than between hospital and nursing home.

RECENT TRENDS

Transfers between hospitals and nursing homes are common. Hospitals have a financial incentive to minimize the length of stay, and they achieve this in part by discharging increasing numbers of patients to nursing homes for post-acute care. Hospital discharges to nursing homes in the U.S. increased from 1.6 million in 1990 to 2.8 million in 1999, while the average hospital length of stay for these patients shortened from 12.8 to 8.1 days (Kozak, 2001). In 1997, 44% of patients admitted to nursing homes in the U.S. were transferred from the hospital (Gabrel & Jones, 2000), which is slightly higher than the proportion in 1995 (Dey, 1997).

Nursing home residents are also prone to hospitalization. Residents are disabled, have multiple medical conditions, and live in an environment that predisposes them to acute nosocomial illness and hospitalization. In national studies 25% to 49% of nursing home residents are hospitalized per year (Castle & Mor, 1996). In 1997, 28.3% of nursing home discharges were to the hospital, representing 40 hospitalizations per 100 nursing home beds (Gabrel & Jones, 2000), a large increase from 1985 (Barker et al., 1994). Although the total number of hospital transfers has increased, the individual risk of hospitalization during a nursing home stay has decreased. This may be due to shorter nursing home stays on average and to federal documentation requirements and staffing standards passed in 1987 as part of the Omnibus Budget Reconciliation Act (OBRA), which have resulted in improved quality of nursing home care (Mor et al., 1997).

REASONS FOR TRANSFER

Studies show that 37% to 59% of nursing home residents experience an acute illness episode each month, commonly urinary tract infection, lower respiratory tract infection, and congestive heart failure (Alessi & Harker, 1998; Boockvar & Lachs, in press; Boockvar & Lachs, 2001). Although any event can lead to hospitalization if sufficiently serious, conditions that are more likely to result in hospital transfer include lower respiratory infection and congestive heart failure (Barker et al., 1994; Bergman & Clarfield, 1991; Boockvar & Lachs, in press; Castle & Mor, 1996; Irvine, Van Buren, & Crossley, 1984; Murtaugh & Freiman, 1995), perhaps because both can precipitate respiratory failure, which nursing homes have limited capacity to address.

Not all acute illnesses in the nursing home result in hospital transfer. Many nursing homes provide on-site medical services that decrease the need for transfer of acutely ill residents to the hospital. These services include full-time physician or nurse practitioner coverage, rapid laboratory testing, intravenous therapies, and special care units. In national studies, the probability of hospitalization has been shown to be lower in facilities that provide these services (Castle & Mor, 1996; Intrator, Castle, & Mor, 1999; Teresi, Holmes, Bloom, Monaco, & Rosen, 1991). In such facilities, one half to two thirds of acute illnesses are treated in the nursing home, and approximately 38% to 50% result in hospitalization (Alessi & Harker, 1998; Boockvar & Lachs, 2001).

ECONOMIC PRESSURES

There are financial incentives and disincentives for nursing homes to transfer residents with acute illness to the hospital. Nursing homes charge and receive a daily payment for provision of skilled nursing and custodial care services, which are the most costly aspects of nursing home care. In general, when ill residents are in the hospital, payments to the nursing home cease, unless residents pay the nursing home to hold their beds or have a Medicaid benefit that pays for a bed-hold (up to 20 days in New York State). By caring for a resident with acute illness, a nursing home maintains occupancy and receives daily payments for the resident's bed.

Nevertheless, caring for acutely ill residents in the nursing home is more expensive than caring for residents without acute illness. Although rates of reimbursement to nursing homes are based on the historical costs of all aspects of care, the actual mechanics of payment generally do not account for acute illness. Nursing homes perform a multidisciplinary assessment of residents' needs on days 5, 14, 30, 60, and 90 of nursing home stay using a standardized instrument (the Minimum Data Set). Each assessment is used to determine the daily Medicare payment until the next assessment. Because an episode of acute illness can occur between the scheduled assessments, the nursing and medical cost (including medications and laboratory testing) of treating an individual episode of acute illness may be missed. Medicare reimburses up to 100 days of post-acute nursing home care and covers about 15% of the nation's nursing home residents at any given time (Gabrel & Jones, 2000). Medicaid covers the majority of those who stay in the nursing home longer than 100 days (Gabrel & Jones, 2000). Medicaid daily payments, which are smaller than Medicare's, also do not cover the medical and nursing cost of acute illness, although Medicaid, unlike Medicare, pays for medications according to use.

Because current financial incentives may not result in optimal use of nursing home- and hospital-based acute care services, alternative models for provision of acute care have been developed. The EverCare program, designed for nursing home residents, receives a capitated payment from Medicare to provide hospital and posthospital nursing home services to patients (Kane & Huck, 2000). Hospital care is much more costly than nursing home care; EverCare has a strong incentive to prevent hospitalization in the case of an acute illness. EverCare helps keep residents in the nursing home by supplying nurse practitioners to provide intensive primary care to enrollees within the nursing home, which has been shown in studies to reduce hospitalization (Ackermann & Kemle, 1998; Castle & Mor, 1996). Nursing homes have an incentive to participate in EverCare because they receive higher payments when residents with acute illness remain in the nursing home. Other Medicare managed-care programs (Reuben et al., 1999) also have incentives to avoid hospitalizations because of capitated contracts with government payers.

TIMING AND RISK FACTORS FOR HOSPITALIZATION

A resident's probability of being hospitalized is highest during the first 2 months of nursing home stay. After 3 to 4 months the risk of hospitalization plateaus at a lower rate (Boockvar & Lachs, 2001). In one study, risk factors for hospitalization in the first 3 months of nursing home stay were stroke, atrial fibrillation, depression, absence of dementia, and receipt of antibiotics (Boockvar & Lachs, 2001). Risk factors for hospitalization after the first 3 months include greater functional disability, older age, male gender, feeding tube, cardiovascular disease, and respiratory disease (Castle & Mor, 1996; Fried & Mor, 1997; Intrator et al., 1999; Murtaugh & Freiman, 1995). These studies suggest that medical condition and stability upon admission are more important predictors of acute illness and hospitalization in the first months of nursing home stay than is physical function, which plays a role later in the course of nursing home care. This may be because progressive medical conditions can directly precipitate acute illness (i.e., stroke can lead to aspiration pneumonia; atrial fibrillation to exacerbation of heart failure). In addition, receipt of antibiotics implies recent recovery from infection and may be a marker of clinical instability.

A number of studies have demonstrated an association between hospitalization and absence of dementia in nursing home residents (Boockvar & Lachs, 2001; Burton et al., 2001; Murtaugh & Freiman, 1995). Avoiding hospitalization may be more consistent with the plan of care for residents with acute illness who are demented than it is for nondemented residents. On the other hand, nondemented nursing home residents usually have significant disability that has resulted from complex medical conditions, which may predispose them to severe acute illness and hospitalization.

Depression has been shown to be a risk factor for short-term acute illness and hospitalization in nursing home residents, independent of comorbid conditions and physical and cognitive function (Barker et al., 1994; Boockvar & Lachs, 2001). The link between depression and mortality in community dwelling elders has been attributed to diminished adaptive skills, accelerated functional decline, and decreased psychosocial support (Covinsky, Fortinsky, Palmer, Kresevic, & Landefeld, 1997). These are not adequate to explain the link between depression and short-term risk of acute illness in nursing home residents. Instead, this relationship may be due to the adverse effects of psychological stress on immune function (Kiecolt-Glaser, Marucha, Malarkey, Mercado, & Glaser, 1995) or vascular flow (Gullette et al., 1997).

In one study, patients anticipated on admission to remain in the nursing home for 2 months or less (i.e., short-stay, rehabilitation residents) were more likely to be hospitalized than those anticipated to remain in the nursing home for long-term care, despite better physical function on admission

(Boockvar & Lachs, 2001). This may be because short-stay residents had less dementia, had more complex or unstable medical conditions, and had more aggressive care plans. In this study a "hospitalization prediction score" made up of five resident characteristics successfully divided residents into groups with widely varying risk of hospitalization within the first 8 weeks of nursing home stay (Boockvar & Lachs, 2001). Although this score has yet to be validated in an independent sample, the ability to identify which nursing home residents are at risk for hospitalization and when would enable development of targeted interventions to prevent acute illness and transfer to the hospital.

BENEFITS AND RISKS OF HOSPITALIZATION

For every nursing home resident, there is a trade-off between the benefits of hospitalization and the potential hazards. Hospitals can provide monitoring, diagnosis, and treatment services that are not available in the nursing home. These may be necessary for timely treatment of the acute condition, recovery of functional status, and prevention of mortality. The difference between nursing home and hospital services is often simply one of intensity. Hospitals offer round-the-clock diagnostic testing and monitoring, whereas nursing-home medical services are usually available only during the day. In addition, many nursing homes can provide intravenous therapy, which, if it is the only treatment required, allows the patient to remain in the nursing home. However, virtually all patients who require a diagnostic or therapeutic procedure need to be transferred to the hospital.

Unfortunately, iatrogenic complications from hospitalization are common and increase with increasing age (Thomas & Brennan, 2000) (see also chapter 8). Nursing home residents are particularly vulnerable to iatrogenic complications because of their medical complexity and physical frailty (Fortinsky, Covinsky, Palmer, & Landefeld, 1999). Inability to walk has been shown to be a risk factor for hospital complications (Lefevre et al., 1992), and age greater than 65 years has been shown to be a risk factor for developing disability from preventable adverse events in the hospital (Thomas & Brennan, 2000). Medication errors are a particular problem for hospitalized nursing home residents who are infrequently followed by their primary care physicians when in the hospital. Case reports and clinician testimony suggest that adverse drug effects (ADEs) occur upon interinstitutional transfer of residents at least in part due to poor communication of medication information (Libow, 1978). Because most nursing homes and hospitals are loosely affiliated and do not share medical records, medication ordering systems, formularies, or pharmacies, medication information may be transcribed by hand. Patients have been observed to incur injury from the inadvertent omission of a medication (Libow, 1978), inadvertent change in medication dosing, or prescription of a medication to which a patient has had a past adverse reaction. Transfer documents are also known to be incomplete. In one study of nursing home transfers to a hospital emergency room, 24% of transfer documents lacked medication information (Jones, Dwyer, White, & Firman, 1997). These studies suggest that nursing home residents with acute illness who can be safely managed in the nursing home might benefit from remaining in the nursing home without transfer to the hospital.

COMMUNICATION BETWEEN NURSING HOMES AND HOSPITALS

Coordination of care between hospital and nursing home providers is important for the well-being of nursing home residents, in particular to avoid duplication of work and mistakes in prescribing. Optimally, a single provider would follow the patient throughout the hospital and nursing home stays. In one study of community-dwelling older adults, 6 months of posthospital home follow-up by advanced practice nurses reduced the risk of rehospitalization (Naylor et al., 1999). It is likely that medical providers who follow their patients from nursing home to hospital confer similar benefit on their patients, although such studies have not yet been performed.

In the absence of a single provider, continuity of care depends on communication between providers in the nursing home and in the hospital. The plan for communication between hospital and nursing home at the time of resident transfer is almost always a transfer of paper documents that occurs with, or just following, the physical transfer of a resident. Transfer of medical information on paper consists of transcribing and gathering information at the site of resident origin, sending the documents (often physically with the patient, but sometimes faxed later), and placing the documents in the chart at the destination institution. If a resident's primary care provider is available in the nursing home at the time of transfer, the PCP will complete the nursing-home-to-hospital transfer documents. Otherwise, the nurse or other clinician covering the resident will do so. For hospital-to-nursing-home transfers, a nursing discharge form and a patient review instrument (PRI), completed by a nurse or social worker, constitutes the transfer documentation. Physicians also complete a hospital summary that may or may not accompany the patient.

The quality of transfer documentation depends on the completeness, accuracy, and legibility of information. Several authors have proposed standards for what type of information should be included in transfer documents (Conger & Snider, 1982; Jones et al., 1997; Madden, Garrett, & Busby-Whitehead, 1998; Tangalos & Freeman, 1988). Nursing home residents often have complex medical histories, long medication lists, physical and cognitive disability, and surrogate decision-makers, so most authors recommend including these classes of information, because each is crucial for care of an acutely ill patient. Specific items considered to be important are physician contact information, family contact information, clinical course, advance directives, history of adverse drug reactions, chronic conditions, vital signs, recent laboratory results, assistive devices, sensory function, cognitive function, and medications (Conger & Snider, 1982; Jones et al., 1997; Madden et al., 1998; Tangalos & Freeman, 1988).

One study (Jones et al., 1997) suggests that medical information such as medications and chronic and acute conditions is more reliably communicated than information on physical and cognitive disability. However, medication information is likely to be transcribed incorrectly at a measurable frequency because transfer forms are often completed hastily, by hand. Medication changes that occur solely on transfer forms (i.e., that do not match the current regimen as prescribed in the nursing home or hospital) are likely to be erroneous or inadvertent. Similarly, a study of continuity of advance directives revealed that hospital do-not-resuscitate (DNR) orders were continued in the nursing home for only 41% of patients discharged to nonhospital-affiliated facilities (Ghusn, Teasdale, & Jordan, 1997). The accuracy and legibility of advance directives and adverse drug reactions as documented on transfer forms have not been studied, but they are also crucial to the appropriate care of the hospitalized nursing home resident.

When transfer documents do not include all the information that a provider needs, other methods of interinstitutional communication should be employed, such as telephone communication between providers or sharing of electronic data. One exemplary system is the U.S. Veterans Administration Medical Center system, in which providers in the hospital and nursing home can look at the complete medical record from medical encounters anywhere in the system, because all records are carried electronically on a common server.

Patients frequently go back and forth between nursing homes and hospitals, so one might expect that strong affiliations would grow between neighboring institutions and that staff would travel between nursing homes and hospitals to ensure the optimal and continuous care of patients. Unfortunately, this is not the case because, except in special circumstances, there is no mechanism for payment for interinstitutional services. Efforts to improve the transfer process are important to the well being of patients, but are unlikely to be successful without payment mechanisms that are flexible to change.

QUALITY OF CARE UPON TRANSFER

Only recently have investigators and policy makers begun to study interinstitutional transfers and the quality of their planning and execution. One study of the appropriateness of hospital transfer suggests that a proportion of hospital transfers are unnecessary or inappropriate in light of the nursing home staff's ability to manage the acute condition and the added cost and risk of harm from hospital transfer (Saliba et al., 2000). Other investigators have begun to look at the quality of the transfer itself from the perspective of patient satisfaction, medical errors, and outcomes like hospital utilization and return to normal function (Ma, Coleman, Lin, & Kramer, 2001). These studies will help direct future research on interventions to improve the quality of care upon inter-institutional transfer. Even in the absence of proven interventions, there are practical approaches to improve the appropriateness of transfers and to optimize the likelihood of good outcomes from hospitalization. The following section contains suggestions for providers caring for nursing home residents who are transferred in and out of the hospital.

OPTIMIZING THE TRANSFER PROCESS: SUGGESTIONS FOR PROVIDERS

Nursing Home to Hospital

• Many decisions to transfer residents to a hospital depend on information conveyed to a physician by staff at the nursing home via a telephone call. Physicians should respond to calls from the nursing home promptly, and nurses should be able to give a report to the physician, including vital signs, without delay. If possible, physicians should speak directly with the nursing home resident over the phone to get additional information or should go to the nursing home to evaluate the resident.

• If stable, a resident with acute symptoms may be safely monitored and treated in the nursing home. This can be done on a trial basis, with hourly or daily follow-up checks.

• For residents who are transferred to the hospital, nursing home providers should complete transfer forms as thoroughly as possible. Information items essential to maintaining continuous care of the transferred resident include, but are not limited to nursing home physician contact information, family contact information, advance directives, medications and dosing, history of adverse drug reactions, chronic medical conditions, presenting signs and symptoms, vital signs, recent laboratory results, assistive devices, and cognitive and physical function.

• Nursing home providers should make efforts to contact the hospital providers by phone to communicate more detailed information. This can occur at many levels (i.e., between physicians, nurses, social workers, physical therapists, and others) at the two institutions. Nursing home providers, especially physicians and physician extenders, should visit residents in the hospital whenever possible. This allows nursing home providers (a) to obtain updates on the resident's hospital condition and (b) to give suggestions on the plan of care to the hospital providers.

• Those providing care for the resident in the hospital should make similar efforts to contact the nursing home providers when questions arise. In particular, when unable to obtain medical histories from aphasic or demented nursing home residents, hospital providers can obtain much-needed recent medical history by calling the nursing home.

Hospital to Nursing Home

• Hospital providers should try to anticipate the date of discharge back to the nursing home several days in advance and have this communicated to the admission office at the nursing home. In many cases the resident can be discharged well before complete resolution of the acute illness if the nursing home can provide appropriate medical monitoring and treatment. Because the hospital can be a hazardous place, early transfer back to the nursing home can benefit the resident.

• Hospital-to-nursing-home transfer documents should include hospital physician contact information, new advance directives, all medications with dosing and planned duration, new adverse drug reactions, new medical conditions, recent laboratory results, new assistive devices, and any changes in cognitive or physical function. In addition, the hospital clinician who knows the resident well should send a written summary of the hospital course with the resident, including diagnostic tests and treatments. Any instructions for treatments to continue in the nursing home and for medical follow-up must be specified in detail.

• Hospital providers should make an effort to contact the nursing home providers by phone at the time of transfer to communicate more detailed information. Again, this can occur at many levels of staffing (i.e., physicians, nurses, social workers, physical therapists, and others). Hospital providers could also contact the nursing home providers by phone several days after transfer to give updated suggestions on the plan of care to the nursing home providers.

• Nursing home providers should anticipate that residents will have increased monitoring and treatment needs when they return from the hospital. They should not assume that medications should be resumed exactly as they were prescribed before hospitalization. When medications on hospital-to-nursing-home transfer documents are significantly different from those the resident was receiving before hospitalization, nursing home providers should contact hospital providers by phone to clarify instructions for treatment (and follow-up) and to ascertain their rationale for making medication changes, especially omissions. If no rationale exists, it may be safe to resume previous therapies.

REFERENCES

Ackermann, R. J., & Kemle, K. A. (1998). The effect of a physician assistant on the hospitalization of nursing home residents. *Journal of the American Geriatrics Society, 46,* 610–614.

Alessi, C., & Harker, J. (1998). A prospective study of acute illness in the nursing home. *Aging Clinical and Experimental Research, 10,* 479–489.

Barker, W. H., Zimmer, J. G., Hall, W. J., Ruff, B. C., Freundlich, C. B., & Eggert, G. M. (1994). Rates, patterns, causes, and costs of hospitalization of nursing home residents: A population-based study. *American Journal of Public Health, 84,* 1615–1620.

Bergman, H., & Clarfield, A. M. (1991). Appropriateness of patient transfer from a nursing home to an acute-care hospital: A study of emergency room visits and hospital admissions. *Journal of the American Geriatrics Society, 39,* 1164–1168.

Boockvar, K. S., & Lachs, M. S. (2001). Measuring risk for inpatient hospitalization in newly admitted nursing home residents. *Journal of the American Geriatrics Society, 49*(4), S96.

Boockvar, K. S., & Lachs, M. S. (in press). Development of definitions for acute illness in nursing home residents based on chart-recorded physical exam findings. *Journal of the American Medical Directors Association.*

Burton, L. C., German, P. S., Gruber-Baldini, A. L., Hebel, J. R., Zimmerman, S., & Magaziner, J. (2001). Medical care for nursing home residents: Differences by dementia status. Epidemiology of Dementia in Nursing Homes Research Group. *Journal of the American Geriatrics Society, 49*(2), 142–147.

Castle, N. G., & Mor, V. (1996). Hospitalization of nursing home residents: A review of the literature, 1980–1995. *Medical Care Research Reviews, 53,* 123–148.

Conger, S. A., & Snider, L. F. (1982). Is there a gap in communication between acute care facilities and nursing homes? *Health and Social Work, 7,* 274–282.

Covinsky, K. E., Fortinsky, R. H., Palmer, R. M., Kresevic, D. M., & Landefeld, C. S. (1997). Relation between symptoms of depression and health status outcomes in acutely ill hospitalized older persons. *Annals of Internal Medicine, 126,* 417–425.

Dey, A. N. (1997). Characteristics of elderly nursing home residents: Data from the 1995 National Nursing Home survey. *Advances in Data, 289*(July 7), 1–8.

Fortinsky, R. H., Covinsky, K. E., Palmer, R. M., & Landefeld, C. S. (1999). Effects of functional status changes before and during hospitalization on nursing home admission of older adults. *Journals of Gerontology A: Biological Sciences and Medial Sciences, 54,* M521–526.

Fried, T. R., & Mor, V. (1997). Frailty and hospitalization of long-term stay nursing home residents. *Journal of the American Geriatrics Society, 45,* 265–269.

Gabrel, C. S., & Jones, A. (2000). The National Nursing Home survey: 1997 summary. *Vital and Health Statistics 13,* 1–121.

Ghusn, H. F., Teasdale, T. A., & Jordan, D. (1997). Continuity of do-not-resuscitate orders between hospital and nursing home settings. *Journal of the American Geriatrics Society, 45,* 465–469.

Gullette, E. C., Blumenthal, J. A., Babyak, M., Jiang, W., Waugh, R. A., Frid, D. J., O'Connor, C. M., Morris, J. J., & Krantz, D. S. (1997). Effects of mental stress on myocardial ischemia during daily life. *Journal of the American Medical Association, 277,* 1521–1526.

Intrator, O., Castle, N. G., & Mor, V. (1999). Facility characteristics associated with hospitalization of nursing home residents: Results of a national study. *Medical Care 37,* 228–237.

Irvine, P. W., Van Buren, N., & Crossley, K. (1984). Causes for hospitalization of nursing home residents: The role of infection. *Journal of the American Geriatrics Society, 32*(2), 103–107.

Jones, J. S., Dwyer, P. R., White, L. J., & Firman, R. (1997). Patient transfer from nursing home to emergency department: Outcomes and policy implications. *Academic Emergency Medicine, 4,* 908–915.

Kane, R. L., & Huck, S. (2000). The implementation of the EverCare demonstration project. *Journal of the American Geriatrics Society, 48,* 218–223.

Kiecolt-Glaser, J. K., Marucha, P. T., Malarkey, W. B., Mercado, A. M., & Glaser, R. (1995). Slowing of wound healing by psychological stress. *Lancet, 346,* 1194–1196.

Kozak, L. (2001). Hospital transfers to long-term care in the 1990s. Paper presented at national meeting of Health Services Research, Atlanta, GA.

Lefevre, F., Feinglass, J., Potts, S., Soglin, L., Yarnold, P., Martin, G. J., & Webster, J. R. (1992). Iatrogenic complications in high-risk, elderly patients. *Archives of Internal Medicine, 152,* 2074–2080.

Libow, L. S. (1978). Another type of iatrogenic problem. *Geriatrics, 33*(3), 92, 94, 99.

Ma, E., Coleman, E. A., Lin, M., & Kramer, A. M. (2001). An analysis of post-hospital care transitions in older patients. *Journal of the American Geriatrics Society, 49*(4), S35.

Madden, C., Garrett, J., & Busby-Whitehead, J. (1998). The interface between nursing homes and emergency departments: A community effort to improve transfer of information. *Academic Emergency Medicine, 5,* 1123–1126.

Mor, V., Intrator, O., Fries, B. E., Phillips, C., Teno, J., Hiris, J., Hawes, C., & Morris, J. (1997). Changes in hospitalization associated with introducing the resident assessment instrument. *Journal of the American Geriatrics Society, 45,* 1002–1010.

Murtaugh, C. M., & Freiman, M. P. (1995). Nursing home residents at risk of hospitalization and the characteristics of their hospital stays. *Gerontologist, 35*(1), 35–43.

Naylor, M. D., Brooten, D., Campbell, R., Jacobsen, B. S., Mezey, M. D., Pauly, M. V., & Schwartz, J. S. (1999). Comprehensive discharge planning and home follow-up of hospitalized elders: A randomized clinical trial. *Journal of the American Medical Association, 281,* 613–620.

Reuben, D. B., Schnelle, J. F., Buchanan, J. L., Kinton, R. S., Zellman, G. L., Farley, D. O., Hirsch, S. H., & Ouslander, J. G. (1999). Primary care of long-stay nursing home residents: Approaches of three health maintenance organizations. *Journal of the American Geriatrics Society, 47,* 131–138.

Saliba, D., Kington, R., Buchanan, J., Bell, R., Wang, M., Lee, M., Herbst, M., Lee, D., Sur, D., & Rubenstein, L. (2000). Appropriateness of the decision to transfer nursing facility residents to the hospital. *Journal of the American Geriatrics Society, 48,* 154–163.

Tangalos, E. G., & Freeman, P. I. (1988). Assessment of geriatric patients—Spreading the word. *Mayo Clinic Proceedings, 63,* 305–307.

Teresi, J. A., Holmes, D., Bloom, H. G., Monaco, C., & Rosen, S. (1991). Factors differentiating hospital transfers form long-term care facilities with high and low transfer rates. *Gerontologist, 31,* 795–806.

Thomas, E. J., & Brennan, T. A. (2000). Incidence and types of preventable adverse events in elderly patients: Population based review of medical records. *British Medical Journal, 320,* 741–744.

■ 18
Discharge Planning

Janice B. Foust and Margaret Dimond

Earlier chapters described the economic pressures that hospitals are facing as federal and state governments and private insurers have tried to limit increases in health care costs. Hospital administrators have viewed discharge planning as a major part of the solution to their financial woes, assuming that good discharge planning will reduce costs and increase reimbursement. Equally important, patients and families value the discharge-planning process, which has become a significant quality indicator for institutional accreditation (Joint Commission for Accreditation of Healthcare Organizations [JCAHO], 2001a, 2001b; see also, Bull, 1994a). Specifically, JCAHO has established expectations that health care providers coordinate care and include patients in their planning of care, and has emphasized that the hospital staff should recognize that they are one part of an integrated system of health care practitioners, settings, and services.

The primary principles of hospital discharge planning include

- determination of a patient's capacity to care for himself;
- assessment of the patient's living conditions;
- identification of health or other community resources necessary to ensure continuity after discharge; and
- counseling of patient and family to prepare them for post hospital care. (American Hospital Association, 1987)

Ideally, discharge planning is a highly collaborative and interdisciplinary process that begins on the day of a patient's admission. This chapter will describe the most critical elements of discharge planning and identify some future challenges; the next chapter will examine services after discharge and the means by which clinicians can promote continuity of care.

MULTIDISCIPLINARY ROLES OF DISCHARGE PLANNING

Effective discharge planning requires input from multiple disciplines. Historically, discharge planners were often social workers who facilitated and coordinated the plan of care for the more complex patients who required formal postdischarge services. Social workers contribute essential support to the health care team in situations that would benefit from community resource linkage or psychosocial intervention with the patient or family. A pediatric social worker, for example, might initiate protective services referrals, foster care placements, or developmental assessments. Master's-level social workers are especially useful in urban academic institutions because they have the knowledge and skills to address the complex needs of patients and families in vulnerable populations. Physicians and nurses have always been involved in the discharge-planning process by using their clinical knowledge to anticipate discharge needs and educate patients and families about post-discharge care.

Not surprisingly, the level of physician and staff nurse involvement is variable. Although attending physicians are ultimately responsible for determining when the patient is ready for discharge and approving the final discharge plan, their active involvement may be quite limited, especially within academic institutions where there are medical residents and teams. Similarly, professional nurses' roles and involvement differ depending on the hospital, clinical unit, and population. In hospitals with primary nursing, for example, the nurse may play a far more active role than a rotating staff nurse in determining discharge needs and collaborating with the health care team to coordinate and implement the discharge plan.

Despite similar roles and responsibilities, people who do discharge planning may have any of a multitude of position titles and job descriptions: discharge planner, case manager, utilization reviewer, and home care liaison. Any of these professionals may be interacting directly with patients, families, and the health care team to help coordinate the patient's discharge from the hospital. Discharge planners may be organizationally linked to the social work department or nursing services. They may be assigned to specific clinical units or perhaps to a clinical program (e.g., oncology). When starting work in a hospital, it is very helpful to determine who is responsible for discharge planning and how the process occurs by addressing the following questions:

- How are discharge planners assigned (Unit? Specialty)?
- Does the discharge planner lead the discharge/transitional planning rounds on the unit?
- Who attends these discharge/transitional planning rounds?

- Who presents the patient at discharge/transitional rounds?
- Does the discharge planner follow the patient across units?
- Who makes referrals, if post-discharge services are needed?
- How are residents/attending physicians included in the process?
- How are nurses included in discharge planning? Expectations?
- How does the discharge planner work with nurses and physicians to determine post-discharge needs?
- Is the discharge planner responsible for reviewing trends in patient care?
- Who reviews variances? Does the discharge planner participate in the process? How is that information shared?
- What, if any, are the feedback mechanisms surrounding discharge plans? Are readmissions reviewed? Are there regular contacts with home care agencies?

STARTING THE DISCHARGE PLANNING PROCESS

Case Finding

Discharge planning begins by screening patients at the time of admission, or in the case of elective surgery, before hospitalization. Many hospitals have developed high-risk-screening tools that can help identify behavior, resource, and functional deficits that may create barriers to a safe hospital discharge. Some common high-risk criteria are

- difficulty with basic or instrumental activities of daily living
- need for skilled nursing after hospital discharge (e.g., wound care, diabetic teaching, and monitoring unstable vital signs)
- need for durable medical equipment in the home (e.g., hospital bed, wheelchair)
- history of nonadherence
- suspected abuse or neglect
- chemical dependency
- high risk-diagnosis (e.g., stroke, fall)
- advanced age
- lack of family or community support (Henry Ford Health System, 1995)

The following are questions that affect plans for discharge:

- Will the patient require rehabilitation or extended-care-facility placement?

- Is the patient capable of realistic decision-making? If not, who is the responsible decision maker?
- Does the patient require major lifestyle changes postdischarge (e.g., a patient with myocardial infarction requiring diet and exercise counseling)?
- Is the patient's diagnosis life-threatening?
- Are patient and family's coping mechanisms intact? If not, will adjustment, behavior, or interpersonal issues cause a discharge delay?

In practice, discharge planners find their well-established working relationships with clinicians and staff nurses are the most effective and efficient means of finding patients in need of care. Nurses and physicians, who know the patient and family best, help the discharge planner understand how the clinical situation affects post-discharge care. In the setting of severe acute illness and short lengths of stay, early identification of patient discharge needs is essential to more timely referrals and efficient coordination of necessary services for the patient and family. Typically, the discharge planner must complete a patient/family assessment, collaborate with various health care professionals, contact the patient's insurer and receiving agency, and ensure that the proper documentation is completed and transmitted to the receiving agency. Inadequate lead-time affects communication and ultimately impedes coordination of discharge care (Bull & Kane, 1996).

After identifying a high-risk patient, the discharge planner works to match the patient's needs with available resources. Typically, the discharge planner completes an assessment that includes information about the patient's physical status, functional abilities, current employment, financial situation, anticipated needs at discharge, willingness and availability of family to meet the patient's discharge needs, and understanding of health condition. Often this assessment requires collaboration between health professionals and interaction with the patient and family. A discharge planner who is familiar with a particular patient population can anticipate needs more easily, guide discussions with the patient and family, and connect them to appropriate inpatient or post-discharge resources.

Insurance Plans

Few people can afford medical services without benefit of some kind of insurance. Discharge planners must ensure the accuracy of insurance information and determine the impact of the patient's insurance on the discharge plan. They must have a sound knowledge of insurance programs (see chapter 2) and reimbursement considerations to follow the appropriate procedures and prevent unexpected or uncovered expenses for patients and families.

Health insurance plans provide guidelines for covered services and any stipulations such as copayment obligations, if and when a primary care provider should be notified of care services, whether or not there is a list of providers within an established network, and financial cost if and when the patient seeks care outside the network. For any insurance coverage, services must meet specified criteria or conditions to qualify for coverage. Some insurers require prior approval. Not surprisingly, which services are covered vary by insurance provider and by their specific programs. For example, in order to receive home care, Medicare beneficiaries must meet the criteria of being homebound, being under a physician's care, and having an intermittent and medically necessary need for skilled nursing or therapy (National Association of Home Care, 2001). As a result, the discharge planner is in a critical position to help negotiate the health care and insurance systems to access available and appropriate resources to meet patients' clinical needs.

Referring to Outside Agencies

The range of postdischarge services is extensive and includes home care, rehabilitation care, skilled nursing facilities, nursing home, and hospice services. The specific care provided by these agencies will vary. For example, some home-care agencies provide infusion therapy services or have expertise in caring for specific patient populations (e.g., heart failure, post-hip-replacement). As mentioned, all of these services will have patient criteria that must be met for the service to be reimbursed. Chapter 19 describes these services in greater detail.

Patients who are functionally dependent or living apart from a caregiver are more likely to receive a referral for home care services (Bull, 1994b; Pohl, Collins, & Given, 1995; Prescott, Soeken, & Griggs, 1995). In one study, almost 90% of older adults had at least one physical complaint after discharge including fatigue, unstable posture, pain, or difficulty sleeping (Mistiaen, Duijnhouwer, Wijkel, deBont, & Veeger, 1997). Seventy-nine percent of these patients wanted more information focused on what they could expect and signs of recovery.

Several studies have demonstrated that home care can help reduce the likelihood of rehospitalizations (Bull, 1994b; Martens & Mellor, 1997). Others have noted that patient needs may be overlooked when they could benefit from a referral to home care (Bowles, Naylor & Foust, in press; Magilvy & Lakomy, 1991; Prescott et al., 1995). And yet, there may be an underutilization of services; in one study, only approximately 50% of older adults with functional limitations received home care, and patients with more problems were rehospitalized and used the emergency room more often (Rosswurm & Lanham, 1998). Collectively, these studies underscore the importance of detecting patient needs and obtaining appropriate postdischarge services.

Developing and Implementing the Plan

The focus of any plan depends on a comprehensive patient assessment that identifies the clinical priorities and possibilities. Interdisciplinary discharge planning or transitional care rounds are common and efficient ways to communicate, modify, and implement a plan. Physicians, nurses, social workers, case managers, physical therapists, occupational therapists, pharmacists, and anyone else involved in the patient's care may attend these meetings. Typically, all patients on a particular unit or clinical program are presented and their plans discussed and revised as needed. The purpose of such rounds is to share relevant clinical, psychosocial information and solve problems collaboratively, drawing on the expertise of the team (see chapter 3 on teams). The most obvious benefit of these rounds is an opportunity to bridge gaps in communication and facilitate the work of the health care team towards common goals. In clinical situations where the plan can change frequently, discharge-planning rounds are an effective strategy to build consensus and provide a consistent plan for the health care team to work with the patient and family.

Patient and family education about the care at home is an important element of any discharge plan. A significant amount of health-care-professionals' time is invested in patient teaching, especially at the time of discharge. Nonetheless, patients and families find it difficult to comprehend all the information they receive. Inadequate information on medications, diet, and treatments can lead to rehospitalization for some patients (Bull & Kane, 1996). Discharge from the hospital is a particularly stressful time for them, and yet it is also when they are given a significant amount of information about the treatment plan. Patients are eager to get home, but are often tired and still recovering from their illness, making it additionally hard for them to absorb new information. Providing relevant and understandable discharge information to patients and families is a challenge for all involved with the discharge plan.

Bull (1994a) described effective communication as a critical aspect of quality discharge planning for both professionals and older adults. Asking questions was one of the most important indicators of this process. Professionals described needing to ask many questions of patient, families, and other professionals in order to have the correct information to develop an appropriate discharge plan. Patients also viewed asking questions as an essential part of a good discharge plan. However, those who were most likely to ask questions were under the age of 70 and had an education greater than high school. Some older adults expected that the health care professionals should provide necessary information automatically.

Physicians may overestimate how effectively they communicate discharge instructions (Calkins et al., 1997). Most patients understand their medication regimen, but are less familiar with medication side effects or when to resume normal activities (Reiley et al., 1996). In this study, patients were more knowledgeable about their medication side effects when a primary nurse was involved with the discharge.

Patient and family participation in planning is essential to ensuring that the plan of care at home is feasible and likely to be implemented. Some of the issues that should be discussed with the patient and family are (a) type of care needed; (b) availability and willingness of the patient and family's ability to perform needed care; (c) agreement to have home care services; (d) geographic proximity of family or informal caregivers; and (e) competing family responsibilities, which could make it difficult to provide needed care. Involving the patient and family minimizes the chance of developing a plan that is unrealistic or impossible to implement. For example, a married patient whose spouse is very supportive may still require a referral for home-health-aide services if the spouse cannot provide the care because of physical limitations or work commitments.

In more complex discharge situations, it is wise to arrange a formal family meeting with the health care team, including the patient (whenever possible), family members, physicians, nurses, social worker, and case manager. Family meetings are particularly effective when family members disagree with the plan or when significant family involvement and responsibility are needed for postdischarge care. It is particularly critical to have everyone involved in the same discussions to resolve conflicts, make decisions, and establish a common goal and plan. Arranging these meetings is time intensive, but it is an efficient strategy when multiple individual conversations could detract from resolving issues, lead to fragmented care, or increase the patient and family's dissatisfaction with care. The discharge planner is a valuable resource to the patient, family, and health care team for information and access to government and community resources. Examples of available programs include pharmaceutical assistance, meal delivery, counseling, educational courses, and caregiver support. Even when these programs have a waiting list, the discharge planner can facilitate the process by making the referral or helping the patient or family to complete the necessary application as soon as possible.

DOES DISCHARGE PLANNING WORK?

Evaluating the cost-effectiveness of discharge planning models is complex and beyond the scope of this chapter. Research has underscored the importance of discharge planning as a quality indicator for patient care and as a process that can lead to improved patient and cost outcomes, at least in specific programs for specific populations (Anderson & Helms, 1994; Brooten et al., 1986; Bull, 1994a; Naylor et al., 1994; Naylor et al., 1999). Specifically, advanced practice nurses (APNs) responsible for implementing a comprehensive discharge plan for older adults contributed to improved patient outcomes. Medical patients receiving discharge planning by APNs were less likely to be readmitted, and if readmitted they had shorter hospital stays (Naylor et al., 1994). In a separate study, Naylor and colleagues (1999) found that patients who received comprehensive discharge planning and home follow-up by APNs experienced fewer hospital readmissions, an increased time to first readmission, and improved quality of life. Nonetheless, it is not clear if these programs can be generalized to a broader, more diverse population. A recent Cochrane review failed to find clear evidence of the effectiveness of discharge planning (Parkes & Shepperd, 2000).

Ironically, discharge planning has been a victim of its own initial successes; shorter lengths of stay can leave clinicians with less time to know the patient and families and collaborate with colleagues, and this can lead to a suboptimal plan of care. Poor communication between health care providers adversely affects the discharge plan (Anderson & Helms, 1994, 1995; Bull, 1994b; Bull & Kane, 1996). Ineffective communication between the hospital and home care agencies has been linked to delays in services and confusion about the treatment plan or additional home care visits (Anderson & Helms, 1994; Bull & Kane, 1996). Other factors that may hinder quality of discharge planning are use of informal or nonstandardized mechanisms, timing of the referral, and fragmented work and role confusion without clear accountability (Anderson & Helms, 1994; McWilliam & Sangster, 1994). Referrals often contain inadequate amounts of information (Anderson & Helms, 1993, 1995), which could further contribute to miscommunication or require additional time to correct.

CONCLUSION

Hospital administrators, insurers, health care providers, patients, and families all want discharge planning to be timely, thorough, effective, and cost saving. Yet this process, which is of such import to so many parties, has developed with little literature to guide it (Potthoff, Kane, & Franco, 1997). The future of discharge planning will depend upon the development of means to determine needs, communicate information, and access services in a way that does not merely make sense, but actually proves to be effective.

REFERENCES

American Hospital Association. (1987). *Discharging hospital patients: Legal implications for institutional providers and health care professionals. Report of the Task Force on Legal Issues in Discharge Planning.* Chicago: Author.

Anderson, M. A., & Helms, L. B. (1993). An assessment of discharge planning models: Communication in referrals for home care. *Orthopaedic Nursing, 12*(4), 41–49.

Anderson, M. A., & Helms, L. B. (1994). Quality improvement in discharge planning: An evaluation of factors in communication between health care providers. *Journal of Nursing Care Quality, 8*(2), 62–72.

Anderson, M. A., & Helms, L. B. (1995). Communications between continuing care organizations. *Research in Nursing and Health, 18,* 49–57.

Bowles, K. H., Naylor, M.D., & Foust, J. B. (in press). Patient characteristics at hospital discharge and a comparison of home care referrals decisions. *Journal of the American Geriatrics Society.*

Brooten, D., Kumar, S., Brown, L. P., Butts, P., Finkler, S.A., Bakewell-Sachs, S., Gibbons, A., & Delivoria-Papadopoulous, M. (1986). A randomized clinical trial of early hospital discharge and home follow-up of very-low-birthweight infants. *New England Journal of Medicine, 315,* 934–939.

Bull, M. J. (1994a). Patients' and professionals' perceptions of quality in discharge planning. *Journal of Nursing Care Quality, 8*(2), 47–57.

Bull, M. J. (1994b). Use of formal community services by elders and their family caregivers 2 weeks following hospital discharge. *Journal of Advanced Nursing, 19,* 503–508.

Bull, M. J., & Kane, R. L. (1996). Gaps in discharge planning. *Journal of Applied Gerontology, 15,* 486–500.

Calkins, D. R., Davis, R. B., Reiley, P., Phillips, R. S., Pineo, K. L., Delbanco, T. L., & Iezzonik L. I. (1997). Patient-physician communication at hospital discharge and patients' understanding of the postdischarge treatment plan. *Archives of Internal Medicine, 157,* 1026–1030.

Henry Ford Health System. (1995). *Department of social work and discharge planning: Consultation/screening assessment.* Detroit, MI: Author.

Joint Commission on Accreditation of Healthcare Organizations. (2001a). *Continuum of care.* [On-line]. Available: http://jcaho.hfhs.org/html. Retrieved August 3, 2001.

Joint Commission on Accreditation of Healthcare Organizations. (2001b). *Standards assessing discharge planning.* [On-line]. Available: www.jcaho.org/standard/dischargepl_rev.html. Accessed October 11, 2001.

Magilvy, J. K., & Lakomy, J. M. (1991). Transitions of older adults to home care. *Home Health Care Services Quarterly, 12*(4), 59–70.

Martens, K. H., & Mellor, S. D. (1997). A study of the relationship between home care services and hospital readmission of patients with congestive heart failure. *Home Healthcare Nurse, 15,* 123–129.

McWilliam, C. L., & Sangster, J. F. (1994). Managing patient discharge to home: The challenges of achieving quality of care. *International Journal for Quality and Health Care, 6,* 147–161.

Mistiaen, P., Duijnhouwer, E., Wijkel, D., de Bont, M., & Veeger, A. (1997). The problems of elderly people at home one week after discharge from an acute care setting. *Journal of Advance Nursing, 25,* 1233–1240.

National Association of Home Care. (2001). How to choose a home care provider: Who pays for home care services?. [On-line]. Available: http://www.nahc.org/consumer/wpfhcs.html. Retrieved June 30, 2001.

Naylor, M. D., Brooten, D., Jones, R., Lavizzo-Mourey, R., Mezey, M., & Pauly, M. (1994). Comprehensive discharge planning for hospitalized elderly. A randomized clinical trial. *Annals of Internal Medicine, 129,* 999–1006.

Naylor, M. D., Brooten, D., Campbell, R., Jacobsen, B. S., Mezey, M., Pauly, M., & Schwartz, S. J. (1999). Comprehensive discharge planning and home follow-up of hospitalized elders. *Journal of American Medical Association, 281,* 613–620.

Parkes, J., & Shepperd, S. (2000). Discharge planning from hospital to home. *Cochrane Database Systematic Review.* 4:CD000313 (latest version 17 August 2000).

Pohl, J. M., Collins, C., & Given, C. W. (1995). Beyond patient dependency: Family characteristics and access of elderly patients to home care services following hospital discharge. *Home Health Services Quarterly, 15*(4), 33–47.

Potthoff, S., Kane, R. L., & Franco, S. J. (1997). Improving hospital discharge planning for elderly patients. *Health Care Financing Review, 19*(2), 47–72.

Prescott, P. A., Soeken, K. L., & Griggs, M. (1995). Identification and referral of hospitalized patients in need of home care. *Research in Nursing and Health, 18,* 85–95.

Reiley, P., Iezzoni, L. I., Phillips, R., Davis, R. B., Turchin, L. I., & Calkins, D. (1996). Discharge planning: Comparison of patients' and nurses' perception of patients following hospital discharge. *IMAGE: Journal of Nursing Scholarship, 28,* 143–147.

Rosswurm, M. A., & Lanham, D. M. (1998). Discharge planning for elderly patients. *Journal of Gerontological Nursing, 24*(5), 14–21.

■ 19
Maintaining the Patient's Health in the Community

Veronica LoFaso

Making the transition from the acute hospital setting back into the community is a critical point in the care of any patient. Each time a patient is admitted, the team must simultaneously treat the acute illness and plan for the patient's discharge to the community. It is appropriate to focus attention on acute medical issues during a patient's hospitalization, but not at the expense of the person as a whole. Although discharge planning plays a fundamental role in helping the patient return safely to the community (see chapter 18), ensuring continuity of care extends beyond accessing of services at the time of discharge (Rich et al., 1993). This chapter will describe the clinician's role in following the patient from hospital to community and the services that are available to maintain the patient's health.

TAKING AN EXPANDED HISTORY

All clinicians appreciate the importance of a complete medical history. Equally important, however, are the social history and functional assessment. This is the essence of who the person is, how she is living, whom she cares about, how she makes a living, what she believes in, and who will be able to help the patient upon discharge. This history begins with a functional assessment of basic and instrumental activities of daily living (BADL and IADL) and also includes family supports, cognition and affect at baseline, and cultural or religious beliefs. Much of this information can be gleaned by good communication with the patient, family, and the assigned social worker.

A clinician who has a clear picture of the patient can better assess progress or setbacks in the hospital. If the hospital course is uneventful, the transition back to home will likely require little intervention. On the other hand, if the patient's social situation is precarious, those external stressors alone can lead a patient to functional dependence, irrespective of the medical course. In this case, creation of a stable home environment requires a great deal of advance work that should be initiated early in the admission. Although gathering functional and social information appears to be time-consuming, these data enable the clinician to provide better care and usually reduce hospital length of stay in the long run (Koenig, 1986).

OPTIONS AT DISCHARGE

Once it is clear that a patient will need services, making the correct choices from the wide array of services and settings can be quite confusing. Options include, but are not limited to the following choices.

Home Health Care

Upon discharge from the hospital, patients may still have active issues that require monitoring by a registered nurse. Almost all medical practitioners will order some form of home care services from either hospital-affiliated or independent certified home health agencies (CHHAs) to manage their patients when they are back in the community. CHHAs can provide home nursing, physical therapy, social work, dietitians, home health aides, and other specialized services. Certain agencies now have specialized programs for chronic diseases, such as congestive heart failure or cancer, which can provide specialized services specific to the disease. Although agencies can provide a variety of services and equipment, the emotional support and caring manner of good nurses may be the key to a patient's recovery.

Patients with the following problems may benefit from referral to a home health care agency:

- new medical conditions or an exacerbation of a chronic medical problem that needs close monitoring
- concern about adherence to complex medical regimens
- wounds that require daily or frequent dressing changes
- frequent falling that necessitates a home safety evaluation
- home rehabilitation needs (physical therapy, occupational therapy, or speech therapy)
- lack of knowledge about equipment or treatments
- diseases or conditions that are appropriate for palliative or hospice care

Medicare, Medicaid, and most insurance companies cover home health services, but benefits may be limited (see chapter 18). A physician must certify that the services are necessary and that the patient is homebound or has significant difficulty coming into the doctor's office to receive those services. The physician should expect to receive and sign an intake form from the home health agency with a plan of care and detailed description of the patient's condition. Updates must be signed periodically if the case extends for weeks or months. Timely completion of these forms and ongoing discussion with the home care team will maximize the services available to the patient.

As important as the communication that occurs between the staff during the hospitalization is the transfer of that information to the community team on discharge (Arras & Dubler, 1994). When arriving home from a hospitalization, patients are still in a weakened state and rely on our planning for their needs upon returning home. This is the real challenge of continuity of care, as hospital discharge does not solve the patient's problems. Patient management continues in the community, but now clinicians, nurses, social service agencies, and patients are no longer located in one place. Communicating despite geographic separation is time-consuming and difficult, and modern technology has not eliminated the need for multiple phone calls and reams of paperwork. Nonetheless, only by making the effort to maintain communications can we help a frail patient stay at home and at maximum level of function.

As part of home care documentation, the agency will submit a list of current medications for review. These forms must be signed by a physician to enable insurance payment to the home care agency. If the patient is receiving home attendant or housekeeping services via Medicaid, then the physician must submit documentation explaining why the patient needs these ongoing services. The thoroughness of the documentation can determine how many hours of home care are allotted to the patient. This has real direct and practical implications for the patient's care. Durable medical-equipment orders will also require the physician to communicate the type of equipment needed and the reason it is required. Often a diagnosis code and an estimation of the expected duration of need must accompany the justification.

Home with Ongoing ("Nonskilled") Services

Most patients want to return home and eventually live independently (Kane, 1995). Some may initially require skilled home care as they recuperate from the acute hospital stay. Although Medicare will pay for these services upon discharge from the hospital, the Medicare Home Health Benefit covers acute, not chronic care. In some states, Medicaid or the Area Agency on Aging may pay for home attendant services over a longer period of time; long-term-care insurance may also provide some benefits to cover chronic home care. Eventually, however, the patient will have to pay for the service out-of-pocket. Some patients do well at home with several hours of home attendant services a few days a week. Others who have significant BADL impairments may require many hours a day of custodial care. Cobbling together a safe support system for a patient requires skill, a sophisticated knowledge of available services, and ongoing monitoring. All too often, custodial care becomes the responsibility of family, and lack of supervision or inadequate teaching can result in rehospitalization for falls, aspiration pneumonia, pressure ulcers, recurrent CHF, or failure to thrive (Rich et al., 1993). The outpatient team should ensure close follow-up, anticipate problems, communicate effectively, and use all available and appropriate community resources. Most often the family members will assume a significant part of in-home care. Although well-meaning, family members are not trained caregivers. It is crucial to have regular, frequently spaced visits by home care nurses or visiting physicians to oversee what is happening in the home, especially for the first few weeks and months after hospitalization. Being available by phone for families can be very helpful in the early discharge period. Family members can become overwhelmed; respite care may be a valuable option that may prevent unnecessary relapses in the patient's health. Coordinating medical, nursing, and social service visits at regular intervals allows the patient to be under close observation and the family to be supported. Once stable, the visits can then be spaced at longer intervals and eventually may not be needed at all.

Adult Day Care

Adult day care is an option for patients whose cognitive or physical deficits necessitate supervision. For example, a patient with moderate dementia who wanders might attend day care 6 hours a day twice a week and socialize, participate in activities, eat lunch, and engage in low-level exercises. The patient can have stimulation under trained supervision and the caregiver receives regular respite. Most adult day care is private pay. Transportation is often available.

Assisted Living

This setting allows individuals with mild dementias or IADL dysfunction to maintain an independent lifestyle. Patients must have few or no impairments of BADLs. Many choose this environment when their family or social circle begins to diminish. This setting offers communal meals, some housekeeping services, and opportunities for socialization. Some facilities have nurses on site. Each assisted-living facility has slightly different services and should be visited by the patient and family prior to transfer.

Acute Rehabilitation

Patients who have had a significant functional decline from events such as closed head trauma, stroke, or spinal cord injury and are able to engage in extensive and aggressive periods of rehabilitation 3 hours a day are appropriate candidates for inpatient rehabilitation. These patients are expected to make significant improvements with aggressive therapy.

Subacute (Geriatric) Rehabilitation

It is quite common to have older patients experience some functional decline during a hospitalization. This can be a direct result of a fractured limb or other acute event or it can be from immobility and delirium during the hospital stay. In these situations, transferring to a nursing home for subacute rehabilitation before returning home can be very helpful. Patients can receive physical, occupational, or speech therapy and can regain some independence. Subacute rehabilitation happens at a slower pace, allowing the patient and family time to see the progression of recovery and determine if permanent placement is necessary.

Outpatient Rehabilitation

Patients who have experienced losses in strength or mobility but are safe to return home may benefit from outpatient rehabilitation. For example, a patient may be hospitalized after a fall that was precipitated by pneumonia and may have sustained a strain, bruises, or fractured ribs. After the pneumonia is treated the patient may still have some gait dysfunction and weakness from extended bed rest, despite some physical therapy during the acute medical stay. Physical therapy can continue after discharge at an outpatient physical therapy facility. These services are intermittent (twice weekly) and of a few weeks' duration. Physical therapy can also take place in the home, but this is reserved for those who are essentially homebound and unable to participate in more aggressive therapy.

Nursing Home

Other patients have more complex medical conditions and require long-term placement. They generally have more intensive custodial needs that require more than one person to perform. These patients may have advanced dementia and require the supervision of an institutional setting. Prior to placement, a detailed evaluation is performed (usually by a registered nurse), which allows the nursing home to determine if the referral is appropriate.

Hospice

Patients with limited life expectancy (usually less than 6 months) from any cause are eligible for hospice. The patient's care needs and availability of caregiver support determine the setting of hospice care: inpatient, outpatient, or nursing home. Hospice care allows for families to be with patients at the end of life and preserves the dignity of the patient at the terminal stages of illness. Although patients who are undergoing aggressive treatment regimens are not eligible for hospice, they can and should receive interventions for palliation of symptoms.

COMMUNITY SUPPORTS

Most practitioners consider community services to be the purview of the social worker and never learn what is available and how to access the help. Understanding the services available in the community and how to access them will greatly improve the effectiveness and satisfaction of patient care.

- *Certified home health agencies* provide skilled services for brief periods in the post-acute period. They were discussed in detail earlier in this chapter.
- *Social service agencies* can provide Meals on Wheels, Friendly Visitors, and other services.
- *Disease-specific support groups* can be easily contacted via phone or the Internet. Organizations such as the American Lung Association or the Alzheimer's Association have local programs that can prove helpful for ongoing support and information.
- *Religious organizations* offer spiritual support and may have outreach programs.
- *Geriatric case managers* can be very helpful to concerned families living at a distance. These individuals take on the case management of patients with impaired function and ensure that all their needs are met (Keenan & Fanale, 1989). This includes financial management, keeping doctor appointments, ensuring medication adherence, and more. These services are not covered by Medicare and are paid for out-of-pocket.
- *Mental health services* are available in every community. Some patients have significant mental health issues. Most communities have outpatient mental health clinics and some offer in-home mental health care.

- *Adult Protective Services* can be a resource if a patient with a mental illness is a danger to himself or others. This agency should also be contacted for concerns about abuse or neglect.
- *Experts in elder law* can provide financial and legal advice to older patients and their families who are preparing for future needs.
- *Local agencies* such as the Area Agency on Aging and city or state departments of health provide a variety of services.

THE POSTDISCHARGE HOME VISIT

Because patients often return home with stable, but still active medical issues that require continued monitoring, many medical practices have started medical home-visit programs to bridge the transition from hospital to home and to augment the services provided by home health nurses. If patients remain homebound after a hospitalization, their care can be given as part of ongoing scheduled home visits. A home visit uncovers an average of four previously unidentified problems (Stuck et al., 1995). Physician home care is an evolving but tenuous field that is shaped by fiscal constraints; nonetheless, technologic advances, new models like the home hospital, and the development of physician practices devoted exclusively to home care offer opportunities for creative care (Leff & Burton, 2001).

Patients who can benefit from medical home visits have a broad range of medical, social, and psychiatric problems with complicated medical regimens and chronic diseases (Mims, Thomas, & Conroy, 1977). Patients may have difficulty with adherence because they misunderstand their disease, lack trust or belief in the therapy, or have early dementia. Another challenge is financial constraints, which may force them to choose between buying their medications or buying food. Medications may make them feel ill and reduce their level of function.

Complicated medication regimens often necessitate close follow-up in the home. Unfortunately, despite our best efforts, problems can occur at the time of discharge. Discharge orders may be written incorrectly or illegibly, and patients may never even receive their discharge prescriptions. Often patients are sent home with complicated regimens that were designed for hospital dosing but are cumbersome and difficult to follow as outpatients. Moreover, even straightforward regimens of diuretics, steroids, or antibiotics that were written correctly and described to the patient before discharge may benefit from monitoring once the patient is at home.

During a house call, the clinician can quickly discover the barriers to adherence. Are there multiple generations of people in the home that lead to confusion and conflicting belief systems? Are other individuals in the home financially abusing the patient, leaving him unable to purchase his medication? Unlike an office visit, a home visit can allow the clinician to observe

- the number of people in the household, their relationships and level of concern about the patient;
- the condition of the house—how clean, how much and what types of furniture are present, and how the patient navigates in the apartment;
- access to the outside world, including the presence of steps, elevator, nearest bus stop, grocery, or pharmacy;
- condition of the kitchen and type of food in the refrigerator;
- methods the patient and family have established to keep track of medications and the timing of administration.

Some patients are discharged with equipment such as nebulizers, oxygen tanks, suction devices, feeding tubes, or more technical equipment such as ventilators. These patients and their caregivers are reassured to have medical follow-up to evaluate their use of these devices at home.

Patients with recurrent falls and mobility problems also benefit from home visits to assess safety. Most patients insist on returning home even at the risk of another fall. Lighting, clutter, slippery surfaces, frayed rugs, and worn tile can be altered to reduce further injuries. Grab bars, commodes, assistive devices, and emergency notification systems can make a big difference. Although an occupational therapist or nurse will often perform a home safety assessment and make appropriate recommendations, physician reinforcement may make a substantial difference in adherence. Hearing these recommendations from physicians can be a powerful stimulus to change.

Many patients, especially older ones, experience some functional decline while hospitalized. When issues of placement arise, a home visit is an excellent way to assess the patient's safety. Sometimes just mobilizing the proper agencies can keep a patient living independently. On the other hand, there are times when, despite the patient's protest to the contrary, it is clear to the team that there are significant issues of hygiene, safety, medical illness, psychiatric illness, or financial irresponsibility. If the patient shows cognitive loss, guardianship proceedings may have to ensue. A visiting team can make those judgments best after seeing the patient in her home setting.

When families face end-of-life concerns, they often feel torn between the medical establishment's need to cure and the wishes of the patient to return home. There is a continuum of levels of intervention at the end of life ranging from aggressive care with chemotherapy to comfort care. Each situation is different and in-home medical care can give patients some reassurance that someone is overseeing their care and listening to their wishes as the disease progresses. If hospice is desired, the medical team can often remain for medical consultation. Allowing for a peaceful death at home is an important intervention for patients and families.

Any situation that requires a team approach would be best served by a home visit program. The input of multiple disciplines can often make overwhelming cases manageable. It is important that the communication between inpatient and outpatient teams be seamless and comprehensive. Patients will have more trust in a well-informed team.

CASE STUDY

Ms. T. was a 90-year-old woman admitted to the hospital with shortness of breath. Her past medical history was notable for coronary artery disease, peripheral vascular disease, and hypertension. Her past surgical history included a hysterectomy and cholecystectomy. Her medications were diltiazem CD 120, enteric-coated aspirin 81 mg PO qD, calcium plus vitamin D, and acetaminophen as needed. She had no known drug allergies.

Ms. T. lived alone in an assisted-living facility that had an elevator. She was personally close to her sister, Ellen, who lived in the same city; her grandchildren lived on the West Coast, in California. She was independent in all BADLs and IADLs, had a cleaning woman who came once a week, and a masseuse whom she visited weekly. Ms. T. was Jewish but not practicing. Her income was moderate and she was not Medicaid-eligible. She did not drink or smoke and had worked in the family bakery but retired many years ago to raise children. She had been living alone and was proud of her ability to remain independent.

On review of systems, Ms. T.'s vision was slightly impaired by cataract OS, her hearing was intact, and she wore dentures. She had no dysphagia or aspiration, and her appetite was good. She attended communal meals at an assisted-living facility and participated in activities. She had no bowel complaints and no urinary incontinence but some urgency. She had had one near fall, and ambulated with a cane inside because of mild balance problems and osteoarthritis in her right knee. Generally Ms. T. had someone with her when she walked outside. There was no evidence of depression or dementia. She had elected to be DNR. Her sister was her health care agent.

Hospital Course

Ms. T. was admitted with shortness of breath. The intern contacted her primary care physician, who provided a detailed summary of her previous health status, cardiology evaluation, current medications, and social history. The resident then called her sister to discuss any concerns she might have and to see if any information could be gleaned about recent symptoms or change in functional status. Ellen faxed over the DNR form and the health proxy form to be placed in the chart.

Evaluation revealed that Ms. T. had an MI, and radiologic and echocardiographic findings were consistent with the diagnosis of congestive heart failure (ejection fraction 30%). Her medications were adjusted to include an ACE-inhibitor, nitrates, and a diuretic. Her diltiazem was changed to a beta-blocker. The admitting team discussed discharge options with the social worker.

Discharge

Ms. T. was now dependent in two BADLs. Discharge options included geriatric rehabilitation at a nearby nursing home for several weeks before returning home or direct discharge home with increased help; she opted for the latter. Her sister and her family in California were contacted with her consent. The inpatient social worker recruited the hospital's home care agency to arrange for a visiting nurse to evaluate the need for home health aides to assist with the transition and monitor her cardiac status. A physical therapist would come to the home to continue therapy. The medical resident called the patient's primary care physician and outlined the plan with her. The social worker faxed a detailed discharge summary to the doctor's office with all test results and a recent medication list. The home care agency would send forms to the primary doctor authorizing initiation of services.

Back in the Community

Ms. T. was now back at home. The visiting nurses came twice a week. They reviewed her medications and arranged them in a box for simple administration. They assessed the home and recommended grab bars and a bedside commode. Forms were sent to the physician to authorize this equipment. Ms. T. had a home health aide 5 days a week for 4 hours to clean and help her bathe and dress, and physical therapy twice a week for exercises and gait training. Ellen, who was 89, was playing an increasing role in providing care as well. Ms. T.'s primary care physician saw her in the office the week after discharge. She came to the office in a wheelchair by ambulette with some difficulty. She was medically stable but looked tired. Ellen, who accompanied her everywhere, expressed concern that Ms. T. was just not herself.

Six Months Postdischarge

Ms. T. made a fair recovery. She was still mildly short of breath with exertion. She no longer was eligible for home nursing or physical therapy and was given exercises to do at home on her own. Home attendants continued to come but were now being paid from her own resources, which were rapidly diminishing.

Nine Months Postdischarge

Ms. T. called her primary physician. Her ankles were very swollen and she was coughing and short of breath. Her sister had fallen and broken her hip and was in a rehabilitation facility, and Ms. T. was afraid to go to the office alone. The primary physician decided that the safest course of action was to call an ambulance and have the patient evaluated in the hospital. The physician called the emergency room staff and discussed the case with the ED physicians. She faxed over the most recent medication regimen and Ms. T.'s most recent EKG. Later that day the primary physician discussed medical and social issues with the admitting team. The physician also spoke with the social worker about the patient's need for more help in the setting of diminishing financial resources.

The patient's heart failure was treated, but delirium prolonged her length of stay to a week. Finally, she returned home on a new medication regimen. The CHHA services were reinstated and in-home physical therapy services were resumed to maximize her strength and mobility. The primary physician completed the intake forms for the CHHA services and ordered a hospital bed for the home.

Eleven Months Postdischarge

Once again the patient became more short of breath, but she made it clear that she did not want to go back to the hospital, recalling her unpleasant stay. Traveling to the physician's office had become very complicated and tiring for the patient, especially without her sister's help. The primary physician agreed to do a house call that afternoon. Ms. T. was in bed and did not appear to have bathed. Her medication bottles were disorganized, and she could not give a reliable medication history. Her affect was flattened and she admitted to loss of appetite and hopelessness, consistent with a diagnosis of depression. Her physical exam was consistent with worsening heart failure, and she refused hospitalization. Her physician discussed the situation with the patient and the family, and all decided that the case would be managed at home at the patient's request.

The physician mobilized the *team*. She first attended to the medical issues, drawing blood samples, contacting *portable radiology services* for in-home chest X-ray and adjusting the medication regimen. The *CHHA* was again contacted to reinstate the case so that *visiting nurses* could monitor Ms. T.'s progress, oversee her medications, and reeducate her about her diet. A *nutritionist* was recommended to the patient. She was started on a low dose of antidepressant, and the *community mental-health agency* was contacted to begin home visits. The CHHA *social worker* assisted with contacting a *geriatric case manager* for the family, as the patient's sister could no longer assume that responsibility of coordinating her sister's care. The social worker also contacted the *community agencies* and *religious groups* for friendly visiting. The telephone numbers of several *elder lawyers* were given to the patient, as she was concerned about the financial implications of spending down all her assets and wondered if she should consider other long-term-care options instead.

Two Months Later
Ms. T. had stabilized a bit. The visiting nurses made regular visits and reported frequently to the primary physician about the patient's lung exam, weights, and adherence to medications. The physician continued to make house calls and reevaluate the patient's progress. The visiting mental health agency had her evaluated by their psychiatrist who adjusted her antidepressant dose with improvement in her mood. She was eating better and more engaged in her surroundings, and a care manager was overseeing her finances and affairs. The community social-service agency sent a friendly visitor once a week, which Ms. T. enjoyed, and the physician made a home visit every 6 to 8 weeks.

One Year Later
The home attendant for Ms. T. called her physician to say that the patient was again short of breath and was having difficulty walking to the bathroom. The physician telephoned the patient, who still refused hospitalization. The physician empirically increased the diuretic dose and contacted the family. All agreed that the patient should be made comfortable and not hospitalized. The physician made a follow-up phone call that week, and in light of the patient's poor prognosis, suggested *outpatient hospice care*. An in-home DNR form was completed, in keeping with the patient's wishes. Home oxygen was obtained. Hospice nurses visited regularly to make sure there was no discomfort or air hunger. The patient remained very comfortable for several months before passing away quietly at home.

CONCLUSION

Making the transition from hospital to the community can be a complex and frightening time for patients. The success or failure of this experience is predicated on the effective use of teamwork and good communication. For patients and families to benefit from all the community agencies and services available, physicians must understand what is available, how to access it, and how to work with agencies and organizations to anticipate and meet the chronically ill patient's ever-changing needs.

REFERENCES

Arras, J., & Dubler, N. (1994). Bringing the hospital home: Ethical and social implications of high tech home care. *Hastings Center Report No. 5*, S19–S28.

Kane, R. A. (1995). Expanding the home care concept: Blurring distinctions among home care, institutional care and other long-term-care services. *Milbank Quarterly, 73*, 161–183.

Keenan, J., & Fanale, J. (1989). Home care: Past and present, problems and potential. *Journal of the American Geriatrics Society, 37*, 1076–1083.

Koenig, H. (1986). The physician and home care of the elderly patient. *Gerontology and Geriatrics Education, 7*, 15–23.

Leff, B., & Burton, J. R. (2001). The future history of home care and physician house calls in the United States. *Journals of Gerontology A: Medical Sciences, 56*, M603–M608.

Mims, R., Thomas, L., & Conroy, M. (1977). Physician house calls: A complement to hospital-based medical care. *Journal of the American Geriatrics Society, 25*, 28–34.

Rich, M., Vinson, J., Sperry, J., Spinner, L., Chung, M., & Davila-Roman, V. (1993). Prevention of readmission in elderly patients with congestive heart failure. *Journal of General Internal Medicine, 8*, 585–590.

Stuck, A. E., Minder, C. E., Peter-Wuest, I., Gillmann, G., Egli, C., Kesselring, A., Leu, R. E., & Beck, J. C. (1995). A trial of annual in-home comprehensive geriatric assessments for elderly people living in the community. *New England Journal of Medicine, 333*, 1184–1189.

Part IV
Common Social and Ethical Issues

■ 20
Families: Roles, Needs, and Expectations

Sona Euster

Family. How can such a simple, familiar word evoke so many interpretations and reactions? Yet it does. Whether we think of our own families, the family of friends, or the family of patients, mixed emotions usually surface. This chapter will explore the complex concept of family as it affects the hospitalized patient and his or her care. It will examine definitions of family, describe a simple theoretical framework of family systems, and discuss the interaction of the family and the physician. Primarily, the chapter will serve as a guide to help hospital personnel understand family behaviors and expectations and as a tool to develop the skill of working effectively with family members and the family unit as a whole.

Families are a part of life. They are the system in which human beings grow and develop, the basic structure of our social fabric. They provide, for most of us, nurturing and a sense of belonging and also give rise to conflict and ambivalence. They are complex, unique, and ultimately, fascinating. In the arena of health care, they are critical allies. While the patient receives the actual medical treatment, the patient and family *as a unit* must be the focus of care. The family cannot be thought of or treated as the patient's unwanted or unnecessary appendage. Family members are not an intrusion on the provider's time and practice. They must be seen and treated as an integral component of the therapeutic process.

DEFINITIONS OF FAMILY

In twenty-first century America, definitions of family must be broad and all-inclusive. The traditional nuclear family (mom, dad, 2.2 kids, and a dog) is no longer the norm. People make all sorts of connections, pursue various lifestyles, and make their own decisions about who is important to them. It is critical that hospital providers recognize this and explore early on how each patient defines family and whom the patient values and trusts.

Family definitions based on kinship may be misleading. Although a patient may have blood relations, he or she may not view them as supportive. Parents, adult children, and siblings may not, in fact, comprise the patient's "emotional family." The patient may well view a partner (of either gender) or close friends as the people who matter. There may be long-standing conflicts among the biological and emotional family members. Even if it appears that the patient has no family, it is crucial to explore what that means.

The definition of family is also related to culture and ethnicity. Extended family plays a much greater role in some cultures; gender and age of family members may have different meaning, and the interactions among family members and between family members and providers will differ. Recognition of cultural affiliations and beliefs help forge alliances with families.

THE FAMILY AS A SYSTEM

These alliances are crucial to patient care; this becomes clearer if one understands the concept of family as a system. A system connotes connectedness, relationships among the parts, and usually predictable patterns of behavior (Minuchin, Colapinto, & Minuchin, 1998). Viewing the family as a system emphasizes the fact that the patient has connections to others and that his illness and treatment will have an impact on them. The family is a discrete entity, not merely a collection of individuals. It is a living system with certain important properties:

- It is an open system with boundaries that are somewhat permeable, accessible to new information from the environment and capable of change.
- It seeks internal balance.
- It requires a sustained, adaptive balance with its environment.

"The family is viewed as an open, transactive, and adaptive system, capable of either self-directed or externally directed growth and change" (Ell & Northen, 1990). The family reacts to systems outside it; it responds to and requires information from the physician. It also responds to changes such as the illness or death of a loved one. The family seeks to adjust to these occurrences, to adapt and, over time, resume a sense of "normalcy."

Family plays a critical role in the patient's life and, therefore, in his or her hospital experience. The illness experience is very much a "family affair" (Ell & Northen, 1990). The patient cannot be seen or treated as an isolated individual. Most patients want family involved and expect them to be included in communications and in decision-making. Supportive family enhances the individual's coping mechanisms and improves health outcomes (Roback, 1984). The converse is true, as well—family conflict or "misdirected" support can have adverse effects. Health care professionals must assess the particular family system and understand how it has functioned, where its strengths lie, and what will help the system adapt to the hospitalization and the illness and treatment. Effective and appropriate family involvement will ease the course of care and often increase the likelihood of adherence to treatment recommendations (Ell & Northen, 1990).

What can hospital personnel expect from families? What responses do families have to the hospitalization of a family member? The answer here is, Anything and everything. Families are as different as individuals. Each comes with a history, a pattern of communication and coping, and particular roles for each member. Hospitalization and illness threaten these patterns. The experience is a crisis for patients and families, and we must understand something of crisis theory to understand family reactions.

CRISIS THEORY AND FAMILY INTERACTIONS

A crisis is an interruption or disruption in the family's homeostasis that appears to be difficult to resolve using past coping mechanisms (Rapoport, 1962). When in crisis, individuals and families feel alienated, isolated, fearful, angry, and anxious. When faced with the crisis of hospitalization, there is often a sense of unreality and fear of the unknown. The hospital environment can be overwhelming, frustrating, and dehumanizing. Families have a myriad of questions and often do not know where to find answers. The hospital culture, systems, and procedures are foreign and frightening. The family is expected to entrust the care of their loved one to this strange and often unfriendly setting. Additionally, family may not understand the nature of the medical problem or the options for, and consequences of, treatment. No handbook prepares families for the hospital experience or teaches them what to expect or how to behave. Even when families are veterans of chronic illness, the hospital is intimidating, and previous negative experiences may color their perceptions.

In this crisis state, the behavior of the family may appear strange and irrational. Often, family members are not thinking clearly; they may not process information effectively and may seem overly aggressive or totally passive. They may wish to be at the patient's bedside 24 hours a day or to avoid visiting if at all possible. They may overwhelm staff with questions or remain almost mute. None of these behaviors is uncommon and most are unpredictable. Family members themselves may not recognize their behavior patterns and wonder, What is happening to me? They may seem to be contradicting themselves and expressing conflicting feelings.

CASE STUDY #1

Mr. N. was a 45-year-old man whose wife recently underwent surgery for breast cancer. He was tearful and very distressed, crying about her "death sentence" and his impending loss. He then commented on the surgeon's excellent reputation and his certainty that "they had gotten it all." He talked about how devastated his wife would be and then about how strong she was and how well she would cope. He expressed his anger, sense of injustice, and the lousy timing of the event. As he began to mobilize his defenses, he stated, "Everything will work out."

This kind of response is actually quite typical. Family members experience wide ranges of reactions and they piece them together in a manner that helps them cope. At the core, all of the behaviors are attempts to make sense of a situation that feels out of control. They are geared toward adaptation and mastery. They may or may not succeed. "The essence of crisis is a struggle—a struggle to cope with and master an upsetting situation and regain a state of balance" (Parad, Selby, & Quinlan, 1976). "Rather than avoid or reject the behaviors, clinicians must recognize the struggle that underlies them and help the family with it (Ell & Northen, 1990).

PROMOTING COPING

To assist the family in that struggle and to promote coping, health care professionals must begin with an assessment of the family system. This necessitates understanding the patient and family as a unit, and learning about the psychosocial and the medical history. Because the hospitalization is often brief, the assessment should be quick, related to the immediate crisis, and part of the totality of care (Ell & Northen, 1990). Clinicians should assess

- the family's perception of the illness and hospitalization;
- their emotional responses to it and their ability to find ways to manage the distress;
- how family members communicate with one another and with staff;
- the influence of their ethnic, cultural, and religious beliefs on their ability to manage the current situation;
- their abilities to understand and synthesize medical information; and

- the strengths they bring—financial security, close extended family, support from the larger community, deep religious convictions, discipline, and humor.

All families have strengths that may be more or less obvious.

Case Study #2

Mr. D., a 62-year-old attorney, was hospitalized with an acute myocardial infarction. His wife was extraordinarily anxious; although she was repeatedly told that the mild heart attack was small and her husband would be fine, her anxiety did not lessen even after a few days in the hospital. Their two adult daughters lived out of town but arrived shortly after the admission. They were physically available to both parents, but staff commented on the fact that no one seemed to be talking. This apparent lack of communication, coupled with Mrs. D.'s unrelenting anxiety, raised concerns. By taking a few moments to learn about the family's previous history, the physician was able to explain the behavior and find strength in the family. The D.'s had lost their only son when he was 14 years old. He died after a prolonged hospitalization secondary to a motor vehicle accident. Mrs. D. had never successfully dealt with her guilt. She believed that her son would be alive if she had been more vigilant when he was in hospital. She believed, accurately or not, that mistakes had been made that somehow she should have prevented. She was attempting to ensure that the same situation was not replicated in her husband's case. She was also unconsciously attempting to "undo" her perceived mistakes of the past. The family's strengths were revealed during this assessment as well. They had a close and loving connection that did not require words. They had survived the tragedy as an intact family, and they valued one another in direct proportion to their loss. They had coped with this previous crisis and were managing to do so again on their terms.

The goals of coping, adaptation, and mastery require significant work on the part of the family system and hospital personnel. Rapoport (1962) has outlined three steps necessary for this successful crisis resolution:

1. achieving the correct cognitive perception of the situation, which is aided by seeking new knowledge and being conscious of the problem at all times
2. managing affect by being aware of feelings and by discharging and mastering tension through appropriate verbalization

3. seeking and using help with actual tasks and feelings by using interpersonal and institutional resources

Only through the alliance of the family system and the health care team can these steps can be taken. Without that partnership, families and providers will struggle with poor communication, misunderstanding, unexpressed feelings, and unmet needs. The health care team must take the lead in assisting families as they move through these stages.

It is critical that the patient/family system understand the facts of the situation. Patient and family need information about the medical problem and the options for treatment. They need to understand potential outcomes and also need time and space to absorb this information. When individuals are under stress, they cannot take in and process as much information as they normally would. This is particularly true when that information is technical and very personal. Clinicians must recognize that people have differing cognitive capacities as well as different educational levels. Language can also be a barrier. Even if some family members speak English, they may be much more comfortable with their native language and will comprehend more if they can speak it.

For patient and families to feel they really understand what is happening, the physician must explain the situation step by step. The communication should be simple and straightforward, without jargon and medical terminology. One must reach for any questions the family may have and explore any confusion. It may be necessary to repeat certain information. The most important message is that no question is stupid and they have a right to information.

Physicians and nurses must communicate frequently with families, informing them about changes and progress. Although talking to families may appear to be too time-consuming, in the long run it will smooth the hospital course considerably. There is nothing as valuable to a family as a clinician who *sits down* with them and discusses what is happening. This approach should include the patient and key family members. It can be helpful to ask who the significant others are and if the family wishes to appoint a spokesperson.

Helping the family system gain a sense of intellectual mastery of the situation can be enhanced through educational tools. Many hospitals have learning centers for patient and family with access to print literature, videotapes, and the Internet. It can be very helpful for family members to have written material they can literally hold onto and take home to read and reread. This meets the need for repetition.

Clearly, families need to talk about their emotional responses to the illness and hospitalization. Families express feelings of fear, anger, and despair in different ways. Some are openly emotive, crying, moaning, laughing loudly and unabashedly. Others appear almost emotionless, with little affect or reaction. There is no single "right" way to deal with emotions, but they *must* be managed or they will impede the entire treatment approach. Clinical staff must hear what families are saying and feeling, even though they do not have to take primary responsibility for the counseling component of care.

It can be very frightening to be with people who are emotionally traumatized. The depth and rawness of the feelings can be overpowering. Clinical staff may often avoid the emotion of the experience for that reason. Listening to families' pain becomes easier over time. As it becomes more familiar, it is easier to witness, and it is frequently the witnessing that is so therapeutic. Families don't always expect clinicians to do something; they simply want them to listen and show compassion.

A key role for the clinician here is as a liaison to mental health providers. Almost all families can benefit from crisis intervention counseling, and hospital social workers are the experts. At times, psychiatric consultation is indicated as well. When a situation is particularly painful and stressful, attendings, house staff, nurses, and others may benefit from discussions with the social worker.

CASE STUDY #3

A first-year resident was treating an older woman with end-stage colon cancer. He insisted on discharging her home although she was clearly about to die. Over the protests of the family and many of the staff, she was discharged and died in the ambulance on her way home. The social worker sought out the resident to discuss what had happened. Through this discussion, the resident realized that he had pushed the discharge because he had heard so many horror stories about patients with cancer "bleeding out," and he could not bear to see it. As he talked with the social worker, he also expressed his guilt about his role in the way this patient died. The interaction helped him understand his reactions and feel better about what had transpired. It also helped him to anticipate future situations with less dread.

The last step of the coping process is obtaining help. Here the concept of the health care team comes into play. The hospital has significant resources to assist families with the myriad of issues they confront. Physicians and other clinical staff should familiarize themselves with what is available and how to access services. Direct and ongoing communication among team members and between team members and the family will allow monitoring of progress and prevent last-minute surprises by identifying and addressing all patient and family needs. Because communication is probably the single most important process to promote successful coping, clinicians must develop and enhance their communication skills. Listening is critical and requires complete attention to the speaker and the conversation; otherwise latent, underlying messages will be missed. It helps to be direct and clear in what we say, then clarify what is said and restate it so that everyone has the same understanding. In addition, we need to express caring and concern. Above all, we need to be willing to take the time necessary to communicate well.

Successful management of illness and hospitalization is a cooperative venture. It requires participation of the patient, family, physician, and other team members. There is an implicit contract in the treatment process that sets out responsibilities for those involved. Families expect that their loved one will receive the best medical care and that they will be involved in that process. They expect explanations, information, and respect and to be treated with dignity. They expect the health care team to be available and to take time and interest in their situation. They expect a partnership with the health care team that will result in positive health outcomes. By and large, families' expectations are essentially reasonable and attainable. They want and need what we all do when a loved one is ill—assistance with decision-making and support during a difficult and distressing time.

Health care professionals have expectations of family members as well. It is important to be sure that these expectations are also reasonable and realistic. We have a right to respect, appropriate information, and cooperation. We have a right to expect that the basic rules of the hospital system are observed and that family behaviors are geared toward positive outcomes. If that is not the case, we have the right to intervene to protect the patient. Conversely, we do not have the right to expect that patients and families will always agree with treatment recommendations and follow through with them. Patients who have decision-making capacity have the right to self-determination and can refuse treatment or seek alternatives that the team perhaps dismisses. The family system should not have to fear retaliation in that kind of a situation. The overarching expectation on all sides is caring, respectful interactions that contribute to the best patient outcomes possible.

Hospital care must move in the direction of family-oriented care (Ell & Northen, 1990). Our daily lives are conducted within the family, and our crises are also centered in that context. Therefore, effective crisis resolution must include family every step of the way. That means paying attention to the people with the patient, incorporating them in all aspects of care, and acknowledging their significance and their contributions. That is the only road to truly compassionate and humane treatment.

REFERENCES

Ell, K. & Northen, H. (1990). *Families and health care—Psychosocial practice.* New York: Aldine De Gruyter.

Minuchin, P., Colapinto, J., & Minuchin, S. (1998). *Working with families of the poor.* New York: Guilford Press.

Parad, H. J., Selby, L., & Quinlan, J. (1976). Crisis intervention in families and groups. In R. W. Roberts and H. Northen (Eds.), *Theories of social work and groups* (pp. 304–330). New York: Columbia University Press.

Rapoport, L. (1962). The state of crisis: Some theoretical considerations. *Social Service Review, 36,* 22–31.

Roback, H. (Ed.). (1984). *Helping patients and their families cope with medical problems.* San Francisco: Jossey-Bass.

SUGGESTED READINGS

Boyd-Franklin, N., & Bry, H. B. (2000). *Reaching Out in Family Therapy—Home-Based, School, and Community Interventions.* New York: Guilford Press.

Carter, B., & McGoldrick, M. (Eds.). (1988). *The Changing Family Life Cycle.* New York: Gardner Press.

Dattilio, F. (Ed.). (1998). *Case Studies in Couple and Family Therapy.* New York: Guilford Press.

Falicov, C. J. (1998). *Latino Families in Therapy.* New York: Guilford Press.

Franklin, C., & Jordan, C. (Eds.). (1999). *Family Practice.* New York: Brooks/Cole.

Hartman, A., & Laird, J. (1983). *Family-Centered Social Work Practice.* New York: The Free Press.

Laird, J. (Ed.). (1999). *Lesbians and Lesbian Families.* New York: Columbia University Press.

Lee, E. (Ed.). (1997). *Working with Asian Americans.* New York: Guilford Press.

Lindemann, E. (1965). "Symptomatology and Management of Acute Grief." In H. J. Parad, (Ed.), *Crisis Intervention: Selected Readings.* New York: Family Service Association of America.

Luepnitz, D. A. (1988). *The Family Interpreted.* New York: Basic Books

■ 21
Providing Culturally Competent Care

*Alexander R. Green, Joseph R. Betancourt,
and J. Emilio Carrillo*

A hospital is a place of hope, healing, and compassion and also one of illness, fear, and isolation. Those who are less familiar with, or less accepting of, the culture of American hospitals may find that these negative characteristics dominate the inpatient experience. Being from a different culture or having a different perspective is often equated with being "difficult" in the busy hospital environment. Countless studies (Kaiser Family Foundation, 1999) have documented disparities in health care based on race, ethnicity, and class that may stem from differences in culture or health care preference, difficulty communicating with the health care team, and biases within the medical system.

These disparities in the delivery of health care are of concern, especially in light of the diversity of this country's population. The term *minority*, which implies difference from a majority, is beginning to lose meaning; in California and in several major U.S. cities, ethnic minorities make up more than half of the population (U.S. Census Bureau, 2000). Moreover, ethnicity is only one component of diversity, which is also influenced by social class, religion, age, profession, sexual orientation, and local environment, among other factors. A one-size-fits-all model of health care delivery, previously the standard, now fits no one. In response, the notion of *patient-centered care* (with *cultural competence* as a large subset) has come to the forefront. This chapter will discuss practical aspects of providing hospital-based care to socioculturally diverse populations and will focus on several core sociocultural issues by providing a framework for problems that commonly arise when health care personnel interact with patients across social and cultural divides. We will emphasize the attitudes, knowledge, and skills that are useful in assessing and managing these situations in the hospital setting.

CULTURAL COMPETENCE

We begin with an explanation of *cultural competence*. Although "culturally competent care" implies that a health care provider is either culturally competent or culturally incompetent, it is clearly more complex than that. Cultural competence should be thought of as a process of learning that incorporates positive attitudes towards cultural differences, knowledge about certain cultural issues, and skills in managing cross-cultural interactions in patient care. Cultural competence may not be an ideal phrase, but it has become widely adopted as a general expression that includes the notions of cultural sensitivity, cultural appropriateness, cultural humility, and multiculturalism. A broad working definition of cultural competence would be providing health care that takes into account the unique sociocul-turally-based perspective of the patient, family, and community, focusing on effective communication, building trust, and a sensitivity to differences in attitude, custom, and belief.

It is also fundamental to understand what cultural competence is *not*. It is not simply learning a laundry list of different cultures and their characteristic ways of thinking or behaving in the medical encounter. This reductionist view oversimplifies the construct of culture. Culture is much more complex than race, ethnicity, or nationality; it is also shaped by factors such as age, gender, socioeconomic status, acculturation, religion, sexual orientation, work experience, and local environment. The laundry-list approach would have us believe that a third generation Chinese American businessman who is Catholic and lives in an upscale neighborhood in Manhattan is culturally similar to a recent Vietnamese immigrant laborer who is Buddhist and living in a poor, gang-infested neighborhood in Los Angeles, because they are both Asian. Given this complexity, it would be impossible to remember all the possible cultural rules of thumb. Additionally, it would lead to stereotypic thinking about certain cultures based on outwardly apparent markers of culture such as race, language, or nationality.

What can you, as a health care provider, do with such a complex subject as culture in the practical, day-to-day world of in-patient care?

1. *Examine your own cultural perspective and keep it in mind at all times.* We have our own personal cultural lens based on the same factors as described above, and we have adopted a professional culture that to a large extent shapes the way we think about health and illness. We are very focused on the diagnosis of scientifically defined disease entities and treatment of these with either medication or surgical intervention. We have our customs of white coats, history and physical examination, rounds, and consultation, and we place a very high value on patient autonomy, scientific study, and extension of life. When a patient has a different perspective, it is our

responsibility to try and understand that perspective, to explain ours in ways that the patient can understand, and to develop recommendations that fit both in the best way possible. We must not look at differences in perspective as right or wrong and we must avoid the temptation to characterize patients as good patients or bad patients. As we explore the various core sociocultural issues, keep in mind your own unique perspective on these issues, how you might act as a patient under similar circumstances, and why.

    2. *Evaluate your attitude towards cultural differences in patient interactions.* You may be able to ask the right questions and understand all the issues, but if you are not able to demonstrate three fundamental attitudes—curiosity, empathy, and respect—barriers will remain (Carillo, Green, & Betancourt, 1999). We are often afraid to be curious about cultural issues in the medical encounter, fearing discomfort on the part of the patient or ourselves. Yet curiosity, when genuine and tactful, is generally welcomed by patients who are happy that health care providers are concerned and interested in their perspectives (Tucket, Boulton, Olson, & Williams, 1985). Showing patients that you have empathy for them by using simple phrases—"That must have been very difficult for you" or "I'm sorry you're in so much pain. I'll try to help you feel better soon"—breaks down barriers and builds trust. We often forget to express this. When dealing with beliefs and perspectives that are different, demonstrating respect can help to open the channels of communication and make the experience of being hospitalized a little less traumatic.

CORE SOCIOCULTURAL ISSUES

Language Barriers and Interpretation

Language discordance is probably the most obvious and easily remedied barrier to effective communication across cultures in the hospital setting. Most information that we learn about patients comes from the medical history, rather than from the physical exam or laboratory studies. Anything that undermines our ability to exchange detailed information with patients also compromises the level of care we can provide. Although persons of limited English proficiency are entitled to interpretation services under recent clarifications of Title VI of the United States Civil Rights Acts of 1964, hospitals are commonly understaffed and ill prepared to handle the true demand effectively. Health care providers commonly adopt a make-do attitude towards interpretation. Rather than using professional interpreters, we often rely on friends or family members of the patient, untrained hospital staff who are pulled from their usual duties, or our own (often limited) foreign language skills combined with the patient's English. This approach has tremendous pitfalls. Family members come with their own biases, which can dramatically affect the way they interpret the health care provider's words and the patient's. They have not been trained in the subtleties of interpretation and medical terminology, nor have hospital staff who are called on to interpret occasionally. Stumbling through with broken English is probably the most dangerous way of dealing with the situation as crucial information may be missed, the important subtleties of curiosity, empathy, and respect are nearly impossible, and trust is compromised (Haffner, 1992).

CASE STUDY #1

A 68-year-old Spanish-speaking man from Ecuador presents to the emergency department for abdominal pain. He brings his granddaughter to interpret. The following is an excerpt from the conversation.

Doctor: Does eating bring on the pain?

Daughter: He wants to know if it hurts when you eat?

Patient: It hurts all the time. It was hurting me at dinnertime yesterday.

Daughter: Yes, it hurts him when he eats dinner.

The doctor may be misled into believing that this pain is worsened by meals. A very important subtlety is lost through ineffective interpretation.

How then should the hospital practitioner approach language discordance with patients? First, evaluate your attitudes towards patients with limited English proficiency. Although many cannot help feeling that communication barriers are the patient's fault, lack of proficiency in English should not intrude upon the clinical encounter. Think what it would be like to be seriously ill in a place where you could not communicate with the health care team, and try to maintain an understanding attitude toward patients with limited English proficiency.

Second, always use professional interpreter services whenever language barriers arise, rather than relying on untrained interpreters or stumbling through without any assistance. Some tips for effective use of medical interpreters are included in Appendix A (Buchwald et al., 1993).

Trust and Mistrust

Advances in medical technology over the past several decades initially gave rise to a surge in respect for the wonders of modern medicine and trust of the medical system. However, those levels of respect and trust are declining for a variety of reasons, including skyrocketing healthcare costs, the emergence of managed care, the lack of miraculous cures for mundane ills such as fatigue and osteoarthritis, medication recalls, high-profile malpractice cases, and the recent focus on medical errors. Fears of prejudice may also precipitate or magnify mistrust among patients of different socioeconomic class, race, ethnicity, nationality, language ability, religion, or sexual orientation from so-called mainstream America for reasons that are not unfounded (Kaiser Family Foundation, 1999).

CASE STUDY #2

Ms. C. is a 32-year-old African American woman with a long history of sickle cell disease who presented to a hospital in a painful crisis when traveling out of town. Her disease course had been marked by numerous painful crises, and through experience she learned that she required 6 mg of Dilaudid (hydromorphone) intravenously every 3 hours to control her pain. The physicians in the ER and on the ward were concerned about giving her that much as she seemed to be "drug-seeking," and instead gave her 3 mg every 6 hours with 2 mg rescue doses every 3 hours. The medication helped briefly, but after about a few hours she would begin screaming in pain, stating that the doctors were trying to torture her. This angered the resident, who felt she was doing the best she could. She began to feel that maybe this patient really was exaggerating her symptoms in order to get more attention or more pain medication. When house staff called Ms. C.'s physician in the morning, they learned that she always received the higher dose every 3 hours. They changed the dose to 6 mg every 3 hours, with substantial relief of her symptoms.

Although this might seem to be an extreme case, it exemplifies how mistrust of physicians can develop. In this case, some combination of racial and disease-based stereotypes, together with the resident's misunderstanding of pain management, led to an emotional reaction by the patient, who ascribed the resident's actions to racism. This set up a vicious circle of mutual mistrust. The first step in correcting this kind of situation is to recognize our own attitudes and response to mistrust. Patients who are mistrustful may make us feel unappreciated and falsely accused. We often retaliate consciously or subconsciously by labeling the patient undeserving of the care we are trying to provide.

Recognize when mistrust is present; it is often hidden or subtle. Use phrases as in Appendix A to explore with patients where the mistrust is coming from, and adapt these to address each unique situation. Mistrust can develop from bad experiences with medical treatment, disrespectful or prejudicial treatment by hospital staff, lack of communication about the patient's diagnosis or prognosis, or general loss of control in the hospital setting, among many other factors. By showing patients that you are interested in their concerns, you take the first step in breaking the vicious circle of mistrust. Once you have "diagnosed" mistrust, you are better able to direct your treatment.

Build trust with patients through good communication, by expressing empathy and respect, by giving patients a sense of control, and by going the extra mile. Although most trust-building is fairly general, in some cases it can be more focused. For example, if a patient is mistrustful because he does not understand what is happening in the hospital and feels he has no control, a conversation can be very helpful. You might discuss the rationale for his hospitalization and treatment decisions. Giving him some choice as decisions arise rather than telling him what he needs to have done could help him feel more engaged in the process of his health care. Going the extra mile—for example, helping set up the breakfast tray—conveys simply and nonverbally that you care about the patient's comfort.

Family and Gender Roles

As health care providers trained in the Western tradition, we place a high value on autonomy and the rights of the individual. This is a cultural (and ethical) perspective that most of us believe in deeply. It affects the way we interact with patients, particularly around medical decision-making and in conveying diagnostic or prognostic information. We address the patient directly, and this is generally accepted. However, it is easy and common to slip into the habit of dealing with the family members of older patients, even when those patients are mentally functional. We may be prejudging the patient's competence and the way the patient and family prefer to interact. These preferences about decision-making are in part due to necessity (e.g., when a patient truly is impaired mentally) and in part due to the cultural norms and unique family dynamics. In some cultures, autonomy is not the norm and the family as a group makes decisions. The family may look to a specific authority figure as the decision-maker. This role may be determined by gender, position in the family, or level of acculturation. Many immigrant families have to rely on their children to help negotiate medical situations because of their limited English proficiency (though as mentioned previously this should be avoided by using professional interpreters). Some patients will not be comfortable with a physician of a different gender. It is best to discuss in an open and thoughtful manner how a patient and family wish to negotiate the medical interaction (see Appendix A).

CASE STUDY #3

Mrs. K. is a 71-year-old, fully functional, widowed Korean woman who began to notice a feeling of early satiety. She ate very little and lost 15 pounds over a month's time. She presented to the emergency room with dehydration and was admitted. She had a microcytic anemia and occult blood was detected in her stool, and she was scheduled for an upper endoscopy. Her son and daughter seemed very anxious though the patient herself appeared quite calm. The hospitalist told the children that the endoscopy would determine whether their mother had cancer or some other upper gastrointestinal condition. They pleaded with the physician not to tell their mother if the endoscopy showed cancer, claiming this would only demoralize her and she would lose her will to live. They told the hospitalist that they would make all of the decisions regarding their mother's health care, stating that this was standard practice in Korea.

Situations of this type arise frequently in the medical encounter and require careful consideration and effective communication with both the patient and the family. American health care professionals generally perceive withholding diagnostic information from a patient as unethical and unreasonable. Yet in many countries, particularly in Asia and the Middle East, it is a common practice condoned by many patients and physicians alike (Elwyn, Gorenflo, & Tsuda, 1998; Harrison et al., 1997; Pang, 1999). A compromise may be reached by asking Mrs. K. to decide how she would prefer her health care decisions to be made prior to starting a workup. If she agrees that she would not want to know her diagnosis and would like her family to manage her medical decisions, she may waive her right to know. In these instances, patients often realize that they may have a serious medical condition. Eventually, family members commonly disclose most of the relevant information to the patient.

Illness/Wellness Beliefs and Complementary/Alternative Practices

Patients may have ways of conceptualizing and understanding their health and illness that differ from those of health care professionals. As the degree and nature of the difference is largely but not exclusively culturally determined, it is essential to explore each patient's unique perspective. For example, a patient from India who was raised with an Ayurvedic medical system of beliefs may avoid taking Western pharmaceutical products, as may a Chinese patient used to acupuncture and herbal medicines or a European American who believes in naturopathic medicine. Any of these patients might interpret pneumonia as a consequence of a system thrown out of balance and be reluctant to take antibiotics, feeling that this would not address the underlying imbalance. However, patients who come to medical attention have generally decided that their condition might require the services of a Western doctor and conventional medicine. In a 1997 U.S. survey, 96%

of patients who saw an alternative practitioner for a particular condition had also seen a medical doctor during the previous year. Almost one fifth of patients seeing a medical doctor were also using an alternative therapy (Eisenberg et al., 1998). Acknowledging and accepting the role of unconventional practices when they are not in conflict with medical therapy can help build trust and improve cooperation.

Patients' conceptualizations and beliefs about illness and its meaning for them are referred to as *explanatory models*. An explanatory model may be as familiar as the one that the common cold is caused by exposure to cold air or as unusual as evil spirits being the cause of chest pain. They may be culturally based and shared, or idiosyncratic, deriving from a unique explanation based on learned information, experience, and common sense. For example, a patient who believes she is able to feel her blood pressure rising and that her hypertension is due to stress or nerves may also be more likely to take medicine episodically rather than regularly and to worry about a stroke being caused by an extremely emotional situation. Appendix A includes a list of questions modified from Arthur Kleinman's original work that guide an exploration of explanatory models and health beliefs (Kleinman, Eisenberg, & Good, 1978).

It can be extremely helpful to explore and understand the patient's explanatory model and beliefs about health in general in order to have a frame of reference from which to explain the biomedical perspective and better negotiate management of the illness. If the hypertensive patient described above presented to the hospital with a stroke, education about hypertension control would best focus on separating the stress component from the disease of hypertension. She could be reassured that her stroke was not self-inflicted due to an emotional state. Negotiation also involves exploring fears and concerns about medical therapy or particular tests or procedures and applying *focused reassurance* when possible. For example, if a patient wishes to avoid antibiotics for fear of interactions with herbal medications, investigate whether such interactions have been documented in the literature, and report your findings to the patient. If a patient is refusing a CT scan of the head, explore their understanding and fears about the CT scan. If the patient is concerned about excessive radiation and brain cancer, for example, alleviate these fears through focused reassurance.

Religion and Spirituality—Death and Dying

Hospitalization for a serious illness is generally a frightening and difficult experience for patient and family alike. Patients may come face to face with their own mortality and the mortality of others around them. In this setting, religious and spiritual beliefs and values are often brought to the forefront as patients try to make sense of things and find meaning in their lives and their illness. Health care providers often feel uncomfortable addressing spiritual matters in the hospital setting as most have not been trained to address them, or may feel uncomfortable with their own sense of spirituality. Religious differences can also heighten the discomfort. Many patients would like their doctors to address spirituality but doctors rarely do (Anderson, Anderson, & Felsenthal, 1993; Ehman, Ott, Short, Ciampa, & Hansen-Flaschen, 1999; Maugans & Wadland, 1991). One study showed that only 16% of patients would not welcome a respectful inquiry into their spiritual or religious beliefs if they were seriously ill (Ehman et al., 1999).

One way to ensure that spiritual issues are addressed in the inpatient setting is to incorporate a spiritual assessment into the standard medical history (Post, Puchalski, & Larson, 2000). Asking about spiritual issues and needs in a carefully worded manner can help promote trust and communication, allow for certain religious considerations and customs, and can direct referral to pastoral services when indicated. Appendix A describes some questions that can be asked as a spiritual screening tool (Puchalski, 1999).

CONCLUSION

One of the great challenges of health care is balancing the scientific aspect of medicine with the humanistic side. This challenge escalates when patients differ socioculturally from their health care practitioners. In the hospital, where patients and families face serious illness and death, health care professionals must overcome social and cultural barriers. This chapter has outlined a practical framework for providing hospital-based care to diverse populations. Nonetheless, although reading can increase knowledge, only active practice can change the attitudes and enhance the skills that are necessary to provide good health care to all.

REFERENCES

Anderson, J. M., Anderson, L. J., & Felsenthal, G. (1993). Pastoral needs for support within an inpatient rehabilitation unit. *Archives of Physical Medicine and Rehabilitation, 74,* 574–578.

Buchwald, D., Caralis, P. V., Gany, F., Hardt, E. J., Muecke, M. A., & Putsch, R. W., III. (1993, April 15). The medical interview across cultures. *Patient Care,* 141–166.

Carillo, J. E., Green, A. R., & Betancourt, J. R. (1999). Cross-cultural primary care: A patient based approach. *Annals of Internal Medicine, 130,* 829–834.

Ehman, J. W., Ott, B. B., Short, T. H., Ciampa, R. C., & Hansen-Flaschen J. (1999). Do patients want physicians to inquire about their spiritual or religious beliefs if they become gravely ill? *Archives of Internal Medicine, 159,* 1803–1806.

Eisenberg, D. M., Davis, R. B., Ettner, S. L., Appel, S., Wilkey, S., Van Rompay, M., & Kessler, R. C. (1998). Trends in alternative medicine use in the United States, 1990–1997: Results of a follow-up national survey. *Journal of the American Medical Association, 280,* 1569–1575.

Elwyn, T. S., Gorenflo, F. W., & Tsuda, T. (1998). Cancer disclosure in Japan: Historical comparisons, current practices. *Social Science and Medicine, 46,* 1151–1163.

Haffner, L. (1992). Translation is not enough. Interpreting in a medical setting. *Western Journal of Medicine, 157,* 255–259.

Harrison, A., al-Saadi, A. M., al-Kaabi, A. S., al-Kaabi, M. R., al-Bedwawi, S. S., al-Kaabi, S. O., & al-Neaimi, S. B. (1997). Should doctors inform terminally ill patients? The opinions of nationals and doctors in the United Arab Emirates. *Journal of Medical Ethics, 23,* 101–107.

Kleinman, A., Eisenberg, L., & Good, B. (1978). Culture, illness, and care: Clinical lessons from anthropologic and cross-cultural research. *Annals of Internal Medicine, 88,* 251–258.

Maugans, T. A., & Wadland, W. C. (1991). Religion and family medicine: A Survey of physicians and patients. *Journal of Family Practice, 32,* 210–213.

Morehouse Medical Treatment Effectiveness Center. (1999). *Racial and ethnic differences in access to medical care. A synthesis of the literature.* Menlo Park, CA: Kaiser Family Foundation.

Pang, M. C. (1999). Protective truthfulness: the Chinese way of safeguarding patients in informed treatment decisions. *Journal of Medical Ethics, 25,* 247–253.

Post, S. G., Puchalski, C. M., & Larson, D. B. (2000). Physicians and patient spirituality: Professional boundaries, competency, and ethics. *Annals of Internal Medicine, 132,* 578–583.

Puchalski, C. M. (1999). Taking a spiritual history: FICA. *Spirituality and Medicine Connection, 3,* 1.

Tucket, D., Boulton, M., Olson, C., & Williams, A. (1985). *Meetings between experts: An approach to sharing ideas in medical consultations.* London and New York: Tavistock.

U.S. Census Bureau. (2000). *United States census 2000.* [On-line]. Available: http://www.census.gov.htm. Retrieved August 3, 2001.

APPENDIX A: CROSS-CULTURAL QUESTIONS AND CONSIDERATIONS

Language barriers and interpretation
- Is a professional interpreter needed in order to provide the best possible care for this patient? If so, set this up in advance if possible.
- Do not rely on friends, family, or untrained staff to interpret, and avoid relying on your own or the patient's limited language skills. This may lead to a biased or inaccurate history.
- Plan what you want to say beforehand as much as possible.
- Position yourself facing the patient with the interpreter to one side of you and slightly behind. This way you are speaking and making eye contact directly with the patient, not with the interpreter.
- Use short, unambiguous questions and explanations or break them into shorter ones when necessary (i.e., avoid compound questions like "Have you had chest pain, shortness of breath, or palpitations?").
- Avoid medical jargon, complex terminology, and slang (e.g., "Is there an *exertional* or *pleuritic* component to the chest pain?").

Trust and mistrust
- Does the patient seem mistrustful of you or the medical system in general?
- Why might this be? (i.e., general mistrust of medicine, previous bad experience, discrimination based on race, nationality, language, gender, sexual orientation, social status, etc.).
- Explore this openly with patient, acknowledge, empathize, and reassure patient of your intentions.
- Build trust by listening to the patient's concerns, trying to address what's important for the patient, avoiding a paternalistic approach, giving the patient a sense of control, going the extra mile.

Family and gender roles
- Does the family play an important role in decision making as opposed to the individual? If so, include them in all decisions.
- Is there one key authority figure? If so, be careful not to undermine that person's role.
- Would the patient be more comfortable with a physician of the same gender? Try to accommodate this when possible.
- Consider involving community leaders or spiritual leaders in very important decisions if the patient or family wishes.

Illness and wellness beliefs and complementary or alternative practices (explanatory model questions)
- What do you think has caused your problem?
- Why do you think it started when it did?
- How does it affect your life?
- How severe is it? What worries you the most?
- What kind of treatment would work (or do you expect to receive)?
- Have you seen anyone else besides a physician about this problem?
- Have you used any nonmedical remedies or treatments for your problem?
- How do you feel about taking medications and about conventional (Western) medicine in general?

Religion and spirituality
- Do you consider yourself spiritual or religious?
- How important are these beliefs to you, and do they influence how you care for yourself?
- Do you belong to a spiritual community?
- How might health care providers best address any needs in this area?

Other issues, customs, and cultural norms
- Be aware of cultural beliefs or concerns regarding taking of blood.
- Be aware of religious fasts such as Ramadan for Muslims (particularly in diabetics)
- Be sensitive to modesty regarding sexual issues, breast and genital exams.
- Pay attention and adapt to both verbal and nonverbal communication styles.
- Allow for customs or rituals that are important (prayer, family at the bedside).
- Allow nonharmful complementary or alternative therapies (cupping, acupuncture).
- Allow and encourage culturally specific diets in the hospital.

The material in Appendix A is adapted from Buchwald et al., 1993; Kleinman, Eisenberg, & Good, 1978; Puchalski, 1999.

■ 22
Ethics Committees and Case Consultation

Shantanu K. Agrawal and Joseph J. Fins

A prominent feature of the modern health care system is the establishment of hospital ethics committees or specific mechanisms to systematically consider ethical dilemmas in the clinical setting. This chapter will address the historic origins of these committees, their organization, and their current functions. We will also consider how to access ethics consultations and identify ethical problems in hospital-based care. We conclude with a consideration of outcomes research in clinical ethics and the future of these activities.

BRIEF HISTORY

The introduction and integration of hospital ethics committees with clinical services is a process that began in the 1960s and 1970s with the widespread recognition of the ethical problems that often arise in patient care (Fletcher, 1995; Ross, Glaser, Rasinski-Gregory, Gibson, & Bayley, 1993; Rothman, 1991). Although human research protocols and the allocation of scarce resources such as dialysis machines were initial concerns, committees today reflect an appreciation of the broad and far-ranging nature of medical ethics.

The earliest hospital ethics committees were "forums for debate and resources for clinicians with difficult cases" (Fletcher & Spencer, 1997). Their role increased in prominence when the courts suggested that ethical dilemmas were best handled at the bedside within institutions and not through the judicial system. A notable example of this was the 1976 case of Karen Ann Quinlan, a young woman in a persistent vegetative state whose family asked that she be removed from life-sustaining treatment. In its deliberations, the New Jersey Supreme Court opined that alternative mechanisms be established to address such dilemmas, specifically suggesting a role for ethics committees *(In re Quinlan)*.

Citing the importance and contribution of ethics committees, the President's Commission for the Study of Ethical Problems in Medicine and Biomedical and Behavioral Research recommended in 1983 that health care organizations have the responsibility

> to ensure that there are appropriate procedures to enhance patients' competence, to provide for the designation of surrogates, to guarantee that patients are adequately informed, to overcome the influence of dominant institutional biases, to provide review of decision making, and to refer cases to the courts appropriately (Tulsky & Fox, 1996)

The commission specifically urged that courts and the legal system be used only as a last resort to resolve contentious decisions. It went on to suggest that "medical staff, along with the trustees and administrators of healthcare institutions, should explore and evaluate various formal and informal administrative arrangements for review and consultations, such as 'ethics committees.'"

Although the recommendations of the President's Commission were influential, they did not establish actual requirements for health care organizations. This situation changed in 1991, when the Joint Commission on Accreditation of Healthcare Organizations (JCAHO) enacted a policy that required accredited organizations to establish a mechanism for "the consideration of ethical issues arising in the care of patients and to provide education to caregivers and patients on ethical issues in health care" (Fletcher & Spencer, 1997; Sexson & Thigpen, 1996). These guidelines drastically increased the number of hospitals and nursing homes with ethics committees because the JCAHO accredits 90% of hospitals and 30% of nursing homes in the United States. Institutions receiving Medicare and Medicaid payments are dependent on this level of accreditation. In 1989 approximately 75% of U.S. hospitals greater than 200 beds and 25% of smaller hospitals had ethics committees. By 1992, about 51% of all hospitals had ethics committees. That number is expected to be about 90% at this time.

Most health care professionals should expect to interact with ethics committees, in light of the high percentage of health care organizations with such committees. But this is not always the case and depends on the activity of the committee, its efforts at educational outreach, and the practice of the clinician. Given this variability, all practitioners should know how these committees function, how to obtain their consultative services, and which types of problems are best served by the involvement of an ethics consultant or a committee. These skills will give clinicians a greater sensitivity to the ethical nuances of practice and help maintain a good balance between the professional autonomy of the practitioner and the need for responsible consultation. Most critically, clinicians who are familiar with these institutional resources know they are not alone when facing difficult ethical problems.

ETHICS COMMITTEE ACTIVITIES

Many clinicians have a vague notion of the function and purpose of ethics committees. The "consideration of ethical issues," as JCAHO required, is a rather broad and ill-defined mandate for any organization, but it arose from a long-demonstrated need in medical practice. Since their inception, ethics committees have sought to address ethical dilemmas in health care settings; safeguard the well-being of patient and family; promote adherence to defined institutional standards; and comply with broader ethical and legal norms. To meet these goals, ethics committees have acquired three basic functions—education, development of policies and procedure, and ethics consultation. Each function is intended to provide the necessary infrastructure and approach to adequately meet JCAHO standards.

Prime among these functions is education. Ethics committees must devote a significant portion of their time to providing forums and materials for the education of clinical care providers, patients, researchers, and their own membership. Educational outreach is especially important to prevent dilemmas and to ensure that practitioners seek assistance when needed. Education can occur in a number of settings: informal rounds, grand rounds, and case presentations and at the bedside. Whatever the venue, the most valuable sessions are those that allow for an open discussion by all those involved, unimpeded by hierarchies or established power dynamics.

In the hospital setting, most educational outreach is related to the care of the dying and end-of-life decision-making. These cases also form the bulk of in-hospital ethics case consultation. Trainees should seek out their hospital ethics consultant when a case is under review in order to maximize their involvement and broaden their expertise. Ideally, every consultation should be a classroom for the dissemination of background information about the ethical, philosophical, and legal aspects of the case.

A second major function of ethics committees is to assist in the development and institution of hospital policies and procedures related to medical ethics. A committee may provide relevant resources, draft guidelines, identify possible options, select between alternatives, or evaluate effects of the new policy. This seemingly bureaucratic function helps to set the norms for behavior when dealing with potentially difficult situations. Establishing these policies in advance improves the deliberative process when cases arise. Although each ethics committee creates and evaluates policies consistent with institutional culture, most will cover several essential domains. At our institution, for example, major policy areas include patients' rights and responsibilities; privacy and confidentiality; informed consent/refusal; do-not-resuscitate orders; advance directives; brain death determination; organ donation; and organizational ethics (New York Presbyterian Hospital, 1999).

The third main function, and the one most often recognized, is ethics case consultation. In this role, ethics committees seek to aid patients, families, and clinicians in assessing and resolving ethical dilemmas that arise from clinical practice. Ethics committees are not meant to replace or contest clinician authority. Instead the role of the committee is to help improve the quality of the analysis of difficult ethical issues that arise in clinical practice and to enhance, not replace, clinician-patient-family communication. *Ethics committees do not make decisions about clinical cases.* This authority resides with doctors and patients. Clinicians should view ethics committees as institutional resources that are available to aid in the deliberative process and should not abdicate their professional responsibilities when engaging an ethics consultant.

Most ethics case consultations in the general hospital setting center around end-of-life care issues. Many of these consults relate to decisions to withhold or withdraw life-sustaining treatment through a do-not-resuscitate (DNR) order or an advance directive such as a durable power of attorney for health care or living will. Other issues that ethics committees frequently address include questions about informed consent and refusal, decision-making capacity, surrogate decision-making, medical futility, genetic testing, transplantation, and brain death. For example, in 1998 and 1999 the ethics consultation service at the Weill Cornell campus of New York Presbyterian Hospital was consulted 124 times. The leading consultative categories are noted in Table 22.1.

Retrospective review of cases brought to ethics consultation services revealed that communication failures between patients, families, and clinicians turn resolvable problems into apparent moral dilemmas (Fins, Bacchetta, & Miller, 1997). These cases do not generally result from fundamental moral questions about the good.

ETHICS COMMITTEE COMPOSITION

To address a broad range of issues, ethics committee must have diverse professional membership and lay representation. Clinicians and staff are more likely to consult and follow the recommendations of ethics committees that reflect the diversity of the health care providers and patients they serve. The entire process of ethics consultation may seem less academic and more realistic when expressing a full range of opinions and voices.

Table 22.1   Leading Consultative Categories

Type of Case	N
Withdrawal of life-sustaining treatment (adult)	50
Determination of capacity	17
DNR	16
Surrogate decision-making	15
Treatment refusal	15
Futility	9
Withdrawal of life-sustaining treatment in neonates	8
Advance directives[a]	5

[a] Cases in which life-sustaining therapy was withdrawn in accordance with a written advance directive are not included in this analysis.

A consensus that arises from a heated discussion among a variety of viewpoints may be more qualified and tenuous than one from a more homogeneous committee. Nonetheless, committee diversity may prevent the rigid interpretation of rules or situations without regard for subtle differences between cases. Being aware of these differences may allow for more effective and specific consultation (Moreno, 1995). Although committee diversity may produce profound disagreement at times over basic philosophical, social, or religious beliefs, this tension more accurately reflects our pluralistic society.

Most ethics committees draw their membership from clinical departments such as medicine and nursing as well as social work, pastoral care, and patient services. Clinicians who serve as members of an ethics committee serve as ambassadors between their home clinical department and the committee. These individuals can help connect the separate "camps" of the ethics committee and the clinical service requesting consultation and build personal relationships between committee members and clinicians, thereby improving education and consultation.

In addition to clinical members, most committees have representatives from hospital administration and legal affairs. An administrative presence on an ethics committee allows the committee a voice in administrative circles and also maintains quality assurance. Lawyers who serve on an ethics committee can provide legal information, although it is important to distinguish ethical deliberation from risk management. In most cases, ethical and legal analyses are mutually reinforcing. However, this is not always the case in novel situations in which case law has not yet evolved.

Members with expertise in philosophy, anthropology, and religious studies are also especially valued. Each discipline helps to bridge the chasm between the art and the science of medicine and provides an analytic framework that helps to guide deliberations. Many committees also have lay members who are drawn from the community. These members represent local values and help to represent the perspectives of patients and families in the committee's deliberations.

Regardless of background, each committee member must possess the ability to engage difficult issues in a collegial and open-minded manner. A number of organizations have established standards for the core competencies required of members of ethics committees, regardless of their professional background (Fletcher & Hoffmann, 1994; Leeman, Fletcher, Spencer, & Fry-Revere, 1997). A major contributor in this area is the joint Society for Health and Human Values (SSHV)-Society for Bioethics Consultation (SBC) Task Force on Standards for Bioethics Consultation, which published a report in 1998 (SHHV-SBC Task Force on Standards for Bioethics Consultation, 1998). This task force was comprised of representatives from the SSHV, SBC, JCAHO, American Medical Association, American Hospital Association, Department of Veterans Affairs, College of Chaplains, and American Association of Critical Care Nurses. Among other requirements, the task force emphasized the need for "advanced knowledge in moral reasoning and skill in ethical analysis," skills necessary to identify value conflicts, the ability to facilitate free and open discussion, facility in conflict resolution, and the ability to build moral consensus. The task force also identified core areas of knowledge and appropriate methods of training to gain the necessary knowledge. These standards have become widely accepted in the bioethics community and inform the activities and composition of most ethics committees. Such standards help to promote quality ethics consultations and foster credibility.

MODELS OF ETHICS CONSULTATION

Although obtaining an ethics consultation requires some knowledge of how services are delivered in a specific institution, consultation follows three broad models (American Academy of Pediatrics, 2001; Fletcher & Siegler, 1996). In one model, an individual consultant responds to a request for consultation. On the opposite end of the spectrum is the second model, in which an entire existing ethics committee responds to a consultation request. In this model, individuals can be added to the ethics committee on a temporary basis as required for individual cases. Finally, the third model is a combination of the previous two, in which consultation is always provided by groups of individuals, though such groups are highly variable and do not necessarily have a stable membership. These consultants may or may not report to an established ethics committee. Regardless of method, consultative process must ensure due process and adequate deliberation (Wolf, 1991).

RECOGNIZING PROBLEMATIC SITUATIONS THAT REQUIRE ETHICS CONSULTATION

Regardless of the richness of an institution's ethics consultative resources, its effectiveness depends on the ability of the clinician to recognize ethical problems that would benefit from expert assistance. Cases in which consultation should have been obtained are always evident in retrospect. The goal is to anticipate problems and engage in timely inquiry that prevents adverse outcomes or mitigates troubling situations.

One approach that may be helpful to the trainee is *clinical pragmatism,* an approach to moral problem-solving that our group has previously articulated (Fins et al., 1997; Fins & Miller, 2000; Fins, Miller, & Bacchetta, 1998; Miller, Fins, & Bacchetta, 1996; Miller, Fletcher, & Fins, 1997). This method seeks to promote what John Dewey called *inquiry.* We engage in this process by considering the full range of medical and narrative facts necessary to reach a judgment about a reasonable course of action. We begin with data collection, interpret our findings, negotiate with patients and their intimates, intervene, and then engage in periodic review. This is comparable to the diagnostic process used by physicians who collect data through the history and physical exam and then interpret the information through the promotion of a differential diagnosis. Here we seek to identify an ethics differential diagnosis.

The process of clinical pragmatism is initiated once a morally problematic situation has been recognized. The hallmark of such a situation is the presence of ethical tensions or conflicts that have gone largely unexplored. Sometimes this can be a gut feeling or the presence of anxiety on a previously well-functioning clinical team. It is important to stop and think about these moral intuitions and allow them to come to surface so that they can be analyzed and addressed, lest they burden the practitioner and adversely affect patient care.

Any health care professional who has identified a conflict or difficult situation should talk to an appropriate supervisor, such as an attending. This will encourage communication about the problem and allow the supervisor to determine if it warrants referral to an ethics committee. Realizing when such a threshold has been reached may require clinical experience and judgment. This further emphasizes the importance of effective supervision and open discourse.

After the initiation of the consultation, the pragmatic method requires the collection of the relevant medical, narrative, and contextual details of the case. Participation in this inquiry phase, when appropriate, may help health care professionals cope with and understand the problem. Information of particular interest at this point includes the medical facts; patient preferences, beliefs, and values; aspects of the family dynamics; institutional arrangements such as the structure and continuity of care; and the broader social norms and context of the case. With such information, the ethics committee or consultants can begin to formulate the *ethics differential diagnosis,* or the range of moral considerations bearing upon the problem.

This stage of interpretation leads then to negotiation, in which the consultant or committee will suggest provisional goals of care and a plan of action. This plan will be negotiated with all involved parties, allowing for equal voice and consideration, until a consensus can be reached. Periodic review follows implementation of the plan to allow for quality assurance and preventive ethics.

This method and others like it commonly used in ethics consultations provide ample opportunity for young or relatively inexperienced health care professionals to be involved in the process of ethical deliberation. Interested readers should consult cited references for more detailed instruction in this method.

EVALUATION OF ETHICS COMMITTEES

Although the mandate for ethics committees has gained momentum in recent years, their activities have not been critically assessed through outcomes research. The importance of such research is increasing in the modern climate of managed care and evidence-based medicine. Although a few studies have been conducted, this field is generally plagued with flawed methodological designs and questionable data (Fox & Tulsky, 1996; Tulsky & Fox, 1996; Tulsky & Stocking, 1996). One of the major reasons for these shortcomings is the nature of ethics committees themselves and the often abstract problems with which they contend.

It is difficult to measure a successful ethical intervention for many reasons. (a) The existence of a conflict often motivates the intervention, but its resolution does not always define success. (b) There is enough heterogeneity across ethics committees to make meaningful comparisons difficult to conduct. (c) Constructing randomized control groups for comparison— usually required for meaningful research—is difficult and may, in fact, be ethically inappropriate because it deprives individuals of potentially beneficial services. (d) Although researchers desire greater knowledge about the role and efficacy of ethics committees, most projects focus on only one of the defined functions of such committees, namely ethics consultation. But without an analysis of how well committees are meeting their full range of obligations, any study of ethics committees would be incomplete.

Nevertheless, some research has been conducted, and it may be useful to get a general idea of these studies. For example, one study published in 1996 measured the perceived effectiveness of three-person-team bioethics consultations by health care staff, patients, and families for 2 years; 22 consultation requests were made during this time (McClung, Kamer, DeLuca, & Barber, 1996). In general, approximately equal proportions of physicians and nurses found the consultations to be of at least some assistance (96% and 95%, respectively). Significantly fewer (65%) patients or family members, however, thought the interventions were helpful. Results were similar when respondents were asked about the impact of the consultation on medical management. These investigators also noted that patients or families who were dissatisfied with the process viewed their level of involvement in decision-making as inadequate.

Another study attempted to compare the consistency in function between five different ethics committees through observations of meetings, chart reviews, and interviews (Kelly, Marshall, Sanders, Raffin, & Koenig, 1997). Four major areas were addressed in this project: access to ethics consultation, the negotiated and contingent nature of ethics consultation, variability of interpretations concerning key issues, and the nature and temporal stability of any achieved consensus. The authors noted great variability in the structure, function, and composition of the ethics committees included in the study, which is in agreement with previous work in this area (Jurchak, 2000). Generally, however, their research revealed that "attending physicians remained the primary gatekeepers to ethics consultation" because of ease of access and prior experience with ethical issues. The authors also noted that most committees did not discuss "formal" ethical concepts and that most consultations were pursued for "disruptions of routine procedures," cultural issues, and disagreements between physicians and nurses.

Our group created a model to assess the economic utility of ethics case consultation (Bacchetta & Fins, 1997), and to date one study has evaluated the cost-effectiveness of medical ethics consultation through a 6-month analysis of the operation of one hospital ethics committee (Heilicser, Meltzer, & Siegler, 2000). This study used a number of outcome measures to evaluate the effectiveness of the committee: educational outcomes, policy changes and revisions, financial indicators, physician satisfaction, and staff satisfaction. The authors of the study concluded that of the 29 consultations included in the analysis, "20 resulted in cost avoidance," estimating savings to the hospital between $288,000 and $337,000 in total costs. This was compared to the hospital's expenses for the ethicist and supporting resources over the 6 months, which amounted to about $12,000. The authors were careful to note, however, that cost savings, while desirable, should not be used to justify ethics committees because of the value of committees beyond just monetary considerations and the rather small amount of savings they offer relative to a hospital's total budget.

Finally, a 1999 study aimed to define the barriers to physician use of ethics consultation services in a large, urban teaching hospital through hour-long interviews of 12 physicians (Davies & Hudson, 1999). The major areas explored in the interviews were experiences with, and opinions about, ethics consultation, physicians' roles in the physician-patient relationship, and education in medical ethics. The authors found that use of consultation services correlated with the interviewees' image of their role as a physician. Those who considered themselves the primary decision-maker in a case did not seek ethics consultations, while those who generally wanted to make a shared decision did find ethics consultation to be useful. The authors also noted that knowledge of medical ethics did not correspond to the use of ethics consultation because, "misperceptions of medical ethics were widely varied, and held by all participating physicians." Studies such as these indicate the need for additional research into educational methods to inform practitioners about the structure and function of ethics committees.

FUTURE DIRECTIONS

Although it is difficult to predict future activities of ethics committees, one likely focus will be an increased emphasis on organizational ethics. Following the 1991 mandate to establish mechanisms for the consideration of ethical issues in patient care, JCAHO in 1995 formalized a requirement for a code of ethical behavior for health care organizations concerning marketing, admission, transfer, discharge, and billing practices and the relationship of health care organizations to their staff members, providers, educational institutions, and payers (Spencer, 1997). This development has begun to transform the traditional hospital-based committee into one that addresses issues in health care systems. We suspect that the consolidation of the health care sector will necessitate an even greater regard for these forces outside the hospital and their impact on the provision of ethically sound medical care.

REFERENCES

American Academy of Pediatrics Committee on Bioethics (2001). Institutional ethics committees. *Pediatrics, 107,* 205–209.

Bacchetta, M. D., & Fins, J. J. (1997). The economics of clinical ethics programs: A quantitative justification. *Cambridge Quarterly of Healthcare Ethics, 6,* 451–460.

Davies, L., & Hudson, L. D. (1999). Why don't physicians use ethics consultation? *Journal of Clinical Ethics, 10,* 116–125.

Fins, J. J., & Miller, F. G. (2000). Clinical pragmatism, ethics consultation, and the elderly patient. *Clinics in Geriatric Medicine, 16,* 71–81.

Fins, J. J., Bacchetta, M. D., & Miller, F. G. (1997). Clinical pragmatism: A method of moral problem solving. *Kennedy Institute of Ethics Journal, 7,* 129–145.

Fins, J. J., Miller, F. G., & Bacchetta, M. D. (1998). Clinical pragmatism: Bridging theory and practice. *Kennedy Institute of Ethics Journal, 8,* 37–42.

Fletcher, J. C. (1995). Clinical bioethics at NIH: History and a new vision. *Kennedy Institute of Ethics Journal, 5,* 355–364.

Fletcher, J. C., & Hoffmann, D. E. (1994). Ethics committees: Time to experiment with standards. *Annals of Internal Medicine, 120,* 335–338.

Fletcher, J. C., & Siegler, M. (1996). What are the goals of ethics consultation? *Journal of Clinical Ethics, 7,* 122–126.

Fletcher, J. C., & Spencer, E. M. (1997). Ethics services in healthcare organizations. In J. C. Fletcher, P. A. Lombardo, M. F. Marshall, & F. G. Miller (Eds.), *Introduction to clinical ethics* (pp. 270–275). Frederick, MD: University Publishing Group.

Fox, E., & Tulsky, J. A. (1996). Evaluation research and the future of ethics consultation. *Journal of Clinical Ethics, 7,* 146–149.

Heilicser, B. J., Meltzer, D., & Siegler, M. (2000). The effect of clinical medical ethics consultation on healthcare costs. *Journal of Clinical Ethics, 11,* 31–38.

In re Quinlan, 355 A 2d 647 (NJ 1976); cert denied 429 U.S. 1992, 1976.

Jurchak, M. (2000). Report of a study to examine the process of ethics case consultation. *Journal of Clinical Ethics, 11,* 49–55.

Kelly, S. E., Marshall, P. A., Sanders, L. M., Raffin, T. A., & Koenig, B. A. (1997). Understanding the practice of ethics consultation: Results of an ethnographic multi-site study. *Journal of Clinical Ethics, 8,* 136–149.

Leeman, C. P., Fletcher, J. C., Spencer, E. M., & Fry-Revere, S. (1997). Quality control for hospitals' clinical ethics services: Proposed standards. *Cambridge Quarterly of Healthcare Ethics, 6,* 257–268.

McClung, J. A., Kamer, R. S., DeLuca, M., & Barber, H. J. (1996). Evaluation of a medical ethics consultation service: Opinions of patients and health care providers. *American Journal of Medicine, 100,* 456–460.

Miller, F. G., Fins, J. J., & Bacchetta, M. D. (1996). Clinical pragmatism: John Dewey and clinical ethics. *Journal of Contemporary Health Law and Policy, 13,* 27–51.

Miller, F. G., Fletcher, J. C., & Fins J. J. (1997). Clinical pragmatism: A case method of moral problem solving. In J. C. Fletcher, P. A. Lombardo, M. F. Marshall, & F. G. Miller (Eds.), *Introduction to clinical ethics* (pp. 21–38). Frederick, MD: University Publishing Group.

Moreno, J. D. (1995). *Deciding together.* New York: Oxford University Press.

New York Presbyterian Hospital Patients' Rights and Organizational Ethics Policy Review Committee (1999, October). *New York Presbyterian Hospital Policies and Procedures Manual.*

Ross, J. W., Glaser, J. W., Rasinski-Gregory, D., Gibson, J. M., & Bayley, C. (1993). *Health care ethics committees: The next generation.* Chicago: American Hospital Publishing.

Rothman, D. J. (1991). *Strangers at the bedside: A history of how law and bioethics transformed medical decision making.* New York: Basic Books.

Sexson, W. R. & Thigpen, J. (1996). Organization and function of a hospital ethics committee. *Clinics in Perinatology, 23,* 429–437.

SHHV-SBC Task Force on Standards for Bioethics Consultation (1998). *Core competencies for health care ethics consultation.* Glenview, IL: Author.

Spencer, E. M. (1997). A new role for institutional ethics committees: Organizational ethics. *Journal of Clinical Ethics, 8,* 372–376.

Tulsky, J. A. & Fox, E. (1996). Evaluating ethics consultation: Framing the questions. *Journal of Clinical Ethics, 7,* 109–115.

Tulsky, J. A. & Stocking, C. B. (1996). Obstacles and opportunities in the design of ethics consultation evaluation. *Journal of Clinical Ethics, 7,* 139–145.

Wolf, S. M. (1991). Ethics committees and due process: Nesting rights in a community of caring. *Maryland Law Review, 50,* 798–858.

■ 23
The Patient as Research Participant

Alice Herb

As a cancer patient and research participant, I am here to tell you that learning about another patient's successful experience might bring hope, but ultimately, such stories do not matter. I'm here to tell you that what really makes a difference is what *you*, my physician and clinical researcher, can do for me. You are the key to my future. (Udycz, 2001, p. 59)

Dr. C. is an oncologist and chief of service at a community hospital. Chemotherapy, a cornucopia of bittersweet choices, is standard treatment for most of her patients like Ms. J. who is recovering from a mastectomy and will have to decide on her course of treatment very quickly. Dr. C. can offer several options including the most commonly recommended standard therapy. But the most promising new treatment is a clinical trial for which Dr. C. is recruiting participants. Ms. J. seems a perfect candidate.

Dr. G. is a geriatrician in a large teaching hospital with a special interest in Alzheimer's disease. He has spent years collaborating with psychiatrists and psychologists in various clinical trials to find treatment modalities to delay the progression of dementia. He is now the principal investigator of a new multisite study to test a new drug on patients like Dr. M., who has been Dr. G.'s private patient for 8 years and who has become increasingly "forgetful."

Dr. H. is a pediatric hematologist/oncologist who remembers vividly her own anguish when she had to tell parents the terrible news that their baby had leukemia and had virtually no chance of survival. Now a few decades later, the odds have changed and the majority of babies are cured. Nonetheless, the percentage of babies and children who do not survive still haunts Dr. H., and she is eager to spearhead a new drug study that was very toxic in the past but that she believes may prove effective in this new protocol. Only terminally ill patients who have tried all other available options are eligible to participate.

THE THERAPEUTIC MISCONCEPTION

These are but three common scenarios encountered in practice sites of nearly every teaching hospital and in many community hospitals. The physicians would likely feel they are integrating gold-standard treatment with high quality innovative science to provide each patient with the best possible outcome. As thoughtful physicians, they are keenly aware of the patient's right to autonomy and the need to act in the best interest of the patient who lacks decision-making capacity. These doctors care about their patients, may have long-standing professional relationships with them, and may therefore be unaware of a most troubling conflict of interest: the dual role of treating physician and researcher.

Can this possibly be a conflict? Isn't the goal of research the same as that of treatment—a cure for the disease, remission of the disease with its concomitant extension of life expectancy, or at the very least the amelioration or palliation of pain and suffering? The blurring of the line between treatment and research is implicit in these questions. Yes, there may be common goals. Nonetheless, treatment is focused on the individual and what will best maximize therapeutic benefit, while research is directed at collecting data to test a hypothesis that usually does not promise any direct benefit to the individual patient. The patient's best interest can easily be overlooked in the search for a positive study outcome. Even research seeking to create new treatment—as opposed to more basic or general research in which there is no prospect of therapeutic benefit—usually does not yield any direct benefit to the patient. Called a *therapeutic misconception* (Applebaum, Roth, Lidz, Benson, & Winslad, 1987), it is a misconception that physicians often do not understand and most patients simply cannot or will not grasp.

In our culture, clinical trials are seen as positive benefits, necessary to achieve therapeutic breakthroughs. Patients often demand access in the expectation that being on the cutting edge of medicine may be their best chance for a cure (Kahn, Mastroianni, & Sugarman, 1998). Even Medicare has been ordered to pay for some research treatment ("Increasing Participation," 2000). At issue is how the physicians-researchers and patients perceive their roles in the conduct of treatment and research. For house officers, physician assistants, nurse practitioners, nurses and other health care providers, it may be useful to see the issues and dilemmas through the prism of the physician-researcher's eye.

The underlying conflict expressed in therapeutic misconception is that the physician may not realize that she is no longer *only* interested in the best possible treatment for her patient but also has a substantial professional and intellectual stake in the outcome of the research. Financial interest also plays a role, primarily because government or private industry sponsorship provides the necessary funds to do the research. Indeed, the pressure on academic physicians-researchers from their institutions to bring in grants is yet another factor in questioning the objectivity of the clinician in evaluating the trial and recruiting participants.

Participating in a clinical trial may not serve the patient's best interest; yet best interest is the primary criterion that should determine the patient's assessment of burdens and benefits of participation. The patient, ill and vulnerable, is apt to cling to the notion that the physician has the patient's best interest at heart and would not suggest or continue the protocol if it were not useful—thus the therapeutic misconception (Applebaum et al., 1987).

In an analysis of physician perceptions, George Annas, attorney and health law professor, calls the conflict "doubling" and "doublethink" (Annas, 1996). The physician sees the experiment as therapy, therefore in the best interest of the patient, and if it is not helpful to the patient, the benefit will nonetheless accrue to future patients and to the greater society. To Annas, the inherent self-deception lies in even characterizing an experiment as treatment. He looks at the U.S. cold war-era radiation experiments and even more contemporary studies with AIDS patients and terminally ill cancer patients to illustrate how physicians have managed to bifurcate their thinking, rationalizing the unspeakable acts they performed on human beings as motivated by an altruistic desire to gain information that could help humankind. In the early radiation experiments, physicians apparently persuaded themselves that they could not harm dying patients and they could study important scientific hypotheses. Later, physicians began to rationalize their experiments as having therapeutic potential. For the terminally ill whose treatment options had been exhausted, it was easy to see a potential therapeutic benefit (something ought to be better than nothing) when realistically none existed. In this way, physicians can rationalize even early studies that offer virtually no benefits and patients can easily be led astray, not actually understanding what entering a clinical trial means, as a 1998 survey of patients indicated (Sugarman et al., 1998). Most people, patients as well as physicians, are reluctant to stand by passively while untoward and often tragic events are happening. The notion that active intervention may cause more harm than good is difficult to accept. And, in some ways, these errors in judgment may contribute to the therapeutic misconception.

Although many physicians do believe that good research "should never be at odds with good patient care" (Lawrence & Bear, 1995), the General

Accounting Office (GAO), in a March 1996 report (GAO, 1996), found that if physicians could not distinguish between treatment and research, they were apt to overstate possible benefits and understate the risks. Applebaum and colleagues (1987) maintain that patients do not weigh risks and benefits accurately because they fail to understand the study design. But that is only one of the criticisms in analyzing the treatment/research conflicts. They also cite some basic considerations that separate treatment from research:

- Although treatment is adjusted to assure maximum outcome for the patient, adjusting medication dosages may be unacceptable on protocol.
- Randomization may not be in the patient's best interest since it can be argued that two treatments will seldom be identical or equivalent for a *particular* individual.
- The treating physician would always know a patient's care plan, while with research in a double-blind randomized study the physician is ignorant of what the patient is receiving.
- Placebo by its very nature is not a treatment modality.
- Additional or comfort medications may be prohibited on protocol.
- Washout periods could be unpleasant for the patient and may even place him or her at risk.

Splitting the roles—having one physician serve as the patient's clinician and another as the researcher—would appear to be an ideal solution. But in many circumstances, this solution is impractical. Often there are not enough specialists available to perform these roles separately. For patients as well, having two physicians—seeing one as a research participant and seeing another as a patient—could be unduly burdensome. Of the many disadvantages in separating the roles, one of the most compelling is that the treatment modality of a research protocol could not be changed anyway if the integrity of the research is to be preserved.

Time and cost are additional considerations. Duplicate records, twice as many appointments, and ongoing communication between researcher and physician are time-intensive and add to an already financially challenged health care system.

Having a single physician serve as clinician and researcher has many advantages. It can be argued that the physician-researcher sees in clinical practice what is effective, what the unacceptable side effects are, and what needs to be improved. These clinicians are probably best equipped to try new modalities and assess their benefits and burdens. A researcher who is also the primary clinician is more likely to know the patient's medical history, to have a full understanding of the patient's illness, and to be familiar with the patient's values and religious beliefs.

PROTECTING RESEARCH PARTICIPANTS

Research is essential, and patients want to participate. The protection of research participants, particularly those who are also patients is, therefore, a major concern. Federal laws and regulations covering federal funding of research have established elaborate methods to address these issues (Food and Drug Administration, 1999; U.S. Department of Health and Human Services [DHHS], 1999). Federal regulations mandate institutional review boards (IRBs) at every facility involved in research and in communities that need a board to review and oversee research. An IRB, as prescribed by the Common Rule and by Food and Drug Administration (FDA) regulations, must be an independent body (though usually operating within an institution) composed of men and women, scientists and nonscientists, community members and health care professionals in order to review protocols (FDA, 1999). The top priority of IRBs is the protection of human research participants. As such, it is the IRB that can eliminate therapeutic misconception by carefully evaluating the risks and benefits of the proposed protocol. One of the focal points of careful IRB evaluation is the *informed consent* that is required for virtually every research protocol. Conscientious IRB members closely peruse informed consent documents to make certain that all information necessary to make an *informed decision* is contained in the document and is written in language that the potential participant will understand. But the document is only one part of the informed consent process. What happens between researcher and potential participant is more difficult to monitor.

Informed consent—routinely obtained to permit treatment, surgery, or any invasive intervention—actively involves not only the physician who *informs* the patient but the patient as well. The patient has to be able to understand the nature and consequences of what she is told. The patient or proxy or a parent must be able to absorb the information in order to make an informed decision. She must keep in mind all of the medical information, options, recommendations, and outcome criteria that she has been told. These are high expectations for someone who is ill and has to deal with bad news. If the patient is also asked to consider a research study in which her physician is the investigator, she must also understand that the study may not benefit her, that she may suffer serious and quite unpleasant side effects; that she may be given a placebo and that, under the most fortuitous of circumstances, if she benefits from the study drug she may not be able to continue on the drug when the study is ended. In addition, the patient must think about confidentiality, privacy, voluntariness, and the specter of a possibly bleak prognosis. Under these circumstances, it should come as no surprise that patients do not retain the distinction between physician as caregiver and physician as researcher; that tensions over the inherent conflict persist, leading to the question, Can *informed* consent ever be obtained?

The difficulty in trusting that the process of informed consent can realistically protect patients is best illustrated by looking back at the three hypothetical cases. Ms. J., an African American, is 55, widowed, has three daughters, a son, two granddaughters, two grandsons, and two surviving sisters. Her mother died of breast cancer when Ms. J. was a child. One of her sisters died at age 36 of ovarian cancer.

Postsurgery, she is now faced with the decision of which course of chemotherapy she should agree to. Dr. C. offered her several options but suggested that she mainly consider the two that are offered at the community hospital—one is the current gold-standard treatment and the other is a research protocol that has a more aggressive approach.

Ms. J. is free to consult other physicians, but she does need to decide soon. Dr. C. also recommended that Ms. J. consider another research study, a study that maps the genes in participants' family trees to determine whether a genetic marker for breast and ovarian cancer can be traced to women of color. Ms. J. is an excellent candidate given her family history. Dr. C. suggests that this study could potentially yield important information for her entire family.

Ms. J. would like to retreat behind locked doors and cry, preferring that her doctor make the decision. Since her diagnosis, she feels that she is in a never-ending nightmare. But she is sensible and knows she has important decisions to make. The chemotherapy decision is the first and most urgent one. If she limits her choices to the two explained by Dr. C., she should consider that the more aggressive research study increases the dose of a cardiotoxic chemical in the first stages of treatment. Ms. J. is hypertensive and diabetic. This regimen conceivably could place her at greater risk. She will also experience physical changes faster, a situation that needs to be thought through. As a social worker who counsels adolescents, her appearance is important to her professional effectiveness.

Even if she chooses to participate in the study, she must face the uncertainty of not knowing what treatment she is receiving. The research hypothesis is that this regimen will increase the likelihood of remission in patients with more advanced, invasive tumors. As a double-blind randomized study, there is a 50-50 chance of her being on the new regimen or in the control group that will be treated with the gold standard.

Although a decision on the genetic mapping study is not critical at this point, the knowledge that her illness could have serious implications for other members of her family, particularly the females, is undoubtedly worrying her. In this connection, she would also have to be advised to consider the confidentiality and privacy implications for herself and her family if she were to enter the study. Information about the family's medical history will perforce be revealed, a situation that could result in a violation of confidentiality. Some family members may be opposed to learning anything about their future potential for illness.

Threats to potential employment and insurance coverage are additional hidden concerns for members of the family, who may be asked about any predisposition to disease when filling out applications. Federal or state laws have not resolved these issues as yet.

No matter how rational, sensible, and dispassionate Ms. J. professes to be, making an informed decision under these circumstances would be difficult for a healthy person who is not under pressure to sort these matters out. But she has a life-threatening illness and must decide on the best option for saving her life.

Dr. C. is obliged to explain and clarify all of these issues as part of the informed consent process, and he should handle it with patience and sensitivity. In sorting out Ms. J.'s options, Dr. C. should be prepared to recommend the optimal medical choices.

Dr. M.'s situation is no less troubling. Dr. G. diagnosed his "forgetfulness" as Alzheimer's disease 6 months ago. At 77, he is physically quite healthy. His only major illness is prostate cancer, which has been in remission for 7 years since Dr. G. diagnosed it and referred him for therapy. A retired physicist, Dr. M. stopped working in his laboratory just 2 years ago. Although Dr. G. has tried gently to make Dr. M. understand his illness, Dr. M. has steadfastly refused to hear it. His wife understandably is devastated. She and her children feel that if Dr. M. ever conceded that he was losing his most precious asset, his intellect, he would not want to live. Once again, the patient suits the research enrollment criteria perfectly. And Dr. G., in empathy with Dr. M.'s predicament, has strongly urged Mrs. M. to agree to her husband's participation.

What is in the patient's best interest? Dr. M., in the early stages of Alzheimer's, may still have the mental capacity to decide, but that would require that he overcome his denial. His wife reports that he is quite happy puttering in the garden, is eating and sleeping well, and seems to be quite content with his life. Placing him on an unproven drug that may have unpleasant or even serious side effects and requires him to submit to periodic medical examinations and mental tests that may not directly benefit him poses serious ethical dilemmas. It may be that as a scientist in his prime, Dr. M. would have wanted to participate, benefit or not, if he had considered it a good study design. Had Dr. M. made his views known while still of sound mind, his preferences would have to be honored. But he did not overtly indicate his wishes and thus his best interest should be paramount in deciding whether the risks are too high.

And what of the terminally ill babies to be recruited in the new leukemia study? Dr. H. is most eloquent when reviewing the history of pediatric leukemia. Treatment could never have been developed without human subject participants. Is that not a worthwhile goal in any event? But will parents understand and believe that *their* baby will not benefit? Will they believe that *their* physician will ask them to subject *their* dying baby to more discomfort for the future benefit of others? Or will they believe that there is probably some hope that their baby will respond? Is the physician truly dedicated to this patient or to the ultimate cure of leukemia?

These questions have no simple answers. If we applaud the enormous advances in medicine in the past 50 or so years, we must also accept that no progress would have been possible without the participation of human beings who with or without their knowledge and consent provided the raw material to prove or disprove a given hypothesis. If we are to respect the autonomy of human beings, to be mindful of their best interest and to do them no harm while at the same time proceed with research, we must examine the conflicts closely.

In this discourse, scarce mention has been made so far of house officers, physician assistants, nurse practitioners, nurses and other health care providers. Yet the physician-researcher and patient-participant could not ordinarily proceed without the assistance of other professionals who often will spend more time with the patient than the attending physician-researcher will. Although the prime responsibility for informing and advising the patient is the attending physician's, all health care providers should see themselves as patient advocates responsible for respecting the patient's autonomy and being vigilant that the best interest of vulnerable, incapacitated patients is observed, that no harm is done them.

Pragmatically, if a health care provider observes that the patient does not understand what he or she is being asked to do, feels that palliative care would be in the patient's best interest, or senses some other ethical dilemma, he or she should feel obligated to speak up on behalf of the patient. The first step would be to discuss the issue with the attending physician. If that is not possible, reporting the situation within the hierarchy of the discipline that is, chief resident or nurse manager, is the next step. If this process is unsatisfactory, informing the IRB chairperson or a member of the bioethics committee would also be appropriate. Protection of the patient-participant is primary.

REASONABLE CHANCE OF BENEFIT

Once the central dilemma of potential physician conflict of interest is identified and understood, we must devise ways to protect the individuals while forging ahead with new ideas. Nancy M. P. King, attorney and professor at the University of North Carolina at Chapel Hill, has published some interesting ideas (King, 2000). Starting with the federal regulations known as the Common Rule (DHHS, 1999)—that for approval of research, "risks to subjects are reasonable in relation to anticipated benefits, if any, to subjects, and the importance of the knowledge that may reasonably be expected to result"—Professor King suggests that there must be a *reasonable chance of benefit* for there to be a *reasonable choice* for a prospective participant to make. Once reasonable chance has been established, IRBs should separate the types of possible benefits and require that these distinctions be explained to prospective subjects.

- direct benefit—benefit directly received from the study intervention
- collateral benefit—benefit from extra medical exams, care, and attention as well as the satisfaction of altruism
- aspirational benefit—benefits to society and to future patients

Dimensions of benefit are also part of King's analysis, meaning that the nature, magnitude, and likelihood of the potential benefit are also part of the equation (King, 2000). When explaining the study to the patient, these more precise definitions can promote more substantive discussion.

Although these distinctions are rational and have great appeal to the analytical and legal mind, a great deal still would depend on how much the patient is able to absorb and process. Perhaps the most helpful aspect of Professor King's analysis is that at the very least, patients must understand in simple terms the following:

- their help is needed to look for better treatment for future patients;
- in exchange for their help, they will receive either the best current treatment or something unproven in a study setting;
- investigators, study sponsors, and IRBs will do their utmost to protect them from harm;
- disclosure and discussion will be thorough and honest, telling them what benefit they can and cannot expect from receiving an unproven intervention and from being a research subject, as compared with receiving standard treatment. (p. 340)

Informed consent endures as the fundamental protection for patients as well as research participants. However, the more that is packed into an informed consent process, the more likely that the patient ultimately does not hear and is unable to marshal the salient facts to make an informed decision in keeping with her best interest and her personal values. The most vital factor is the ability to communicate effectively. Moreover, the time and patience that these discussions require may tax already beleaguered physician-researchers. And, as has been pointed out, physicians themselves are often oblivious to the inherent conflict.

Clearly the greatest responsibility to resolve the conflicts rests with the physician. IRBs can demand that greater protections be put in place; sponsors, whether governmental or private industry, can help write the necessary protocols in comprehensible, straightforward language. But the physician who has established or is building a trust relationship with the patient must put safeguards into effect. If this responsibility is delegated to a house officer, a research nurse or others, the same rules must apply. Physicians and all health care providers must, therefore, be overtly aware that

- a potential conflict exists between treatment and research aims;
- a distinction between treatment and research exists;
- time and effort must be invested in explaining again and again, if necessary, for informed decision-making;
- acknowledgement from the patient that he understands and has processed the information is essential;
- the patient-participant is a "member of the team" and is entitled to know whatever happens in the course of treatment and in the conduct of the study.

Most important for any physician-researcher is that patient care should supersede all research requirements. Patients-participants must be closely monitored. If the individual is being harmed, he should be withdrawn from the study. Only through such careful surveillance can both patient care and greater knowledge occur simultaneously and ethically.

REFERENCES

Annas, J. G. (1996). Questing for grails: Duplicity, betrayal and self-deception in post-modern medical research. *Journal of Contemporary Health Law and Policy, 12,* 297–324.

Applebaum, P. S., Roth, L. H, Lidz, C. W., Benson, P., & Winslad, W. (1987). False hopes and best data: Consent to research and the therapeutic misconception. *Hastings Center Report, 17*(2), 20–24.

Food and Drug Administration. (1999). 21 C.F.R Pts. 50, 56. [On-line]. Available: http://ohrp.osophs.dhhs.gov/references/comrulp4.pdf Accessed 1/4/02.

General Accounting Office. (1996, March 8). *Scientific research: Continued vigilance critical to protecting human subjects.* GAO/HEHS-96-72. Washington, DC.

Increasing participation of Medicare beneficiaries in clinical trials. (2000, June 7). Executive Memorandum to the Secretary, HHS. [On-line]. Available: http://www.nhlbi.nih.gov/public/9_00.htm#medicare. Accessed 1/4/02.

Kahn, J. P., Mastroianni, A. C., & Sugarman, J. (Eds.). (1998). *Beyond consent: Seeking justice in research.* New York: Oxford University Press.

King, N. (2000). Defining and describing benefit appropriately in clinical trials. *Journal of Law, Medicine and Ethics, 28,* 332–343.

Lawrence, W., Jr., & Bear, H. D. (1995). Is there really an ethical conflict in clinical trials? *Cancer, 75,* 2407–2409.

Sugarman, J., Kass, N., Goodman, S. N., Perentesis, P., Fernandes, P., & Faden, R. (1998). What patients say about medical research. *Institutional Review Board, 20*(4), 1–6.

Udycz, C. (2001). A presentation at the weekly meeting of the institutional review board. *Annals of Internal Medicine, 135,* 58–59.

■ 24
End-of-Life Care Planning

Jessica B. Scholder, Abraham A. Brody,
and Melissa M. Bottrell

Advance care planning enables patients to explore the kind of care they wish to receive at the end of life and to express those wishes and preferences in a formal document called an advance directive. Because it has legal and ethical support, an advance directive is one of the few written documents that patients, families, and health care providers can utilize to respect a patient's personal decisions about end-of-life care.

In the United States, patients can implement two primary types of written advance directives—the living will and the durable power of attorney for health care (DPAHC) or health care proxy (HCP). A living will is a set of specific instructions from a patient about what type of life-sustaining interventions are or are not wanted. The instructions can vary from a simple do-not-resuscitate order to complex instructions for different illness scenarios. On the other hand, the DPAHC/HPC is a legal means for an individual to designate another person—generally called a health care agent, health care proxy, attorney-in-fact, or surrogate—to make health care decisions should the patient lose health-care decision-making capacity.

DPAHCs in many states specifically address the patient's wishes and an agent's right to make decisions about the provision of artificial nutrition and hydration and organ donation. A decision by a duly appointed agent supersedes the wishes of a patient's family or significant other, the traditional decision-maker in the absence of a DPAHC. DPAHCs are especially important when a patient wishes to appoint a nonrelative to make health care decisions. In particular, execution of a DPAHC or HCP becomes important for gay men and lesbians who wish their partners to be their proxies or for patients who have a live-in significant other to whom they are not married: Surrogacy laws in most states do not afford such proxies the same legal decision-making rights as are available to married couples. State surrogacy laws and regulations should be considered when a health care proxy has not been designated.

DPAHCs and living wills are not mutually exclusive and can be executed concurrently. The standard of decision-making known as *substituted judgment* stands behind a DPAHC and requires that the decision maker who is acting on behalf of the patient be aware of the patient's wishes and preferences. Thus, executing both a DPAHC and living will can help clarify a patient's stance on certain treatments, while at the same time allowing the proxy to act in ambiguous cases.

Although a written advance directive is preferable, most states will accept an oral advance directive in lieu of a written document. When patients with decision-making capacity make statements about forgoing end-of-life treatment, health care providers must consider the authenticity of such contemporaneous statements. Courts have held oral advance directives as valid, particularly when the statements are consistently repeated, made in a serious and solemn manner, made shortly before the need for treatment decision, are consistent with the patient's general values about life, and are specific to the patient's actual condition (Furrow, Greaney, Johnson, Jost, & Schwartz, 1995).

Other end-of-life care directives with legal status in several states include the Physician's Order for Life-Sustaining Treatment (POLST) and the Five Wishes document. The POLST encourages patients to select options about types and intensity of end-of-life care using a simple check-box system. Four sections relate to treatment: resuscitation, medical intervention, antibiotic administration, and artificially administered fluids and nutrition. The POLST includes a list of other directives the patient previously executed and documents periodic reviews subsequent to execution of the form for reasons such as change in health status. The most significant aspect of the POLST is that the physician signs the document as a doctor's order. By translating the advance directive wishes and updates (when the patient's health status changes) into orders, the POLST is an active document that follows the patient throughout the illness trajectory. Furthermore, the POLST can be transferred between health care settings and is of value across the entire continuum of care. The POLST form is valid in 42 states, either by regulation or state statute (Center for Ethics in Healthcare, 2001).

The Five Wishes document (Aging with Dignity, 2000) combines a number of end-of-life care questions into a single document. Unlike the POLST, it does not function as physician's order and thus does not have the same utility as the POLST.

- *Wish 1* requires the patient to choose a health care agent and then allows the patient to "cross out" or opt out of the potential decisions the agent can make.

- *Wish 2* allows patients to describe, using check boxes, what type of treatment they want under different circumstances, such as being close to death, in a coma and not expected to recover, or in a state of permanent and severe brain damage.
- *Wish 3* covers pain management.
- *Wish 4* permits patients to express desires about how they want to be treated by others, who is to be informed about their illness, and their preferred location of death.
- *Wish 5* addresses what patients want their loved ones to know and how they want their death and burial to be handled.

The document, which must be signed, witnessed, and notarized, is accepted by statute or regulation in 35 states.

In addition to describing treatment preferences at the end-of-life, some states have policies that enable patients to express their wishes about organ donation on the advance directive. Although disease and organ system failure may preclude organ donation at the end of life, organ donation may allow some patients to feel that they can contribute to the life of another individual or to the societal good.

IMPORTANCE OF ADVANCE DIRECTIVES TO HEALTH CARE PROVIDERS

Advance care planning should be a routine activity for clinicians. Although patients may express the desire to die in their homes, the location of death has moved out of the home and into the institutional setting. In one study, 43% of patients faced with a serious illness stated a preference to die at home, but only 17% actually ended up doing so (Fried, Doorn, O'Leary, Tinetti, & Drickamer, 1999). Currently 51.8% of deaths in the United States occur in the hospital (Center for Gerontology and Health Care Research, 1997).

Health care providers have a unique and important opportunity to initiate discussions with hospitalized patients about their end-of-life care. Nonetheless, dying patients are often unaware of the choices available to them. Many patients and their families tend to overestimate or be overly optimistic about their prognosis (Covinsky et al., 2000). Covinsky and colleagues found that among patients with metastatic colon cancer, 75% reported they had at least a 90% chance of 6-month survival, whereas only 5% of their physicians concurred with that assessment. The physician estimates were generally accurate (Covinsky et al., 2000). Without advance care planning, patients and families risk missing the opportunity to smoothly transition from curative care to aggressive palliative care.

In the absence of an advance directive stating a patient's preferences, physicians often feel compelled to treat (Gabany, 2000) without knowing whether the patient would have desired the intervention if given the option. Studies show that physician, nurse, and surrogate understanding of their patient's treatment preferences are only moderately better than chance (Covinsky et al., 2000). Absent the guidance offered by an advance directive, the medical team and family are forced to make assumptions on the patient's behalf, and care may be inconsistent with actual patient preferences had an advance directive been executed.

Do-not-resuscitate (DNR) orders are another source of confusion for staff, patients and families. Although a DNR order may be put into place based on wishes expressed in an advance directive, a DNR order is too limited to be construed as an advance directive. Clinicians should take care to counsel both family members and patients that imposition of a DNR order should not be interpreted as a patient (or family's) wish for *no* treatment. Moreover, the absence of a DNR order should not be interpreted as a patent's wish for a full, aggressive end-of-life course of care.

In the course of transitioning from a curative to a palliative plan of care, discussions about ethical differences between withholding or withdrawing care are common. Clinicians should counsel patients and families that there is no legal or ethical difference between not starting life-sustaining treatment and discontinuing a previously initiated life-sustaining treatment. Often, the underlying and commonly stated ethical concerns about withholding or withdrawing care is fear that treatment withdrawal will result in neglect or abandonment of the patient and family by the physician and other clinical care staff. Patients and families should be assured that an aggressive palliative course of treatment requires the full involvement of clinical professionals who will remain to support the patient's care and emotional needs.

Health care providers have a responsibility to make patients aware of their rights and help them make the difficult decisions that are part of end-of-life care. This responsibility is also supported by hospitals' legal requirements, particularly those specified by the Patient Self-Determination Act.

PATIENT SELF-DETERMINATION ACT

The Patient Self-Determination Act (PSDA) is a federal law passed in 1991 aimed at ensuring that patients are made aware of their rights to accept or refuse medical treatment (Parkman, 1997). The PSDA requires that organizations participating in the Medicare and Medicaid programs do the following (Parkman, 1997):

1. Provide their patients with written information regarding advance directives upon admission to the facility.

2. Provide each adult patient with written policies that explain how the facility will implement these rights of self-determination.

3. Document that a discussion about end-of-life planning and advance directives has occurred.

4. Place a copy of any advance directive in the patient's medical record.

5. Provide the patient with a written statement that the facility will not condition the provision of health care or otherwise discriminate against the patient based on whether an advance directive has been executed.

6. Educate institutional staff and the community on medical and legal issues concerning advance directives.

The PSDA leaves to each state the authority to establish and define legislation regarding advance directives (Parkman, 1997). Living wills and DPAHCs are described, constructed, and protected by state statutes in 46 states. Health care providers must learn about their state's available documents, surrogacy considerations, and other regulations applicable to expression of end-of-life care preferences.

BARRIERS TO ADVANCE CARE PLANNING

Despite the intent of the PSDA, less than 25% of the public have actually executed an advance directive (Larson & Tobin, 2000). The reasons for low completion rates are complex and revolve around socioeconomic, educational, cultural, religious, and personal histories. Clinicians often assume that patients are fully informed of their choices; this is not always the case (Silveira, DiPiero, Gerrity, & Feudtner, 2000). Advance care-planning information is generally given to patients along with other admissions materials by admission clerks, who do not review the material with the patient or are not properly educated to do so (Mezey, Leitman, Mitty, Bottrell, & Ramsey, 2000). Physicians and nurses are in the best position to discuss advance-care planning with patients, to answer questions, and to address concerns. Yet communication between patients, families, and providers about advance care planning often fails to occur because of culturally insensitive approaches to discussions about end-of-life care and dying, concerns about the patient's competence to make decisions, attitudes towards dying, and the need to make quick decisions often without comprehensive discussion.

Cultural Issues

Culture plays an important role in the discussion of end-of-life care and decisions about completing an advance directive (Larson & Tobin, 2000).

In general, patients who execute an advance directive tend to be non-Hispanic, White, and highly educated. Several studies found that in comparison to Black patients, non-Hispanic Whites are more receptive to advance directives and more likely to forgo life-sustaining treatments than Black and Spanish-speaking patients, even when the rates are controlled for education (Blackhall, Murphy, Frank, Midel, & Azen, 1995; Eleazer et al., 1996; Hopp, 2000; Mezey, Leitman, et al., 2000). In one study of nursing homes, 65% of White patients had executed advance directives compared to 11% of Black patients (Mezey, Leitman, et al., 2000).

Cugliari and colleagues have suggested a reason for the differences in the execution rates of advance directives; they propose that low-income and non-White patients (particularly Hispanic and Black patients) already have limited access to health care and thus may distrust mechanisms that could further limit their access to treatment options (Cugliari, Miller, & Sobol, 1996). Some patients may also prefer not to complete an advance directive because they believe that if a particular family member knows their wishes or is the appropriate health-care decision maker (such as an oldest son or daughter), there is no need for a written document. In some cultures, talking about death is taboo, for fear that it will bring on precisely the thing that is being discussed and most feared.

Patients' religious beliefs can also affect the way they view the end of life and the decisions they make (Daaleman & VandeCreek, 2000). For instance, many Catholics believe that God will work a miracle, or that life-support cannot be removed once it is in place (Connors & Smith, 1996). Most Native American beliefs call for letting a patient be treated without any heroic measures (Hepburn & Reed, 1995). Informed and supportive communication with a caring health-care provider can often remedy ignorance and attitudes that advance directives are irrelevant. Clinicians should proceed cautiously. Never assume that a non-White patient would not want information about advance directives; recognize that culture influences end-of-life care-planning and decision-making, but do not allow cultural stereotypes to impede patients' autonomous decision-making. All patients should be included in end-of-life care discussions (Morrison, Zayas, Mulvihill, Baskin, & Meier, 1998).

Decision-Making Capacity

Although patients should determine advance directives before they become ill, advance care planning often first occurs when a patient's poor prognosis necessitates decisions about the transition from curative interventions to palliative care. Often in such circumstances, moderate to severe loss of cognitive function from dementia, strokes, end-stage disease (e.g., metastatic cancer), organ failure, and treatment complications (e.g., infection, adverse drug reactions, and depression) leads to questions about the patient's capacity to make decisions. Furthermore, clinicians should not immediately assume that a patient who is unable to make complicated choices about personal finances or other needs cannot be included in advance-care-planning decisions. A patient who is unable to make complex end-of-life treatment decisions can often consistently designate a health care proxy or express an end-of-life care preference (Mezey, Teresi, Ramsey, Mitty, & Bobrowitz, 2000). Delirious patients may also have periods of lucidity in which they may be able to comprehend and consistently express preferences for treatments or a health care proxy. Statements made during such lucid opportunities should be considered authentic, valid expressions of treatment preferences.

Attitudes Towards End-of-Life Discussions

A major barrier to end-of-life care planning can be discomfort and apprehension about discussing dying on the part of patients, families, and health care professionals. Patients cite shyness, confusion, and fears of death and dying as reasons for not addressing advance care planning (Larson & Tobin, 2000). Few physicians feel they are sufficiently trained to communicate with patients about end-of-life care. One study showed that nearly 50% of a group of oncologists rated their own ability to break bad news to a patient as poor to fair (Wenrich et al., 2001). Clinicians should not allow such discomfort or fear to be a barrier to advance care planning. Patients expect and want their physicians to raise these discussions (Emanuel, von Gunten, & Ferris, 2000b). Without adequate communication between the patients and the health care provider, even the execution and use of advance directives is unlikely to increase a patient's chance of receiving end-of-life care in the manner that was so carefully specified.

TOOLS OF END-OF-LIFE CARE PLANNING

In advance care planning, the skill most important to patients and their families is the clinician's ability to establish trust, address patients in an honest and straightforward way, and listen to them. Emanuel and colleagues have described five steps of communication for health care providers to address end-of-life care in the hospital setting (Emanuel, von Gunten, & Ferris, 2000a).

1. *Introduce the topic.* Often the most difficult aspect of discussing advance care planning is introducing the topic. Health care providers themselves have a host of concerns that make them reluctant to do so, including fear of

frightening the patient, of relaying the wrong message, or of disappointing the patient whom they cannot cure. In fact, patients welcome the opportunity to address advance care planning with their providers. Although some patients seem more likely candidates for this kind of discussion, particularly those who are chronically ill and old, healthy people hospitalized with an unexpected, significant, life-threatening illness or major trauma are often the ones most in need of advance directives (Emanuel et al., 2000a). Health care professionals in the hospital should make discussion of advance directives a routine part of the medical process with every adult patient, regardless of age or status of health.

Upon introduction of the topic, the clinician should ask the patient how familiar he or she is with advance care planning. Some patients may already have a living will or DPAHC, and these should be reviewed and amended as necessary. Clinicians should be prepared to explain the nature of the process of advance care planning. If patients are unfamiliar with the topic, providing educational materials can be very helpful (Emanuel et al., 2000a). Most hospitals and health clinics have useful materials for this purpose; additional tools are available from the resources at the end of this chapter.

2. *Engage in structured discussions.* The attending physician and other staff should convey a commitment to respect the patient's wishes. The health care proxy or agent, if available, should also be included in the discussion of treatment options so that the patient, the proxy, and the health care team have a thorough understanding of the patient's preferences and wishes regarding treatment. Both the patient and the proxy need to feel that they can make decisions and that clinicians will support them. Staff can discuss various medical scenarios and explain medical terms to ensure complete understanding and insight into care choices. Throughout this discussion, clinicians should remain sensitive to the patient's specific values, including religious beliefs and spirituality.

Using a work sheet to ensure that a patient's attitudes and values are addressed through a variety of potential scenarios can help ensure structured discussions with all patients. Clinicians can choose from several different work sheets, including the Five Wishes document mentioned earlier, which provide a consistent and structured approach to document a patient's wishes. Copies should be given to the patient and to the proxy (Emanuel et al., 2000a).

3. *Document patient preferences.* To reduce ambiguity and avoid possible future conflict, the attending physician should review the advance directives with the patient and the proxy once decisions have been made. The directive should then be formally documented in the patient's medical record, so that all health care providers working with the patient know the patient's treatment preferences (Emanuel et al., 2000a). Copies of the

advance directive should also be provided to the patient, proxy, family members, and necessary health care providers (Emanuel et al., 2000a).

4. *Review and update the directive.* If an advance directive already exists, patients and agents should regularly review it, because major life events such as changes in health care status or prognosis can alter the patient's attitudes or preferences. Any changes in the advance directive should be thoroughly discussed with all involved parties and carefully documented (Emanuel et al., 2000a).

5. *Apply directives to actual circumstances.* An advance directive becomes effective when a patient is no longer able to articulate treatment preferences, and hospital staff must then refer to and follow the wishes stated in the document as best they can. If and when the patient regains health-care decisional capacity, the advance directive is no longer active. The document will not always apply exactly to the variety of potential health or treatment scenarios. Therefore, the staff should also consult the proxy and or other family members and together attempt to reach the best decision regarding the patient's wishes (Emanuel et al., 2000a).

EDUCATION

Information about advance directives, palliative care, and end-of-life care decision-making may be available through the hospital, professional associations, and community and government resources. Clinicians, patients, and health care proxies will find valuable information available on the Web sites included at the end of this section.

Physicians can refer to the Education for Physicians on End-of-Life Care (EPEC), a project funded by the Robert Wood Johnson Foundation, to educate themselves on the essential clinical competencies in end-of-life care. A resource guide, information on obtaining EPEC curriculum, and a list of EPEC conference attendees can be found on their Web site (see Resources). Physicians can also contact the End of Life Physician Education Resource Center (EPERC), an initiative of the Medical College of Wisconsin and the Robert Wood Johnson Foundation. EPERC provides information to physician educators about end-of-life training materials, publications, and conferences (see Resources).

Nurses can refer to the End-of-Life Nursing Education Consortium (ELNEC), funded by the Robert Wood Johnson Foundation, which is a comprehensive, national education program to improve end-of-life care by nurses. Its primary project goals are to develop a core of expert nursing educators and to coordinate national nursing education efforts in end-of-life care. Information on ELNEC can be found on their Web site (see Resources).

A health care agent is an essential resource in end-of-life decision-making. An informed agent with assertive skills can provide the best chance for compassionate and appropriate treatment decisions for a dying patient (Post, Blustein, & Dubler, 1999). Health care agents and clinicians who would like to support them can refer to the Center for Bioethics (1999).

CONCLUSION

Advance care planning, including the execution of advance directives, is a formidable process that can empower patients to direct their end-of-life care and treatments. Supportive patient-physician communication, awareness of particular cultural preferences, and efforts to include patients irrespective of lessened cognitive capacity can enhance advance directive completion rates and improve the process of decision making at the end of life. Physicians, nurses, and other involved health care providers in the hospital setting must take an active role in informing hospital patients about their advance-care-planning options. To achieve this, providers must learn about advance directives and effective communication skills in order to earn their patient's trust and mutual respect.

ADVANCE DIRECTIVE RESOURCES

Association for Death Education and Counseling
638 Prospect Avenue
Hartford, CT 06105
(203) 232-4825
www.adec.org

Partnership for Caring
1620 Eye Street NW, Suite 202,
Washington, DC 20007
(202) 296-8071
www.partnershipforcaring.org

Center for Bioethics of the University of Pennsylvania
3401 Market Street, Suite 320
Philadelphia, PA 19104
(215)898-7136
www.med.upenn.edu/bioethic/center/

Education for Physicians on End-of-Life Care (EPEC)
Feinberg School of Medicine
Northwestern University
Chicago, IL
www.epec.net

End-of-Life Nursing Education Consortium (ELNEC)
American Association of Colleges of Nursing
Washington, DC
www.aacn.nche.edu/elnec/about.htm

End-of-Life Physician Education Resource Center (EPERC)
Medical College of Wisconsin
Milwaukee, Wisconsin
www.eperc.mcw.edu

Last Acts
Stewart Communications, Ltd.
325 West Huron, Suite 300
Chicago, IL 60610
(312) 751-1297
www.lastacts.org

WNET
On Our Own Terms: Moyers on Dying
Bill Moyers, Executive Producer
www.pbs.org/wnet/onourownterms

REFERENCES

Aging with Dignity. (2000). Five wishes. [On-line]. Available: www.agingwith-dignity.org/5wishes. Accessed August 16, 2002.

Blackhall, L. J., Murphy, S. T., Frank, G., Midel, V., & Azen, S. (1995). Ethnicity and attitudes toward patient autonomy. *Journal of the American Medical Association, 274,* 820–829.

Center for Bioethics. (1999). *Making health care decisions for others: A guide to being a health care proxy or surrogate—A quick reference for physicians.* [On-line]. Available: www.montefiore.org/bioethics (accessed August 13, 2001).

Center for Gerontology and Health Care Research. (1997). *Facts on dying.* [On-line]. Available: www.chcr.brown.edu/DYING/usa_statistics.htm (accessed August 9, 2001).

Center for Ethics in Health Care. (2001). *Physician orders for life-sustaining treatment program.* [On-line]. Available: www.ohsu.edu/ethics/polst. Accessed August 16, 2002.

Connors, R. B., & Smith, M. L. (1996). Religious insistence on medical treatment. Christian theology and re-imagination. *Hastings Center Report, 26*(4), 23–30.

Covinsky, K., Fuller, J., Yaffe, K., Johnston, C., Hamel, M., Lynn, J., Teno, J., & Phillips, R. (2000). Communication and decision-making in seriously ill patients: Findings of the SUPPORT project. The study to understand prognoses and preferences for outcomes and risks of treatments. *Journal of the American Geriatrics Society, 48*(Suppl. 5), S187–93.

Cugliari, A., Miller, T., & Sobol, J. (1996). Race and health care: An American dilemma? *New England Journal of Medicine, 155,* 1893–1998.

Daaleman, T., & VandeCreek, L. (2000). Placing religion and spirituality in end-of-life care. *Journal of the American Medical Association, 284,* 2514–2517.

Eleazer, G. P., Hornung, C. A., Egbert, C. B., Eghert, J. R., Eng, C., Hedgepeth, J., McCann, R., Strothers, H., Sapir, M., Wei, M., & Wilson, M. (1996). The relationship between ethnicity and advance directives in the frail older population. *Journal of the American Geriatrics Society, 44,* 938–943.

Emanuel, L., von Gunten, C., & Ferris, F. (2000a). Advance care planning. *Archives of Family Medicine, 9,* 1181–1187.

Emanuel, L., von Gunten, C., & Ferris, F. (2000b). Gaps in end of life care. *Archives of Family Medicine, 9,* 1176–1180.

Fried, T. R., Doorn, C. U., O'Leary, J. R., Tinetti, M. E., & Drickamer, M. A. (1999). Older person's preferences for site of terminal care. *Annals of Internal Medicine, 131,* 109–112.

Furrow, B., Greaney, T., Johnson, S. S., Jost, J. S., & Schwartz, R. (1995). *Health law* (p. 369). St. Paul, MN: West.

Gabany, J. (2000). Factors contributing to the quality of end of life care. *Journal of the American Academy of Nurse Practitioners, 15,* 472–474.

Hepburn, K., & Reed, R. (1995). Ethical and clinical issues with Native American elderly. *Clinics in Geriatric Medicine, 11*(1), 97–111.

Hopp, F. P. (2000). Preferences for surrogate decision makers, informal communication, and advance directives among community-dwelling elders: Results from a national study. *Gerontologist, 40,* 449–457.

Larson, D., & Tobin, D. (2000). End-of-life conversations. *Journal of the American Medical Association, 284,* 1573–1578.

Mezey, M., Leitman, R., Mitty, E. L., Bottrell, M. M., & Ramsey, G. C. (2000). Why hospital patients do and do not execute an advance directive. *Nursing Outlook, 48,* 165–171.

Mezey, M., Teresi, J., Ramsey, G., Mitty, E., & Bobrowitz, T. (2000). Decision-making capacity to execute a health care proxy: Development and testing of guidelines. *Journal of the American Geriatrics Society, 48,* 179–187.

Morrison, R., Zayas, L., Mulvihill, M., Baskin, S., & Meier, D. (1998). Barriers to completion of health care proxies. *Archives of Internal Medicine, 158,* 2493–2497.

Parkman, C. (1997). The Patient Self-Determination Act: Measuring its outcomes. *Nursing Management*. [On-line]. Available: www.springnet.com

Post, L. F., Blustein, J., & Dubler, N. N. (1999). The doctor-proxy relationship: An untapped resource. *Journal of Law, Medicine and Ethics, 27*(1), 5–12.

Silveira, M., DiPiero, A., Gerrity, M., & Feudtner, C. (2000). Patients' knowledge of options at the end of life. *Journal of the American Medical Association, 284*, 2483–2488.

Wenrich, M., Curtis, J., Shannon, S., Carline, J., Ambrozy, D., & Ramsey, P. (2001). Communicating with dying patients within the spectrum of medical care from diagnosis to death. *Archives of Internal Medicine, 161*, 868–874.

Part V
Improving Quality of Care

■ 25
Preventing Errors

Molla Sloane Donaldson

A patient has the wrong leg amputated or dies from a drug overdose during chemotherapy. A child dies during "minor" surgery because of a drug mix-up (Cook, Woods, & Miller, 1998). Although such events make headline news, house staff, advance practice nurses, pharmacists, and other hospital personnel recognize and correct errors and usually prevent harm every day. Despite our acknowledgment that to err is human, health care professionals have customarily viewed errors as a sign of incompetence, not humanity. As a result, rather than learning from such events and using this information to improve safety, they have had difficulty admitting or even discussing adverse events or "near misses," often because of fear of professional censure, administrative blame, or lawsuits.

Error is "the failure of a planned action to be completed as intended or the use of a wrong plan to achieve an aim" (Institute of Medicine, 1999). Not all errors result in injury, but those that do are sometimes called *preventable adverse events;* injury is thought due to a medical intervention, not the underlying condition of the patient. Although there is some controversy about the actual number of preventable hospital deaths (Hayward & Hofer, 2001), the Institute of Medicine (IOM) reported that as many as 98,000 Americans die each year as a result of preventable medical errors (IOM, 1999; Leape et al., 1991). Two large studies, one conducted in Colorado and Utah and another in New York, found that adverse events occurred in 2.9% and 3.7% of hospitalizations, respectively (Brennan et al., 1991; Leape et al., 1991; Thomas et al., 2000). In both studies, more than half of these adverse events resulted from medical errors and could have been prevented. Medication errors alone, occurring either in or out of the hospital, are estimated to account for more than 7,000 deaths annually (Phillips, Christenfeld, & Glynn, 1998). Reacting to such reports, health professionals have begun to ask how hospitals can be made safer. Questions like the following come from many quarters:

- During my first month as a resident, a patient suffered and died because I missed seeing the results of an electrocardiogram that showed she was having a myocardial infarction. The strip was in with a pile of X rays, and though I had ordered it, I never saw it. What should I have done when I realized what had happened? What should my superiors have done? What should I have told the family?
- Who is responsible for making sure that the gas lines are hooked up correctly before anesthesia is administered?
- We are really short-staffed. Sometimes I am so busy and distracted that I am sure I must make mistakes when calculating the doses of meds. I haven't killed anyone, but I probably don't even know sometimes when I've made a mistake. How can I make sure I don't make errors?

These questions are not unusual. Health care is a complex system that is prone to harm from errors—especially in operating rooms, intensive care units, and emergency departments where there is little time to react to unexpected events; consequences can be serious. Although many of the available studies have focused on the hospital setting, medical errors present a problem in all settings, including outpatient surgical centers, physician offices and clinics, nursing homes, and the home, when patients and families use complicated equipment.

Patients should not be harmed by the health care system that is supposed to help them, but the solution does not lie in assigning blame or urging health professionals to be more careful. In what seems to be a simple example, an ICU nurse was wheeling a patient to radiology on a gurney when his knee struck a fire extinguisher hanging on the wall, and the patient needed extra care. The error appears obvious. Perhaps the nurse was scolded by her supervisor and told to be more careful. In some hospitals she would be punished, and everyone would feel the problem had been solved. Would that make the hospital safer? That is, would it prevent other similar events from happening with other staff and patients in other units?

The answer is an emphatic *no*. Experts in accident analysis distinguish between the "sharp" end of an error, when the event occurs, and the "blunt" end during which many "latent" errors develop that may be attributable to a faulty system, equipment design or maintenance, poor working conditions, failures of communication, and so forth. Improving safety, defined as *"freedom from accidental injury"* (IOM, 1999), arises from attention to the often multiple latent factors that contribute to errors. In this case, such factors included (a) the nurse's need to move the patient herself because transport had never arrived; (b) a change in hospital policy, allowing one instead of two people to guide the gurney; (c) the failure to mount the fire extinguisher in a recessed niche; (d) the decision to transport a seriously ill patient rather than having mobile equipment come to him, requiring extra handoffs and opportunities for injury; and (e) poor gurney design, making steering difficult. Much can be learned from the analysis of errors, and still other latent factors may have played a part in the accident.

Certainly, all adverse events resulting in serious injury or death should be evaluated to identify such latent factors and guide system improvements. Safety does not reside in a person, department, or device, even if the device was developed to make care safer. Large, complex problems require thoughtful, multifaceted responses; that is, preventing errors and improving safety require a systems approach to the design of processes, tasks, training, and conditions of work in order to modify the conditions that contribute to errors.

Fortunately, there is no need to start from scratch. A great deal is already known and could be put in practice today. Designing for safety requires a commitment to safety, a thorough knowledge of the technical processes of care, an understanding of likely sources of error, and effective ways to reduce them. Hospital leadership must provide resources and time to improve safety and foster an organizational culture that encourages recognizing and learning from errors. However, a culture of safety cannot develop without the keen observation, trust, extensive knowledge of care processes, and support from those on the front lines of health care.

When errors occur, individuals must be held responsible for their actions. Nonetheless, accountability is not the same as making systems safer. Redesigning care processes reduces errors more effectively than blaming individuals. There are many opportunities for individuals to prevent error. Some actions are clinically oriented and have considerable evidence to support them, such as the use of antibiotic-impregnated catheters to prevent infection and real-time ultrasound guidance to prevent morbidity during central line insertion (Agency for Healthcare Research and Quality, 2001). Others are broader in focus or address the work environment. Although less evidence supports them, students of patient safety believe they have strong face validity. They include

- communicating clearly to other team members
- requesting and giving feedback for all verbal orders
- being alert to "accidents waiting to happen"
- simplifying processes to reduce handoffs
- participating in multidisciplinary training
- involving patients in their care
- being receptive to discussions about errors and near misses
- paying respectful attention when any member of the hospital staff challenges the safety of a course of action.

The remainder of this chapter offers a framework for preventing error and the harm that results when error does occur, and it offers examples of good practices to bring to the task of improving the safety of patients and their visitors as well as those who work in these institutions.

UNDERSTANDING ERROR

One approach to understanding how to reduce error is to focus on human factors and likely sources of error. Human beings have many intellectual strengths, such as their large memory capacity, a diverse repertoire of responses, flexibility in applying these responses to information, and an ability to react creatively and effectively to the unexpected. They also have well-known limitations, including difficulty attending carefully to several things at once and recalling detailed information quickly and generally poor computational ability, especially when tired (Haberstroh, 1965). Respecting human abilities involves designs that recognize the strengths of human beings as problem solvers but that limit reliance on weaker traits such as memory and vigilance.

Human beings commit errors for a variety of reasons that have little to do with lack of good intention or knowledge. Leape (1999) has described the "pathophysiology of error" that distinguishes two types of cognitive tasks. The first type of cognitive task occurs when people engage in well-known, oft-repeated processes. Tasks are handled rapidly, effortlessly, in parallel with other tasks, and with little direct attention. An example is driving to work or making a pot of coffee. Errors may occur because of interruptions, fatigue, time pressure, anger, distraction, anxiety, fear, or boredom. Errors of this sort are to be expected, but conditions of work can make them less likely.

By contrast, other tasks require problem solving. They are done more slowly and sequentially (rather than in parallel with other tasks), are perceived as more difficult, and require conscious attention. Examples are making a differential diagnosis and readying several types of surgical equipment made by different manufacturers. Here, errors are due to misinterpretation of the problem that must be solved, habits of thought that cause us to see what we expect to see, and sometimes lack of knowledge to bring to the task (e.g., which physical findings are significant, how the equipment differs from others one has used). Attention to safe design includes simplification of processes so that users who are unfamiliar with them can understand quickly how to proceed, and making accurate information readily available.

User-Centered Design

Understanding how to reduce errors depends on linking knowledge of likely sources of error with effective ways to reduce their likelihood. User-centered design of processes and technologies (Norman, 1988) builds on human strengths and avoids weaknesses. The first strategy of user-centered design is to make things visible—including the conceptual model of the process—so that the user can determine what actions are possible at any moment, for example, how to turn off a piece of equipment, how to change settings, and what is likely to happen if a step in a process is skipped.

Avoid Reliance on Memory

The next strategy is to *standardize* and *simplify* the structure of tasks to limit the demand on working memory, planning, or problem solving.

Standardize Process and Equipment

Standardization reduces reliance on memory. It also allows newcomers who are unfamiliar with a given process or device to use it safely. In general, standardizing device displays (e.g., readout units), operations, and doses is important to reduce the likelihood of error. Examples of standardizing include avoiding look-alike products and using standard order forms, administration times, prescribing protocols, and types of equipment. Sometimes devices or medications cannot be standardized. When variation is unavoidable, differentiate clearly. For example, one can identify look-alike, but different, strengths of a narcotic by labeling the higher concentration with bright orange tape.

When developed and used wisely, protocols and checklists can enhance safety. Protocols for the use of heparin and insulin, for example, have gained widespread acceptance. Software that checks drug-drug interaction and laminated dosing cards that include standard order times, doses of antibiotics, formulas for calculating pediatric doses, and common chemotherapy protocols can reduce reliance on memory (Leape, Kabcenell, Berwick, & Roessner, 1998). Even with excellent protocols, not all steps may be appropriate for a given patient, of course, and rapid increases in knowledge and changing technology necessitate regular updating of protocols.

Simplify Key Processes

Simplifying key processes can greatly reduce the likelihood of error. Simplifying includes reducing the number of handoffs required for a process to be completed. Examples of processes that can usually be simplified are writing an order, then transcribing and entering it in a computer, or having several people record and enter the same data in different databases. Other examples of simplification include limiting the choice of drugs and dose strengths available in the pharmacy, maintaining an inventory of frequently prepared drugs, reducing the number of times per day a drug is administered, keeping a single medication administration record, automating dispensing, and purchasing equipment that is easy to use and maintain.

Incorporate Affordances, Natural Mappings, Constraints, and Forcing Functions into Designs

Another strategy of user-centered design is the use of affordances, natural mappings, constraints, and forcing functions. An *affordance* is a characteristic of equipment or work space that communicates how it is to be used, such as a push bar on an outward opening door that indicates where to push, or a telephone handset that is uncomfortable to hold in any position but the correct one. *Natural mapping* refers to the relationship between a control and its movement; for example, in steering a car to the right, one turns the wheel right. Other examples include using louder sound or a brighter light to indicate a greater amount.

Constraints and *forcing functions* guide the user to the next appropriate action or decision. A constraint makes it hard to do the wrong thing; a forcing function makes it impossible. For example, one cannot start a car that is in gear. Forcing functions include the use of special luer locks for syringes and indwelling lines that have to be matched before fluid can be infused, and different connections for oxygen and other gas lines to prevent their being inadvertently switched. Removing concentrated potassium chloride from patient units is a negative forcing function.

Attend to Safety in Conditions of Work

Jobs should be designed with attention to the effect of human factors such as work hours, workloads, staffing ratios, sources of distraction, and shift changes (which affect one's circadian rhythm) and their relationship to fatigue, alertness, and sleep deprivation. For example, reassigning some tasks can allow residents to have periods of uninterrupted sleep and greatly improve their performance. Distraction can be decreased by setting aside times, places, or personnel for specific tasks such as calculating doses or mixing intravenous solutions.

Avoid Reliance on Vigilance

Individuals cannot remain vigilant for long periods of inaction, and it is unreasonable to expect them to do so. Approaches for accommodating the need for vigilance include providing checklists and requiring their use at regular intervals, limiting long shifts, and rotating staff who must perform repetitive functions. Automation such as robotic dispensing systems in the pharmacy and infusion pumps that regulate the flow of intravenous fluids can reduce reliance on vigilance. There are pitfalls in relying on automation, however, if a user learns to ignore alarms that are often wrong, becomes inattentive or inexpert in a given process, or if the effects of errors remain invisible until it is too late to correct them. Well-designed equipment provides information about the reason for an alarm and has moderate sensitivity.

Train in Teams Those Who Are Expected to Work in Teams

People work together throughout health care in multispecialty group practices, interdisciplinary teams assembled for the care of a specific clinical condition, operating rooms, and ICUs. Whenever it is possible, hospitals should establish team training programs for personnel in critical care areas (see chapter 3). People make fewer errors when they work in teams. When processes are planned and standardized, members look out for one another, noticing errors before they cause an accident. In an effective interdisciplinary team, members come to trust one another's judgments and attend to one another's safety concerns.

Involve Patients in Their Care

Patients and their family or other caregivers should be part of the care process. Clinicians must obtain accurate information about each patient's medications and allergies and make certain this information is readily available at the patient's bedside. In addition, safety improves when patients know their condition, treatments (including medications), and technologies that are used in their care.

At the time of discharge patients should receive a list of their medications, doses, dosing schedule, precautions about interactions with alternative therapies or with alcohol, possible side effects, and any activities that should be avoided such as driving or using machinery. Patients also require written information about the next steps after discharge such as follow-up visits to monitor their progress and whom to contact if problems or questions arise (Hwang, 1999).

Anticipate the Unexpected

Some technologies such as computerized physician order entry systems (CPOE) are engineered specifically to prevent error. Despite the best intentions of designers, *ALL technology introduces new errors, even when its sole purpose is to prevent errors.* Indeed, future failures cannot be forestalled by simply adding another layer of defense against failure (Cook, 1998). Safe equipment design and use depend on a chain of involvement and commitment that begins with the manufacturer and continues with careful attention to the vulnerabilities of a new device or system. Health care professionals should expect any new technology to introduce new sources of error and should adopt the custom of automating cautiously, alert to the possibility of unintended harm.

Anticipating the unexpected also applies to times of organizational and financial change. The likelihood of error increases when reorganization, mergers, and other organization-wide changes result in new patterns of care.

Design for Recovery

The next strategy for user-centered design is to assume that errors will occur and to design and plan for recovery by duplicating critical functions and by making it easy to reverse operations and making it hard to carry out nonreversible ones. An example is the Windows® computer operating system that asks if the user really intends to delete a file, and if so puts it in a recycle folder so that it can still be retrieved.

Examples of ways to mitigate injury are keeping antidotes for high-risk drugs up-to-date and easily accessible and having standardized, well-rehearsed procedures in place for responding quickly to adverse events. Another way to mitigate harm is simulation training, a feedback method in which learners practice tasks and processes in lifelike circumstances using models or virtual reality. In simulation for crisis management, small groups that work together learn to respond to a crisis in an efficient, effective, and coordinated manner. Such simulation should involve all key players because many problems occur at the interface between disciplines.

Improve Access to Accurate, Timely Information

The final stage for user-centered design is to improve access to information. Information about the patient, medications, and other therapies should be available at the point of patient care, whether they are routinely or rarely used. For example:

- Include a pharmacist on rounds. Pharmacists are much more valuable if they are present when the patient care team is making decisions and writing orders.
- Use computer programs that alert clinicians to abnormal lab values.
- Put lab reports and medication administration records at the patient's bedside.
- Place protocols in the patient's chart.

- Use color-coded wristbands to alert for allergies and bar codes to identify patients.
- Ensure easy access to formularies, Web sites, and other resources for ordering, dispensing, and administering medications.

MEDICATION SAFETY

Because the burden of harm to patients is great and we know how to prevent the most common kinds of drug errors, medication safety is a high priority area. Errors increase with complexity. Complexity in the medication system arises from several sources, including the extensive knowledge and information necessary to prescribe correctly; the intermingling of medications of varying hazard in the pharmacy, during transport, and on the patient care units; and the multiple tasks performed by nurses, only two of which are medication preparation and administration. The practices that follow have been shown to reduce medication errors and should be implemented in all appropriate health care organizations.

1. Ask for feedback on all orders. If instructions are verbal (in person or by phone), ask the recipient to repeat your instructions to verify them. Welcome requests for clarification.

2. Implement standard processes for medication doses, dose timing, and dose scales in a given patient care unit. Standardization facilitates recall, checking, and cross-checking.

3. Standardize prescription writing and prescribing rules. Many common shortcuts in prescribing have been found to cause errors. Abbreviations are the major offender because they can have more than one meaning. Other frequent sources of error include the use of *q* (as in qid, qod, qd, qh), which is easily misread, and the use of the letter *u* for "unit." Failure to specify all of the elements of an order (form, dose, frequency, route) also leads to errors.

4. Limit the number of different kinds of common equipment. Limit the types of equipment available on a single patient-care unit unless all such equipment has the same method of setup and operation. When a device fails, it should always default to the safest mode; for example, an infusion pump should default to shutoff, rather than free flow. Unfortunately, both sorts of pumps are in use in hospitals today.

5. Use physician order entry (CPOE). Having physicians enter and transmit medication orders on-line is a powerful method for preventing medication errors due to misinterpretation of handwritten orders. It can ensure that the dose, form, and timing are correct and can also check for

potential drug-drug or drug-allergy interactions and patient conditions such as renal function. In one before-and-after comparison (Bates et al., 1998) nonintercepted serious medication errors decreased by more than half (from 10.7 to 4.86 events per 1,000 patient-days). If CPOE is not available, much of the safety benefit can be realized by manual systems that use standard order forms for common conditions (e.g., myocardial infection, use of heparin) if the forms are completed by clinicians and not transcribed.

6. Use pharmaceutical-decision-support software that checks for duplicate drug therapies; potential drug-drug and drug-allergy interactions; and out-of-range doses, timing, and routes of administration.

7. Have the central pharmacy supply high-risk intravenous medications. Having the pharmacy place additives in IV solutions or purchasing them already mixed, rather than having nurses prepare IV solutions on patient care units, reduces the chance of calculation and mixing errors.

8. Use special procedures and written protocols for the use of high-risk medications. A relatively small number of medications carry a risk of death or serious injury when given in excessive dose. Some, like heparin, warfarin, insulin, lidocaine, magnesium, chemotherapeutic agents, and potassium chloride (see below), narcotics, adrenergic agents, and immunoglobin are among the most powerful and useful in the therapeutic armamentarium (Leape et al., 1998). Special protocols and processes should be used for high-alert drugs. Such protocols might include written and computerized guidelines, checklists, preprinted orders, double-checks, special packaging, and labeling.

9. Do not store concentrated solutions of hazardous medications on patient care units. Potassium chloride (KCl) is an especially deadly drug that is never used undiluted and should never be stored on a patient care unit.

10. Make relevant patient information available at the point of patient care. Bar coding to identify patients or colored wristbands to alert personnel to allergies are useful strategies to prevent improper prescribing or administration.

11. Improve patients' knowledge about their treatment. Patients should know the medications they are receiving and for what reasons, the expected effects and possible complications, what the pills or injections look like, and how often they are to receive them. Patients should be involved in reviewing and confirming allergy information in their records. They should be encouraged to notify their doctors or staff of discrepancies in medication administration or the occurrence of side effects.

CONCLUSION

This chapter suggests ways to think about error and encourages attention to safety problems that may have been unnoticed. It also describes actions that health care professionals can take now in their own institutions. Still other actions, which are discussed in greater detail in the Institute of Medicine's report *To Err Is Human* (IOM, 1999), require resources and authority to develop new policies and systems.

REFERENCES

Agency for Healthcare Research and Quality. (July 2001). *Making health care safer. A critical analysis of patient safety practices: Summary.* AHRQ Publication No. 01-E057. Rockville, MD: Author. Available: http://www.ahrq.gov./clinic/ptsafety/ Accessed July 20, 2001.

Bates, D. W., Leape, L. L., Cullen, D. J., Laird, N., Petersen, L. A., Teich, J. M., Burdick, E., Hickey, M., Kleefield, S., Shea, B., Vander Vliet, M., & Seger, D. L. (1998). Effect of computerized physician order entry and a team intervention on prevention of serious medical error. *Journal of the American Medical Association, 280,* 1311–1316.

Brennan, T. A., Leape, L. L., Laird, N. M., Hebert, L., Localio, A. R., Lawthers, A. G., Newhouse, J. P., Weiler, P. C., & Hiatt, H. H. (1991). Incidence of adverse events and negligence in hospitalized patients: Results of the Harvard Medical Practice Study I. *New England Journal of Medicine, 324,* 370–376.

Cook, R. I. (1998, November). *Two years before the mast: Learning how to learn about patient safety. Enhancing patient safety and reducing errors in health care.* Proceedings of the conference on enhancing patient safety and reducing errors in health care. Annenberg Center for Health Sciences, Rancho Mirage, CA.

Cook, R. I., Woods, D., & Miller, C. (1998). *A tale of two stories: Contrasting views of patient safety.* Chicago: National Patient Safety Foundation.

Haberstroh, C. H. (1965). Organization, design and systems analysis. In J. J. March (Ed.), *Handbook of organizations.* Chicago: Rand McNally.

Hayward, R. A., & Hofer, T. P. (2001). Estimating hospital deaths due to medical errors. *Journal of the American Medical Association, 286,* 415–420.

Hwang, M. Y. (1999). Take your medications as prescribed. [Patient page]. *Journal of the American Medical Association, 282,* 298.

Institute of Medicine. (1999). *To err is human. Building a safer health system.* L. T. Kohn, J. M. Corrigan, & M.S. Donaldson (Eds.). Washington, DC: National Academy Press.

Leape, L. L., Brennan, T., Laird, N. M., Lawthers, A. G., Localio, A. R., Barnes, B. A., Hebert, L., Newhouse, J. P., Weiler, P. C., & Hiatt, H. (1991). The nature of adverse events in hospitalized patients. Results of the Harvard Medical Practice Study II. *New England Journal of Medicine, 324,* 377–384.

Leape, L. L., Kabcenell, A, Berwick, D. M., & Roessner, J. (1998). *Reducing adverse drug events.* Boston: Institute for Healthcare Improvement.

Leape, L. L. (1999, May 14). Reducing medical error. Can you be as safe in a hospital as you are in a jet? National Health Policy Forum.

Norman, D. A. (1988). *The design of everyday things.* New York: Doubleday/ Currency.

Phillips, D. P., Christenfeld, N., & Glynn, L. M. (1998). Increase in US medication-error deaths between 1983 and 1993. *Lancet, 351,* 643–644.

Thomas, E. J., Studdert, D. M., Burstin, H. R., Orav, E. J., Zeena, T., Williams, E. J., Howard, K. M., Weiler, P. C., & Brennan, T. A. (2000). Incidence and types of adverse events and negligent care in Utah and Colorado. *Medical Care, 38,* 261–271.

■ 26
Risk Management

Brian K. Regan

The call to the risk manager is terse and frightening. The nurse manager reports that a small fire has occurred in the operating room and a patient is hurt. The risk manager reaches for a pad and confirms that the fire is out and all other patients and staff are safe. It seems a 68-year-old patient was prepared and draped for an excision of a cyst from her right flank when fire erupted on the patient's hip.

The fire was contained and quickly extinguished, so quickly in fact that no fire alarms or protection sprinklers were triggered. The patient herself has sustained a third-degree burn and is being tended by the medical and nursing staff. The patient is anesthetized and her husband and son are in the waiting room adjacent to the OR, as yet unaware of the incident.

The risk manager knows the physician in this case is an experienced and well-respected member of the professional staff. The risk manager reviews the events with the physician and others who report that a routine laser excision of the cyst was planned; before the procedure could begin, however, the laser had suddenly fired, igniting the drapes that covered the operative site. The cause of the event is unknown.

As with all invasive procedures, the physician has obtained the informed consent of the patient and has discussed the risks, benefits, and alternatives to this procedure, including the alternative of no treatment. The risks of anesthesia had also been reviewed with the patient and her consent was obtained and documented on the standard form used by the hospital. The patient is married with two children, a son and daughter. The surgeon knows them well and has cared for them on many occasions. It is clear to the risk manager that the physician is the best person to speak with the family and carefully plans this difficult conversation with the physician.

The family is waiting anxiously. They know the patient is in the OR. They have seen the frantic activity in and out of the OR area, but no one has been willing or able to tell them what was happening inside.

The physician starts by telling them the patient is safe, that the patient sustained a small burn but is stabilized and being treated. The family is angry and upset. "What went wrong?" The surgeon knows from experience that he must repeat and reiterate, over and over, that the patient is safe and that her injuries are not life-threatening and are relatively minor. He explains that he too is upset about this incident and he too wants to know what went wrong. The physician explains that no one knows what happened and that a full investigation is underway. Most important, he tells them that the patient and family will be kept fully involved in the investigation. The physician tells them he will find out what happened and that they will know as soon as he does.

After a time, the family accepts his word. The physician introduces them to the director of patient relations who will stay with them while he attends to the patient. He knows the patient will be fine physically. He also knows that as soon as the patient is recovered from anesthesia he will have this same difficult conversation with her.

OVERVIEW

This accident is not typical, but it is representative of the problems faced by a hospital risk manager. Hospitals can be very dangerous places. According to the Institute of Medicine, more than 40,000 medical errors occur in the United States each year (Kohn, Corrigan, & Donaldson, 1999) (see also chapter 25). For this reason, hospitals have instituted clinical risk management "to identify, evaluate, and reduce the risk of injury associated with care" (Joint Commission on Accreditation of Health Care Organizations, [JCAHO], 1991, p. 1). The risk manager works for the hospital to reduce the risk of such events and to coordinate a response to them.

The risk manager is often a nurse by education who has had training in medical-legal issues as well as ethics, patient relations, and insurance issues, although more attorneys and physicians are taking this role. Risk managers often coordinate all reports of incidents and accidents, most of which involve no injury at all. They analyze incidents and adverse events to find patterns and trends over time and to identify potential problem areas. Often, they use specialized tools such as "root cause analysis" or "failure mode analysis" to investigate problems in hospital systems and to assess faults in procedures, resources, equipment, the environment, or individual job roles. When serious accidents occur, they may initiate a peer review process to bring together experts from within the hospital in order to review the care rendered by an individual practitioner.

If an accident with injury has occurred, the risk manager will coordinate steps to ameliorate damages and provide a plan of action to avoid recurrence. A serious event may lead to adverse publicity for the organization and may severely harm public opinion and community relations. In such cases, the risk manager will work with hospital staff or outside consultants on press relations and communication.

In many cases, regulatory authorities will also be involved. State and local authorities usually have direct oversight agencies that are dispatched to the hospital to ensure investigation and follow-up. Moreover, federal review may result: The Food and Drug Administration (FDA) will be interested in any potential problem with a medical device or pharmaceutical. The Center for Medicare and Medicaid Services (CMS) may also review the hospital's compliance with Federal regulations and "conditions of participation" that must be met by any facility receiving federal payments (e.g., Medicare). The Joint Commission on Accreditation of Healthcare Organizations (JCAHO) has very specific standards that must be met by any hospital it accredits; they also conduct important oversight. All of these organizations are important to ensure enforcement of standards of care and to provide public assurance that health care facilities are safe and effective.

Nonetheless, after an untoward event, the first concern of the risk manager is to secure the current safety of the facility, its staff, and patients. Once this is done, the risk manager will ensure that the primary focus is on the medical care of the patient who has been injured: *Staff must do what is best for the patient and must not be distracted by medical-legal concerns.*

COMMUNICATION

Communication with the patient and family is next in order of priority. The staff member who is closest to the patient and family must communicate what is known. In the event of accidental injury, the most common reaction of staff is to avoid this important communication, because it is unpleasant and because they fear being blamed for the event and getting involved in litigation. Experience has shown that any attempt to suppress information or to cover up the incident will result in far worse consequences than openness will. If patients or their families are angry and are uninformed, the lack of information will increase frustration and destroy any sense of trust with the facility and practitioner. Patients and families may seek out the media to help them get answers or turn to law enforcement or the courts to get information (or in some cases revenge). Once the risk manager is sure that a communication link has been forged, it must be maintained with regular updates to the patient and family whenever new information becomes available. All communication should be centralized through a single source, usually the attending physician, in order to avoid conflicting or confusing reports to the family. Although other members of the care team and administration can be involved, the attending physician is usually the leader. If the attending physician is unable or unwilling to assume the role, another leader must be designated, preferably a senior physician with a leadership role in the organization.

DOCUMENTATION

Next, the risk manager must act quickly to secure the medical record and to ensure that each involved member of the care team will properly document the factual events of the accident. In the case of the fire in the OR, the patient's preparation and placement prior to the accident, as well as the burn and its treatment must be documented. In short, *involved staff must document all aspects of the event that are important to the patient's care and treatment.* Fearful of litigation, involved staff may want to avoid the necessary chart notes that are routinely documented in other cases. However, omissions or gaps in the chart will likely be interpreted as gaps in care or a lack of accountability. Staff must also resist the urge to engage in finger-pointing and accusatory comments in an attempt to blame others for the accident. Such comments may become an admission of liability in a lawsuit and will be difficult to defend even if the comments are later shown to be obviously false. Finger-pointing does not absolve accusers, who will be asked what action they took in response to any defect or departure they noted. Finally, such behavior shatters any perception that health care providers work as a team, and this can be very upsetting to a lay jury. It is also inappropriate for one member of the care team to volunteer to write a lengthy explanation, part hearsay and part fact, to "explain everything." The risk manager may have to remind the staff that the primary purpose of the medical record is communication of patient care.

Many hospitals use incident report or occurrence report forms and require staff to complete one for each accident (or "near miss"). These forms are the proper place to record particulars of the event that are not directly related to the care of the individual patient. Such forms may be protected from discovery in civil litigation, depending on state law.

Medical records are legal documents and subject to external review. In case of patient injury, the chart may well be a legal exhibit in litigation proceedings. Entries should be legible and should be dated and timed concurrently. Any necessary deletion should be marked with a line through it and initialed by the writer, with the deleted passage clearly visible beneath the strike-through. Late additions to the record may be written as an addendum and should also be concurrently dated and timed. No part of the record may be destroyed. Any attempt to scribble over or white-out an entry will certainly be viewed suspiciously by a jury.

Staff must also be cautioned to avoid self-serving "corrections" that are documented with hindsight long after the events. For example, a physician who received an attorney letter of request for a copy of the chart may be tempted to review the record and "clarify" the documentation. This is not only bad practice but potentially fraudulent.

In most cases the risk manager will coordinate the investigation of any accident involving an injury. The medical record must be reviewed and interviews must be conducted with involved staff. In matters likely to involve litigation, outside counsel may also be needed to preserve attorney-client privilege and to look after the legal interest of the hospital and staff. However, the investigation for purposes of quality improvement and communication with the family is paramount.

> Investigation of the OR fire began with the removal of the laser machine to a locked closet to protect other patients and to preserve the chain of evidence for potential litigation. Bioengineering review (conducted by an outside consultant to ensure impartiality and expertise) found no defect in the laser. Had a product defect or flaw been found in the laser, the hospital would have notified the FDA (and the manufacturer would have a potential product liability exposure in court).
>
> Upon investigation, it was determined that policies and procedures for laser surgery were current and complete and staff had been trained in the use of the device. According to the procedure, the patient was to be prepped and draped. Upon arrival of the physician the laser was to be positioned, with the foot-pedal switch (to activate the laser) placed at the foot of the physician.
>
> After all involved staff were interviewed, it was found that this procedure had not been followed. Instead, the laser had been brought to the OR table first. The switch had been placed on the floor, and the nurse who was positioning the patient accidentally stepped on the foot pedal activation switch, firing the laser at the patient. Also contrary to policy, disposable paper drapes had been used instead of cloth, literally adding fuel to the fire.

PREVENTING FURTHER ACCIDENTS

What happens once the investigation has revealed the steps leading to the incident? Until recently, the primary administrative response to an accident was to find the person responsible for the error and to punish him. This often involved disciplinary action, including termination. This approach certainly discouraged open reporting procedures, to say the least. A more enlightened response would be to see the error as a failure of education and to mandate counseling and in-service training for the involved person. This approach still involves assigning blame, while trying to help the person who made the error.

It is now widely recognized that most medical accidents are the result of a failure in a system. Punishing or training an individual is not likely to prevent recurrence. Rather, the methodologies of performance improvement should be used to prevent accidents (see chapter 28).

> An analysis of the system in the OR found that the technician placing the laser and the nurse preparing the patient had no means of communication. The machine could be dropped off hours or minutes before the procedure. The nurse had no chance to speak with the technician about any questions or concerns. After review, this practice was changed to ensure that the technician would hand off the machine to a nurse who was required to accept it and assume responsibility for final positioning of the laser. Another problem was identified in this case: Staff had been oriented to the machine when it was purchased several years before, but it was not part of their annual orientation schedule. This oversight was remedied and all staff in the OR were promptly in-serviced on the laser. These findings precipitated a review of the training schedule to ensure that each piece of equipment was included at least annually.

In this case, the lessons learned from an accident with one type of equipment were used to reduce the risk of injury with all types of equipment in the hospital. Moreover, the nonpunitive approach toward involved staff was meant to encourage other staff to report real or potential accidents in the future.

LEGAL LIABILITY

When an accident occurs, the risk manager is also concerned about the elements of legal liability. In fact, risk managers have been criticized in some quarters for risk-adverse decisions and for being more concerned with protecting the hospital from lawsuits than with protecting the patient (Dubler & Nimmons, 1992). Nevertheless, medical staff who are involved in an adverse event are at risk of suit, and are themselves properly fearful of the time and expense involved, in addition to the potential consequences to their reputation (and perhaps their license to practice). Civil liability or malpractice will be assessed if there is a breach in the standard of care that is the proximate cause of injury or other damages. In the most egregious circumstances, a district attorney may even be convinced that criminal negligence has occurred.

In the case study, the overriding duty to do no harm was breached. An accident of this type is clearly not a foreseeable risk of the procedure; a patient is not supposed to sustain a burn in the hospital. It seems the actions of the staff were the proximate cause of a burn that resulted in damage to the patient. But how are these damages quantified?

The risk manager determined that the patient's burn measured four centimeters in diameter and required full-thickness grafting, which involved a second operative procedure after the one originally planned. Aside from an extended hospital stay, the patient also sustained significant pain and suffering, as well as limitation on her activity over a period of many weeks after the injury. The patient will also have a permanent scar from the burn.

These damages can be quantified by reviewing what juries have awarded in similar cases. Additional damages include the loss of services to her husband because she could not help with the cooking, cleaning, and other household activities during her convalescence. In court, the claim could include loss of consortium as the injury prevented sexual activity with her husband. A jury could assign a dollar value to this, as well.

If the patient had been employed and sustained a loss of income, if projected longevity had been decreased by the injury, or if she required ongoing medical care, equipment, or supplies, these costs would be projected over her lifetime and would contribute to the dollar value of the case.

The risk manager consulted with the hospital's malpractice defense attorney and the insurance carriers who had been put on notice at the time of the accident. Based on similar cases in this jurisdiction, the value of this case was assessed at $400,000. If the case were to go to trial, the value could be more, given the sympathetic appeal of this case to a jury.

Faced with a clear liability and a moderate likelihood that a lawsuit would ensue, the risk manager concluded that a presuit settlement would be in the best interest of the hospital. Such a settlement would save the hospital the expenses of staff time dedicated to preparation for trial and testimony in court. It would also save the fees for a legal defense, which can escalate quickly if expert fees and investigative costs are a factor.

From the patient's standpoint, a malpractice suit would take many years and would also involve a significant time commitment. The patient might be responsible for paying her attorney to prepare the case, unless it was handled on a contingency fee basis, where the patient's attorney would typically receive one third of any eventual award by a jury.

Given all these factors, it is often in the interests of a patient to settle prior to litigation. Of course, all such settlement agreements should be reviewed by an attorney for the patient (paid on a fee basis, not on contingency) in order to ensure the patient's interests are protected.

> In this case, the patient had recovered well and had been kept well informed by her doctor and the hospital staff. She knew that errors had occurred and that she had been injured as a result. She was comforted when she was informed that hospital procedures and training had changed to ensure that this accident would not happen to another patient. Her friends had told her to sue, but she wasn't sure.
>
> She was surprised when the hospital risk manager told her that the hospital wanted to compensate her for her injuries. The dollar value they agreed upon was $200,000. This seemed fair to her and to the attorney she consulted, and she was glad to put the whole thing behind her. So was the hospital.

Of course this case is not typical. The vast majority of injuries that occur in a hospital do not have clear and specific causative events, and it is left for juries to determine whether a complication is an ordinary risk of the procedure or whether the community standard of care has been violated. The jury is then faced with dueling experts: The plaintiff's and defendant's experts will each present their cases in a very convincing way; this is what they are paid well to do.

Most cases are not settled on a presuit basis and will involve lengthy (and costly) litigation. There are many reasons why such settlements are not common: Often the elements of causation are unclear. There is also a relatively low probability that an individual will sue. In fact, the Harvard Medical Malpractice Study found that only one out of seven potentially compensable injuries actually resulted in litigation (Brennan et al., 1991).

Even in cases of clear departure involving a litigious patient, it may be difficult to negotiate a pre-suit settlement in the aftermath of an accident. This is because one side or the other may have an unrealistic expectation of the value of the claim or because the extent of damages may be unclear in the period immediately after the injury. In these cases, a medical malpractice suit can be brought against the hospital and the caregivers involved in the patient's care.

Often those named as parties to the malpractice suit will include many physicians, nurses, and other licensed professionals. The plaintiff's attorney will have culled their names from the patient's medical record, which highlights the importance of clear and objective documentation. Staff who were peripheral to the accident or injury may be surprised to find themselves involved in a lawsuit. However, in the early stages of a lawsuit before the process of discovery and deposition, the plaintiff's attorney may not be sure who was responsible for an alleged error. If the plaintiff's attorney fails to name defendants in a timely way, the applicable statute of limitations may prevent them from ever being sued. In addition, by naming a person in the suit, the plaintiff may find it easier to depose him or her about the case.

"Patient falls are responsible for more lawsuits alleging negligence on the part of hospitals and nurses than any other kind of injury" (Feutz-Harter, p. 120). A fall in the hospital may be defensible if there was no prior indication of risk. For hospitalized patients, a risk-assessment checklist can be used to estimate the risk of falls, and fall precautions can be implemented by the care team and documented in the patient's medical record. Multiple falls are difficult to defend for obvious reasons: Once the patient has fallen, proper precautions should be taken.

Another common cause of claims in the geriatric population is the development of pressure ulcers (see chapter 12). Even when infection or other complications do not develop, the appearance of the open wound can be reason enough for a jury to consider an award for the plaintiff. A well-documented program of skin assessments and care plans for those at risk of skin breakdown is essential.

Medication errors can also result in suit. According to the Institute of Medicine (IOM), medication errors result in more than 7,000 deaths in the U.S. each year (Kohn et al., 1999). Partly as a result of the IOM report, medication errors are likely to result in more risk than ever before. Severe medication errors that result in injury or death carry the risk of public exposure, a demand for response by the patient and family, and high award value in the event of litigation (Boswell, 2000). Systematic organizational responses have focused on high-risk medications (such as heparin and insulin), sound-alike and look-alike medications, and dangerous abbreviations that can lead to misinterpretation of the physician orders.

Another potentially high-risk area is the use of seclusion and restraints, where mistakes can lead to injury and death. Errors include inappropriate use, inadequate training of those who apply them, improper application of the restraint devices, and insufficient monitoring of the patient in restraints. Because of the public perceptions and because the use of restraints is highly regulated (see chapter 10), an injury or death involving restraints is difficult to defend (Maloney & Domaleski, 2001).

Other common sources of liability involve the failure to properly monitor the patient's condition and the failure to properly notify the responsible physician of any pertinent information. In general, if the physician is not given timely notice of significant changes in the patient's condition or is not provided sufficient information to respond appropriately, the physician will not be liable, although the responsible nurse may be (Feutz-Harter, 1993).

CONCLUSION

Risk managers must be able to foster communication and synthesize information from patients and caregivers, with the advice of medical experts, legal counsel, regulators, insurance officers, investigators, safety experts, and others. They must be able to work with all involved parties to analyze complex systems and develop safer ones. The concerns of the experts, however, should always be peripheral to the central dyad of patient and practitioner. Health care providers should always remember that "good medicine is good risk management." Careful documentation will reduce the risk of lawsuit, but it will also facilitate care and allow all members of the team to be fully informed about the progress of treatment. Empathetic support, good communication, and a caring approach to the patient may avoid a malpractice case, but these are also at the heart of the relationship that all patients want and deserve when they put their lives and trust in the hands of a health care provider.

Hospitals, nursing homes, and even the physician's office are not danger-free environments for the patient and practitioner. The risk manager knows that all risks cannot be controlled. The risk manager's role is not to eliminate risk but to reduce the number of adverse events, control damages when such events occur, and to prevent their recurrence. In this sense, the risk manager is an ally of both the patient and health care professional.

REFERENCES

Boswell, D. J. (2000). *The medication prioritization matrix: Prioritizing medication errors using severity and process indices.* [On-line]. Available: www.ashrm.org/asp/membership/medicationmatrix2000.asp. Accessed December 4, 2001.

Brennan, T. A., Leape, L. L., Laird, N. M., Hebert, L., Localio, A. R., Lawthers, A. G., Newhouse, J. P., Weiler, P. C., & Hiatt, H. H. (1991). Incidence of adverse events and negligence in hospitalized patients: Results of the Harvard Medical Practice Study I. *New England Journal of Medicine, 324,* 370–384.

Dubler, N. N., & Nimmons, D. (1992). *Ethics on call.* New York: Harmony Press.

Feutz-Harter, S. A. (1993). Common sources of liability. In *Nursing and the law.* Eau Claire, WI: Professional Education Systems.

Kohn, L., Corrigan, J., & Donaldson, M. (1999). *To err is human: Building a safer health system.* Washington, DC: National Academy Press.

Joint Commission on Accreditation of Health Care Organizations. (1991). *Risk management strategies.* Oakbrook Terrace, IL: Author.

Maloney, B. A. M., & Domaleski, V. O. (Winter, 2001). Law and practice hand in hand: The use of seclusion and restraint interventions in the healthcare setting. *Journal of Healthcare Risk Management.* [On-line]. Available: www.ashrm.org/asp/membership/lawwinter2001.asp. Accessed December 30, 2001.

■ 27
The Role of
Outcomes Research

Mark A. Callahan, Nathaniel Hupert,
and David S. Battleman

Quality improvement has become a central theme in health care. To a large extent, the mounting concerns of payers, regulators, and consumers over medical errors, defects in quality, and unexplainable regional variation in the use of medical and surgical services have driven this change (Ashton et al., 1999; Berwick & Leape, 1999; Brennan et al., 1991; Chassin et al., 1986; Chassin & Galvin, 1998; Leape et al., 1991; McPherson, Wennberg, Hovind, & Clifford, 1982; Phillips, Christenfeld, & Glynn, 1998; Wennberg, Freeman, & Culp, 1987). To improve quality, one must be able to measure it accurately; this need has given rise to the field of outcomes measurement and research.

Donabedian (1988) provided a framework for measuring quality of care based on operational engineering principles. The framework divides quality into structural measures, process measures, and outcomes measures. *Structural measures* are the characteristics of hospitals and providers that may be associated with quality (i.e., Are the physicians board certified? Is there a quality assurance committee at the hospital?). *Process measures* are the activities performed during the course of treatment. Process measures include such items as giving the appropriate medication for a given condition, the timeliness with which health care interventions occur, and charting of delivered care. *Outcomes measures* evaluate the patient's health state after treatment has occurred (i.e., mortality rate, blood pressure levels in hypertension). This chapter focuses on outcomes measurement in health care and how it applies to the hospital setting.

TYPES OF OUTCOMES MEASURES

Outcomes measures can be divided into three subgroups: generic measures, condition-specific measures, and patient satisfaction measures. All these approaches have their strengths and limitations, and often combinations of measures are appropriate to understand quality for a given clinical setting or condition.

Generic outcomes measures come in a variety of forms. The simplest are measures of mortality and morbidity, for example, survival rates after treatment for acute myocardial infarction or surgical mortality rates. These types of measures are relatively easy to quantify and are often used to compare populations or providers. However, there are significant limitations to their use, and they provide a fairly crude measure of quality of care. Additionally, mortality is a rare or infrequent event for many conditions and may fail to provide useful information in many settings.

To evaluate outcomes beyond simple measures of morbidity and mortality, a number of scales and questionnaires have been developed over the years. These instruments evaluate the patient's quality of life, usually across multiple domains (such as physical, social, and emotional functioning, ability to carry out activities of daily living, and level of pain). Research has confirmed the validity, reliability, and sensitivity of these instruments across multiple disease conditions, age groups, clinical settings, and ethnic groups. As a result, instruments such as the Sickness Impact Profile (SIP) (Bergner, Bobbitt, Carter, & Gilson, 1981) and the Short Form-36 (SF-36) (Ware & Sherbourne, 1992) serve as outcomes measures for a number of scenarios in the hospital setting.

Condition-specific outcomes measures examine parameters specific to a given disease. Condition-specific measures can include laboratory values such as the hemoglobin A1c as a measure of how well diabetes mellitus is controlled; physiologic measures such as average blood pressure readings in hypertensive patients, or questionnaire scales designed for a medical condition, such as the Minnesota Living with Heart Failure Scale (Rector & Cohn, 1972). These types of outcomes measures are often used in clinical trials, as they provide information centered on the clinical condition under study. Additionally, because these outcomes measures are rooted in clinical measurement, physicians and nurses are often more receptive to them.

Patient satisfaction is another outcomes measure. An extensive literature exists on the predictors of patient satisfaction, and these measures are often a key focus of payers and providers of care. Hospitals, health plans, and medical groups measure patient satisfaction and use the results to make decisions about marketing strategies and selection of providers and to identify areas for improvement in customer service activities. As such, patient satisfaction is an important and widely used outcome measure. Patient satisfaction and technical measures of the quality of medical care often correlate poorly, however (Maciejewski, Kawiecki, & Rockwood, 1997).

When evaluating an outcome study, it is critical to understand the characteristics of the patients for which the measure was derived. Underlying differences in patient characteristics have a major impact on the incidence, treatment, and outcomes of illnesses. For example, older patients with more comorbid conditions have worse outcomes (higher death rates and more complications) when examining mortality for most diseases. Patients from lower socioeconomic groups often have worse outcomes and higher underlying rates of certain diseases. Taking these patient characteristics into consideration when looking at outcomes is referred to as risk adjustment: statistically adjusting the outcome measure of interest for underlying population-based risk factors. These underlying population-based risk factors represent the measured preexisting characteristics (demographic and clinical) of the patient population studied. There is a complex science related to risk adjustment methodologies, the scope of which is beyond this chapter.

UTILITY OF OUTCOMES RESEARCH MEASURES

A variety of organizations use outcomes research for internal quality improvement and external benchmarking. Individual physicians and hospitals measure patient satisfaction, condition-specific outcomes, and measures of morbidity and mortality for a variety of reasons. These measures identify the strengths and weaknesses of hospital care and help to direct quality improvement activities. Benchmarking against regional or national norms allows physicians and hospitals to understand how their performance compares to their peer institutions.

Additionally, regulators and payers of health care have also begun to use outcome measures in their review and oversight processes. The Joint Commission on Accreditation of Healthcare Organizations (JCAHO), for example, has recently initiated their ORYX program (JCAHO 2001; see also Campbell, 1997; DeMott, 1997). This program incorporates outcomes-related data into the hospital accreditation process. JCAHO has developed a standardized set of core performance measures across several clinical domains. The initial set of core measures spans four clinical domains (i.e., acute myocardial infarction, community-acquired pneumonia, congestive heart failure, and pregnancy-related conditions). Within each clinical domain, specific quality measures have been defined. In acute myocardial infarction, for example, thrombolytic door-to-needle time for eligible patients is one of the disease-specific process measures that is used to assess clinical quality of care. The statewide peer review organizations (PROs), commissioned by the Center for Medicare and Medicaid Services (CMS, formerly HCFA), have adopted similar benchmarking and profiling approaches to evaluate the quality of care delivered by physicians and hospitals participating in federally funded health insurance programs (Brass, Krumholz, Scinto, Mathur, & Radford, 1998; Caldwell, Berg, Pritchard, & Lewis, 1998; Cooperative Cardiovascular Project Best Practices Working Group, 1998; Graff et al., 1999; Meehan et al., 2001; Weinmann, 1998).

In some cases, combinations of outcomes measures can provide a more comprehensive view of the quality of care delivered by a hospital, physician, or health plan. These combined measures, or "report cards," may be used for internal quality improvement or by external parties (such as regulators, purchaser, and patients) who are interested in quality.

For example, three states (California, New York, and Pennsylvania) and one major metropolitan area (Cleveland, Ohio) now collect and publish hospital-level outcomes data on selected medical conditions and procedures; New York and Pennsylvania also provide patient mortality reports for individual cardiac surgeons. Over the past decade, researchers have investigated the impact of public disclosure of hospital-based morbidity and mortality data on subsequent outcomes. Several large studies have shown that many hospitals in these regions have been able to demonstrate quality of care improvements in risk-adjusted outcome measures over sustained periods of time (Dudley, Johansen, Brand, Rennie, & Milstein, 2000; Hannan, Kilburn, Racz, Shields, & Chassin, 1994). Additionally, research comparing disease-specific outcomes of high- and low-volume centers indicates that selective referral policies may improve clinical outcomes in meaningful ways (Dudley et al., 2000). These reports support the claim that publication of outcomes data has the potential to improve patient care (Hannan et al., 1994; Meehan et al., 2001). Some are concerned that outcome measures and report cards may have an impact only on a small subset of preselected clinical activities within an institution, leaving others unaffected. For example, institutions often focus on outcome measures and quality improvement programs that address specific topics of interest to health care regulators (i.e., JCAHO and CMS) and payers. It is possible that quality may improve in some targeted areas, while at the same time the overall quality of care within an institution may remain unchanged or, in fact, decline due to the large number of clinical programs for which no outcomes measures or quality programs have been undertaken (Casalino, 1999; Chassin, Hannan, & DeBuono, 1996).

Additionally, there is ongoing debate over the ability of outcomes data to reflect underlying clinical quality (Brook et al., 1990) and the potential for summary measures to misrepresent care for high-risk, high-mortality cases as poor care (Wyatt et al., 1997). This concern has hampered the use of health-care-performance report cards that include provider- and hospital-level outcomes. Cardiologists in Pennsylvania, for example, have found it more difficult to find surgeons who are willing to take high-risk patients due to the potential adverse impact of these high-risk patients upon their "quality of care standings" (Schneider & Epstein, 1996). Thus, in some regions of the United States, the concern about adverse selection and the impact that adverse selection has upon individual physician performance profiles has had the unintended consequence of encouraging physicians to avoid sick or unusually complex patients—clearly, a disutility of outcome measurement efforts (Chassin et al., 1996).

Practical barriers also limit the effective use of outcomes measures by consumers, health care purchasers, and managed care organizations (MCOs). The majority of MCOs in New York appear not to base their selection of surgeons on available outcomes data, despite public statements to the contrary (Mukamel et al., 2000). Similarly, corporate health care purchasers for 1.8 million employees nationwide place far more emphasis on consumer satisfaction ratings (i.e., Health Plan Employer Data and Information Set [HEDIS] measures) than on outcomes data for health-plan-affiliated hospitals (Hibbard, Jewett, Legnini, & Tusler, 1997). In fact, only 25% of purchasers surveyed considered outcome reports at all in contracting decisions. Consumers, too, seem to favor using satisfaction measures over outcomes data in choosing health plans and providers (Schauffler & Mordavsky, 2001), although there are occasional reports suggesting that outcomes data can have an impact on patient choice (Mukamel & Mushlin, 1998).

Clearly, some uncertainty surrounds the impact and use of outcomes research efforts and the appropriate use of health care performance reports; nonetheless, there is also evidence that the benchmarks they set and the quality improvement efforts they stimulate significantly improve current hospital performance and future disease-specific outcomes. Outcomes research and quality measurement in health care have developed considerably from the original framework proposed by Avedis Donabedian nearly 30 years ago (Donabedian, 1966). Future research should elucidate which components of health care constitute quality from a consumer perspective, which measures are both accurate and acceptable to physicians, and what types of information reflect most accurately the performance of managed care plans and the hospitals and physician groups they utilize.

REFERENCES

Ashton, C. M., Petersen, N. J., Souchek, J., Menke, T. J., Yu, H. J., Pietz, K., Eigenbrodt, M. L., Barbour, G., Kizer, K. W., & Wray, N. P. (1999).

Geographic variations in utilization rates in Veterans Affairs hospitals and clinics. *New England Journal of Medicine, 340*(1), 32–39.

Bergner, M., Bobbitt, R. A., Carter, W. B., & Gilson, B. S. (1981). The Sickness Impact Profile: Development and final revision of a health status measure. *Medical Care, 19,* 787–805.

Berwick, D. M., & Leape, L. L. (1999). Reducing errors in medicine. *British Medical Journal, 319,* 136–137.

Brass, L. M., Krumholz, H. M., Scinto, J. D., Mathur, D., & Radford, M. (1998). Warfarin use following ischemic stroke among Medicare patients with atrial fibrillation. *Archives of Internal Medicine, 158,* 2093–2100.

Brennan, T. A., Leape, L. L., Laird, N. M., Hebert, L., Localio, A. R., Lawthers, A. G., Newhouse, J. P., Weiler, P. C., & Hiatt, H. H. (1991). Incidence of adverse events and negligence in hospitalized patients. Results of the Harvard Medical Practice Study I. *New England Journal of Medicine, 324,* 370–376.

Brook, R. H., Park, R. E., Chassin, M. R., Kosecoff, J., Keesey, J., & Solomon, D. H. (1990). Carotid endarterectomy for elderly patients: Predicting complications. *Annals of Internal Medicine, 113,* 747–753.

Caldwell, G. G., Berg, P., Pritchard, C., & Lewis, J. N. (1998). Quality improvement in the diagnosis and treatment of heart failure by participating Indiana and Kentucky hospitals. *Evaluation and the Health Professions, 21,* 461–471.

Campbell, S. (1997). Outcomes-based accreditation evolves slowly with JCAHO's ORYX initiative. *Health Care Strategic Management, 15(4),* 12–13.

Casalino, L. P. (1999). The unintended consequences of measuring quality on the quality of medical care. *New England Journal of Medicine, 341,* 1147–1150.

Chassin, M. R., Brook, R. H., Park, R. E., Keesey, J., Fink, A., Kosecoff, J., Kahn, K., Merrick, N., & Solomon, D. H. (1986). Variations in the use of medical and surgical services by the Medicare population. *New England Journal of Medicine, 314,* 285–290.

Chassin, M. R., & Galvin, R. W. (1998). The urgent need to improve health care quality. Institute of Medicine National Roundtable on Health Care Quality. *Journal of the American Medical Association, 280,* 1000–1005.

Chassin, M. R., Hannan, E. L., & DeBuono, B. A. (1996). Benefits and hazards of reporting medical outcomes publicly. *New England Journal of Medicine, 334,* 394–398.

Cooperative Cardiovascular Project Best Practices Working Group. (1998). Improving care for acute myocardial infarction: Experience from the Cooperative Cardiovascular Project. *Joint Commission Journal of Quality Improvement, 24,* 480–490.

DeMott, K. (1997). JCAHO introduces ORYX for outcomes-based accreditation. *Quality Letter for Healthcare Leaders, 9*(3), 18–19.

Donabedian, A. (1966). Evaluating the quality of medical care. *Milbank Memorial Fund Quarterly, 44*(Suppl.), 166–206.

Donabedian, A. (1988). The quality of care. How can it be assessed? *Journal of the American Medical Association, 260,* 1743–1748.

Dudley, R. A., Johansen, K. L., Brand, R., Rennie, D. J., & Milstein, A. (2000). Selective referral to high-volume hospitals: Estimating potentially avoidable deaths. *Journal of the American Medical Association, 283,* 1159–1166.

Graff, L., Orledge, J., Radford, M. J., Wang, Y., Petrillo, M., & Maag, R. (1999). Correlation of the Agency for Health Care Policy and Research congestive heart failure admission guideline with mortality: Peer review organization voluntary hospital association initiative to decrease events (PROVIDE) for congestive heart failure (Pt. 1). *Annals of Emergency Medicine, 34,* 429–437.

Hannan, E. L., Kilburn, H., Jr., Racz, M., Shields, E., & Chassin, M. R. (1994). Improving the outcomes of coronary artery bypass surgery in New York State. *Journal of the American Medical Association, 271,* 761–766.

Hibbard, J. H., Jewett, J. J., Legnini, M. W., & Tusler, M. (1997). Choosing a health plan: Do large employers use the data? *Health Affairs (Millwood), 16,* 172–180.

JCAHO (2001). Getting hospital core measures on track. The continued evolution of ORYX. *Joint Commission Perspectives, 21*(7), 5.

Leape, L. L., Brennan, T. A., Laird, N., Lawthers, A. G., Localio, A. R., Barnes, B. A., Hebert, L., Newhouse, J. P., Weiler, P. C., & Hiatt, H. (1991). The nature of adverse events in hospitalized patients. Results of the Harvard Medical Practice Study II. *New England Journal of Medicine, 324,* 377–384.

Maciejewski, M., Kawiecki, J., & Rockwood, T. (1997). Satisfaction. In R. L. Kane (Ed.), *Understanding health care outcomes research* (pp. 67–92). Gathersburg, MD: Aspen.

McPherson, K., Wennberg, J. E., Hovind, O. B., & Clifford, P. (1982). Small-area variations in the use of common surgical procedures: An international comparison of New England, England, and Norway. *New England Journal of Medicine, 307,* 1310–1314.

Meehan, T. P., Weingarten, S. R., Holmboe, E. S., Mathur, D., Wang, Y., Petrillo, M. K., Tu, G. S., & Fine, J. M. (2001). A statewide initiative to improve the care of hospitalized pneumonia patients: The Connecticut Pneumonia Pathway Project. *American Journal of Medicine, 111,* 203–210.

Mukamel, D. B., & Mushlin, A. I. (1998). Quality of care information makes a difference: An analysis of market share and price changes after publication of the New York State cardiac surgery mortality reports. *Medical Care, 36,* 945–954.

Mukamel, D. B., Mushlin, A. I., Weimer, D., Zwanziger, J., Parker, T., & Indridason, I. (2000). Do quality report cards play a role in HMOs' contracting practices? Evidence from New York State (Pt. 2). *Health Services Research, 35,* 319–332.

Phillips, D. P., Christenfeld, N., & Glynn, L. M. (1998). Increase in US medication-error deaths between 1983 and 1993. *Lancet, 351,* 643–644.

Rector, T. S., & Cohn, J. N. (1992). Assessment of patient outcome with the Minnesota Living with Heart Failure questionnaire. *American Heart Journal, 124,* 1017–1025.

Schauffler, H. H., & Mordavsky, J. K. (2001). Consumer reports in health care: Do they make a difference? *Annual Review of Public Health, 22,* 69–89.

Schneider, E. C., & Epstein, A. M. (1996). Influence of cardiac-surgery performance reports on referral practices and access to care. A survey of cardiovascular specialists. *New England Journal of Medicine, 335,* 251–256.

Ware, J. E., Jr., & Sherbourne, C. D. (1992). The MOS 36-item short-form health survey (SF-36). I. Conceptual framework and item selection. *Medical Care, 30,* 473–483.

Weinmann, C. (1998). Quality improvement in health care. A brief history of the Medicare Peer Review Organization (PRO) initiative. *Evaluation and the Health Professions, 21,* 413–418.

Wennberg, J. E., Freeman, J. L., & Culp, W. J. (1987). Are hospital services rationed in New Haven or over-utilized in Boston? *Lancet, 1,* 1185–1189.

Wyatt, S. M., Moy, E., Levin, R. J., Lawton, K. B., Witter, D. M., Jr., Valente, E., Jr., Lala, R., & Griner, P. F. (1997). Patients transferred to academic medical centers and other hospitals: Characteristics, resource use, and outcomes. *Academic Medicine, 72,* 921–930.

■ 28
Creating Quality Improvement Projects

Robert J. Rosati

The Institute of Medicine (IOM) report on medical errors (IOM, 1999) caught the attention of clinicians, consumers, payers, and government by clearly delineating the direct relationship between quality of care and patient outcomes. Becher and Chassin (2001) have pointed out that patients suffer harm because of three types of quality issues: underuse, overuse and misuse. First, patients may not receive beneficial health services. Second, patients may undergo treatments or procedures from which they do not benefit. Third, patients may receive appropriate medical services that are provided poorly, exposing them to added risk of preventable complications. Physicians are often involved in quality improvement initiatives that are meant to address these problems and improve the outcome of those under care.

Very few physicians would be opposed to investing in quality improvement efforts. Most would agree that the literature has shown a strong relationship between underuse, overuse, and misuse on patient outcomes. At the most practical level, modern methods of quality improvement (QI) have freed physicians from the need to respond to numerous citations for quality-of-care issues from within and outside the hospital. The traditional quality assurance (QA) focus was to review care on a case-by-case basis and identify problems. This subjective approach rarely identified issues that could be improved, and it often infuriated providers. Every citation left the physician defending clinical decisions. The QI approach, on the other hand, has created the opportunity to identify *systems* problems and helped eliminate placing the blame on a few individuals. This transition has increased the likelihood that care can improve. The chief disadvantage of QI is not ineffectiveness (it works), but rather the tremendous commitment that each participant must make to implement improvements and bring about change. The key dilemma is how to convince more physicians with limited time to participate actively.

THE REAL VALUE OF QI

Benefits to the providers. Berwick and Nolan (1998) observed that physicians are taught to work *within* the system and to perfect themselves by improving their skills and knowledge. In general, physicians are not trained to challenge the system of health care delivery. Therefore, the first important transition that physicians must make is to acknowledge that a specific aspect of care must improve and become involved in changing the system. By actively participating in the process, physicians will help bring about change, and they will have less reason to complain that their input was not included. They will also benefit by working more efficiently, with fewer frustrations and reduced burden on their time. There may actually be an economic incentive because more efficient systems will allow a physician to treat more patients.

Benefits to the organization. Patients want high-quality service, and they do not believe that is what they receive (Kenagy, Berwick, & Shore, 1999). How patients view the quality, availability of service, and convenience factors affects their loyalty to the organization. Therefore, organizations that focus on QI can increase patient satisfaction, reduce costs, and create a competitive advantage in the market place. Further, organizational interest in QI can improve physician satisfaction, increasing their loyalty to the institution and market share.

Benefits to the patients. The true value of QI is measured in the benefits to the patients. A QI project should begin with a goal of improving care and ensuring that patients will notice the difference. Even an improvement in something as basic as turnaround time of laboratory results can have significant impact on the patients' view of the care provided in the emergency room. Improvement in clinical outcomes should be the ultimate goal, but this is often difficult to define and obtain (Berwick & Knapp, 1987). In addition, QI projects that limit the risk patients can encounter in the hospital environment are also essential.

WHAT ARE QUALITY IMPROVEMENT PROJECTS?

Most QI projects are designed to improve care, reduce turnaround time, decrease cost, and enhance customer satisfaction. For example, a physician who typically admits geriatric patients from a skilled nursing facility may believe that the number of pressure ulcers at time of discharge is above acceptable norms for several nursing units. More formally, the Department of Emergency Medicine may decide that all patients who arrive with a potential myocardial infarction receive an aspirin because several recent studies have shown this to be effective treatment. Another major reason is that the Joint Commission on Accreditation of Healthcare Organizations (JCAHO) mandates that all hospitals use QI methods to improve the care being delivered.

Much of what we know today about QI is influenced by the work of Deming (1986) and Juran (Juran, 1988; Juran & Gryna, 1988). These early pioneers of QI established a standard set of tools for businesses to increase quality and productivity. The philosophy behind their work has been to improve products and services continually by putting resources into research and the education of employees. Deming stated that organizations should not tolerate mistakes and defects and that the goal of every organization should be continuous improvement until perfection is obtained. He further stated that finding errors by inspection was inefficient and implies "rework." Deming also realized that quality was dependent on the organization environment, staff training, and leadership characteristics. These characteristics of quality lead to a systems approach to improving and maintaining quality.

Over the past 10 years, the systems approach to improving quality has been extended to health care. Berwick (1989) noted that there were far too many examples of waste, rework, and errors in hospitals and that quality was suffering because systems failed. Berwick suggested that to improve quality in health care we analyze systems and processes and not focus solely on individual performance. The IOM (1999) report adds further support in the analysis of medical errors. The report states that the majority of medical errors do not result from individual carelessness but from basic flaws in the way the health system is organized (see chapter 25).

HOW TO PLAN A QI PROJECT

Organizational priorities. Before any improvement effort can begin, one must assess whether the initiative will fit into the current set of organization priorities. The project will be doomed to failure if it lacks organizational support for implementing the systems changes. Typically the support should come from the administrative and clinical leadership. However, support at the level of the board of trustees or the finance division of the hospital may be necessary for a project to be successful. Identifying the set of organizational priorities may be difficult in some organizations and may be a source of friction between the clinical and administrative leadership.

Available resources. Two kinds of critical resources must be identified before a project begins: personnel and financial. Staff must volunteer their time despite competing priorities within the hospital. Additionally, they must learn to take on defined roles such as team leader, facilitator, and secretary. Some organizations have paid personnel within the quality management department who are responsible for supporting QI teams, but most organizations lack these resources.

Because the QI team's final recommendations may have financial implications for the hospital, a budget that will support the improvement initiative must be established early in the planning process. The finance division may require a cost-benefit analysis to demonstrate the potential long-term savings to the hospital after an initial investment in new equipment, purchasing certain supplies, or hiring staff.

Develop a timeline. Although QI is often described as continuous (CQI), there must be a well-defined timeline for implementation and accomplishing goals. Good project management is essential, and a well-defined timeline will increase the success of the QI efforts. Furthermore, *most projects should not go beyond 6 months* without meeting certain objectives. QI projects often fail because they begin as open-end endeavors and everyone involved loses interest. The best approach is to set deadlines for completing specific tasks using the 10-step process for implementing QI projects described in the next section. Continuous quality improvement is defined as an approach with cycles that are repeated until the process is completely under control. This may be a long process for physicians to be involved in over an extended period of time. Once initial improvements have been made, the goals of the team should continue and consideration given to recruiting new members.

Getting "buy-in." QI efforts require two key organizational elements to succeed. First, there must be a *commitment* to participate actively and take on responsibility. Individuals cannot sit back passively and hope others will volunteer. QI is a team effort and requires that everyone involved take ownership of the process. Therefore, selecting people to work on the QI project requires knowing in advance who is likely be an active participant. Second, there must be *cooperation* among the team members. Clemmer, Spuhler, Berwick and Nolan (1998) describe five elements that foster cooperation: Develop a shared purpose, create a safe environment, encourage diverse viewpoints, work toward negotiating agreement, and use fair and equitable rules for everyone involved. Individuals who cannot abide by these principles may undermine a team's effectiveness and should not participate in the QI process.

Where are the data? The most important difference between traditional QA and QI is the use of data. Traditional QA tends to rely on small, non-random chart reviews to identify problems. The reviews are tabulated to show levels of compliance. QI uses more formal statistical analysis to identify areas for improvement and to measure the impact of changes to the system. Because the more advanced analysis requires sufficient data to conduct appropriate statistical tests, QI requires a significant investment in time and effort to gather data. The data collection may necessitate the development of new instruments, protected time for staff to gather information, and construction and maintenance of a database unless the necessary data are already being captured in systems throughout the organization. If the data are available in the hospital's systems, this may create a new challenge to determine how to extract information in a format that can be analyzed.

Sampling issues. As described above, QI studies require sufficient data to conduct appropriate analyses. The data set, like that of a research study, should be of sufficient size and representative of the population under review. Representativeness can be achieved using an acceptable sampling method such as simple random, systematic, or stratified methods. Evidence from prior studies or power analysis is essential to estimate sample size needs. Consultation with statistician may be helpful to define the sample size before the QI project begins.

TEN-STEP PROCESS FOR IMPLEMENTING QI

1. *Focus on the consumer* (identify the consumer of interest). The first important step in QI is identifying at the start of the project who will likely benefit from the changes to the system. Improvements in quality should be meaningful to the consumer. Identification of the appropriate consumer can be difficult. In health care, the most likely consumers include patients, families, physicians, nurses, laboratory technicians, pharmacists, ancillary personnel—anyone involved in the delivery of services. Most QI initiatives will affect multiple consumers.

2. *Collect and analyze data* (identify the outcome that needs to be improved). Understand the products and services that are important to the consumers and assess whether their expectations are being met. In health care, this translates into whether we are relieving pain, improving the quality of life, keeping the amount of risk to patients low, providing a warm meal, not conducting unnecessary procedures, treating patients with dignity, and so forth. Focused studies conducted by quality assurance or utilization review, physician research, surveys, audits and statistical analysis of information maintained by the hospital's information systems department are also useful sources of preliminary data. The main focus of all data collection should be to determine objective criteria for assessing outcomes.

3. *Analyze the process* (identify the process that produces the outcome). Assemble a team of individuals who have a fundamental knowledge of the

process that needs improvement. These individuals should be involved daily in the process (frontline workers). The team should be able to identify the sequence of events in the process and must use the tools of quality improvement to document the process. These tools include the following: brainstorming, multi-voting, selection grids, affinity diagrams, and cause-and-effect diagrams. Any combination of tools may be useful for understanding the inputs, outputs, procedural components and problems that exist in the system. Brassard and Ritter (1994) have assembled a useful pocket guide that summarizes these procedures.

The team must also identify two types of variation in the system. Random variation (or common cause) is variability that is built into the system and normally occurring. An example would be random functions in turn-around time for lab results throughout the year. Specific variation (or special cause) is variability that is caused by specific components within the process that are not working appropriately, that is, lab turnaround time that has doubled since the hospital has consolidated the service at one facility that serves several institutions. Specific variation is typically what the QI team is interested in reducing. Figure 28.1 is a control chart of a patient outcome that shows random variation for approximately 10 months and then a change to specific variation.

4. *Flowchart* (document the process that produces the outcome). Based on the information collected about the process gained in step 3, begin to diagram the process using flowcharting methods. Include information on the standard procedures and known variations in process. The flowchart will help to understand the actual path the service follows to identify inefficiencies, redundancies, and misunderstandings. Figure 28.2 shows an example of a flowchart tracking a patient admitted through the emergency room.

5. *Set goals* (develop measurable expectations that will produce benefits to the consumer). Develop a flowchart of the ideal path of service delivery as a goal for the team. Establish objective criteria for improvements. This would include setting standards for improvement such as reducing emergency-room waiting time 25%, decreasing length of stay by 1 day for a particular diagnosis, or increasing overall patient satisfaction ratings by 10 points. The standards that are developed are not meant to be thresholds as in traditional QA, but intermittent goals for continuous quality improvement. In traditional QA, thresholds were established as triggers for when a process was thought to be below acceptable standards, for example, surgical infection rates of greater than 10%, or less than 99% of all medical records signed within 30 days. With QI, the goals should be revised as the process becomes more controlled and variability is reduced.

6. *Propose changes to the system* (identify methods for changing the process). After gathering all the information about the process, the team should use methods similar to those in step 3 to suggest modifications to the

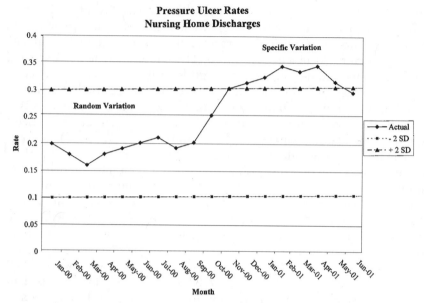

FIGURE 28.1 Control chart of a patient outcome.

system. This can include standardizing procedures, developing enhanced staff training, changing staffing patterns, improving the physical environment, moving the location of a department, or choosing a different supplier. Basically, the team must recommend specific changes in behavior and organization that can produce tangible outcomes.

7. *Make changes to the system* (implement improvements). Changes that the team has recommended in step 6 must be implemented during a trial period, which should be a reasonable period of time that will allow for the changes to have an impact. Furthermore, the team must specify objective and quantitative measures to assess whether goals established in step 5 can be reached. An example would be a reduction of lab turnaround time of 30 minutes within an 8-week period. Also, some measurement of the extent to which the process is changing must occur. This would include documentation of how positions were restructured, staff changes, new equipment purchased, and any other information that shows how the system has changed.

8. *Collect more data* (monitor the impact of the changes). As part of trial phase, the team should repeat step 2 (collecting and analyzing data). These data will be used to assess the impact of the changes to the system. In a sense, the team will be conducting an experimental study that will compare the initial period before the changes to the current phase. The team should use similar statistical methods as in step 2, as well.

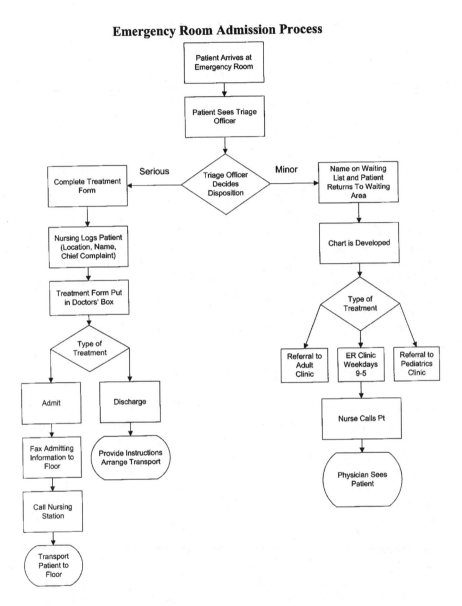

FIGURE 28.2 Flowchart tracking a patient admitted through the emergency room.

9. *Continuously improve* (assess the impact of the changes and continue to modify the system if necessary). Based on the data collected and analyzed in step 8, the team should determine the effectiveness of the changes to the system by making comparisons to the initial goals set in step 5 for improvement. If the goals have not been meet, the team must propose new changes to the system and continue to measure the impact of the changes. If the changes have been met, the team then has two responsibilities. First, the team must propose permanent changes to the system that incorporate the findings of the QI process. Second, the team should establish new goals for improving the process that go beyond those established in step 5 and continue to better the system.

10. *Evaluate* (appraise the success of the QI project over time). The team should prepare to evaluate over time the overall success of the system changes in meeting the consumers' expectations. At specified points in the future (3 months, 6 months, 1 year, etc.) it should repeat evaluations to determine whether the goals are still being met and whether changes are being maintained. This step is critical, because continuous quality improvement requires that the process be periodically assessed to be sure that consumers are satisfied. If problems are identified, the team must begin again and identify why the changes are not being maintained.

EXAMPLE OF THE 10-STEP PROCESS

An urban medical center with a large number of patients who are referred from nursing homes is receiving complaints that patients are returning after discharge with hospital-acquired pressure ulcers. The data are anecdotal, but the hospital's chief medical officer has decided that the complaints must be investigated. Instead of conducting a traditional QA review of a sample of patient records, she decides to start a QI project. She has determined that the effort fits into the organizational priorities because the percentage of patients that are being referred from nursing homes is significant and many of the physicians at the nursing homes are affiliated with the hospital.

Step 1. Three distinct consumers can be identified: patients, physicians, and administrators of the nursing homes. Patients will directly benefit from the efforts to reduce the incidence of hospital-acquired pressure ulcers. The physicians and administrators are responsible for the referrals to the hospital. If they believe the care provided at the hospital puts their patients at risk, it is unlikely they will continue to refer patients. The QI efforts must address the patient care issues and reassure the nursing homes that the problem has been resolved.

Step 2. Data collection will focus on establishing whether the nursing homes are correct that the rate of pressure ulcers is "abnormally" high. A source within the hospital must be identified to provide the data. If the data do not already exist, data collection must be implemented. The information necessary for in-depth understanding of the problem will require information for each patient about referral source, age, diagnoses, comorbidities, incontinence, length of stay, and hospital ward. To assess whether there has been a change in the frequency of pressure ulcers over time, data should cover at least 6 months, and preferably a year. Another piece of valuable information would be to find out from the nursing homes when they believe the rates started to rise. The data would then be analyzed using appropriate methods to determine whether there is support for the anecdotal information and whether the QI team should be formed. One way to look at the data would be to use a control chart that helps to identify if the frequency of pressure ulcers has gone beyond normal limits. Figure 28.1 provides an example of a control chart for the pressure ulcer data.

Step 3. The QI team needs to be constituted for reviewing the process of care and making recommendations for improvements. A multidisciplinary team is necessary, including physicians, nurses, physical therapy, central supply, administration, and quality management staff. The team must cover various areas of the hospital from the emergency room to the critical care units, because issues may vary by location. The team should start by using brainstorming techniques to identify an initial list of systems issues that could be potential causes of increased pressure ulcer rates for the geriatric population. The brainstorming could be used to produce a cause-and-effect diagram that describes the process. Figure 28.3 is an example of a cause-and-effect diagram.

Step 4. The team has determined that delays in admission from the emergency room have caused patients to spend greater than 24 hours on stretchers before being moved to the units. Additional data analysis has shown that the increased pressure ulcer rates correspond to considerably longer wait times over the past several months. The team then flowcharts the admission process from the emergency room to the patient floor to help identify where potential systems problems are causing the delays (see Figure 28.2).

Step 5. The team develops a new flowchart showing the ideal admission process for patients who are admitted directly from nursing homes. The redesigned process stipulates that patients should not spend more than 6 hours in the emergency room. Furthermore, the team develops procedures to provide the patient with a special mattress from central supply when it is not possible to move the patient quickly. The team also sets a goal of reducing the pressure ulcer rate from 20% to 10% in 3 months and to 3% within a year, which is the current rate at the hospital for non-nursing-home patients.

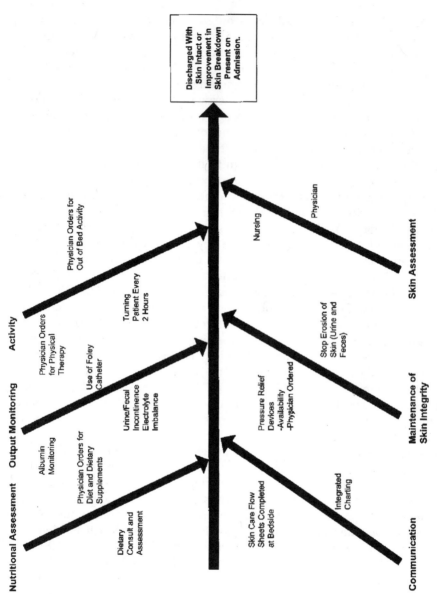

FIGURE 28.3   Cause-and-effect diagram.

Step 6. For the new admission process to work appropriately, processes must change. The team will have to develop recommendations to expedite patient flow. By reviewing the analysis, flowcharts, and suggestions from the prior meetings, the team should have enough information to make the system changes. For example, they may recommend that certain patients be admitted directly to the floors from the nursing homes. Instituting the change will require the coordinated effort of many people, from the admitting department in the hospital to the referring physicians in the nursing homes. Policy and procedure manuals will require rewriting and staff training must occur. The QI team is responsible for overseeing that all these components be documented so that staff can implement the changes.

Step 7. Formal testing of the system changes requires that the new admission procedures be piloted for several months. During the test phase the team may not need to meet as frequently unless a problem arises.

Step 8. While the testing phase occurs, data collection will be ongoing. In addition to the pressure ulcer data discussed in step 2, the team should collect information on speed of the admission process for the nursing home patients.

Step 9. All of the data will be analyzed and compared to baseline statistics to determine the impact of the system changes. If the changes seem to have a positive impact, they will become permanent. If not, the team will need to reevaluate the process and make new recommendations.

Step 10. Approximately 1 year after the project is initiated, the team should meet again to review the current status of the patient outcomes and satisfaction of the physicians and nursing home administrators with the changes. If the outcomes and feedback are not satisfactory, the QI team must reconvene.

SUMMARY

Frequently in health care, a process that on the surface appears simple is likely to be very complex. Trying to fix a process is likely to be much more difficult than complaining to the CEO of the hospital and demanding he or she make some changes. QI is a tool that can be used to get at the root causes of poor outcomes and to identify suggestions for improving the system. The approach is empirically based, allowing for a true assessment of the impact of the changes. Furthermore, QI is a team process that allows for input across disciplines. Understanding and actively participating in the QI process provides physicians the opportunity to bring about positive change that will impact patient care. Physician leadership of QI initiatives can have tremendous influence on the organizational culture of a hospital by demonstrating a commitment to bringing about process improvements that will benefit the patient, organization, and other practitioners.

REFERENCES

Becher, E. C., & Chassin, M. R. (2001). Improving the quality of health care: Who will lead? *Health Affairs, 20,* 164–179.

Berwick, D. M. (1989). Continuous improvement as an ideal in health care. *New England Journal of Medicine, 320*(1), 53–56.

Berwick, D. M., & Knapp, M. G. (1987). Theory and practice for measuring health care quality. *Health Care Finance Review* (suppl.), 49–55.

Berwick, D. M., & Nolan, T. W. (1998). Physicians as leaders in improving health care. *Annals of Internal Medicine, 128,* 289–292.

Brassard, M., & Ritter, D. (1994). *The memory jogger II: A pocket guide to continuous improvement and effective planning.* Methuen, MA: GOAL/QPC.

Clemmer, T. P., Spuhler, V. J., Berwick, D. M., & Nolan, T. W. (1998). Cooperation: The foundation of improvement. *Annals of Internal Medicine, 128,* 1004–1009.

Deming, W. E. (1986). *Out of the crisis.* Cambridge, MA: MIT Center for Advanced Engineering Study.

Institute of Medicine. (1999). *To err is human: Building a safer health system.* Washington, DC: National Academy Press.

Juran, J. M. (1988). *Juran on planning for quality.* New York: Free Press.

Juran, J. M., & Gryna, F. M. (1988). *Juran's quality control handbook* (4th ed.). New York: McGraw-Hill.

Kenagy, J. W., Berwick, D. M., & Shore, M. F. (1999). Service quality in health care. *Journal of the American Medical Association, 281,* 661–665.

Index